MERGER

Published by Melbourne Books
Level 9, 100 Collins Street,
Melbourne, VIC 3000
Australia
www.melbournebooks.com.au
info@melbournebooks.com.au

Copyright © William Westerman 2021

All rights reserved. No part of this publication may be reproduced, stored in a retrieval system, or transmitted in any form or any means electronic, mechanical, photocopying, recording or otherwise without the prior permission of the publisher.

Title: Merger: The Fitzroy Lions and the Tragedy of 1996
Author: William Westerman
ISBN: 9781925556858
Front and back cover image artist: Mitchell Toy

A catalogue record for this book is available from the National Library of Australia

MERGER

THE FITZROY LIONS AND THE TRAGEDY OF 1996

WILLIAM WESTERMAN

M
MELBOURNE BOOKS

Lovingly dedicated to
David Keith Westerman (1952 – 2017)
A noble man still dearly missed

Should old acquaintance be forgot.
And never thought upon,
The flames of love extinguished,
And freely past and gone?
Is thy kind heart now grown so cold
In that loving breast of thine,
That thou canst never once reflect
On old long syne?

A Choice Collection of Comic and Serious Scots Poems Both Ancient and Modern, Part III, 1711

CONTENTS

8	FOREWORD	
13	PROLOGUE	
21	INTRODUCTION	THE POOR CITIZENS
31	CHAPTER ONE	HEART AND SOUL
44	CHAPTER TWO	THE BOYS FROM OLD FITZROY
56	CHAPTER THREE	THE PEOPLE'S CLUB
73	CHAPTER FOUR	THE CENTENARY
86	CHAPTER FIVE	THE OPTION OF LAST RESORT
102	CHAPTER SIX	ONCE MORE TO THE BARRICADES
116	CHAPTER SEVEN	DEALS, RUMOURS AND ULTIMATUMS
131	CHAPTER EIGHT	EXPLORING OTHER OPTIONS
146	CHAPTER NINE	THE HIGH-WATER MARK
162	CHAPTER TEN	SEALING THE DEAL
177	CHAPTER ELEVEN	A TOUGH DAY AT THE OFFICE
192	CHAPTER TWELVE	THE LONG WEEK

209	CHAPTER THIRTEEN	ONE DAY IN JULY
220	CHAPTER FOURTEEN	A MIXED RESPONSE
237	CHAPTER FIFTEEN	SELLING THE MERGER
253	CHAPTER SIXTEEN	CUSTODIANS OF THE JUMPER
269	CHAPTER SEVENTEEN	THE LONG GOODBYE
283	CHAPTER EIGHTEEN	A TOUCH OF SADNESS
300	CHAPTER NINETEEN	LOOSE ENDS
316	CHAPTER TWENTY	DEATH IS NOT THE END
326	CONCLUSION	COUNTING THE COST
337	EPILOGUE	
343	BIBLIOGRAPHY	
346	ENDNOTES	
388	ACKNOWLEDGEMENTS	
391	THE AUTHOR	

FOREWORD

In the existential crisis prompted by the Covid-19 shutdown of March 2020, the AFL industry faced questions not contemplated for more than two decades.

The rivers of television rights gold had long carried the notion of survival away. The AFL landscape was awash with money to fund all manner of enterprise, innovation and excess. And the finances were predicated on the existence of the eighteen clubs. It seemed the perfect circle of life.

The one eventuality that had never been countenanced was the incapacity to stage the game. Without the footy itself there would be no revenue and the ecosystem was doomed to collapse.

It was declared the greatest threat the Australian Football League had faced and the task of saving the industry fell to incumbent Chief Executive Gillon McLachlan as surely as Allen Aylett and Jack Hamilton had been tasked with salvaging the Victorian Football League a generation prior.

In the early days of the Coronavirus crisis many a President lay with their head on the pillow restlessly wondering how their club would survive as sport was shockingly revealed to be more perilously positioned than anyone would have forecast or cared to imagine.

Amidst the furrowed brows came long dormant grumblings.

They were targeted at the financially weak. Those politely depicted as the 'recipient clubs'. Those who lived on the teat of AFL funding.

The subtext was lost on few. Those clubs were to be seen as a drain on the industry. Those who relied for their existence on central funding. Those that couldn't pay their way through historical disadvantage or accumulated debt, low attendance or a dearth of sponsorship dollars.

Some of the murmurings were subtle. Some more explicit. They stretched from the football community in Western Australia to the Premier's Office in Tasmania. The new economy necessitated a cull, natural selection to rationalise the competition for the next era.

The targets were the smaller Victorian clubs.

At its worst, Hawthorn President Jeff Kennett penned his manifesto insisting strict financial criteria be applied to all clubs and those that failed to meet the benchmarks in a prescribed period be relegated from the AFL. He meant expelled. Permanently.

The end point of such a dogmatic policy could only have resulted in the death of a club. Likely more than one.

There were those who agreed with Kennett. He had after all once orchestrated landslide victory in a popular election with such philosophies. But only one. And the former leader of Victoria was filling a role previously performed by another Liberal heavyweight, Carlton President John Elliott, who dreamed of a super league sans the burden of the financial strugglers.

Such logic is to lose sight of the football in the forest that is the industry. It's to discount the affection for and connection to the indigenous game because it isn't measurable in a column on a spreadsheet.

Australian Football Hall of Fame broadcaster Tony Charlton espoused the mantra: 'Know your history.'

As the threat to existence returned to the terrain, it forced the football family to revisit a death that had long haunted the corners of the game. The outcome would reveal whether history had been heeded or forgotten.

When last the economic rationalists held sway, they killed Fitzroy. It was justified, even encouraged, as assisted dying. But it was dealt out with an executioner's hand.

Fitzroy was seen as a relic. Rich in history but with little modern relevance and no foreseeable future. It had been allowed to decay. The most influential voices of the era all seemed to arrive at the same conclusion. It was said there were too few who cared. The displaced were either expendable or could be rehomed.

The acolytes were wrong.

The demise of Fitzroy is a deep wound rather than a scar. A tear in the fabric of the game that will never truly repair.

History has judged it unnecessary. The club's demise didn't spark the desired reduction in the crowded Victorian market. Eleven teams became ten, just as would have been the case if the Lions had merged with a team in their home city. The removal of Fitzroy wasn't the catalyst for the AFL to become the country's dominant domestic sporting code. It merely hacked off the weakest limb to meet the overriding sentiment and thinking of the time. Its legacy is one of pain not progress.

Fitzroy was incapable of saving itself and its right to say it couldn't meet the aspirations the League harboured without intervention.

The history of missteps is a dismal long-term litany. The missed opportunity for relocation. The scuppered attempt to merge with Melbourne that failed over the composition of board numbers. Pressure to amalgamate with the Bulldogs, rebuffed by the Footscray faithful. The desired and denied marriage with North Melbourne. The shotgun wedding with Brisbane.

There is farce and misjudgement, doubtless incompetence and absolute bastardry.

It even has its exotic twists. The entrée of Nauru in the survival tale really does beggar belief in its retelling.

But the genre overall is misery.

The AFL could have chosen to assist Fitzroy in renewal prior to the grim throes of death rather than aiding and abetting its expiration. Future administrations would appoint handpicked executives armed with hefty assistance packages to refloat sinking clubs. No such rescue strategy was afforded Fitzroy.

By 1996, the club couldn't be saved. But its final wishes might have been honoured.

The partnership with North Melbourne is one of the great *what ifs* in footy. A natural and willing blending. Perversely it was precisely what League Headquarters had wished for — two Melbourne teams reaching an accord to merge — but could never quite consummate.

As Fitzroy's final season unfolded, preparations were being made that saw Melbourne and Hawthorn heading for the altar. When the time came the Demons members voted in favour of the union. Don Scott famously rallied the Hawks to turn away. It was the impetus that led Hawthorn to become a modern powerhouse but left Melbourne to struggle along.

It was even more pointed for North Melbourne in the aftermath of the abandoned Fitzroy merger. They were never far from talk of relocation or collapse and eventually went within one vote of becoming the AFL's Gold Coast team.

Few recognise the imposed merger with the Brisbane Bears as the continuation of the Fitzroy history. It was too cynical then. Too unscrupulous now.

Fitzroy exists in the archive and in the aching memories of those that loved the Roy Boys. In the ghosts and the amateurs at Brunswick Street Oval. Hayden Bunton Sr and Kevin Murray carry its torch in the pantheon of Legends. And in modern pop culture Fitzroy lives in just the right blend of kitsch and connoisseur in the perfectly dressed pub frequented by television's brilliantly conceived Jack Irish.

Not to be romanticised, Fitzroy is a remnant of what was lost. What was judged expendable. What wasn't worth saving. What was deemed superfluous, unprofitable and unsustainable rather than a treasured foundation stone worth preserving and reinventing.

The tale that follows is morbid but necessary. It fulfills the provision to know your history.

Almost a quarter of a century on, when next the custodians of the game confronted the question of survival and the callus demands for sacrifice, they stared down the elitists and enacted their policy: eighteen teams in, eighteen teams out. No-one would be left behind.

No club would again suffer the fate of Fitzroy.

Gerard Whateley

PROLOGUE

In the early 1880s, Gertrude Street, Fitzroy, was a bustling commercial precinct. With no large factories and a limited residential area at its western end, the street was dominated by small double-story brick and stone buildings, each with a business on the ground floor and either a shopkeeper's residence or a room to let above.

In 1883, Mr D. Morgan, a caterer, pastry cook and confectioner, purchased the lease for 83 and 85 Gertrude Street and set up a catering business. In addition to advertising his ability to cater for balls, weddings, breakfasts and suppers at short notice, Morgan's Café (as it was known) boasted an elegant and comfortable dining and luncheon room.[1] Morgan soon established an excellent reputation for himself; throughout 1883, he was employed for many local community events, with his spreads equal to 'the best houses of the metropolis'.[2]

Later that year John McMahon, an Irish tailor and habit maker who owned a business at 99 Brunswick Street, held a banquet at the Fitzroy Town Hall. Formerly mayor of the City of Fitzroy, McMahon wished to honour the work of the current Fitzroy City Council. He employed Morgan to cater the event and was not disappointed. The menu was 'the choicest description and replete with every delicacy of the season'. The tables were 'very richly and handsomely decorated', with two of the largest champagne bottles possibly seen in the colony of Victoria at the head of the central table.[3] Impressed with Morgan's efforts, McMahon enlisted his services the following year for a function on the evening of 30 September 1884. In addition to his commercial and political endeavours, McMahon was the president of the local Australian rules football club, which had just completed its inaugural season in the Victorian Football Association (VFA). McMahon wished to celebrate the auspicious occasion by inviting players and officials to Morgan's Café for an evening of supper and festivities. Mr Morgan 'fully sustained his reputation', and everyone present thoroughly enjoyed themselves.[4] There was, to be sure, much to celebrate.

By the 1880s, the city of Melbourne was thriving. The monarch, Alexandrina Victoria of the House of Hanover, had been Queen of the United Kingdom of Great Britain and Ireland since 1837 and Empress of India since 1876. Mother of nine and ruler of millions, her empire sprawled across the globe, driven by industry, finance and commerce, safeguarded by the Royal Navy and maintained with a powerful sense of its purpose as a force for civilization and modernity. In a distant corner of her realm, on land traditionally owned by the peoples of the Kulin Nation, Melbourne stood as the capital of the colony that bore her name. George Augustus Sala, a well-known London journalist, dubbed it 'Marvellous Melbourne'.[5] Its moniker was well earned — massive borrowing from British banks enabled large amounts of money to flow in, driving business investment, railway construction and property speculation. At its most ambitious, it compared itself to London, the empire's grand and ancient capital.[6]

As well as a prosperous economy, Melbourne was also experiencing the growth of its local sporting product, Australian rules football. Following the creation of the Melbourne Football Club in 1858, other clubs had formed all over the city and the colony to play friendly matches against each other. In 1877, several clubs came together to form the VFA, providing a competitive structure to their games. As the number of clubs expanded, one suburb notably without representation was the relatively affluent Fitzroy. A junior side, the Normanby Football Club, had been active in the area since at least 1882. Eventually, those affiliated with Normanby and with the Fitzroy Cricket Club, tenants of the cricket ground at the Edinburgh Gardens, began discussing the prospect of creating a senior football team in the area.[7]

Then, on 22 September 1883, a notice ran in the local papers:

> Football
>
> A meeting will be held on Wednesday, 26th September at the Brunswick hotel, Brunswick Street, Fitzroy, at 8 o'clock p.m. for the purpose of forming a Senior Football Club in Fitzroy. Footballers and others interested are requested to attend.
>
> G. Toms, Hon. Sec. *pro tem*.[8]

Although Toms called the meeting, McMahon had the honour of chairing it. That evening, about seventy people attended, and McMahon told them that he saw no reason why there should not be a senior Australian rules football club in Fitzroy. There was no lack of 'good and reliable' players in the district, and they had an excellent venue available at the Fitzroy Cricket Ground in the Edinburgh Gardens.[9] Toms moved the motion to establish the Fitzroy Football Club, and it was carried unanimously. McMahon became the club's first president, a managing committee was elected, as was James Henry Simpson (associated with the manufacturing perfumery firm of Simpson's in Burnley) to the position of honorary secretary.[10] The local press reported that the meeting was 'very hearty and unanimous, all seeming agreed that it was time Fitzroy awoke from its lethargy and came forward to honourably hold its own against any of the surrounding districts'.[11]

Club officials met again on 10 October at the Brunswick Hotel. They established many of the club's foundations, including opening the member's roll (they settled subscription at five shillings) and selecting the club's colours and uniform: a blue cap and knickerbockers, maroon jersey and hose. The secretary was instructed to write to the VFA for information regarding the condition of entry.[12] Needing wait until the following year before its admission was confirmed, in the interim, the club began putting together a team. Normanby provided several men, while others were poached from neighbouring clubs. Soon, Fitzroy had a colourful team of footballers, ready for the 1884 season.

A prominent early recruit was Patrick McShane, one of the best athletes in the colony of Victoria. His 9–45 at the Sydney Cricket Ground in March 1881 while playing for a combined Victoria/New South Wales XI against the Australian team was legendary.[13] Alongside his prowess as a cricketer, he was also an accomplished footballer. One observer wrote that he 'always plays with great dash and untiring energy; runs well with the ball; is a fair kick and good mark; judges time and ball with success'.[14] He was already vice-captain of the Essendon Football Club when a relative, Sarah McShane, acquired the publican's license for the Leicester Arms Hotel at 81 Leicester Street, Fitzroy.[15] Paddy was soon drawn into the orbit of the new Fitzroy club, which no doubt welcomed such a talented and established footballer and leader.[16] He became a fixture of the club in its early days, and the players would often use the Leicester Arms Hotel for formal and informal gatherings.[17] 'Broad-shouldered, massively moustachioed, arms akimbo,' wrote one historian, he looked 'impatient for action in Fitzroy's first team photograph'.[18]

Other early clubmen included Jack Worrall, who club secretary James Simpson had seen at a game in Ballarat. Short and stocky, broad-shouldered and clean-shaven, Worrall was a nuggety and determined rover who could soar for marks and kick accurately with either foot.[19] Like McShane, he was both a prodigious footballer and cricketer and would captain the Victorian cricket team on sixteen occasions. A natural leader, he was regarded as 'undoubtedly one of the greatest players Australian football has produced' and was later club captain.[20] 'Dummy' Muir was another addition to the club. Dummy was so named because he was both deaf and dumb. Long and wiry, Muir also had a head of grey hair, and when he left his cap at the pavilion (which he often did), spectators found it difficult to believe that the 22-year-old was not at least twice that age. Despite his impairments, he was a good player that could swing forward or back and proved one of the club's better shots on goal in its early seasons.[21]

On Tuesday, 11 March 1884, the club held its first annual meeting at the Fitzroy Town Hall on Napier Street. About 400 people attended, including many past and present footballers. McMahon, chairing the meeting, promised to present a gold medal to the best all-round player in the club's inaugural season, as well as a silver medal for the member who rendered the best services to the club. Members were signed up and officer-bearers formally elected. Several local politicians, including the Fitzroy mayor and members of the Victorian Legislative Council and Assembly were appointed as club patrons. McMahon remained president, Simpson as secretary and 25-year-old McShane appointed the inaugural captain. All that remained was to join the league formally.

On the night of 25 April 1884, the VFA held its annual meeting at Young & Jackson's Hotel and admitted Fitzroy into what was then the colony's premier Australian rules football competition.[22] The following day, Fitzroy had its first competitive game as a member of the Association. Led by McShane, they played a 'scratch match' against Richmond Union, a junior team. Approximately one thousand spectators made their way to the Brunswick Street Oval for the game. Inclement weather dampened the occasion, but the Fitzroy City Brass Band did its best to liven the atmosphere with some 'choice selections'.[23] The slippery conditions made displays of skill rare — fumbles and dropped marks became the order of the day, much to the amusement of the crowd. Both teams tried hard, but neither managed a goal for the entire game. The final score, Fitzroy 0.14 to Richmond Union 0.2, was designated a draw with the rules of the time, as neither side had kicked a goal. Although it was disappointing to see Fitzroy struggle against junior opposition, one correspondent wrote: 'No doubt when the team have played together for some time they will be able to hold their own.'[24]

Fitzroy did not need to wait long to secure its first win. The following week, the team travelled across the city to play Williamstown, a club also playing its first senior season in the VFA. In front of 400 spectators at Gardens' Reserve, Fitzroy stormed over Williamstown in the first half, too 'fleet of foot' for the opposition. At half-time, Fitzroy was 1.4 with Williamstown yet to score. By the end of the contest, Fitzroy were victors 2.9 to 0.4, both goals from Dummy Muir, who became a 'tower of strength' in the ruck during these early years.[25] Graciously, the local Williamstown press applauded Fitzroy for their team performance: 'It would be invidious to individualise any [player], play being excellent throughout the whole team.'[26]

Fitzroy would play twenty-two games that season (at a time when the number of matches, even for the recognised senior teams, was not standardised), sixteen of which were against fellow VFA senior clubs. The highlight of the season was perhaps the 2.5 to 1.7 away victory over Hotham (the once and future North Melbourne Football Club, name temporarily altered due to the renaming of the suburb), the only win over an opponent that finished higher on the ladder that year. Fitzroy was, alas, unable to defeat Geelong — premiers in 1883 and premiers-in-waiting in 1884 — despite two attempts. In their first encounter at Corio in May, Fitzroy was defeated 4.17 to 2.6. The Fitzroyites (they would not come by the nickname of the Maroons until later) had their opponents initially 'under the whip', showing 'dash and brilliance all round', but allowed Geelong to fight back and eventually overrun them.[27] In the return fixture at the Edinburgh Gardens in August, Fitzroy fared much worse, losing 5.14 to 0.10. In front of a large crowd, Fitzroy 'came to the attack with all the confidence begot of a long succession of luck this season', but was 'taken down several pegs'. The defeat, one correspondent wrote, was 'one of the most crushing instilled in the present year'.[28] At least these matches were 'highly picturesque', an observer noted, given the contrast between the maroon of Fitzroy and the light blue and white of Geelong.[29]

Fitzroy played its final game of 1884 against South Melbourne at Albert Park on Saturday, 27 September, where poor conditions and Fitzroy's 'wretched kicking' condemned it to a 3.6 to 1.15 defeat. The game was notable for the late inclusion of Worrall, who was playing cricket for South Melbourne nearby. Before the game, Fitzroy officials told Worrall they needed him, and he obliged, playing the game still wearing his cricket whites.[30] So ended Fitzroy's inaugural season. Against VFA clubs, they finished with a respectable seven wins, eight losses and a draw. Writing in *The Australasian*, Peter Pindar declared it a 'highly creditable outcome for a first year', and believed that the individual strength of the team compared favourably to any afield.[31]

McMahon was seemingly delighted at the performance of his club, and the Tuesday following the final game, he invited the players and officials to Morgan's Café to celebrate the season.[32] During the evening, loyal toasts were duly proposed and honoured. McMahon presented medals, rewarding Mr Williams as the best all-round player and acknowledging club secretary James Simpson for his service. McShane toasted McMahon's health as president, calling him 'the father of the club' and attributing to him a great deal of the club's success. McMahon responded that he had sought to do his duty, and he was glad that his efforts were appreciated. He was pleased with how Fitzroy had progressed and believed that the club had a big future — even suggesting that if they amalgamated with the Fitzroy Cricket Club, there was no reason they could not build a stand at Brunswick Street Oval comparable to that of the Melbourne Cricket Club. After additional toasts to the future health and success of the club, and a special one to Mr Morgan, the proceedings, 'which had been of the most harmonious and pleasant character', were brought to a close with a rendition of 'Auld Lang Syne'.[33]

Over the following years the club's pioneers gradually drifted away. McMahon handed over presidency of the club to Sir Robert Best in 1888. He died thirty years later, having lost most of his assets in the depression of the 1890s.[34] Dedicated club secretary and life member James Simpson lived until the age of seventy-one. For many years his photograph hung on the Fitzroy committee room, honouring his contribution to the founding of the club.[35] Jack Worrall had a long and successful sporting career, coaching Carlton and then Essendon to multiple premierships, playing several Tests for Australia and then working as a journalist for many years.[36] Dummy Muir's fate is unknown, but for decades he was remembered as the man with white hair who always played without a cap.[37] Paddy McShane had a sad end, struggling financially before being committed to the Kew Asylum in 1901, dying two years later.[38] Whatever their fate, the Fitzroy Football Club was destined to outlive them all.

Yet the passage of time changed their club profoundly; many aspects of the modern Fitzroy Lions would have been unrecognisable to those involved in the club's foundation. As with the football club, the suburb of Fitzroy underwent a radical transformation: from a respectable area to an industrial slum, to its modern incarnation as a trendy, bohemian enclave. While some of the nineteenth-century hotels still exist on Gertrude Street, all the old shops have gone. Morgan's Café vanished quickly, with Mr Morgan selling the goodwill and stock of his business in 1885. Still, after so much change over the decades, odd details gain poignant resonance. A seemingly innocuous legacy from Fitzroy's first season, the singing of 'Auld Lang Syne', re-emerged many years later. Robert Burns' eighteenth-century poem set to music was sung to mark the end of another Fitzroy season, one remembered for entirely different reasons.

INTRODUCTION

THE POOR CITIZENS

Amid the barracking and general murmur of the crowd, the sound of the final siren pierced the chilly winter's air and brought the game to an anti-climactic end. It was Round 13 of the 1996 AFL season, and at the windswept Whitten Oval in Melbourne's inner west, the Fitzroy Lions had hosted Geelong. The result was beyond doubt; indeed, those of a pessimistic disposition likely pronounced Fitzroy beaten well before the first ball was bounced. For two years the Lions had been undersized and overwhelmed by almost every opponent, losing was now practically a fact of life. That day, Geelong won by 127 points. Fitzroy put up a fight in the first half but then completely capitulated after half-time, adding only two points to its total score, while conceding eleven goals and six behinds. The defeated players were left exhausted, battered and bereft. The victors could have celebrated, but there would have been little dignity in the act and even less grace.

It is an inevitability of competitive sport that football clubs will lose games, and although Fitzroy had lost more than its fair share in recent years, this had been no ordinary Saturday afternoon defeat.

Barely twenty-four hours before, an administrator had been appointed to oversee the affairs of the club. After an initial meeting with club officials, he had publicly declared that Fitzroy might be insolvent. The players were not stupid, they knew the club had been in financial difficulty for some time, but the severity and suddenness of the events caught them by surprise. That Friday night they were unsure whether they would even be playing the next day. League administrators, determined that the game would go ahead, rushed to secure funds to cover the match expenses. In the longer term, however, no-one knew what would happen. For some time, the AFL had been looking to reduce the number of teams in Melbourne and the prevailing view at AFL House was that if clubs could not pay their own way, they would need to go. It did not bode well for the Lions. After the game, the players trudged slowly and despondently off the ground and descended into the run-down dressing rooms under the E.J. Whitten Stand. The rooms were like a morgue; no-one spoke. Not the captain, not the coach. Individually, every player must have been thinking about their future, nervous and full of questions. Even if finances became available to fund their remaining nine games of the season, one journalist believed it was hardly fair to put the players through nine more 'humiliating and pointless performances' because Fitzroy was 'dead in body and soul'.[1]

This Fitzroy team, with an average age of twenty-two, was a shadow of what it had been even three years earlier. 'Fitzroy had become the equivalent of those Motown outfits,' one writer commented, 'who kept touring long after everyone who sang on the original records had retired, died or ambled into dissolute insanity, to be replaced by imitators in similar costumes.'[2] An uncharitable assessment to be sure, but that afternoon there were no proven champions like Paul Roos or Alastair Lynch wearing red, blue and gold. Instead, there were twenty-one young men with an average of forty-four games each. Their 24-year-old captain was close to tears as he led the team off the ground. He had played sixty-two games for the club for only sixteen wins. Today was another to add to a long list of losses.

For one player, this had been his first game. He had waited a year and a half to make his senior debut, and had done well with twelve disposals and seven tackles. For all he knew, however, his first game might also be his last. Fitzroy's oldest player had been playing senior football since 1986 and was formerly the captain of another club — that was, before he was considered surplus to requirements and traded to the Lions. He had not thrived at Fitzroy and looked to give the game away. The new coach had convinced him to stay, but he soon found himself out of favour and was dropped. This had been his first game in seven weeks, but he had managed only four disposals, and his professional future was looking bleak. Another player's concerns were more personal. The previous month his nineteen-year-old wife had given birth to their second daughter, twelve weeks premature. They had come across from Adelaide when the Lions drafted him and thus lacked family nearby to provide support. He had been juggling the demands of his family situation while trying to establish himself as a regular in his first season of AFL football. The club's current predicament was the last thing he needed.

Given the circumstances, the players had done their best. Throughout the afternoon, they were cheered on, as always, by their small band of loyal supporters. They did what supporters had always done, barracked for their boys and booed the umpires. Their mood was sombre and many experienced deep feelings of despair.[3] One supporter, who had followed the Lions for half a century, had been 'howling' all night. It was as if someone had cut out her heart with a knife, she said, and she vowed never to go to another game of AFL or give the league a cent.[4] Yet they were not entirely defeated. Many made light of the situation, if only in the form of gallows humour.[5] Sitting in the stands was the 1969 Brownlow medallist, Kevin Murray. When the Lions scored one of their two points for the second half, Murray heard a supporter behind him sigh, 'Closing the gap, Roys.'[6] The 1981 Brownlow medallist, Bernie Quinlan, was watching on too. The previous year the club legend stepped in when offered the position of Fitzroy's senior coach. It had been a bruising year, where his team had only won two games. Sacked before the end of the season and well before his contract expired, he doubted Fitzroy had the funds to pay out its remainder.[7]

All the Fitzroy supporters at the Whitten Oval that day and many more who had not made it to the ground had the same question: what would become of their club — the club, as their song proclaimed, that they held so dear? This may well have been the last time the Fitzroy Lions took the field. When the final siren sounded fans had spontaneously swarmed onto the field. One elderly woman rushed out to hug and kiss as many Fitzroy players as she could, 'as if kissing her boys goodbye'.[8] Supporters wept, the club's theme song was played and played again, and some players almost broke down in tears. Even when the players had disappeared up the race, the supporters lingered at the ground. 'Like saying goodbye to a terminally ill friend,' one reporter observed, 'they were not sure what to say. Not sure if they'd ever see that dear friend again.'[9] One elderly gentleman surveyed the scene, wiping away tears from his eyes before his wife clasped his hand and nodded in the direction of the exit. It was time to say farewell, possibly for the last time.[10]

The small number of spectators began drifting back to their cars to return home. As one Fitzroy supporter walked along the terraces, several Geelong supporters made a point of stopping to offer their condolences, state their fondness for her club and generally express their disgust at what was happening.[11] Driving back down the Princes Freeway, one young Geelong supporter, unaware of the larger machinations at play, asked his father whether they had just killed Fitzroy. His concern was touching, if misplaced. A small group of Fitzroy fans had remained in front of the main stand after the game, and they knew who to blame, chanting angrily about the League's chief executive officer, Ross Oakley. One man yelled, 'I hate the AFL! I hate the AFL!' as the Fitzroy club song played over the ground's loudspeakers.[12] For some time they continued their show of defiance, but soon they too capitulated and quietly headed home. There was nothing they could say or do to change the course of events.

The Fitzroy Football Club, its players, supporters and officials, would experience many poignant moments that year, but the scene of desolation after the conclusion of the Round 13 game against Geelong was perhaps the most powerful. Unlike the orchestrated commemorations later in the season, this was spontaneous; there was no time to prepare, there was no time to think — there was only the raw emotion of it. The following day, the injuries listed in *The Age*'s match report captured the tragedy of what had occurred that day, 29 June 1996:[13]

Injuries

Geelong: Mensch (ankle) replaced by Handley
Fitzroy: The club (broken heart)

...

'I don't talk about it anymore,' said Alan McConnell, the snow-haired veteran coach, as he sat across the table from me at a café in Canberra. The 61-year-old had been Fitzroy's assistant coach that Saturday in June 1996. Now, on a sunny Friday in August, he was in the nation's capital as the advance party for the Greater Western Sydney Giants' game against Adelaide at Manuka Oval the following evening. We met for coffee in one of the more pleasant shopping strips in Canberra to talk about his time at Fitzroy. McConnell has been around football all his life. Born and raised in the Victorian country town of Terang ('where football was God'), he has worked professionally in coaching and player development roles since the early nineties. He earned such a prodigious reputation within the 'industry' that he was the first person appointed to the Giants' football department. In time he was named the Director of Coaching, subsequently adopting a concurrent role as the club's AFLW Coach in 2018.

McConnell had a long and close history with Fitzroy, particularly during its tumultuous final years in the AFL. Recruited from the Hampden Football League in Victoria's south-west (the Lions' rural zone), he won a best and fairest playing for the Fitzroy Under 19s before illness prevented his progression towards the senior team. After a decade away from the club, he returned in the early nineties as Under 19s coach, development coach and then assistant coach. His 1996 season was as challenging as they came. Thrust into the position of caretaker coach after Round 14 he oversaw the slow disintegration of his club and the team of young men in his care. In a 1997 interview with *The Age*, he put a positive spin on these dreadful years. Acknowledging that there were some horrific moments, he believed that he had come out the other side 'a richer and more rounded person' in terms of his AFL experience.[14] Whatever he gained from his time at Fitzroy, he was nevertheless acutely affected by the club's demise.

Few involved with Fitzroy, be they officials, players or supporters, escaped the trauma of that year. Former committeeman and club official Arthur Wilson called 1996 'bloody awful'.[15] 'No-one enjoyed it,' reflected Greg Swann, the man who effectively ran the club during the final weeks of the season, 'no-one was happy about the whole thing, but it was what it was.'[16] Fitzroy captain Brad Boyd offered the understated, 'it was a bit of a sad time', while the club's 1996 best and fairest, Martin Pike, summed it up succinctly: 'It really was a year from hell.'[17] Indeed, it is difficult to find anyone involved with Fitzroy who does not share these sentiments. Writing, reading and reflecting on Fitzroy's 1996 season is a painful endeavour, and one not undertaken lightly. The year left broken hearts and deep scars, many of which have yet to heal completely. When McConnell and I spoke, however, he clarified that the reason he did not talk about Fitzroy was not that he did not want to, but because no-one was interested in the club anymore: 'Everyone's forgotten,' he said.[18]

This admission is unsurprising for an 'industry' biased towards the present and the future. Historical reflection and contextualisation are not in the vocabulary of the League in its modern incarnation: 'where are they at' and 'how far away are they from their next premiership' are the two key questions. In the contemporary AFL media cycle, the afterglow of a grand final will have barely dimmed before trade speculation begins in earnest — the seventeen clubs that did not win the premiership are each looking to build towards *their* moment of glory. Embedded within Collingwood in 2009, journalist Peter Ryan observed that the assistant coaches often struggled to recall the opponents they had played the previous month. A relentless focus on the upcoming game required them to 'discard any useless remnants from the past' if they were to be successful in the future.[19] Even at the end of 1996, after a year of historical celebrations, the AFL Commission chairman, John Kennedy Sr, suggested it was perhaps futile to look backwards.[20] For many, Fitzroy has become another useless remnant from the past to be discarded.

For those too young or unable to reach back into the recesses of memory, the Fitzroy Football Club was a foundation member of the VFL, known variously as the Maroons, the Gorillas, the Lions or simply the Roys. Inasmuch as a football club has a character or essence, Fitzroy's was very well defined. 'We were culture rich and cash poor,' said McConnell, perfectly describing the poor working-class club from Melbourne's inner suburbs that rarely met on-field success but was nevertheless proud of its history and its people.[21] After winning one VFA and seven VFL premierships in its first four decades, Fitzroy struggled both on and off the field. The club lacked a large catchment area from which to draw supporters and was squeezed out by larger neighbours Collingwood and Carlton. From then on, despite a final VFL premiership in 1944, it was a club perpetually short on resources and support. Evicted from its home at Brunswick Street in the late sixties, it also lost a physical connection to its place of origin. Still, all the challenges pulled Fitzroy people together into a tight community. 'We were downtrodden in a way,' reflected Matt Rendell, who played for Fitzroy from 1981 to 1991, 'but it didn't affect us, and it brought us close together. We were the poor citizens.'[22] The endearing intimacy between officials, players and the small number of supporters made the club what it was, but it was also a symptom of the more significant problem: Fitzroy never seemed able to progress beyond being a suburban club.

By 1996, the club's financial struggles were too great, and it was forced into a merger with the Brisbane Bears — the AFL's first, and thus far only, merger. For years, League administrators had been declaring that Melbourne could not sustain ten professional football clubs. The League's governing body, the AFL Commission, did not want to see clubs fold, but was unable and unwilling to offer much financial support to weaker teams. Their solution was to push for mergers, bringing together two smaller, less successful Melbourne clubs to pool supporters, players and resources and create new entities that could compete with the larger clubs. At the same time, the League was expanding from its suburban roots. South Melbourne had relocated to Sydney in 1982 (another painful event also slipping out of collective memory), and new clubs were established in Perth, Brisbane and Adelaide to create a national competition. The merger of lowly Fitzroy with the Brisbane Bears represented the best of both worlds for the Commission: removing a team from the crowded Melbourne market and bolstering a club in a non-traditional AFL state. To some, it was a masterstroke. 'Fitzroy has been exhumed from the grave it largely dug for itself to survive as a partner in a vibrant new force in Australian football,' wrote Mike Sheahan in the *Herald Sun* the day after the merger was completed.[23] Fitzroy president, Dyson Hore-Lacy, saw things differently. Calling it 'one of the most cynical and insensitive acts ever perpetrated in the history of sport', he denounced the merger, declaring that the club and its supporters had been 'obliterated by the stroke of a corporately-driven pen'.[24]

This book tells the story of the club's tumultuous final year in the AFL and the drama, politics and intrigue around the completion of the merger agreement. The historical significance of Fitzroy's 1996 season speaks for itself. As the editor of the *Footy Record*, Greg Hobbs, wrote in August 1996, Fitzroy's demise was the most significant football upheaval in League history: the 'loss of a foundation club in the centenary year beats everything else in terms of emotion and ramifications to the competition'.[25] Because of this, it is a story that needs to be conveyed anew to every generation. *Merger* is not necessarily an attempt to explain in extensive and forensic detail what happened to Fitzroy and why it was the only club to succumb to this miserable fate. That story is far too complicated; it stretches back into the late seventies and concerns the broader evolution of the League through the decades. Instead, this book will explore the devastating year of 1996, telling the story of both the merger and the experience of those affected by it. This matters because, beyond its historical significance, the story of Fitzroy's demise as an AFL club had human consequences; as Alan McConnell noted, football clubs are, above all else, about the people who are involved with them.[26] Narrowing the timeframe to a single year allows for a much deeper and richer understanding of what the players, supporters, club officials and volunteers endured during that *annus horribilis*. These perspectives are vital in fully appreciating the Fitzroy story; it is insufficient merely to understand how and why Fitzroy's merger occurred — one must also understand why it mattered.

Writing about Fitzroy's demise as an AFL club also allows space for philosophical musings on the nature and character of the modern AFL. The merger asked profound questions about the AFL's relationship with the people who love and support Australian rules football — questions that were never satisfactorily answered. Who are the actual custodians of the game? What obligations do the League's administrators owe to the supporters, those who make the game what it is? What place do history and tradition have in the modern AFL? At what point do commercial decisions and imperatives detract from the essence of the sport and harm supporters' engagement with the League? In short, how does the AFL Commission fulfil its role as being the 'keeper of the code', not just the entity responsible for ensuring the competition remains financially viable? These questions seemed to fall by the wayside very quickly after the merger and are just as pertinent now as they were in 1996.

Finally, notwithstanding the drama and the anguish of the merger, it is essential to note that the Fitzroy Football Club still exists, despite its seeming death in 1996. Fitzroy limped on as a football club without a competition in which to play football — that was until it merged with the University Reds in 2008 and began competing in the Victorian Amateur Football Association (VAFA). The Fitzroy Football Club is now a thriving suburban club, with both men's and women's teams, playing home games at Brunswick Street Oval on Saturday afternoons, just as their forebears had done, in front of healthy and dedicated crowds.

Yet despite the success of Fitzroy in its modern incarnation, the significance, trauma and tragedy of the club's departure from professional football should not be minimised, or worse, forgotten. When Fitzroy left the AFL, part of Melbourne's cultural fabric was torn away. The club of Bunton, Smallhorn, Ruthven, Murray, Wilson, Quinlan and Roos that won eight VFL premierships was lost to the league it helped create. As author and Roys supporter Adam Muyt argued, Fitzroy deserves better than being a mere footnote in VFL/AFL history.[27] The history and heritage of Australian rules football belong to those of us that love the game, but we are mere custodians of it — we own it for a time, nurture it, and then pass it on to our children and future generations. For them, the story of the Fitzroy Football Club in 1996 is a worthy tale to tell.

CHAPTER ONE

HEART AND SOUL

'Where are the Fitzroy people? The battle-weary few who remained like a strung-out battalion decimated by too much time in the front line'

— Simon Hawking, Fitzroy player.[1]

Debutante balls were an excellent place to meet a future spouse, or so Pat Ryan discovered. It was the mid-fifties, and sixteen-year-old Pat needed a tall young man to accompany her to such an occasion. Accordingly, Ward Leydon, whom she had never met, was selected as her partner. Looking to overcome the awkwardness of their arranged pairing, they searched around for any common interests. Soon enough, they discovered a mutual love of the Fitzroy Football Club. Pat was born and bred in Fitzroy, and she and her sister Doreen had been attending games since the late forties. Ward shared Pat's deep affection for their local club, and by 1958 the couple were married. Fitzroy was central to family life; following the birth of their son,

David, they draped a small, knitted Fitzroy jumper at the end of his cot before he left the hospital. Along with their daughter, Kelly, the family followed the Lions across Melbourne at five different home grounds and an assortment of opposition venues. Standing in the outer over all these years, the family of Fitzroy supporters went through plenty of thin and not much thick. But that was their lot — fate selected them to be a family of Roys, and you never took sides against the family. When Ward and Pat's first grandson, Sean, was born in 1992, he too was welcomed into this sprawling familial narrative, with Pat taking him to his first Fitzroy game at the age of two.[2] 'The Fitzroy thing was always a family thing,' David reflected.[3] Week in, week out, the Leydon clan would go to games as a family, stand in the same spot at the various grounds, engage in the same rituals. There was just no other way to do football.

Anyone can watch a well-played game of Australian rules football and, with an open mind, appreciate it as a spectacle. Arthur Conan Doyle attended the 1920 VFL Grand Final between Richmond and Collingwood and was impressed by the athleticism and the skill the game demanded of its participants.[4] The AFL's famous 1994 advertising campaign highlighted the game's appealing and distinctive aspects: the physicality of the contest, high marking, fast-paced action, goals from seventy metres out, and, according to the lone female contributor, 'thirty-six big guys in very tight shorts'. Few, however, remain passive and neutral observers of this impressive sporting spectacle. Instead, they become invested, either by chance or by choice, in supporting one particular club.[5]

The attraction of club support is multifaceted. There is, of course, the pure exhilaration of being emotionally invested in a team, where the outcome of a game may rest on a piece of individual skill or collective determination to hold their nerve, leaving fans to ride the emotions. It is a life of great highs and lows, of bitter disappointments and all too brief moments of triumph. Each season, supporters are transported into 'an intense drama', wrote academics John Cash and

Joy Damousi in their 2009 book *Footy Passions*, riding a roller-coaster of 'triumph and despair, mourning and melancholy, joy and fulfilment, sacrifice and resurrection'.⁶ With such attachment inevitably brings much trauma and heartache, yet the rewards of passionate support are often ample recompense, with supporters warmed by the memories of great games, brilliant players and moments of glory.

What Fitzroy supporter could forget that Elimination Final at a sodden Waverley Park, where Mick Conlan's terrible game was redeemed by the greatest goal of his career that sealed an improbable one-point victory over the reigning premiers. Or in 1979, when the Lions defeated Melbourne by 238 points at Waverley Park, the highest winning margin in League history. Fitzroy historian Pete Carter considered the 150-point demolition of North Melbourne at the Junction Oval in 1983 (which saw Quinlan, Rendell and Conlan kick twenty-two between them) one of the greatest home-and-away performances of all time.⁷ Then there was the underdog victory against Richmond in 1980 (when Warwick Irwin had a feast in the middle) or the three-point victory over Collingwood in 1992 thanks to a Paul Roos goal with eleven seconds remaining.⁸ Fans live for these moments.

Beyond the drama that each new season brings, club affiliation has deeper resonance, both personally and communally. Football clubs occupy a special place in the hearts of those who follow them. 'In telling us about their support for a beloved team,' Cash and Damousi wrote, 'supporters also tell us about themselves, their life stories, their family relations, their friendships and their anxieties; disappointments, hopes and fears.'⁹ Football clubs can be crucial to personal identity, and could be part of someone's life from as early as birth, when family members place club colours on a newborn baby as a form of secular baptism, until their death, when those same colours could be draped over a coffin at a funeral. In addition, one Fitzroy supporter suggested that many fans viewed their club as one of the few concrete links back to their own childhood, and, in many cases, the club made them feel relevant through passing on their own passions to the next generation.[10]

Clubs also provide a communal identity beyond self or family (although family history and sporting allegiances are often tightly linked) and enable individuals to combine together in pursuit of a collective purpose.'[11] In many cases, a child might have been the only Fitzroy supporter at their school. This was the case for Steven Smith, a cheer squad member. At games, however, he would be surrounded by fellow Roys: 'You felt like you were part of something,' he declared.[12] For many, the community of Fitzroy supporters became something of a surrogate family. Skott Dean was another lone Royboy at school, and coming from an unstable family background (with none of his family supporting Fitzroy) football was a welcome escape. Attending games alone as a teenager, older supporters would look after him, helping him develop a lifelong love of the club.[13]

In the beginning, the club's supporters were Fitzroy residents, for whom the Maroons were their local team. At the club's 1892 AGM, president Robert Best, MLA, proclaimed that the team afforded 'great pleasure' to locals, with several matches garnering impressive attendances. Fitzroy games were apparently 'freer from roughness' than most other clubs, one of the reasons the citizens of Fitzroy were proud of their team.[14] Even by 1996, there were still many Roys who could trace their origins back to the suburb itself. Paul Noone was born in Fitzroy and lived at 528 Brunswick Street for his first twenty-five years, being baptised, educated and married at St Brigid's on Nicholson Street.[15] Phyllis Walker grew up in North Fitzroy. She and her husband opened a fruit shop opposite Brunswick Street Oval, and on Saturdays, they would go upstairs and watch the game out their window.[16] Stuart Winstanley's grandfather emigrated from Estonia in the fifties. Living on Gore Street, he began supporting Fitzroy as a way to assimilate into his new society, especially when he drank at the Builders' Arms or the Union Club Hotel.[17] Jan Wright and her siblings were born and raised in Fitzroy: 'There was absolutely *no way* you'd ever think of barracking for anybody else, ever.'[18]

As Melbourne expanded and the VFL's tribal, suburban character changed, families became the primary emotional tether to Fitzroy. For matriarch Norma Burnie, her whole family revolved around football. Her daughter, Janelle, met her future husband when they were members of the Fitzroy cheer squad, and each new child entering the family was either named after a player or adorned in a Fitzroy jumper at a young age.[19] Kevin Power grew up around the corner from the Brunswick Street Oval and would walk to Fitzroy games with his brothers. When his three sons, Ben, Luke and Sam, were old enough, they would travel up together from Oakleigh every week to watch the Lions, dressed in Fitzroy jumpers, socks, shorts and boots.[20] Jason Wellman's grandfather had given him a Fitzroy jumper when he was two days old and took him to his first game as a six-month-old. By 1996, Jason was thirteen and fully committed to the club allegiance into which he was born.[21] Family ties did not necessarily overcome all obstacles, however. 'I was the only one of four boys to follow my dad in barracking for Fitzroy,' Troy Selwood recalled, 'probably because they were pretty woeful at the time.'[22] Sam Lord's family was divided down gender lines: he and his brother followed his father in barracking for Fitzroy, while his sister adopted their mother's allegiance for Essendon.[23]

Other supporters came to the club through alternative pathways, developing a passion and love for the club just as strong as if it had been passed down through the generations. Kev Court grew up in a Collingwood family before switching to St Kilda and then to Fitzroy. His reason for eventually settling on the Roys was the colours: 'I was still young enough to be impressed just by the colourful uniform.'[24] As a child, Chris Donald's grandparents gave him a toy lion, named 'Larry Lion', and decided to begin supporting Fitzroy based on his affection for Larry.[25] Philip Mendes' father had devoutly followed both the St Kilda Football Club and, his first love, the St Kilda Cricket Club. When the football club left the Junction Oval for Moorabbin in 1964, he viewed it as treachery and ceased his support. When Fitzroy began playing at the oval in 1970, he adopted the Lions as his new team.[26]

Of all the reasons people arrived at Fitzroy, one reason never given was the expectation of success. Following their 1944 premiership, Fitzroy made the finals only nine more times. If anything, the club's poor on-field record did more to cause those born and raised in Fitzroy families to fall away from the club, rather than enticing others to flock to the colours.

Whatever the source of supply, however, once people embraced the club, their bonds often grew deeper. Fans gave their time, their money and their emotional and physical energy. Dedication to the club could mean giving up several hours on the weekend from time to time, or it could be a lifelong commitment, living and breathing their team. Many volunteered around the club, receiving nothing in return but the satisfaction of being part of something they loved. Jessie Crump was the daughter of Goldie Waterford, who played for Fitzroy in 1887. For twenty years Jessie had been repairing players' guernseys, often being asked to sew a number onto a jumper at the last minute due to a late change in the starting team. 'That's just the way Fitzroy does things,' remarked Jessie's son, Ross, who, like the rest of his family, was devoted to the club.[27] Other supporters showed their commitment by just turning up, week after week, to barrack from the outer irrespective of Fitzroy's chances of winning. Rob Clancy's father, Jack, had one game for Fitzroy in 1957, spending all four quarters on the bench. Rob started going to see the Roys in the mid-seventies, and by the nineties he was going to every game in Melbourne. 'Fitzroy Football Club was a huge part of my identity,' he reflected.[28]

Supporters had their rituals: packing the thermos and lunch for the day before the game, buying a record or some paraphernalia outside the ground, standing or sitting at a familiar spot in the outer, running onto the ground after the final siren, maybe to get close to a favourite player or simply to have a kick with family or mates. At games, the most energetic of the barrackers joined the cheer squad, often wearing the ubiquitous duffle coat adorned with an array of badges, labels, names and numbers and ready to launch into songs and chants.²⁹ Lorraine Duncan was six weeks old when she went to her first Fitzroy game but needed to wait until she was six before she could pay the $1 fee and join the cheer squad. The group was a big family, she recalled: 'Fitzroy was my life. I lived and breathed Fitzroy. I knew no different.'³⁰ Other groups, such as Kev Court's so-called 'Lynch Mob', offered a different experience for fans. Finding the cheer squad restrictive and comprised of too many young children, Court and his mates gathered together away from the goals to sing songs, scream obscenities and be generally uncouth in support of the Roys.³¹

Everyone had their favourite players. Gordon Chaundy had been friends with Haydn Bunton, the club's Depression-era triple Brownlow medallist, who was blessed with supreme athletic prowess and matinee idol good looks. Gordon's daughter, Jean, followed her father and started supporting Fitzroy as a seven-year-old. Her favourite player, 1944 premiership captain Freddie Hughson, was also her local constable.³² As a child, Karen Scott would go to school and tell everyone that she barracked for Fitzroy *and* Kevin Murray. Bernie Quinlan was Nancy Stokes' idol, naming her blue heeler 'Bernie' in his honour.³³ Rod Walsh wore Garry Wilson's number 29 to the games, enamoured with his courage, skill and commitment to fair play.³⁴ Young Jonathan Brown had, at various times, Richard Osborne's '44', Alastair Lynch's '11' and Paul Roos' '1' on the back of his Fitzroy jumper.³⁵ And who did not love Darren Wheildon, the very definition of a Fitzroy cult hero? Supporter Liz Crompton converted from Geelong to Fitzroy after meeting 'Doc'. 'I guess I am addicted to him,' she admitted. When Wheildon left Fitzroy for West Adelaide at the end of 1994, she and her husband Ken personally threw him a farewell party at their Dandenong North home.³⁶

Despite their lowly status, Fitzroy had its share of prominent supporters. The number one ticket holder, Tom Reynolds, had been the state Member of Parliament for Gisborne since 1979. In 1996, he was Minister for Sport, Recreation and Racing, as well as Minister for Rural Development. Former Labor Opposition Leader Frank Wilkes was also a passionate Roys supporter. 'Political commitments that clashed with Fitzroy games,' a former staffer declared, 'were never given high priority.'[37] Local celebrity supporters ranged from television personalities Bert Newton and John Blackman, to several members of the Channel Seven police drama *Cop Shop* (Gil Tucker, John Orcsik and Paula Duncan) to car salesman Ken Morgan. Playwright Barry Dickins was also a well-known Royboy.[38] Among the many and varied topics about which he chose to write, Fitzroy was a constant theme, eliciting great passion. His 'A Sentimental Roymance' columns in *The Melbourne Times* were required reading, and he even wrote a play about the club, simply titled 'Royboys', that was first performed in 1987. Another writer, South African-born Peter Temple, moved to Melbourne in 1982. Once he realised the importance of football to his new home, he started following his local team: Fitzroy. Temple infused his passion for the Lions into his work. His debut novel, *Bad Debts* (published in 1996), featured the alcoholic, former lawyer turned investigator protagonist, Jack Irish, whose father was said to have played for the Roys in the forties.

Focusing on Fitzroy supporters should not imply that they were somehow more passionate or dedicated than supporters of other clubs. All clubs have their share of fanatics who give their whole lives to the colours, casuals who drift in and out as the team's fortunes wax and wane, and those who fall somewhere between the two. What separates supporters of different clubs is the nature of the team they support. Some supporters live in blissful ignorance of what it means to follow a club that is truly struggling; others understand this pain all too well. Footscray, for instance, knew many of the same financial worries as Roys, particularly in the late eighties, while St Kilda's on-field record was much more dismal than Fitzroy's, finishing last twenty-five times between 1897 and 1996. Yet by the mid-nineties, extinction was not looming over their heads in quite the same way as it was for the Roys. One Lions fan recalled the years before 1996 were 'pretty hard because you were going to the games and not knowing whether Fitzroy was going to be around the year after. You just had that eerie feeling about going to games; it was a really desperate battle.'[39]

The mid-nineties were not a good time to be a Fitzroy supporter. 'Deep in our hearts everyone barracks for Fitzroy,' Greg Champion sang, a claim that could only ring true about a club so bereft of success and so unthreatening as the Lions. The rare period of on-field strength and assuredness from 1979 to 1986 was a fading memory, as the club had not played a final since that glorious September in 1986. They had narrowly missed the finals in 1989 and then struggled in the wrong half of the ladder from then on. Tenth place in 1992 was followed by eleventh in 1993, although the Roys were competitive early in both seasons before falling away as winter set in. In 1994, they finished fourteenth and then sixteenth in 1995, earning the club's seventh wooden spoon.

Fitzroy supporters had been through slumps before, but something was different this time. Multiple clubs were in financial trouble, and the dreaded 'M' word — merger — was being spoken aloud again. Fans read the papers each year, seeing story after story about the club's woes and predicting its imminent decline. 'Merge or bust' was the headline of a Mike Sheahan piece in the *Sunday Age* in July 1993, in which he described the 'chronically ill' Fitzroy as sliding 'inexorably to its grave'.[40] In 1994, Roys fans read articles such as 'Fitzroy's future again at risk' and 'AFL plan dooms Lions'.[41] In 1995, when the AFL Commission imposed a rule to ensure clubs met minimum income criteria, Stephen Linnell wrote in *The Age* that Fitzroy 'would face almost certain extinction' unless it merged.[42] One supporter came to dread the Monday newspaper, not because of the match reports of Fitzroy's losses, but for fear of yet another story about the club's financial plight.[43] Even with a healthy scepticism of the media's accuracy and its agenda, many suspected there was no smoke without fire.

Ailing financial health was at the root of Fitzroy's decline, and the club's condition was not just evident on annual reports and balance sheets; the exodus of talent from the club spoke volumes. Despite losing Gary Pert in 1990 and Richard Osborne in 1992, the core of the senior team had remained intact. A positive 1993 was undermined, however, when at the end of the season, 25-year-old Alastair Lynch announced he was moving to Brisbane, giving an emotional farewell to the Lynch Mob at the Fitzroy Club Hotel after he had officially signed.[44] Club captain Paul Roos considered Lynch to be the most valuable player in the League at the time, and some thought his departure was the beginning of the end for Fitzroy.[45] Soon the floodgates opened: Ross Lyon, Paul Broderick, Michael Gale, Matthew Armstrong, John Blakey, Darren Kappler, Jamie Elliott, Marcus Seecamp, Matthew Dundas, Peter Caven and Michael Dunstan had all left by 1995.[46] Other clubs offered more money, better facilities and the chance to play in successful teams. Compared with Fitzroy, it was hard to say no.

All of this took a toll: losing players not only affected the team's competitiveness, but it also hit morale among players and supporters alike. Finally, it all became too much for the last major hold-out, Paul Roos. He had been a great servant of the club, starting with the Lions when he was fifteen, and playing for thirteen seasons in the seniors, six as captain. During that time he had been one of the League's best players and had resisted offers from larger clubs like Collingwood and Carlton. But by 1994, the state of the club, its challenges and the lack of hope about its future were telling. Out of contract at the end of the season, he took an offer to play for Sydney.[47] Many supporters were disappointed, but Kevin Murray (with whom he shared Fitzroy's No. 1 jumper) understood his plight and wrote him an encouraging letter to let him know he had made the right decision.[48]

As supporters watched player after player drift away, insult was added to injury at the start of the 1994 season when the Western Oval (renamed the Whitten Oval following the death of Ted Whitten in 1995) became the Lions' new 'home'. After leaving Brunswick Street, they played at Princes Park from 1967 to 1969, before moving to the Junction Oval for a successful period still looked back upon with fondness.

Ground rationalisation forced Fitzroy to relocate in 1984 to Victoria Park until 1986, when it returned to Princes Park in 1987 and remained there until 1993. While never properly 'home', Princes Park had served the Lions well in the early nineties. Financial constraints, however, compelled the board to save money where they could, which led Fitzroy into an agreement as a co-tenant with Footscray at the Western Oval.

Like Lynch's departure, some considered the move to the Western Oval in 1994 the mortal blow from which the club never recovered.[49] After the board announced the move, several senior players voiced their displeasure internally. Within a year, most of these players, including Paul Roos (who now struggled to see the club ever becoming successful again) departed.[50] Commonly referred to as windswept, the ground was inhospitable in winter; aside from its two main stands on the western wing, spectators stood on the terraces. To the north, the Barkly Street end was difficult to kick to, as a stiff breeze came from behind the goals; to the south, if a forward kicked forcefully towards the Geelong Road end they may never see the ball again. While the playing surface started each season in pristine condition, after several games and a little Melbourne rain it became a quagmire.[51] Towards the end of the 1996 season, clubs petitioned to have games moved as the surface was so bad it was considered a workplace health and safety issue for the players, umpires and staff.

Footscray players and fans faced these problems too, but for them, the Western Oval was their home — both the ground and the Footscray people belonged in and to the western suburbs. For Fitzroy, this was a foreign place, too far away from their heartland. At a Footscray v Fitzroy game at the Western Oval some years before, Roys supporter Rob Clancy was walking around the outer when a voice boomed out: 'Go back to fucking Brunswick Street you latte-sipping bastard!'[52] Many Fitzroy supporters and players did not want to be there either.[53] Barry Dickins described the ground as 'a bloody disgrace', a 'filthy, squalid, ferret-box not fit for decent mums and dads and kids to barrack from.'[54] It was neither comfortable nor popular; attendances for Fitzroy home games at the Western Oval dropped by twenty-five per cent from their Princes Park levels.[55] Worse still, Fitzroy's form at their new 'home' was dismal — two wins and thirteen loses in 1994 and 1995. Each loss in 1995 had been by an average of eleven goals, including a 126-point thrashing by Sydney in Round 19, when Tony Lockett kicked sixteen straight. A dwindling but dedicated group of fans still came week after week to support their team and, much more often than not, watch them lose. One supporter recalled being at the Western Oval for a sparsely attended game in the pouring rain: 'We were all just kind of drowned, wet and freezing cold and getting done, and there I was thinking, "So this is as good as it gets." It was pathetic really.'[56]

Without many supporters even in the best of times, by 1996 the recent years of turmoil had not been kind to the club's membership drives. Only 8806 members signed up in 1995, and this fell to 7628 in 1996.[57] No-one could doubt the commitment of this small band; as Martin Flanagan wrote: 'You have to be a person with some depth in your being to hang in with a footy club that has gone years without winning a game, which has been threatened with extinction on a weekly basis for most of the past decade.'[58] What was one of the club's strengths, intimacy and closeness among the 'happy few', was also in no small part the cause of its downfall — there were simply too few people paying to watch and support the club, and not enough to come to its rescue when needed. Since 1986, Fitzroy's average home attendance was 12,631, the lowest Melbourne-based club by some margin. In 1995, the so-called 'big four' clubs — Collingwood, Richmond, Carlton and Essendon — each drew over 40,000 to their games, while Fitzroy could only muster 11,587.[59]

The bonds of family, tribal commitment and a sense of community and belonging kept these few supporters coming back, week after week, to watch their team get flogged. It was hard, but they did it because they knew no other way to be. 'Fitzroy was a cause,' wrote Martin Flanagan, 'a lost cause for most of the past decade perhaps, but, for all that, something which gave meaning to a lot of people's lives.'[60] Pat and Ward Leydon would agree. In 1991, Ward had taken long-service leave to volunteer week after week at a fundraising appeal for the club, with son David coming to work the night shift — all to no avail.[61] Alan McConnell summed up the mentality of the few Roys supporters who remained faithful: 'If you loved Fitzroy, you loved them to death.'[62] Ominously, death seemed too near for comfort come the start of the 1996 AFL season.

CHAPTER TWO

THE BOYS FROM OLD FITZROY

'I'm here to be successful and I'll be extremely disappointed if I don't find over a period of time sufficient people to make an impact on what you might call a new Fitzroy culture'

— Michael Nunan, Fitzroy senior coach.[1]

Standing to the side of the oval at Trinity Grammar School's sports grounds in Bulleen, Michael Nunan watched as his players went about their pre-season training. Under the glaring eyes of their new senior coach, men blew away the cobwebs of the all-too-brief break since their last game two months ago: a 103-point loss to North Melbourne in the final round of the 1995 home and away season. A rover in his playing days, 46-year-old Nunan was not the tallest man on the training ground that evening, but what he lacked in physical presence he made up for in force of personality; Nunan had the stature of a terrier, journalist Joyce Brown observed, but the bark of a Rottweiler.[2] Very soon, every player knew precisely what he expected. Rather than easing into the pre-season, after a ten-kilometre run, Nunan let his players loose with footballs; assessing their technique, accuracy and control by hand and foot. He punished players for bad skill: Martin Pike did twenty-five sit-ups for 'bad hands', while Chris Johnson missed three passes and found himself doing 150 sit-ups (although Nunan let him go with thirty or so remaining).[3]

It was October 1995. Two weeks had passed since Nunan was announced as Fitzroy's latest senior coach, succeeding the much-loved but underqualified Bernie Quinlan. In that time he had familiarised himself with the club, sitting down to interview almost every player and staff member individually.[4] His goal was clear: make Fitzroy competitive. He had been given two years (with the option of a third) for this ambitious task, and he firmly believed he needed all three at a minimum to rebuild the team to meet his exacting requirements.[5] With the national draft looming at the end of the year, he signalled his intent early by trimming his list. One player culled was Doug Hawkins, the 35-year-old 350-game Footscray legend who had come across to Fitzroy at the end of 1994. After a decent 1995 season, many around the club felt he should stay on another year and be an on-field leader for the young playing group. Nunan had other ideas and swiftly dispensed of his services.[6] For the remainder of the pre-season, the coach studied and tested his players, determining who would be part of his core team and who, like Hawkins, was surplus to requirements.

Just as he was learning about his new team, his players were learning more about their new coach. Michael Allen Nunan had played 254 games in the SANFL, winning four premierships with Sturt, before coaching North Adelaide from 1981 to 1992. Those unfamiliar with South Australian football had known little about him, but, at his first Fitzroy press conference, he clearly outlined his *modus operandi*: 'I guess I'm a reasonably hard taskmaster who has a very strong emphasis on the accuracy and development of skill and a coach who doesn't like errors.'[7] He was also a strong-minded perfectionist who had an unshakable belief in his philosophy with little concern for offending sensibilities. Depending on one's perspective, he was either arrogant, or he simply had high standards.[8] He also had a pedigree as a thinking coach with a sophisticated football mind, a devotee of sports science and a man not afraid of integrating new technology into football. Holding the licence to sell Polar heart-rate monitors in Australia, he used these devices to measure the performance of his players at training and in practice matches.[9] And, most of all, he was successful: in his twelve years at North Adelaide, the Roosters played in five grand finals, winning two.

Nunan had not been the club's first preference to replace Bernie Quinlan, that distinction belonged to North Melbourne reserves coach Rodney Eade. The former Hawthorn premiership player had accepted the position but reneged when the Sydney Swans unexpectedly accepted an ambit claim Eade had put to them. They were searching for a replacement for Ron Barrassi, and Swans president Richard Colless overruled his board to make the appointment.[10] Other names were considered, such as Terry Wallace, Jeff Gieschen, Fitzroy's caretaker coach Alan McConnell and former club captain John Murphy. Yet the selection committee ultimately decided on Nunan. His credentials as a premiership-winning senior coach in the SANFL stood out, as did his willingness to work for reportedly $65,000 per season (compared to salaries between $200,000 and $300,000 for leading AFL coaches), making him the lowest-paid senior coach in the AFL.[11] Nunan was a successful businessman and did not need the income from football. 'The issue was not the salary,' he said at the time of his appointment. 'The issue is coaching. The issue is making Fitzroy successful.'[12] He had been out of football since leaving North Adelaide at the end of 1992, working as the director of the South Australian Institute of Sport. A competitive man, he could not stay away from the game for too long and when Fitzroy approached him, he jumped at the opportunity to coach again.[13]

Nunan needed supreme self-confidence to take on one of football's most difficult jobs and was fully committed to implementing his system and his philosophy at Fitzroy. Not long into his tenure, however, he realised how far from competitive his team was. Watching his players fumble through their early training sessions was sobering and he was devastated by the realisation that the club was paying players in a 'so-called professional competition' that had 'such poor levels of skill and poor levels of conditioning'.[14] Skill was central to Nunan's football philosophy, something ingrained from his playing days at Sturt where he had been under the tutelage of the legendary South Australian coach Jack Oatey. Rather than kicking long to contests, Oatey wanted his players to maintain possession of the ball and then distribute it effectively by hand or foot.[15] Echoing his former coach, Nunan would say there were two facets to his coaching style: getting the ball and retaining it — and both required a high level of skill.[16] Nunan 'worshipped at the altar of skill', one observer wrote, and skill development became his main effort during the pre-season.[17] On his desk, he had a chart showing how long his players maintained possession and another plotting the efficiency of their use.[18]

Nothing typified his approach like handballs. Fitzroy's players had various reflections about Nunan, but his obsession with handballs stood out prominently.[19] Like Oatey, he thought of the handball as a formidable weapon, and he developed a game plan around it. The ball would come out from defence by hand to a fast, skilled midfield that would navigate their way through opposition with a series of handballs (defender Frank Bizzotto recalled that Nunan demanded four or five handballs before players took a kick) before kicking into the forward line.[20] He drilled this game plan into his players and left an indelible imprint. Fellow South Australian Martin Pike could spot the Jack Oatey style instantly, with its emphasis on fitness, handball receives and running to assist teammates.[21] Midfielder Brett Chandler summed up Nunan's approach as: 'Run, handball, run, handball.'[22]

He also sought to centralise control of football operations to an almost unprecedented degree.[23] He had no chairman of selectors (a position formerly held by 37-year-old Grant Lawrie, who had played

151 games for the Lions in the seventies and eighties), personally taking the responsibility with the match committee for selecting the team each week. He tightened the player rules, systematised training and imposed stricter policies around allowing supporters access to the rooms on game days. Even the football directors, Colin Hobbs and David McMahon, were kept at arm's length from the football department, with Nunan adopting a 'my way or the high way' approach.[24] The board initially welcomed these changes, pleased to see some regimentation in the football department. Club president Dyson Hore-Lacy later admitted that they had allowed themselves 'a moment or two of optimism'.[25]

At his first press conference, Nunan declared that the whole club had to move into a much more positive frame of mind and begin accepting what was required for a winning environment.[26] The malaise at Fitzroy was a genuine problem. One of the promising young players, Chris Johnson, believed that the culture of the club reinforced the belief that they were not good enough to win and that every other team was better.[27] Brett Chandler similarly confessed that the players probably went out some weeks expecting to be beaten.[28] To Simon Hawking, this attitude was merely a reflection of the grim reality: by 1996, he knew the players would turn up and do their best, but he often doubted that such effort would translate into a win.[29] It was an understandable mentality among a young team for whom winning in Fitzroy colours was rare. Of the thirty-one players returning for the 1996 season, only six had won more than ten games at Fitzroy. The pillaging of so many senior players over the years left the club with little corporate memory of being a competitive side. 'It was basically a bunch of kids with a few older blokes thrown into the mix,' recalled 22-year-old ruckman, Brett Cook.[30]

Being so young had other downsides: not only did the team lack the experience and physical maturity to be competitive, but many players were being given senior games before they had earned them. By rewarding performances that were not at a proper AFL standard, it became difficult to change attitudes and work rate. It did not help that most of the experienced players, those who could set the necessary standards in training and during games, had left the club. Furthermore, giving young men senior games without years of pre-season conditioning had ramifications for their longevity in the game and their general physical wellbeing. These were difficult issues for Nunan to navigate, and despite his best efforts, there was no short-term solution.

Over the summer months, Fitzroy's players became more familiar with Nunan's preferred style of play, and Nunan learned more about the strengths and weaknesses of the list. The team he inherited from Bernie Quinlan won two games in the 1995 season and was derided in a post-season assessment in the *Sunday Age* as 'a laughing stock, [their] lack of skill, game plan or fundamental on (or off)-field discipline ridiculed by opponents'.[31] Some said Fitzroy had the poorest list in recent history.[32] Promisingly, the draft process had been working to bring in talented youngsters such as Chris Johnson, Jarrod Molloy, John Barker and Simon Hawking, all of whom were nominated for the Norwich Rising Star award in 1994. To increase the club's stocks of young talent, Nunan went to the draft at the end of 1995. With pick number two, the Lions acquired 21-year-old Matthew Primus, whom commentator Gerard Healy believed was the club's best recruit since Paul Roos.[33] With three of their other five picks inside the top twenty, Fitzroy also selected Scott Bamford, Shane Clayton and Nick Carter. Later in the year, Jake Niall found himself impressed with the 'surprising level of youthful talent' at Fitzroy.[34]

Some older players had defied the exodus and remained at Fitzroy while their peers left for higher ground. Jason Baldwin played his first senior game for Fitzroy in 1989, while Stephen Paxman and Frank Bizzotto played theirs in 1991. Their commendable loyalty came at a professional cost, however, as none had seen many victories since 1993. Most of the other 'older blokes' on Fitzroy's list had come from other clubs. The team needed mature players to carry the physical burden during games and, in theory, set an example for the younger players about the standards necessary to be competitive in the AFL. Half-back flanker Martin Pike, forward Darren Holmes and self-professed 'Poly Gap filler' John McCarthy were dependable additions to the Lions' squad.[35] Experienced Tasmanian on-baller Simon Atkins had been a good acquisition from Footscray in 1995. The Dogs delisted the Axe (as he was known) due to concerns he was a one-position player. By 1996, he was Fitzroy's deputy vice-captain, giving the midfield a much-needed touch of class and experience. One of Fitzroy's better players in the 1995 season, he readily acknowledged that Nunan's emphasis on developing skill was sorely required and wanting the Lions to take the ball from one end of the ground to the other without making a mistake.[36] Other mature players were less successful, leading to some candid reflections from their younger teammates. 'They weren't your gun players,' Chris Johnson suggested. 'They were good at other clubs, but they were probably good because they had gun players around them.'[37]

During the pre-season, Nunan put the team through their paces. Each week there would be five skill sessions, five fitness sessions and three weight sessions — training designed to develop his players' ability to retain the ball and run flat out for the whole game.[38] As with handballs, running was also central to Nunan's approach. He believed it was important to put kilometres into players' legs in the pre-season as a necessary part of conditioning players' bodies.[39] Jason Baldwin later criticised Nunan's approach: doing nineteen-kilometre runs three times per week, he argued, did not replicate the requirements of game situations.[40] The skill sessions were also demanding. One journalist watched Fitzroy train one evening, observing a solid forty-five minutes of free-flowing quick ball movement through chains of handpasses and accurate kicking to the leading space. Sustained accuracy and skill were not up to standard, but, she noted, was already better than the previous year.[41]

As Nunan had not put the playing list together himself, there were those who did not suit the style he wanted to play. Spending the summer evaluating the team, he developed a list of those who were not going to be in the club's future. Nine from 1995 would not return in 1996, including wantaway Ben Holland (traded to Richmond).[42] Nunan would have dispensed with more if he could — by March 1996, he had earmarked ten to fifteen players to delist at the end of the season.[43] Several learnt very early on that they were not part of his vision.[44] Nineteen-year-old Rowan Warfe was on the outer, with Nunan commenting the following year that he 'had some deficiencies' but given time he might 'make the grade'.[45] Brett Cook also learnt that he was not Nunan's preferred ruckman, despite being a fellow South Australian.[46] Jason Baldwin had been vice-captain in 1995, but he was dropped from the leadership role and came to believe that Nunan favoured younger players: 'If you weren't in the age bracket of 17 to 24, you pretty much weren't in his plans,' he said at the end of the year.[47] Other players met with bad luck. Nick Mitchell sustained a pre-season knee injury that ruled him out for the entire season, while injury forced popular veteran defender Mark Zanotti into early retirement.[48]

Within the group, there were obvious leaders. Some had held leadership positions at other clubs, while others, like Martin Pike and John McCarthy, were naturally inclined to be vocal and demand performances from the younger players. Yet standing above the rest, both as a leader and the best player in the team, was the club's young captain, 24-year-old Brad Boyd. No club captain in the AFL looked as boyish as Boyd. Then again, none were as young. Only Wayne Carey at North Melbourne was born the same year (1971, Carey in May, Boyd in August), but where Boyd appeared lithe, Carey, even at twenty-four years old, was already imposing as a centre half-forward. Boyd was over a decade younger than Roger Merrett at Brisbane; 'Sticks' Kernahan at Carlton had ten centimetres and sixteen kilograms on him; Jason Dunstall at Hawthorn had won 159 games by the start of 1996, while Boyd had only played fifty-four games in total.

Yet even at twenty-four, he was well on his way to being a great player — and arguably Nunan's most important. *Football Record* listed him as one of the top 100 players for the 1996 season, he won the club's best and fairest in 1995 (after being runner-up behind Paul Roos in 1994) and had represented Victoria in State of Origin in 1994 and 1995.[49] A talented junior footballer from Bundoora, he had impressed Collingwood's recruiters, and in time was appointed captain of their Under 19s side. By 1991, however, the twenty-year-old lacked a degree of professional commitment and was naïve about the mental and physical requirements to play AFL. He also did a couple of self-confessed 'silly things', such as joining two high profile senior players in a $360 taxi ride from the pre-season camp at Marysville to the Tunnel Nightclub back in Melbourne.[50]

The Magpies were looking to unload Boyd and they developed a trade with Fitzroy for Tony Woods. The Lions' recruiting manager, Neville Stibbard, thought Boyd 'wasn't getting a go' and could play over one hundred senior games if given a chance.[51] Boyd was not sure he was fully committed to professional football, but eventually, he decided to continue his career with the Lions. His senior debut came in 1992 against Hawthorn at Waverley Park. After his second game, he was sent back to the reserves, not to play another senior game that year. At the end of the season, he knew he would need to put in more effort and bulk up if he was to play regularly in the seniors.[52] Five rounds into the 1993 season he was beginning to lose faith. He had excelled in the reserves but did not think playing on the half-back line suited him — again he looked to give AFL away. Teammate Ross Lyon encouraged him to tell the coach and the match committee that if he did not get a run in the seniors, he would leave. With some trepidation, he approached coach Robert Shaw and reserves coach Alan McConnell the next day. Not only did Boyd issue his ultimatum, but he declared that he was best suited to playing as a ruck-rover. Shaw and McConnell were not sure Boyd was right but respected his courage in coming to them and McConnell played him on the ball for the next four reserves games. Boyd's self-confidence paid off — very soon he was a fixture in the senior team.[53]

Once established, he began to produce his best football. Shaw initially played him as a tagger, but soon came around to Boyd's way of thinking and played him as a ruck-rover who could go forward or back when required. His size proved challenging for opponents: he was much taller than the average ruck-rover at 189 centimetres. Ross Lyon called him the quintessential footballer of the future, and one observer marvelled at his combination of exceptional aerobic fitness, ball gathering ability and marking strength.[54] Against Hawthorn in Round 13 of the 1995 season, he kicked five goals, the following week against Footscray he amassed thirty-eight disposals.[55] Round 2, 1994 was perhaps his best game for Fitzroy. In a come-from-behind thirteen-point victory over reigning premiers Essendon at Princes Park, Boyd had thirty-seven possessions and kicked three goals — earning him his first three Brownlow votes.[56]

As Boyd grew in confidence and stature, Fitzroy's fortunes began to wane. Many senior players saw the writing on the wall and encouraged Boyd to leave with them. He elected to stay, knocking back offers from several clubs: 'I felt a real sense of loyalty to the place,' he recalled, 'I was never going, just not interested in leaving Fitzroy.'[57] He came to the captaincy as something of a last man standing. With the departure of captain Paul Roos, vice-captain Ross Lyon and deputy vice-captain Matthew Armstrong, several players were in contention for a leadership position during the 1995 pre-season. The match committee strongly considered Jason Baldwin, but Boyd won in a narrow vote, impressing Bernie Quinlan with his work ethic and approach to football.[58] If he had been at any other club, the burden of captaincy would not have been on his shoulders, but at Fitzroy, there was no-one else to assume the mantle.

Injuries proved his most significant obstacle as a footballer. He suffered two stress fractures to his lower back as a nineteen-year-old, which got worse over time. After a while, he started to develop groin and hamstring problems associated with his back injury.[59] In contemporary terminology, Boyd was an inside midfielder, a 'fall-of-the-ball footballer' as Alan McConnell described him. Yet his injuries forced him to play an outside style of game, which, McConnell believed, suited neither his skill-set nor his psyche.[60] Furthermore,

Boyd was forced to play in other positions that did not necessarily suit him due to the lack of options on the list. Had he been surrounded by more mature players and been supported by more significant football department resources, his career might have been very different. Nevertheless, he led the young team as best he could.

Despite the factors inhibiting his ability to perform at his peak, Boyd stood out as a player and a leader. He was an 'exceptional player', recalled his vice-captain, Stephen Paxman, who led by example 'as much as his body would allow him to'.[61] Chris Johnson concurred: 'He meant business every time he went out.'[62] After Matthew Primus arrived at the club, he saw very quickly why Boyd was so highly regarded: he was fit, he was hard, and he was skilful.[63] John Rombotis believed he could have won a Brownlow if he did not have a bad back: 'That's how good he was.'[64] John Barker loved the way he played; he was a hard, smart footballer who could move beautifully, the prototype of a large-bodied midfielder.[65] Jarrod Molloy noted that even with his burdens Boyd 'handled himself brilliantly', and the closeness of the playing group was mainly due to Boyd, as he was the only stable leadership figure at the time.[66]

While Boyd was a unifying figure within the team, Nunan was more divisive. Some older hands were unconvinced about the chances of Nunan achieving anything other than another last place finish.[67] Some got on well with him, however, and were optimistic about where he could take them. It took a while for John McCarthy to understand Nunan's approach. After three months in the role, he believed Nunan was doing an excellent job, teaching a first-class game plan that generated plenty of excitement among the players before the season.[68] Others, usually those who did not fit into Nunan's plans, were less enamoured with him. But he was not at Fitzroy to be liked; he was there to build a competitive, skilful team. He was also there to prove a point. Within the Victorian football establishment, there was a suspicion of styles of football played in other states (the mockery of West Australian Gerard Neesham's so-called 'chip and draw' style was a prime example).⁶⁹ Nunan, a proud and parochial South Australian, was going to beat the Victorians at their own game. The upcoming season would be his thirteenth year as a senior coach, and it would be his most challenging and eventful. 'I came over here for an experience,' Nunan said at one point during the year, 'and I'm certainly getting it.'⁷⁰

In other circumstances, Nunan would have made an excellent addition to the AFL, but context was everything. The club's financial position undermined much of what he was trying to achieve. One fundamental assumption underpinned his approach — that he would have several years to develop the young team so that at the end of that time they would be playing in a manner that made them competitive.⁷¹ Yet Nunan was not at any regular club, he was at Fitzroy, and he had to struggle with all its problems: inadequate facilities, no money and a very inexperienced playing list. While other clubs went on exotic pre-season trips, the Lions went to Rawson in eastern Victoria. From his public remarks later in the year he was not informed about the club's financial state for some time. But looking around the club, at the quality of its facilities and the threadbare playing list (not to mention the constant newspaper reporting), he must have become aware very quickly of how difficult his task would be. Nevertheless, he rolled up his sleeves and got to work shaping the Fitzroy Lions to his will.

CHAPTER THREE

THE PEOPLE'S CLUB

'People say you should not get too emotional with your job, but when it comes to Fitzroy it's just very hard not to'

— Fran Tascone, Fitzroy receptionist.[1]

The core business of a football club is to win games of football — a simple proposition often immensely challenging to execute consistently over a sustained period. Achieving this objective is not merely the work of eighteen players on the field and a coach to direct them. Clubs require dozens (if not hundreds) of people mobilised throughout the year for training, match-day preparations, player support and welfare, recruitment, administration, membership services, fundraising and a host of other tasks. This work often goes unthought-of but is nevertheless vital to the smooth and effective running of a professional club. Even in its impoverished state, Fitzroy still employed dozens of staff, volunteers and supporter groups to ensure the club continued to function.

Working conditions were rudimentary, resources were tight and the prospect of seeing any on-field success was slim. Volunteers and supporters had little or no remuneration for their time and effort beyond the satisfaction of helping their club. The commitment shown by those who worked at Fitzroy reflected a deep love of the club and the community around it.

Before exploring the various behind-the-scenes facets of the Fitzroy Football Club, it is worth sketching out the off-field experience of the club's most visible element: the players themselves. The young men who wore the jumper and competed each weekend were more than just blunt instruments. Somewhere between being an object of idolisation to supporters and a commodity to club officials was the real, lived experience of AFL footballers. For the purpose of player contracts and financial reporting, the footballing year began on 1 November and ended on 31 October. Clubs could have forty-two players on their senior list, fielding teams of twenty-one on game day (eighteen on the field with three on the bench). Most clubs also had a reserves team in the Victorian State Football League (VSFL), although the Under 19s competition, which had been a staple of player development within clubs for half a century, ceased in 1991. In its place came the Under 18s competition, a pathway for young players to enter the AFL, via the national draft. The draft, one of the League's key equalisation measures, was first run in its modern form in 1986, and by the mid-nineties it had replaced the old metropolitan and rural zoning system. By 1996, the majority of Fitzroy's young list had entered the AFL system through the national draft.

Many matches were still played at 2.10pm on Saturday afternoons, although night fixtures and Sunday games were now common. On the field, players generally remained in their positions against a direct opponent and the three interchange players were used sparingly. Training was usually held on Monday, Tuesday and Thursday nights, leaving coaches with very little time to drill complicated game plans into them. In this semi-professional era, clubs lacked many aspects that modern footballers take for granted: generous remuneration, elite infrastructure, access to sports science and rehabilitation facilities and the benefits of full-time, professional coaching and development.[2] Instead, it was training after work, beers for post-match recovery and three-figure win bonuses.

The AFL had not professionalised to the point where football was a viable full-time occupation for all, and many players either worked or studied full-time. Still, the salary cap was set at $2.55 million per club and the average player earnt $77,695.[3] The most recent Collective Bargaining Agreement (CBA) had established a minimum base salary of $15,000 and a minimum senior game payment of $1000 per game for the 1996 season. On top of that, a player's earning capacity fluctuated, often depending on how well they or their management could negotiate with the club.[4] For 20-year-old Brett Chandler, the money was not a significant factor, 'it was more just wanting to play senior footy', he recalled.[5] Stephen Paxman was older than most of his teammates. He already had a degree in manufacturing engineering in 1993 and was working for a breaks company in East Bentleigh. To arrive on time to training at 5.00pm required him to make the arduous journey across Melbourne just before peak hour.[6] Chris Johnson had left school at fifteen and had been working as an apprentice painter and decorator for Higgins Coatings during his first years at the club. He would often leave home at 6.00am, spend his day sanding, grinding, cutting in or rolling walls, before heading off to train with Fitzroy. It was not unusual for him to arrive at training with bleeding fingertips from a day working with sandpaper. By the time he arrived home, it could be as late as 9.00pm.[7]

Some Fitzroy players were employed by the club. John McCarthy had worked as a sales representative, and took up a role as a projects officer in Fitzroy's marketing team.[8] Several younger players, including John Rombotis and Marty Warry, were part of the AFL traineeship course, working as 'administration assistants/trainees' in between studying sports administration at Western Melbourne Institute of TAFE.[9] Chris Johnson joined this program in 1996, spending several days each week at the club's administrative headquarters, helping around the club ('We probably weren't too much help,' he later joked), before spending one or two days in class.[10] Some players undertook normal tertiary education, such as John Barker, who had been studying Commerce part-time at the University of Melbourne.[11] Others took the third option. Matthew Primus was neither working nor studying, preferring to concentrate on establishing himself as an AFL footballer.[12]

As a group, Rowan Warfe remembered that the players 'stuck tight' despite the 'whole heap of crap going on'.[13] Club events, particularly the post-match functions at the Fitzroy Club Hotel, were always well represented by seniors and reserves players.[14] 'We drank a lot of piss,' recalled Cook, which no doubt reflected the need to release tension and anxiety in stressful circumstances.[15] The whole group got on well, according to Martin Pike, 'There weren't any egos around the place, there wasn't anything like that.'[16] As with any club, there was a mixture of personalities: jokers and characters, as well as deep thinkers and introverts. Danny Morton, for instance, was known for his practical jokes and generally inserting humour into any situation (a helpful attribute later in the season when some levity was required).[17] There was a youthful complexion to the side, bringing with it a naivete about Fitzroy's financial predicament. While some senior players were aware of the club's issues, most younger players just concentrated on playing in the senior team and were not interested in anything else.[18] 'As a young guy you're just excited to get drafted and play AFL footy,' 21-year-old Scott Bamford reflected.[19] 'I was young and naïve,' echoed Chandler, who was just happy to be playing top-flight football.[20]

But the players were only the most visible section of the club and behind them was an entire organisation enabling the team to play football week after week. At the top sat Fitzroy's board of directors, led by the irrepressible Queen's Counsel, Dyson Hore-Lacy (he would subsequently adopt the less monarchical 'Senior Counsel' title some years later). By 1996, he was one of the more vocal club presidents in the AFL, partially because of Fitzroy's predicament and partly because of his somewhat combative public persona. When not at the head of a struggling football club, Hore-Lacy was a prominent criminal barrister. Working predominantly as a defence lawyer, his propensity to take on clients in seemingly hopeless positions built his reputation as a 'quixotic defender of underdogs' (and his involvement with Fitzroy only enhanced this image).[21] His most notable trait, aside from his inclination to defend the defenceless and a droll sense of humour, was his determination and tenacity — Dyson Hore-Lacy was a fighter. One Supreme Court judge remarked: 'I haven't always agreed with him, but the one thing anyone who had Dyson represent them could *not* say was that he didn't fight their case as hard as humanly possible.'[22] He seemed perfectly suited for one of the most challenging jobs within the AFL.

Born in Tasmania, Hore-Lacy briefly attempted a career in football before studying Law at the University of Melbourne.[23] Admitted to the Victorian Bar in 1967, he spent ten years 'marking time' in the Magistrates Court before he moved to Darwin to work for Aboriginal Legal Aid. His time in the Northern Territory and his interaction with indigenous people nuanced his views on certain issues, and he returned to Melbourne twelve months later with 'a much greater commitment to less privileged people'.[24] He soon developed a reputation as a St Jude-like figure (the patron saint of lost causes), yet the reality was more complicated. 'I'd prefer patron saint of unpopular causes or unfashionable causes,' he remarked, 'but they're not lost causes.'[25] He spoke on behalf of notorious prisoner Garry David, whom the State Government had detained indefinitely, and represented the family of Gary Abdallah, the man suspected of having been a getaway driver during the 1988 Walsh Street murders and who was shot and killed a year later by police.[26] He became a larger-than-life figure in legal circles, known for his fearlessness and commitment to clients, as well as the occasional lack of diplomatic tact and outbursts of passion. 'If

I were in trouble,' a fellow barrister declared, 'I would want to have Dyson appearing for me — and there are not many of my colleagues about whom I would say that.'[27]

When not in his chambers or in a courtroom, he maintained his interest in football, and following a move to North Fitzroy, he gradually began supporting the Lions.[28] The club's underdog character and his propensity for defending the downtrodden was a perfect marriage. Standing in the outer at Fitzroy games, he soon met Leon Wiegard, Fitzroy's president since 1985, and became more involved in the club, putting his legal expertise to good use. His first formal engagement came when the board requested his services in a wrongful dismissal case. The club was less impressed that he won than by the fact he did not charge a fee.[29] His involvement solidified in 1990 when Wiegard approached him to join the board of directors. He was happy to help the club and believed his contribution would be limited to a monthly meeting and the provision of some legal advice.[30] Then, barely a year later, the 51-year-old became Fitzroy's president after Wiegard resigned over Gary Pert's controversial contract renegotiations and subsequent move to Collingwood. On assuming the role, he faced an unenviable task. As president, he led a club with dwindling revenue and increased debts, battling against (what was perceived to be) a hostile AFL administration always happy to leak negative stories about the club to the press.[31] Regardless of the obstacles, he brought the same approach to running the football club as he did to representing clients: fighting doggedly.

As chairman of the club's board of directors, Hore-Lacy led a group with a wealth of corporate experience and expertise, as well as a deep commitment to Fitzroy. His vice-president was Elaine Findlay, the club's longest-serving board member. Born into a Fitzroy family (her brothers were friends with Kevin Murray), Findlay became treasurer of the Lion Hunters' coterie group in 1982, and then secretary shortly thereafter. Her excellent management of the coterie's affairs attracted attention, and she was soon asked to join the board. Concerns about how the exclusively male board would react to a female joining their ranks made her cautious about accepting and she stipulated that she would only do so if the invitation were unanimous. Sure enough, a unanimous request came, and in 1985 she became the first female board member of a VFL club.[32] 'When the contribution of women in AFL football is assessed historically,' Hore-Lacy remarked, 'Elaine should be at the forefront of discussions. She worked tirelessly for the club and loved it to death.'[33]

The Fitzroy board functioned like a Cabinet, with different members responsible for different 'portfolios'. At the start of 1996, there were ten members (including Hore-Lacy and Findlay). Colin Hobbs and David McMahon, both former players, were football directors. Hobbs, a teacher turned businessman, had played sixty-four games between 1966 and 1971. McMahon had a more significant on-field contribution, playing 218 games between 1973 and 1984. Findlay was responsible for the social club and engagement with the coterie groups, which she did with John Pettinella, a successful fruit and vegetable grower and long-time club supporter.[34] Two directors oversaw the club's finances: John Stewart was a chartered accountant, and Kevin Ryan was formerly the club's general manager. Rounding out the board, Robert Eales was an insurance broker and Robert Johnstone was a vice-president at McDonald's Australia. Among the directors, the odd man out was Kinza Clodumar, whose unique role at Fitzroy will be discussed later.

In 1992, Fitzroy's directors acquired the lease for the Charles Albion Hotel at 2 Charles Street, Northcote. Established in 1887 as the Albion Family Hotel, the architecturally unremarkable three-storey hotel dominated the convoluted intersection where Merri Parade meets St Georges Road. It had operated as a local hotel for decades, until members of the Fitzroy board purchased the lease through a complex series of corporate and legal manoeuvres (including the use of a shelf company). They then established a trust to direct hotel revenue to Fitzroy, thus keeping the hotel separate from the club.[35]

Renamed the Fitzroy Club Hotel, it brought in a modest income, accommodated the club's administrative office and provided a venue for club functions. After games, players would go there for dinner and then spend as much time as they wanted with the supporters.[36] For Chris Johnson, it was the one place they could call home, where the players could go and simply enjoy each other's company.[37]

To give the hotel a more 'Fitzroy' feel, the club decorated it with memorabilia. The 'Alan "Butch" Gale Room' had photos of the club's Brownlow Medallists guarding the front door, while premiership teams looked down upon those heading up the hotel's old wooden staircase: 'Tough men with folded arms,' one observer wrote. 'Committeemen with starched white collars, suits and waistcoats. Handlebar moustaches and brilliantined hair, parted in the middle. Proud men from proud glad days.'[38] The club's administrative headquarters was on the second and third floors, where approximately a dozen staff ran the club in surrounds that were Spartan by any standard. Membership details were still recorded physically on cards, long after every other AFL club (and many VFA clubs) had shifted to computers.[39] Andrew Ireland, CEO of the Brisbane Bears, had worked in Portacom offices during his early years at the Bears, but even he was taken aback at the dilapidated condition of the offices.[40]

The day-to-day running of the club was in the hands of its chief executive officer, 59-year-old John Birt. A former Essendon premiership rover and best and fairest, he had come from Collingwood in the middle of 1994. As CEO, Birt was running a football club with no money and a very uncertain future in an austere environment. For encouragement, he had a quote from former West Indian cricket captain Richie Richardson pinned to his diary: 'When things are tough, I hang in even more. I'm not going to run away from what's happening. I'm just going to keep working hard ... and if my best isn't good enough, then that's the way it is.'[41] A warm and avuncular man, Birt was widely loved and respected among Fitzroy's staff.[42] While other clubs had more prominent chief executives, he tended to remain in the background during the events of 1996. He was often unable to confirm or deny what was happening at board level due to a lack of involvement in the critical decisions. This was probably to his benefit: running the club was stressful enough without becoming involved in the weightier matters troubling the board.

Working for Birt were the usual assortment of staff necessary for a football club to operate. Finance and accounts were run by finance manager Susan Cornish, while the marketing team (charged with selling the increasingly unsellable) was run by Michael Rodriquez, and included several players as marketing officers. Sandra Hounslow was Birt's secretary (and surrogate mother for the office staff), while the club's receptionist, Fran Tascone, was on the front line when it came to fielding the constant enquiries from AFL House or journalists about the state of the club. She would also greet the many supporters who made their way to the Fitzroy Club Hotel for whatever reason, and particularly enjoyed spending time with older supporters, hearing their stories about how they came to follow Fitzroy and learning about how much the club meant to them.[43] Resources were often spread thin, with key people often undertaking multiple roles. Hounslow, for instance, doubled as the football secretary. When Rodriquez resigned mid-year (with legitimate complaints about the difficulty of marketing the club to potential sponsors) Birt reportedly took on the role himself.[44] Fortunately, if the office needed to undertake large tasks such as mailouts, volunteers would always be on hand to assist.

Internally, the club's financial predicament was well known. As one staff member noted, Fitzroy had become a club where if a lightbulb broke you would not replace it — you would swap it with one from an area in less pressing need of illumination.[45] Despite assumptions to the contrary, however, morale among the administration staff had remained healthy. Birt never let any private concerns permeate through the office, Sandra Hounslow made sure everyone was well and helped to keep spirits high and there was a good sense of camaraderie among the staff and the volunteers.[46]

As such, the Fitzroy Club Hotel was often an enjoyable place to work, belying the club's dire circumstances. Eighteen-year-old Melanie Gibb was enrolled in the AFL traineeship course at Western Melbourne Institute of TAFE and at the start of 1996 was placed at Fitzroy for the practical component of her course. Working three days per week as a receptionist (which freed up Tascone to work in other parts of the office), she found the small staff welcoming and friendly and quickly became enamoured with the club, despite barracking for Melbourne. Such was her enthusiasm that after discovering the club's lion mascot costume in a back room, John Birt gave her permission to wear it for the Round 10 game against Sydney.[47]

Within the football department, the football manager, Glenn Warry, had been with Fitzroy since 1986, first as the metropolitan development manager before assuming his current role. He was responsible for running football operations, managing the playing list, the coaches and the football staff, working with Birt to manage the salary cap, working with the recruiting staff in preparation for the draft and assisting the relocation of players who were drafted. On top of that, he was also the secretary to the match committee.[48] Although a divisive figure with a terse personality, he was nevertheless very good at his job. One colleague called him a 'hard arse', and with the club in a perpetual state of siege, he needed to be.[49] He had been a longstanding critic of the board's 'survival first' policy, which had relegated the development of the club's football operations and made the team uncompetitive. Despite such reservations, a sense of obligation to the players he had drafted compelled him to remain at Fitzroy.[50]

Another permanent staff member was the senior assistant coach, Alan McConnell. Invited by Warry to coach Fitzroy's Under 19s for the 1991 season, he moved into a development role once that competition was abolished. He became the reserves coach and then the senior assistant coach to Bernie Quinlan and Michael Nunan.[51] Outside his coaching role, McConnell had a range of administrative and welfare duties. One difficult task was to organise training locations each week, communicating to the players and staff about which of several locations evening training would be held.[52] Some within the club called him 'Micky Mouse' due to his squeaky voice, but such jokes were made with deep respect, and he was a much-loved figure at the club.[53] There was no full-time recruiting officer (a vital fixture at every other club), which no doubt contributed to some poor trading and drafting decisions.[54] When the former full-time recruiting manager Neville Stibbard was enticed away to North Melbourne in 1993, there was insufficient money to replace him and thus Warry was left to fill the gap.

Other members of the modest football department included Leon Harris, who had played 186 games for the Lions and had captained its 1989 reserves premiership team. He had been assistant coach to Robert Shaw in 1993 and 1994, but, wishing to coach in his own right, left in 1995 to coach the Western Jets in the Under 18s TAC Cup. He returned to Fitzroy for the 1996 season as the part-time reserves coach (he worked full-time at Ross Faulkner Sporting Goods).[55] Another former player from the eighties, Ross Thornton, was the senior team manager. Greg Freemantle had played for Fitzroy's Under 19s and reserves but was unable to break into the senior side. A school PE teacher who did some club fitness work in his spare time, he had known Warry and McConnell from his time at Fitzroy, and when Robert Shaw was looking for a fitness advisor at the Lions, he was offered the job. He worked part-time alongside weights and rehab staff, until Michael Nunan swept in and criticised the conditioning of the players. All of a sudden, Freemantle was offered a full-time position. He also filled in as the runner when the first choice, Nunan's friend and former test batsman David Hookes, was unavailable.[56]

The football department was aided by a large number of part-time and volunteer personnel, working as trainers, bootstudders, stewards, timekeepers and statisticians, as well as other singular specialist roles. Among the volunteers were some of the club's most dedicated and colourful personalities. Doorman Tommy Couch was an imposing figure, and it was said that not even Atilla the Hun could get into the rooms if he was on the door.[57] Room steward Jim Moloney had been with Fitzroy for years. When Alastair Lynch was recruited from Tasmania, Moloney picked him up from the airport and drove him straight to a practice match in Bundoora. Taking Lynch back to the airport after the game, Moloney stopped off at a bottle-shop and picked up some 'travellers' for the two of them.[58]

The football department attracted both loyal Roys and those with specialist skills who just wanted to work at an AFL club, regardless of their affiliations. Many in the latter group, however, were won over to Fitzroy by the culture and the people. One of the club's statisticians, Tony Mazoski, was a Collingwood supporter but became so enamoured with the sense of belonging at the Lions that he contemplated transferring his allegiance.[59]

While players and coaches came and went, the bootstudders and trainers — men with white hair and strong hands — were the true custodians of Fitzroy's heritage and history. They were 'fantastic people', remarked defender Simon Hawking, and 'great servants of the club'.[60] One trainer, Lance Upton, had family connections with the club going back well over a century.[61] He himself grew up in North Fitzroy, and would often go to the Brunswick Street Oval during the week to watch the Lions train. When he was invited to become a trainer in the eighties, he joined an experienced and knowledgeable group. 'They were solid men,' Upton recalled, 'loyal and very good at their jobs.'[62]

From these men, one could get a sense of the real Fitzroy Football Club. They were always prepared to greet players and staff with a smile, make them feel welcome and regale them with a story or two.[63] Many had been around the club for decades; in 1963, 23-year-old Arthur Aylward answered an advertisement Fitzroy had placed in the *Football Record* for backroom staff. He was hired as the club's bootstudder, and had held the job ever since.[64] Glen Ford had been with the Lions for seven years, first as the assistant timekeeper, then the property steward. His father, John, began volunteering for Fitzroy in 1968, leaving the club when he started shift work. He returned in 1988 and by 1996 was an assistant property steward under his son. While Glen was the boss, Jack did all the washing at his home (Glen pitched in if Jack got 'snowed under').[65] The pair were the backbone of the club, tireless workers who had dedicated their lives to Fitzroy.[66] Even Troy Hall, one of the youngest trainers at the club, was deeply enmeshed within Fitzroy's history. His mother, Carolyn Hall, was the manager of the Fitzroy Club Hotel and her grandfather, Les McMaster, had been a committeeman in the forties and fifties.[67]

Few at Fitzroy had been around the club as long as its head trainer, the irrepressible Kevin Elms. Born in George Street, Fitzroy, he had earned a living through a variety of jobs, including wharfie, truckie, working at a meatworks and as an amateur weightlifter and one-time professional wrestler, nicknamed 'Ivan the Terrible'.[68] He began working for Fitzroy in 1962 and as a trainer, he was one of the best in the business. One colleague called him 'the back whisperer' because he had such an intuitive understanding of athletes and their injuries.[69] Not only did he work for Fitzroy, but he was a trainer for the Victorian state sides in the eighties and for the Australian Olympic Team on two occasions. 'I've just got a feel for it,' he stated years later, 'I can pick injuries, even watching the telly. I had a lot of blues with physios, and nine times out of ten I was right.'[70] Elms was so dedicated to Fitzroy that when his daughter was deciding on a wedding date, he warned her: 'Don't get married in the footy season or I won't be coming.'[71]

A quintessentially Fitzroy story involves the move from the Lakeside Oval to Coburg as a training venue, the end of the line for Fitzroy as far as training facilities went. More so than the club's nomadic search for a home ground, its quest for a training facility took them all over Melbourne. For many years the club had trained at the Lakeside Oval, but Melbourne's successful bid for the Formula One Grand Prix forced them from the premises.[72] At the start of 1995, Warry and McConnell were tasked with finding a new training facility.

They looked high and low, but continually faced rejection, many organisations turning them away due to concerns over their financial position. Eventually, they secured the City Oval in Coburg near Bell Street and Sydney Road, due in part to the assistance of Phil Cleary, former Coburg Football Club legend and at that time a Member of Parliament for the Federal seat of Wills. With Cleary's intervention, Fitzroy had a training base for its final years in the competition. Still, they faced two problems: getting their equipment out of the Lakeside Oval and bringing the Coburg City Oval up to a standard that was sufficient for an AFL club.[73]

To move the equipment from Lakeside, McConnell organised the logistics while the Fords did the hack work. When they arrived to collect the lockers from the Lakeside Oval they were locked out because their bills were unpaid. Fortunately Geelong legend Doug Wade owned the gym next door, and allowed them to move their equipment through his premises. They stored everything at a facility owned by one of the board members while they renovated the Coburg City Oval.[74] The club had signed a lease agreement with the Coburg Football Club for approximately $30,000 (which included the provision of lighting plus several working bees).[75] The working bees were essential. Volunteers knocked out walls to enlarge the space and player-apprentices John Rombotis, Marty Warry and Rowan Warfe repainted the dressing rooms.[76] Even with all the hard work, the Coburg facilities were substandard. With so much sand on the surface of the oval, the players nicknamed it the 'Williamstown beach'.[77] Occasionally the lights would not work during an evening training session, and players needed to navigate through exposed drainage pipes yet to be remediated.[78] Chris Johnson later called the facilities a 'disgrace', pointing to the leaking ceiling and poor showers. There was also only two toilets to service well over fifty staff and players during training sessions. 'It was definitely very unprofessional,' he recalled, 'but I didn't know any better, I'd never been at another AFL club.'[79]

...

To make any improvements in the quality of the club's facilities and equipment or to employ additional staff required Fitzroy to generate greater income. Successive marketing managers had strived to raise revenue for the club, and while sponsorships brought in valuable income, it fell to the rank and file to assist. Regular income came from memberships (in 1996 an adult membership cost $80) and gate receipts, with supporters also rattling tins, buying raffle tickets and helping with fundraising drives. Fitzroy also had a diverse and active collection of coteries and supporter groups, such as the Gold Lions, the Lionesses, the Lion Hunters, The Pride, The Roys, The Cheer Squad, the Roy Girls and the Cheerleaders, as well as the less imaginatively named Social Fundraising Group and the Social Club, dedicated to fundraising for the club.

Each group was distinct. Some, like the Gold Lions and the Pride, catered to corporate supporters. Others, like the Lionesses, were more modest in their endeavours. The first Lionesses luncheon of 1996, for instance, was held at the Fitzroy Club Hotel. Members met the new sponsored players, special guests and, for $26 per head, enjoy a two-course meal and a complimentary glass of wine.[80] Another group, the Lion Hunters, was one of the oldest coteries in the League. Founded in 1963, they had been a prominent part of the club's history. Kevin Murray had been at a Lion Hunters' dinner at the Bookmakers' Club on Queen Street when he learned he had won the 1969 Brownlow Medal. Before long, Murray's teammates and several Lion Hunters carried him aloft through the street in celebration.[81]

The Ladies Auxiliary had also been a longstanding Fitzroy staple, selling handmade Fitzroy trinkets from a kiosk during home games. In 1965, several ladies began knitting scarves, beanies and dolls to sell at the football to raise money for the club, with the auxiliary developing from there.[82] So important was the group to Fitzroy that two stalwarts, Lorna Duncan and Dot Thompson, were made life members of the club in 1987, with fellow members Deidre Worn and Alvie Phillips similarly honoured in 1996.[83] At the other end of the spectrum, the

Fitzroy Foundation was a trust established by Warren O'Neale and Bill Atherton. In 1994, Atherton had suggested to Elaine Findlay that the club establish a bequest fund. Findlay agreed and asked Atherton, a public accountant, to be the bookkeeper, with O'Neale the upfront salesman. By 1996, they had raised approximately $100,000.[84]

One of the most prominent groups was the Fitzroy Supporters' Group, which, according to its co-founder, Jan Wright, was the 'poor man's coterie'. It comprised a colourful collection of characters. In addition to Wright, there were Nancye and John Cain (the former Victorian premier), Brian Rix (a senior Victorian policeman) and his wife, Shirley Hardy-Rix, along with Shirley's brother Alan Hardy and his wife Galia (both of whom worked in television). The Supporter's Group developed two roles that set it apart from the other coteries. First, it provided support for the very young players being drafted from all over the country. The group held player welfare breakfasts on Friday mornings, attended by the captain, several players and often the coach or members of the coaching staff, particularly for young, interstate players who had no connections in Melbourne. Each group member offered assistance to players from their own particular expertise: Jan Wright would work with players about writing CVs and encouraging them to consider tertiary education, John Cain could provide legal advice, the Hardys offered media training, while Brian Rix could get players out of jail on a Sunday morning if necessary. During his time at the club, Ross Lyon functioned as the players' representative for welfare activities.[85]

Since 1994, the group's second role was to run a weekly function, known as the Ins and Outs Night, on Thursday evenings at the Fitzroy Club Hotel. For $10, supporters would receive a two-course meal and be the first to hear the weekend's team from the match committee. For an additional $2, they could enter a competition to guess the twenty-one players selected for the round (without needing to guess the exact starting positions) with a prize on offer for any winners.[86] There would also be a raffle, trivia and guest speakers (such as past players, prominent supporters or local celebrities) and appearances by current team members. Journalist and supporter Chris Donald would call Wright each Monday and find out who that week's guest would be, allowing him to prepare statistics on the player to help with the interview.[87] Once the formalities concluded, the organisers would turn on *The Footy Show* at 9.30pm. 'They were great nights,' recalled supporter Rick Lang, who would often attend after watching Fitzroy train at Coburg City Oval before then heading off to a night shift.[88]

Fitzroy officials had adopted the moniker 'the people's club' for the Lions, which appeared on letterheads, reports and other documentation. While not a particularly original claim, it nevertheless suited the Lions. 'The best thing about Fitzroy was the people,' remarked Norm Brown, the three-time club champion and president of the Past Players' Association. 'They were the lifeblood of the club.'[89] As a club without recent premiership success, with few remaining physical ties to its suburb of origin and a lack of geographic distinctiveness, the club's culture and ethos, at least within the inner circle of the players, staff, volunteers and loyal supporters, was defined by personal relationships.[90]

At Fitzroy, players and supporters shared much closer and more frequent contact than other professional clubs, with many players comparing the 'really tight-knit' environment (as ruckman Brett Cook described it) to a local footy club.[91] This was prominent at Ins and Outs Nights or in post-match functions at the Fitzroy Club Hotel (where players and supporters would mingle freely), as well as in many other parts of the life of the club. Every Monday or Tuesday night, for instance, four or five players would have dinner at the house of a supporter who financially sponsored several players.[92] At its heart, Fitzroy never developed much beyond being a suburban club, neither in size nor in culture. It was one of the aspects that made it special to those who loved it. Unfortunately, this great strength was also the club's greatest weakness. A local football club had no place in the AFL — or so those who ran the League thought as the world approached the new millennium.

CHAPTER FOUR

THE CENTENARY

'My [New Year's] resolution is to make the AFL centenary year a year to remember'

— Ross Oakley, AFL chief executive officer.[1]

It was an inauspicious start to the new year. Heavy rains swept across Melbourne on the night of 31 December 1995, leaving only a hardy and sodden crowd in the streets to celebrate. The rain stopped just before midnight, but most events had already been cancelled.[2] Nevertheless, the customary rituals were observed, and at the stroke of midnight revellers ushered in the new year. What would be in store for 1996? Victorians already expected several events, such as federal and state elections, as well as the Games of the XXVI Olympiad in Atlanta. For greater clarity about the unanticipated, the *Sunday Age* had called *New Idea*'s astrologer-at-large, Milton Black, to see what he could proffer about the year ahead. Labor will win the federal election, he declared, and Prince Charles and Lady Diana would not divorce.[3] Neither prognostication came to pass: John Howard became the country's twenty-fifth Prime Minister on 11 March, and the Royal Couple finalised their divorce on 28 August. He certainly did not see the Macarena coming. The catchy Spanish dance song spent nine weeks atop the ARIA charts and together with the corresponding dance became the global cultural peculiarity of 1996.

The world was inching closer to the new millennium, but while it was a time of technological and information advancement, looking back, the era appears distinctly analogue. Many demographic studies have 1996 as the final year one could belong to the millennial generation — anyone born after that would not be able to remember a world without the internet.[4] And it was a different internet in 1996. People could 'surf the net', but it was absent of social media, online shopping, streaming services and a gamut of other now-standard websites. At the offices of the *Sunday Age*, they had one computer with internet access, rarely used due to the lack of useful or relevant content on the World Wide Web.[5] Most people received their news from physical newspapers, radio and the nightly news. Mobile phones were neither smart nor widespread, and there were few digital cameras. Foxtel was founded in 1995 and started operating later that year, but it was the free-to-air channels that people turned to for their news, sport and other entertainment.

Victoria's population was 4.373 million (with Australia's not yet above twenty million).[6] The state was still rebounding from the recession we had to have, where the average adult male working full-time earned approximately $760 per week, and the median house price in Melbourne was only $131,000.[7] Defining the state's political and economic (and perhaps cultural) landscape was Victoria's larger-than-life premier, Jeffrey Kennett, described by Martin Flanagan as a 'modern-day Caesar'.[8] The 'Kennett Revolution' brought privatisation, public sector reductions and high-profile capital works.[9] In 1996, he was at the peak of his power, with a confident victory in the March

1996 state election suggesting he would be premier for many years to come. When asked for his new year's resolution, Kennett wanted 'to deliver in 1996 to the state the rewards that have been promised as a result of the changes we have made over the last three years. I think it will be a wonderful and exciting year.'[10]

Another prominent and divisive Victorian, AFL CEO Ross Oakley, was also looking forward to 1996, but for different reasons. Ensconced at AFL House, Level 2 of the MCG's Great Southern Stand, the 53-year-old was entering his tenth year as the League's chief executive officer. Oakley's was not an easy job, and few, if they were honest, envied the man who ran the League, a task where one was guaranteed to incur criticism and hostility from every conceivable corner of the footballing landscape. As CEO he was responsible for the AFL's operating performance and the implementation of policy as decided by the seven-man AFL Commission, as well as generally being the public face of the League's governing body.

As a testament to the rigours of office, his grey hairs were becoming more prominent, particularly on his distinctive moustache, yet he retained the assertive confidence and swagger that had typified both his personality and his approach to running the League. 'Everything he does or says tells you he is confident,' one journalist wrote in 1996, 'and right.'[11] He had a solid history in the game, playing sixty-two games for St Kilda and narrowly missing the 1966 Grand Final (and carrying the injuries from his playing days long after he had hung up his boots) before sitting on the board of directors at Hawthorn in the early eighties. It was, however, primarily his commercial, governance and marketing experience — most recently as managing director of Royal Insurance — that earned him his appointment as CEO in 1986 (and, in a very eighties set-up, concurrently Commission chairman until 1993).[12] After his initial appointment, some asked whether he was tough enough for football's most difficult job. In response, he would point them to the difficult decisions he had made in the business career, including sacking 250 people while at Royal Insurance.

He would have preferred not to, of course, but the situation demanded action be taken, and, as journalist Garry Linnell wrote, 'The buck had stopped with him.'[13]

Tough decisions, as well as a bold vision, were required from Oakley. He worked with tenacity and passion, but often alienated many within the wider football community who believed that he was destroying the game they loved. Whatever the merits of their arguments, their pleas were insufficient to sway him from the task at hand. While Oakley had watched the game romantically as a boy and had maintained a strong emotional attachment to it through the years, as CEO he had separated himself for such sentiments: 'This was a business under threat that needed dispassionate and logical attention,' he noted years later, 'which is exactly what the Commission was engaged to deliver and was prepared to deliver.'[14] This approach left him reviled by many, yet he had overseen the most profound changes in the League's history; changes, Oakley argued, that were necessary for the League to survive.

In the mid-eighties the VFL had been in a state of emergency and the word 'crisis' was freely used in VFL House without any sense of hyperbole. A confidential report revealed that in 1984, the League's twelve clubs had lost a combined total of $1.9 million, and six — Geelong, Sydney, Footscray, Collingwood, St Kilda and Fitzroy — were technically bankrupt, with their continued existence largely due to the leniency of lending institutions.[15] The parlous state of many clubs had been of their own making. In the late seventies, clubs began spending reckless amounts on their players, eventually driving some to the brink of financial ruin. A weak governance structure had done little to address the issue. For decades the clubs essentially governed themselves in the form of the VFL Board — there was no independent authority to manage and administer the competition in the best interests of all. As a result, League officials began contemplating the unthinkable — VFL football clubs, those seemingly immutable pillars of Melbourne's cultural landscape, were at risk of disappearing due to a lack of money. It was a vulgar prospect, but it was also perilously real.[16] Indeed, the rival VFA would experience precisely this scenario, with twenty-four clubs in 1983 reduced to twelve by 1991. This rationalisation, it was argued, was that for the health of the Association, only its strongest and most financially viable clubs should remain.

The League's crisis brought about much-needed governance reform, introducing the independent VFL Commission in 1985, but there was still more to do. Due to a limited pool of sponsorship money in Melbourne, modest broadcast deals and, for the first time in decades, dropping attendances, there was insufficient income to meet the League's rising costs. With the advent of the VFL Commission, three men rose to prominence: Peter Scanlon, Graeme Samuel and Ross Oakley. Scanlon and Samuel were inaugural Commissioners from 1985 and they acted as kingmakers to appoint Oakley as the CEO in 1986. All three had corporate experience, and together they understood how to 'fix' the VFL's problems. Unlike the VFA, which sought to retain its Melbourne-centric identity, the VFL needed to move away from being a suburban competition, with all games played on Saturday afternoons at local grounds with poor facilities, to a national competition, drawing sponsorship and broadcast money from across Australia. This transformation had already begun with the move of South Melbourne to Sydney in 1982, but it gained serious momentum under the new Commission. Advancing this agenda was controversial and unpopular, but was, nevertheless, effective. Broadcast revenue slowly increased, and the AFL sold licences to establish new clubs in Brisbane and Perth, raising $8 million for the League's coffers.

The push interstate had helped set up the AFL to enter the new millennium, but it was only half of the equation. While non-Victorian clubs offered greater revenue, struggling clubs in Melbourne were a liability. In October 1985, a report, *VFL Football: Establishing the Basis For Future Success* (more commonly known as the Blue Report), argued that eleven professional teams in Victoria were not viable — the League and its clubs would be trying to extract too much money from a single sporting market.[17] Heavily in debt itself, the League could not bail out its cash-strapped clubs, particularly those with smaller supporter bases. If nationalising the game was the solution to generating greater income, any excess revenue needed to be used to support clubs in non-traditional Australian rules states, particularly the Swans in the lucrative Sydney market, for the betterment of the competition's long-term future. Attrition would likely occur naturally, as weaker Melbourne-based clubs would eventually succumb to commercial pressures and fold.

While the League lacked the ability to help Victorian clubs it also, in part, lacked the will. The Commission, influenced by Graeme Samuel, had embraced a philosophy of 'economic rationalism', which championed economic liberalism and free-market primacy. While Scanlon stepped off the Commission in 1992, Samuel had remained and became Oakley's wartime consigliere.[18] He was a 'quintessential 80s figure', as one journalist described him, who made his money first as a lawyer and then as a merchant banker.[19] He had also never played the game and knew little about it before becoming a Commissioner, yet he left an indelible mark on the competition. Samuel openly acknowledged bringing 'the values of economic rationalism to football'.[20] This found expression in the Commission's intention not to 'prop up clubs which in the longer term are fundamentally not viable'.[21] It had introduced some equalisation to produce an even competition and avoid a 'survival of the fittest' mentality developing, yet the League did not want to be a banker to struggling clubs and keep them on life support. To do so would guarantee immunity for inefficient clubs and thereby destroy financial discipline at club level.[22]

Still, no-one on the Commission wanted to see clubs disappear entirely, despite suggestions to the contrary from the football public (Ross Oakley would lament that the Commission was being portrayed as 'football Svengalis', plotting the demise of Victorian clubs).[23]

The way to save clubs from anticipated financial collapse was with mergers between weaker Melbourne-based clubs. A merged club would keep the identity and heritage of both, creating a stronger financial entity and removing one club competing for the limited sponsorship money available. The Commission's policy to encourage mergers predated Oakley's arrival, but the new boss adopted and owned it. All of his dealings with clubs on this issue, and with Fitzroy in particular, need to be seen in the context of his belief that for weaker clubs, it was a choice between a merger or inevitable and terminal financial decline. Commercial loans, fundraising and capital injections might keep a club going in the short-term, but in the end, clubs with smaller supporter bases simply could not compete and would be drowned by the rising costs of professional football. While he recognised that contemplating this option was emotional for supporters, he believed supporters would, eventually, prefer to see their club merge rather than disappear altogether.[24]

By the end of 1995, the Commission still had not achieved its first merger, but the AFL's general position was much healthier than it had been ten years earlier. The League's debt was down to $11.22 million and was slowly being reduced with each passing season. In 1995, AFL operating revenue was $68 million, which, after expenses, produced an operating profit of $1.855 million. Of the outgoings, just over $22 million was distributed equally to the sixteen clubs, $1.402 million each. Coca-Cola was the AFL's major sponsor until 2001, and Channel Seven extended its contract for broadcast rights until 1999.[25] In 1995, over five million people had attended matches during the home and away season for the first time in League history, while club membership hit a new record of 261,067.[26] TV and radio audiences, media coverage and corporate support all continue to grow and reach record levels. All in all, the AFL, under Oakley's leadership, was in a strong position.

After ten years as CEO, it seemed appropriate and fortuitous that in 1996 the League would be taking stock of its evolution and achievements by celebrating its centenary season. Oakley wanted to make it an event to remember, promising that the 1996 season would be bigger and better than what had come before.[27] Pomp and pageantry would feature prominently, from a lavish launch to the grand final featuring a gold premiership cup, and a formal dinner on the MCG surface for thousands of dignitaries and guests. There would also be an additional pre-season tournament (the Lightning Premiership), a centenary round in the middle of the season and exclusive centenary merchandise, including a series of unique postage stamps. The League's history would receive appropriate emphasis, with a 'Team of the Century' selected and a two-hour documentary, *100 Years of Australian Football*, to air on television. If that was not enough, seventies singer-songwriter Kevin Johnson rerecorded 'Rock 'N' Roll (I Gave You the Best Years of My Life)' as 'Aussie Rules I Thank You for the Best Years of Our Lives'. In all, 1996 would be a grand occasion for the League — and Oakley.

There was just one problem — the League's centenary season was 1997. Australian rules football as a game was first formally played in 1858, with the VFA established in 1877. The breakaway VFL was established in 1896, yet its inaugural season was the following year. Claims that 1996 represented the League's centenary season were one year premature and evident to those on the AFL Commission and in the administration. In his memoirs, Oakley dismissed these concerns with a hand wave; he wanted to celebrate 'many events that were the 100th of their kind'.[28] While it was indeed the 100th season, it would only be the 100th grand final if the replays of 1948 and 1977 were counted twice, as the VFL had not held grand finals in 1897 and 1924. The 'centenary' made even less sense for other events, such as the re-enactment of the first League round, played on 8 May 1897. Cynics suggested that there were ulterior motives for celebrating the centenary a year early. While it was not yet public knowledge, Oakley had determined that 1996 would be his final year as CEO.[29] He believed that the time was right for him to leave, and the centenary year was the 'perfect opportunity not just to leave but also to celebrate a turbulent 10 years in the big job'.[30] For Oakley, this was his chance to leave in style.

Many Lions supporters were looking forward to seeing the back of Ross Oakley. The emphasis on nationalisation, mergers and a doctrinaire insistence on economic rationalism left the struggling Fitzroy in a perilous position. By 1996, the perception had become entrenched that Oakley and the Commission were doing everything they could to remove Fitzroy from the competition (which would, among other things, pave the way for a second team from Adelaide to enter the AFL). While Lions supporters held divergent opinions on a variety of issues, a uniting factor was their suspicion of and animosity towards the AFL. In April 1996, a lifelong Fitzroy supporter wrote to the *Herald Sun* expressing their contempt towards the present AFL administration, accusing Ross Oakley and other officials of engaging in a campaign of 'subterfuge and intimidation' against Fitzroy for almost a decade.[31] These views were not uncommon, and it was the type of sentiment that Dyson Hore-Lacy stoked to galvanise the supporters and cast the AFL as the villains of the piece. The narrative of the perfidious football league set against the battling football club suited Hore-Lacy, who made full use of the David and Goliath overtones to stir up the passions of the supporters and generate sympathy in the wider public.

That the Commission had been looking for Victorian clubs to merge was no secret: it had been a very public part of their thinking since the Blue Report in 1985. And Fitzroy, as one of the weakest clubs in the competition by the early nineties, was undoubtedly seen as low hanging fruit. Yet Fitzroy's supporters argued that the AFL's interest in merging Fitzroy went beyond light encouragement. There was always a belief that the Commission proactively sought Fitzroy's demise through undermining it as a financial and competitive entity, actively taking steps to block the club from generating money. To this day, supporters can recite a litany of grievances as if they were a catechism:

Fitzroy had proposed playing home games in Tasmania and Canberra to raise revenue, but both offers were rebuffed.³² Allegedly, after the proposal for Fitzroy to play games in Canberra was shot down, a Commissioner came to see Hore-Lacy in his chambers, explaining that the Commission wanted to bring Port Adelaide into the competition and wanted to keep the pressure on Fitzroy to merge.³³

There were also several high-profile sponsorship deals kyboshed by the League in previous years.³⁴ One recent case involved sponsorship from short-lived pay-TV operator Galaxy. The AFL had rejected the deal on the not unreasonable grounds that Channel Seven, having paid a significant amount for the rights to broadcast AFL football, did not want to have a competitor's name and logo shown over their broadcasts. Yet Channel Seven were happy to air ads for Galaxy during their regular programming. Furthermore, the AFL's position was utterly undermined in late February 1996 when they welcomed a deal with Optus Vision, another pay-TV operator with plans to launch a 24-hour football network. As ambitious and ultimately ill-fated as the Optus Vision proposal was, it added grist to the mill for those who believed the AFL was deliberately attempting to deny revenue to Fitzroy to force it out of the competition. In *The Age*, Patrick Smith thought that there was 'no doubt the overriding decision to stop Fitzroy's Galaxy sponsorship was to pressure the Lions, not ease pressure on Channel Seven.'³⁵

Adding fuel to Fitzroy's grievances was the notion, real or imagined, that Sydney and Brisbane were the beneficiaries of significant financial support and favourable treatment from the Commission while it denied the same to many established Melbourne-based clubs. While Sydney, in particular, was a recipient of AFL largesse, there was also heavy parochialism from Victorians who were still trying to come to terms with the 'VFL' becoming the 'AFL'. South Melbourne had moved to Sydney in 1982, West Coast and Brisbane joined the League in 1987, Adelaide in 1991 and Fremantle in 1995, yet even in 1996 there was still a cultural war to convince Victorians that these 'interstate' clubs deserved a place in what had, until recently, been a Victorian competition. The success of West Coast in the early nineties attracted opprobrium from some quarters and led to the not-too-clever 'West Coast Wankers' sobriquet. Victoria, and Melbourne in particular, felt it had ownership of Australian rules football. The city that gave birth to Australian rules football, guarded it with proprietary zeal. Unsurprisingly, many Victorians treated interstate clubs with suspicion, if not downright hostility.

The attitude many Victorians held regarding Sydney and Brisbane ignored the real difficulties both clubs faced in establishing themselves in challenging markets, often with little support from the Victorian clubs. Strategically, the Commission needed to support teams in non-traditional Australian rules states for the benefit of the League as a whole — if this meant that Victorian clubs had their noses bent out of joint, so be it. This crude calculus was little consolation to Victorian supporters. In May, two fans wrote to *The Age*, suggesting that by offering concessions to Sydney and Brisbane while undermining Melbourne-based clubs, the Commission had 'angered and alienated many football supporters and galvanised their resistance to the merger path'.[36] Similarly, one prominent Fitzroy supporter lamented that his club had become a byword for merger while interstate clubs were 'given everything but the keys to the Treasury'.[37]

The football media did not help Fitzroy's insecurity. Sitting just behind the AFL Commission in the rogues' gallery of the club's villains, the media, particularly newspapers, were a constant source of frustration and depression. One fan was demoralised every time they picked up a paper with the headline 'Fitzroy gone' or 'Fitzroy doomed', with articles declaring that the club could not pay its players.[38] In a 1995 children's book, *Carn the Lions*, the young supporter mentions that his grandfather 'looks sad when people say the Fitzroy club won't last much longer', and shows the grandfather ripping up a newspaper with the headline 'Roys Look Finished This Time'.[39] The constant stream of articles on Fitzroy were part running commentary, part

Greek chorus. They helped shape the public perception, either through editorials, or by breaking stories that shed light on the sometimes-opaque world in which the clubs and the AFL operated. Newspapers generated speculation, with negative articles creating the perception of a club in crisis, potentially scaring off future sponsors. Television and radio provided platforms for discussion, multiplying the effect of a single, negative article. Many journalists were well-connected within AFL House, and there were suspicions about how they received their information and what the intended effect was on Fitzroy once it was published. In particular, Mike Sheahan, writing for the *Herald Sun*, had earned the ire of many Lions supporters by running an editorial line that not only should Fitzroy merge, but it would be in their best interest to do so with Brisbane. Such commentary fuelled the belief at Fitzroy that the media was against them, actively trying to frustrate the club's attempts at survival.

By 1996, the AFL environment was bleak for Fitzroy people. Many felt besieged, with too many enemies and not enough friends. Adding insult to injury was the timing of the League's centenary year of celebrations. Not only was the AFL trumpeting the worth of its history while letting a foundation club sink into oblivion, many supporters believed the amount spent on the celebrations could be put to better use. The season launch on 8 February at the MCG was a perfect example. The event was a spectacle barely worthy of the name, hokey and quaint by the standards of the AFL's later, slicker productions. Those planning the event likely predicted a big crowd on a balmy summer's evening. Instead, only 10,000 people came out on an unseasonably cold and windswept Thursday night to watch the AFL's attempts at spectacle fall flat. As 'entertainment', Brad Boyd joined Leon Cameron, John Platten and Tony Woods to dance to a Beatles melody with cardboard guitars, before Billy Brownless, David Schwarz, Justin Madden and Stephen Alessio mimed Robert Palmer's 'Simply Irresistible'. Inexplicably, Dorothy the Dinosaur also made an appearance.[40]

The AFL's 1996 promotional advertisements reprised the famous 'I'd Like To See That' campaign. This time, the League's marketing department secured legendary American comedian George Burns (who, symbolically, had just turned one hundred), blues singer John Lee Hooker, *Melrose Place* actress Heather Locklear and Archbishop Desmond Tutu. None of the contributors were able to attend, although a George Burns impersonator arrived via helicopter with two nurses to partake in the 'festivities'. Tragically, the real Burns died thirty days later, suffering a cardiac arrest. The evening, attended by far fewer supporters than the AFL would have preferred, was a flop as a spectacle and gave those already suspicious of the AFL's motivations more ammunition with which to mock the League's pretentions. At the end of the night, the crowd, cold and uninspired, headed for the exits; 'they no doubt felt grateful,' Patrick Smith wrote, 'that an AFL centenary launch comes about just once every 100 years.'[41] It was a warning of what was to come: Ross Oakley wanted 1996 to be a joyful celebration. Instead, it would be one of the most sombre and depressing years in VFL/AFL history.

CHAPTER FIVE

THE OPTION OF LAST RESORT

'[W]e took the view that we were duty bound to preserve what we could of Fitzroy, and if that meant merging, it had to be done'

— Dyson Hore-Lacy, Fitzroy president.[1]

At the start of 1996, Dyson Hore-Lacy was a man bereft of options. The fifteenth successor to John McMahon as the president of the Fitzroy Football Club may well have thought he might be the last. For much of its existence, Fitzroy had been poor. This reality was baked into the club's culture and, for better or worse, was an intrinsic part of its identity. While the quest for financial stability had occupied generations of Fitzroy committeemen and board members, by the middle of 1995 the club's current board of directors had become acutely conscious of Fitzroy's financial position and its deficiencies relative to its competitors in the AFL. As such, the board determined that additional finance was necessary to cover operational costs and entice quality players. They settled on the amount of $1 million, and set about exploring how to raise the required funds.[2] After six months chasing several seemingly promising avenues, on 12 January 1996 Hore-Lacy had been informed that one of the few remaining options would be closed to him. This was not the news he needed to start the new year.

It was no secret that Fitzroy was struggling financially. For years, media reporting and the club's own annual accounts gave a clear picture of the club's plight. For the 1995 season just past, the club recorded an operating loss of $263,834 with only $138,345 cash-on-hand at the end of the financial year. It had generated $4.07 million in revenue, of which $1.402 million came from the AFL distributions. Another thirty per cent came from marketing, functions and other activities, leaving fifteen per cent from sponsorships, eleven per cent from memberships and a meagre two per cent (or $89,575) from gate receipts. The Fitzroy Club Hotel earned a further $2.751 million, but this only resulted in a $132,000 profit when balanced against the hotel's expenses.[3] By comparison, that same season Carlton recorded a profit of $581,000 (*excluding* gaming and social club revenue), Essendon posted a $1.04 million profit while Geelong turned over $10.9 million from its football operations and social club resulting in a group profit of $707,261.[4] If the AFL was split between the 'haves' and the 'have nots', Fitzroy was not only in the latter group but its poor financial position was slowly becoming terminal.

Fitzroy, however, was not the only club struggling financially. In 1986, the Commissioner for Corporate Affairs declared that seven clubs — Fitzroy, Geelong, Footscray, Collingwood, Melbourne, North Melbourne and Richmond — were technically insolvent.[5] By the mid-nineties many clubs had stabilised but few had become truly secure. Furthermore, the eighties powerhouse Hawthorn had accumulated $1 million debt since 1990 and reported a $700,000 operating loss for the 1996 season.[6] To address their various financial ailments, clubs needed to increase their ability to generate revenue while also raising capital by one-off means to pay down their debt. Geelong borrowed

$1.6 million to build the Hickey Stand at Kardinia Park — adding to their debt in the short-term but giving them greater earning capacity in the long term.[7] North Melbourne became inventive, pioneering Friday night games and floating the club in 1986 for $3 million. When Collingwood began playing seven home games at the MCG in 1994 it was able to reap the rewards of having a large supporter base in the form of gate takings. Several clubs ran fundraising campaigns to raise cash when desperately needed. During Footscray's 1989 crisis, the club called upon the support of the entire western suburbs of Melbourne; when Richmond struggled financially in the early nineties, its sizeable (if latent) army of supporters responded to the Save Our Skins campaign and raised $1 million.

Unfortunately, Fitzroy was different. It lacked several significant historical and structural assets available to other clubs. It did not have a large supporter base or catchment area from which to draw members or raise funds. What little money they could raise was quickly eaten up in pre-existing debt and interest repayments. There were also few wealthy benefactors associated with the club who could be elected to the board and invest their millions; they had no facilities to develop, no home ground to support them and none of their alternative revenue-raising methods met with success. The Fitzroy board had considered something drastic in 1986, being tempted to follow the precedent of South Melbourne and relocate to Brisbane. Despite support from the players, the board ultimately rejected the move.[8] After that, Fitzroy teetered on the precipice, managing to wriggle out of its predicaments, often at the eleventh hour. Last minute rescues, financiers appearing and deals being struck when all hope seemed lost had allowed the club to cling on to life for one or two more years until the next crisis. Yet an uncertain hand-to-mouth existence and a VFL Commission intent on reducing the number of clubs in Melbourne did not bode well for the Lions in the longer-term.

Pressure slowly mounted on Fitzroy. As top-flight football became more expensive the club's costs grew and revenue either stagnated or went backwards. By the nineties, all manner of football operations expenditure needed to increase, most notably for player wages and more full-time staff. Full-time assistant coaches were not only becoming standard among AFL teams but necessary if they wanted to compete for premierships. AFL Players' Association (AFLPA) negotiations and the threat of industrial action in early 1993 led to a rise in player payments in their next CBA.[9] While this was a win for the players, higher salaries were not met by increased AFL dividends to the clubs. Despite the League's revenue increasing dramatically, much of its expenditure was directed at its own debt relief and to developing the game in New South Wales and Queensland.[10]

The widening resources gap between Fitzroy and its competitors had on-field ramifications, which in turn affected its ability to generate greater income and close the gap. 'Every time they kicked a point,' reflected director Colin Hobbs, 'every time someone dropped a mark, it was another nail in the coffin.'[11] Poor performances were not conducive to gaining sponsors, and if the club did manage to secure a sponsorship, arrangements often ran afoul of the AFL for various reasons. As the team's on-field performance dipped, fewer companies wanted their brands to be associated with the failing club. VicHealth, via the Quit campaign, sponsored Fitzroy since the eighties, but they had been reducing the amount for years. By the start of the 1996 season, it was contributing just $125,000 per year (compared to $400,000 most clubs received from their major sponsors). Worse, Fitzroy started the year with no 'back of the guernsey' sponsor, despite extensive efforts to attain one.[12]

To be able to continue operating, the club took out short-term commercial loans, but banks were increasingly unwilling to lend to Fitzroy, fearing it would collapse and default (fears, Fitzroy people argued, that were stoked by the AFL administration). A loan arrangement from Westpac ended in 1993, and the board was struggling to find replacement finance. Fortunately a 'white knight' had emerged in the form of trucking tycoon Bernie Ahern. In an inventive solution, he proposed loaning the AFL $750,000 (the value of its dividend to Fitzroy) at the start of the year, forwarded to Fitzroy. The League would then repay Ahern at the end of the year, with Fitzroy paying the interest upfront. While the AFL administration accepted that arrangement for 1994, it would not endorse similar unorthodox loan deals in the future, even though Ahern was prepared to roll the deal over into 1995.[13]

By 1994, the AFL Commission had become very serious about ensuring that, for the general welfare of the competition, all clubs were financially viable and robust (knowing, of course, that some were not). It also had more power to enact its vision for the League, with the implementation of the 1993 Crawford Report completing the transfer of power from the clubs to the independent commission. As a statement of intent, in August 1994, the Commission released a five-year strategic plan.[14] In some respects, the 192-page document simply repeated well-worn arguments and positions: Victoria could not support eleven near-professional clubs, while the League would be a generator of income it was not prepared to act as banker to the clubs and mergers remained the preference for struggling clubs, rather than seeing them fail financially.[15]

In addition, the Commission also imposed a financial solvency rule, with expulsion from the AFL as a penalty.[16] Seven months before the pre-season, each club needed to satisfy the Commission that it could meet its debts when they fell due for the entirety of the following season. This requirement was more stringent than mandated by Australia's corporate regulator, the Australian Securities Commission (ASC, which would become ASIC in 1998). If a club failed to satisfy the Commission, it could seek to revoke the club's licence or appoint an administrator to run the club.[17]

As outlined in the five-year plan, the Commission wanted to see the game flourishing in Sydney and Brisbane at the plan's end and favoured retaining a sixteen-team league, but with one fewer team in Melbourne and an additional club in Adelaide.[18] While the document never explicitly mentioned Fitzroy as the Melbourne-based club to make way, this failed to reassure the Lions that they were not the prime target. 'The AFL Commission does not accept that 100 years of history automatically qualifies a club for participation in the AFL into the next century,' noted the document pointedly. One journalist expressed it even more bluntly: 'The future gained at the expense of the past.'[19] Fitzroy looked doomed, but then, in late 1994, help came from an unlikely source — the Republic of Nauru.

The full complexity and curiosity of Nauru's involvement with the Fitzroy Football Club will be explained in due course. For now, it is sufficient to know that in October 1994 the phosphate-rich island nation decided to provide Fitzroy with a loan via the Nauru Insurance Corporation (an instrument of the Nauruan Government) of $1.2 million.[20] Nauru became Fitzroy's only secured creditor, with a 'floating charge' (i.e. a security interest over unspecified assets) placed over the club as security. As part of the deal, a representative of the Nauruan Government, Kinza Clodumar (who had played for the Fitzroy Under 19s side), was elected to the board.[21] Nauru's intervention was the lifeline Fitzroy needed. The loan eased Fitzroy's reliance on the AFL's dividend to have sufficient cash-on-hand to meet its debts.[22] Dyson Hore-Lacy was bullish about its implications for Fitzroy: 'We'll no longer have to worry about our future at the end of every year,' he said. As long as the club kept to its budget it would 'be around forever'.[23] Fitzroy only needed to remain solvent, although this was a task easier said than done.[24] While Nauru provided support in the short run, in the long-term it merely added to the club's liabilities. There was no benefit to the club in accruing higher debt and buying time for itself if it did not use that time to find additional means to raise revenue.

Nevertheless, the loan had rescued the club from a precarious financial position. By the following year, a Fitzroy-facilitated partnership was developing between Nauru, which was always looking for Australian-based commercial opportunities as a means of investing its phosphate-generated wealth, and property developer

Bruno Grollo.[25] With both parties seemingly happy, in September 1995 Fitzroy asked for $500,000 from each to support the club — meeting the board's need to raise $1 million for the 1996 season.[26] Initially, the response seemed positive. The Nauruan Cabinet had agreed to give the requested financial assistance, confirming Clodumar's assertion that they were in for the 'long haul' with Fitzroy (although Grollo's contribution was still up in the air).[27] While Nauru and Grollo negotiated, the directors personally lent the club $235,000 of their own money (some needed to borrow themselves to forward it to the club) in late December for outstanding player payments.[28]

Then, an election in Nauru in November 1995 removed President Bernard Dowiyogo resulting in Clodumar's loss of influence. Almost overnight Nauru's relationship with Fitzroy cooled. Nervous negotiations took place over the Christmas period to ensure Nauru's ongoing support. Unfortunately, on 12 January 1996, Hore-Lacy was told unequivocally that the club would not get one cent more; Nauru, it seemed, were concerned that Fitzroy was insolvent and did not want to risk any more of their money.[29] Soon after that, the club learnt that sponsorship from Bruno Grollo would also not be forthcoming. Fitzroy's options narrowed dramatically. Without the injection of cash, the club would struggle to pay its debts if and when they became due. At that point, the club's board would need to make some tough decisions.

...

Having dismissed relocation in 1986, the option of last resort for Fitzroy was to merge with another club, thereby retaining something of the club's history, heritage and identity within the AFL. The alternative, if the necessary income could not be secured, was to see the club be wound up. None of the directors wanted to merge — Hore-Lacy did not, and neither had Leon Wiegard. The club's policy was that merger was the last option before liquidation, a statement of resignation to the fact that the club could not stay afloat on its own. But if the directors believed they had exhausted all options to keep the club going, they felt duty-bound to preserve what they could of Fitzroy, and as Hore-Lacy later wrote, 'If that meant merging, it had to be done.'[30]

The Fitzroy board had engaged in merger discussions on and off for years depending on the health of the club at the time. In 1986, it had discussions with Melbourne, St Kilda and North Melbourne, all of which came to nothing. Often, the negotiations would break down over club colours or who would be the president.[31] Despite placing it high on their agenda, the VFL Commission was unable to secure any mergers in the years after 1985. In desperation, in mid-1989, the League offered an incentive: if two teams merged, the AFL would pay their outstanding debts.[32] Finally, this seemed a sufficient inducement to take a merger seriously. By late 1989, Footscray was insolvent and on the verge of being placed into administration. Fitzroy, by no means in a healthy financial state itself, had nevertheless been positioned as a senior partner in a prospective merger with the Bulldogs. By the time the VFL Commission met on 3 October 1989, there was an in-principle agreement between the two parties.[33] In a merger favourable to Fitzroy, the new club would be the 'Fitzroy Bulldogs', playing in Fitzroy's colours with the Bulldogs' symbol, training at the Western Oval, playing at Princes Park, coached by Fitzroy's Rod Austin. After agreement from the Footscray board, the deal was done with Fitzroy and announced to the public that evening.[34]

Public reaction, particularly from the Footscray supporters, was visceral. Peter Gordon, a 31-year-old lawyer and rising star from the western suburbs, organised a 'Save the Dogs' campaign, and after a court-ordered injunction, the Commission gave Footscray three weeks to raise $1.5 million to save their club. The ensuing campaign, featuring the sale of the memorable 'Up Yours Oakley' stickers, raised the required cash and then some.[35] The Commission reversed its decision; Footscray people had saved their club. For the Sons of the West, it was a triumph. The amount their supporters raised not only covered Footscray's debt, but it set them up in advance for the following season. For Fitzroy, it was a disaster. While Footscray were able to build from their near-death experience, Fitzroy lost sponsors and were still $700,000 in debt.[36] 'We did everything pretty right and ended up with a black eye,' lamented the club's president, Leon Wiegard.[37] Footscray and Fitzroy had travelled down the merger path in 1989 because they both believed they needed a merger to survive. Footscray found resilience and a renewed optimism about its future through the process; Fitzroy did not.

The failure of the 'Fitzroy Bulldogs' did not discourage Fitzroy's board from continuing to explore the option of a merger when it seemed necessary. Before Nauru's intervention in late 1994, things were looking dire. As a result, in August 1994, Fitzroy and Melbourne were engaged in discussions, to the point where Hore-Lacy and Melbourne's president, Ian Ridley, fronted the AFL Commission with a merger proposal. The plan fell apart in early September after it was revealed in the press, reinforcing to Dyson Hore-Lacy the risks once negotiations were made public. The two clubs also fell out over the new club's name and colours — another important aspect in any merger negotiation.[38] Looking back, Ross Oakley considered the failure of the Melbourne/Fitzroy merger 'close to the last roll of the dice for Fitzroy'.[39] Nauru's intervention late in 1994 propped them up for at least another season, but by the end of 1995, the situation again was looking grim.

From the AFL Commission's perspective, it had been badly burnt by the 1989 Footscray experience, with Oakley becoming the target of severe public vitriol. It still believed that the underlying financial situation had not altered, and it remained committed to finding mergers among its Melbourne-based teams.[40] Recent experience, however, demonstrated that supporters reacted very badly to the prospect of seeing their club merge and this would place pressure on club boards to reject merger proposals. While the club directors had a fiduciary obligation to examine a merger if they believed it was in the best interest of the club and its creditors, extra incentives were necessary to make a merger more than just a last resort before liquidation. The AFL Commission decided to employ both the carrot and the stick to get what they wanted. On 13 June 1995, AFL House made its strongest push for a merger yet, presenting a $4 million merger incentive package to the clubs. In addition to a lump sum payment and some playing list concessions, there were also some punitive measures, such as minimum revenue criteria and a financial solvency rule, to encourage struggling clubs to think more closely about pursuing a merger.[41]

The scheme was aimed directly at Fitzroy and the Commission made little attempt to hide it. A month earlier, Graeme Samuel spoke at a luncheon where he discussed the Commission's vision for the League and the place of mergers:

> I do think that Fitzroy needs to focus on the market realities, and I am well aware of the traditions associated with the club, the length of time it has been in the competition, but it ought to face the market realities before they are hit from external sources and the external sources put increasing pressure on them which makes it impossible for them to survive as a significant club in the competition. If I were Fitzroy I would be seriously looking at establishing for themselves a future but a future in a different guise to what they currently have.[42]

At the subsequent meeting between the Commission and the clubs at the Leonda By The Yarra function centre in Hawthorn on the night of Monday, 19 June 1995, the clubs voted to increase the merger incentive package to $6 million for the first two teams to merge before 31 October 1995.[43] In *The Age*, Patrick Smith described the increase in the incentive as a move from 'enticement to downright bribery', arguing that the Commission was 'begging' for mergers and looking for 'a way to kill off Fitzroy'.[44] Crucially (although little remarked upon at the time), the package included an extra $700,000 above the annual salary cap of $2.3 million over three years to accommodate an expanded playing list from forty-two to between forty-four and fifty (depending on the seedings of the merging clubs).[45]

Dyson Hore-Lacy condemned the Commission's plan, knowing that the coercive aspects would see Fitzroy face inevitable extinction if it did not find a merger partner.[46] Yet despite the jeopardy, neither Fitzroy, nor any other club, finalised a merger by October; the deadline came and went. While some incentives, such as the playing list and salary cap, were formally withdrawn, the $6 million remained on the table. Failure in 1995 did not preclude the Commission offering other incentives in any future deal, but they would need to be worked out via negotiation (with the Leonda agreement as a template).[47] With Port Adelaide knocking at the door to enter the AFL and thus fulfil the Commission's aim of having a second team in Adelaide, a merger remained a timely and appropriate solution to address several of the Commission's issues as it headed into 1996.

Merging also remained a viable path for the Lions, but by the time the additional Nauru financing and a sponsorship deal from Bruno Grollo had come to nothing, it had moved from the option of last resort to the only course of action. As Hore-Lacy would later write, 'Our last real hope for avoiding a merger faded dramatically.'[48] The directors would later tell members that a new fundraising campaign might have seen Fitzroy through to the end of 1996, and perhaps through 1997 as well.[49] Internally, however, they projected the club would not survive to the end of the year, and they made the 'unpalatable' decision that they would seek AFL funding to see them through the season in return for agreeing to attempt to conclude a merger at the end of the year.[50] Completing a merger, however unpopular, would salvage something of the 113-year-old club. Dyson Hore-Lacy would later argue that the time had come to 'turn a negative into a positive' and take advantage of the lucrative carrot offered to the first two clubs to merge.[51] Privately, it must have been a devastating decision, to believe that they had financially secured their position in late 1994 with the Nauru assistance, only to be forced back into considering such a painful option.

Before the board got too far ahead of itself, however, there were some preliminary matters to consider. Deciding to pursue a merger was one thing, successfully completing the delicate alchemy required in merger negotiations was a different matter. 'Negotiating a merger would be a painstaking exercise which would take time,' Hore-Lacy later commented, 'time which we did not have.'[52] With club finances never particularly healthy, the board needed to buy time for negotiations and agreement with another club in case cash ran out. The directors' personal financial intervention at the end of 1995 did not bode well for the club's cash position. The distribution of Fitzroy's $1.48 million dividend from AFL was scheduled for several points during the year, but there was no guarantee cash-on-hand would last until then.

One solution came through director Robert Johnstone, who was not only a Fitzroy board member but also a senior executive at McDonald's who had been negotiating a large sponsorship deal with the AFL in late 1995 and early 1996.[53] Intimately aware of Fitzroy's financial difficulties, during personal negotiations with Ross Oakley in his capacity with McDonald's, he raised a proposal with him — sanctioned by the club's directors — regarding Fitzroy's future. Playing to the Commission's desire to see a merger between two clubs, Johnstone put it to Oakley that the Commission could underwrite the Lions $750,000 for the remainder of the season on the basis that the AFL could appoint an administrator (and merge the club to their liking) if it could not repay the money by 31 October 1996. The proposal was initially received positively from the Commission and Graeme Samuel nominated an independent solicitor to draw up the necessary documents.[54]

Yet one sticking point reoccurred throughout the club's discussions with the AFL — the directors could not provide an unequivocal undertaking to the League that it would merge, as Fitzroy's memorandum of articles stated that the club required approval from members and stakeholders before any merger was finalised (in 1986, Fitzroy raised $580,000 selling shares in a limited float, giving the club a number of shareholders with enhanced voting power over ordinary members).[55] Sensing their opportunity to secure their first merger, the Commission did not want to give Fitzroy any assistance unless the club could guarantee a merger. Samuel seemed concerned that a 'white knight' might arise and secure Fitzroy financially, leading Hore-Lacy to reflect sardonically that the League 'seemed to fear our survival more than our demise.'[56] To expedite the whole process, the Commission wanted Fitzroy to hold a meeting of members and shareholders immediately to change the articles of association to allow the club to merge without gaining their support beforehand. The directors were concerned about the message this would give to the club before the start of the season. Without promising what it could not deliver, Fitzroy's board guaranteed the AFL administration its best endeavours to find a merger partner.[57]

From the AFL's perspective, Fitzroy's overtures and their willingness to look at a merger again was welcome news. The Commission had kept a close eye on the club's financial position, particularly since the collapse of the potential Fitzroy/Melbourne merger in 1994 (while the Commission monitored several clubs, Fitzroy seemed most in peril). Regardless of any wider machinations about removing a club from the Victorian football landscape, the AFL needed to ensure that its clubs would be financially solvent for the duration of each season (not an unreasonable request, as the Commission wanted to ensure that Fitzroy — or any club — would play all its scheduled matches each year). Clearly concerned about Fitzroy's financial state, once the new financial solvency rule was ratified, the Commission instructed Oakley to apply greater stringency to the Lions and, if necessary, apply the rule. From the middle of 1995, Fitzroy and the AFL administration had been in constant communication over the club's finances for the 1996 season.⁵⁸ At the start of 1996, the Commission remained concerned and on 23 January they decided to write to Fitzroy, formally seeking advice about the club's financial position (the second time in as many years the Commission had given the Lions a solvency notice).⁵⁹

Any concerns the Commission was harbouring were likely amplified by a request from Dyson Hore-Lacy shortly thereafter for an advance of $100,000 on Fitzroy's next AFL dividend payment, not scheduled for another fortnight. Oakley agreed to advance $60,000 to the Lions, and the suspicions of the AFL's administrators was seemingly confirmed.⁶⁰ When the Commission met on 9 February, it expressed doubts as to whether Fitzroy could pay its debts through to 31 October 1996. They wanted assurances from Fitzroy that they were, and would be, solvent for the foreseeable future.⁶¹ It was at this point that Johnstone put Fitzroy's proposal to Oakley. While that deal was being negotiated, the Commission agreed to give the club an extension until 1 March to provide the necessary information regarding its solvency.⁶²

By now, it was not just AFL House that was monitoring Fitzroy's financial position closely. At the end of 1995, the AFLPA were concerned that Fitzroy was unable to pay its players. While the cash intervention from the directors had covered all back payments to the start of 1996, there were lingering concerns within the association about the upcoming season.⁶³ When news of the Commission's solvency notice to Fitzroy was broken by Stephen Linnell in *The Age* on 1 March, the AFLPA's executive director, Peter Allen, publicly described Fitzroy's future as 'extremely uncertain'.⁶⁴ Allen called on the AFL to assist the club in meeting its contractual obligations, stating: 'I don't believe for one moment that Fitzroy has the capacity to do this on their own.'⁶⁵ This was the type of media attention Dyson Hore-Lacy hated, as it perpetuated the narrative of a club in financial crisis. Hore-Lacy had, for many years, wanted to exude confidence about the club, lest it deter potential sponsors and investors. Responding to this latest story, Hore-Lacy made strong public statements about the club's ability to continue to operate. 'This is not the first time we've received notice,' he said. 'We've satisfied them before and we'll satisfy them again.'[66] Oakley too was downplaying the severity of the situation, stating that the action the League had taken was 'no more or less than [what] we've been doing constantly over the last nine to twelve months.'[67]

Fitzroy provided the necessary information to the AFL, but the Commission was unsatisfied and called on the club to provide further details (an outcome that was immediately leaked to the media and published the following day).[68] The situation was deemed so serious that a contingency plan had been developed and presented to the Commission in the event that the club was unable to field a team that season.[69] Publicly, however, Oakley was not too alarmist. When asked whether it was 'crunch time' for Fitzroy, he replied: 'No more so than it's been for the past three years. Fitzroy, as we all know, have got a fairly substantial debt and they're trying to address that.'[70] Others could see that time was running out for the club. In *The Age*, Patrick Smith wrote: 'If Fitzroy doesn't drop dead this winter, then it will the next … Sadly, money ran out for Fitzroy years ago. Now, it appears time has as well.'[71]

Fitzroy's directors had come to this conclusion too. While publicly Hore-Lacy was defiant about Fitzroy's survival, privately the directors were resigned to the need to merge or else face the possibility of extinction by the end of the year. At a portentous board meeting on 6 March, Fitzroy's directors resolved that:

> Dyson Hore-Lacy, Elaine Findlay and Robert Johnstone be empowered to enter into any agreement that they deemed necessary in the interests of the Fitzroy Football Club provided that no agreement shall be entered into which irrevocably commits the Fitzroy Football Club to cease operating in the AFL past the 1996 season.[72]

Fitzroy's directors had entered into merger discussions before, and at times of great financial peril, but now there was little hope of a 'white knight' coming to the rescue. The challenge for Hore-Lacy and the other directors was to conclude a favourable merger agreement before the club ran out of money. The suggestion that the League underwrite its season was being considered by the AFL Commission throughout March, but the signs were not positive. One afternoon, Ross Oakley and Dyson Hore-Lacy had a heated conversation, with the Fitzroy chairman ending the discussion by telling Oakley that he had better 'batten down the hatches. This would be a Centenary Year to remember.'[73]

CHAPTER SIX

ONCE MORE TO THE BARRICADES

'By the year's end Fitzroy supporters will have experienced some obvious lows, but should be content in the fact that their club is on the improve'

— Gerard Healy, Brownlow medallist.[1]

There are few better times of the year to be a football supporter than at the start of a season. With each new year, supporters are thrown into 'a ritual of hope, anxiety and despair as their beloved team takes the field'.[2] Fans give themselves the opportunity to dream before the reality of twenty-two often-bruising games sets in. 'We only won two games last year,' 15-year-old Fitzroy supporter Rebecca Cullen told the *Football Record* before the start of the season, 'so we can't really go much worse than that.' Optimistic about what Michael Nunan could bring to the Lions, she could not wait for the season to start: 'I went to the cricket the other day and I just wanted the goalposts there!'[3]

Round 1 of the 1996 AFL Season found Fitzroy hosting Hawthorn at the Whitten Oval. Their previous encounter had seen the Hawks defeat a lacklustre Lions by ninety-nine points at Princes Park, where Brad Boyd had kicked five of Fitzroy's seven goals. Since then, both clubs had new coaches: Nunan at Fitzroy and Ken Judge at Hawthorn (replacing the ineffectual Peter Knights). Nunan's mission was to turn Fitzroy's fortunes around, and this was the place to start. A 'Centenary Gala & Guernsey Day' had been held at Brunswick Street Oval on Sunday, 24 March, where he had presented the 1996 playing list with their jumpers.[4] The following Thursday night, just before Round 1, supporters gathered at the Fitzroy Club Hotel for the first Ins and Outs Night of the season (with Simon Atkins as the special guest). As was custom, prizes were offered for anyone who could guess the correct team as selected by Nunan and the match committee.

The pre-season competitions had informed much of the committee's thinking. The AFL Lightning Premiership, a short, knockout tournament with modified rules played before the formal pre-season tournament over the weekend of 9–11 February had been Nunan's first chance to give his team and his game plan a run against external opposition. Fitzroy did not stay in the competition long, being knocked out in the first round by Collingwood. The game, as with the whole tournament, was something of a disappointment, and how much Nunan was able to learn was questionable. Essendon eventually won the competition, but there were no real winners from the Lightning Premiership. Unpopular with clubs and spectators, despite early suggestions to the contrary, the Lightning Premiership never reappeared.[5]

The next pre-season competition, the Ansett Cup, began in late February and was played through March, with other practice matches scheduled around it. Fitzroy lost its first game against Richmond and Nunan was not impressed. He believed that teams that had remained near the bottom of the ladder for long periods developed the habit of not committing themselves to the contest, an attitude he wanted to redress.⁶ The players responded positively and showed more fight against Footscray, with the team starting to show signs of his system in the way they played. Nunan kept his pleasure at his team's improved performance contained, however, noting that they still had a long way to go.⁷ Unluckily, Simon Hawking rolled his ankle in the first quarter and was expected to miss three weeks, while Matthew Dent was suspended for two weeks for headbutting former Lion Richard Osborne.⁸ Fitzroy was narrowly beaten by Geelong in their third pre-season game, thanks primarily to the brilliance of Gary Ablett Senior.⁹ Cruelly for Fitzroy, Brad Boyd picked up a hamstring injury, and was expected to be out for two to four weeks.¹⁰ The following weekend, Fitzroy played Fremantle in their final practice match of the pre-season and were soundly defeated.¹¹

Despite the string of pre-season losses, by the start of the season proper, several players felt energised. Nunan had brought fresh ideas and a new approach to the club. They had shown that they could play some reasonable football, despite being a young group.¹² Nunan himself was positive about his team's chances in the coming season. While acknowledging the gap that needed to be made up from the previous year, he told *The Age*: 'I've spent five and a half months trying to teach the boys a range of skills and to play the sort of footy I'm looking for.'¹³ He had come to the club wanting to develop skill, fitness and work rate among the players. Round 1 would prove whether Nunan's labours had borne fruit.

Selecting the senior team for the first game of the season, Nunan and the match committee were without the injured Boyd and the suspended Dent. Simon Hawking was fit and selected at full forward, with Trent Cummings and Jarrod Molloy on either side of him. He had an experienced half-forward line, with Jeff Hogg in the centre and John McCarthy and Mick Dwyer on the flanks. Anthony Mellington, Rowan Warfe and Martin Pike were the half-backs, with Stephen Paxman (acting as captain in Boyd's absence) at full-back, flanked by Darren Holmes and Chris Johnson. The centre comprised

John Rombotis, Simon Atkins, Danny Morton and Matthew Primus in the ruck. John Barker, Brad Cassidy and Wayne Lamb were on the bench.[14]

Three players — Bamford, Cassidy and Primus — would be making their AFL debuts, but it was the latter who was the most eagerly anticipated. The 21-year-old Primus was the grandson of Geelong legend Reg Hickey. Recruited by the Cats when he was sixteen, he languished in their reserves for two years before a scout from the Norwood Football Club spotted him and brought him to South Australia.[15] He played two seasons for Norwood (under Nunan's friend, Neil Craig), the first when he was in Year 12. In his second, in 1995, he was awarded as the club's best and fairest. Still, he wanted another chance to play AFL football before the opportunity passed him by. 'A lot of people were saying to me that I wasn't good enough,' he remarked, 'but I just wanted another crack at it.'[16] Nominating for the 1995 national draft, Fitzroy selected him with pick two.[17] It was, he recalled, 'pure excitement' moving back to Melbourne to play in the AFL.[18] The club expected big things from Primus, and he was not to disappoint them. Fitzroy's other ruckman, the 22-year-old, 194-centimetre Brett Cook had been with the Lions since 1991, but waited until 1994 to make his senior debut. Nunan was positive about Cook as a ruckman, praising the quality of his mobility, agility, kicking and marking that he had seen on the training ground.[19] But Primus, two years younger and four centimetres taller, played all of Fitzroy's pre-season games, shining in each and cementing his spot as the team's number one ruckman for Round 1.

On Friday morning, both major newspapers declared that Round 1 was an excellent chance for the Lions to snatch a win against a Hawthorn side that lost its last seven games of the 1995 season, had its worst season in thirty years and was a shadow of the powerful side that had dominated the previous decade. In *The Age*, Charles Happell wrote that 'on their home ground against a weakened opponent, [Fitzroy] will realise what a golden opening fixture this could be'.[20]

Through the day, Melbourne was a buzz with anticipation for the start of the season. The AFL set a target of 340,000 to attend the eight matches across Melbourne, Adelaide, Perth and Brisbane, which would shatter the previous record, set in 1995, of 245,308.[21] That night, the League's oldest clubs, Geelong and Melbourne, began the Centenary Season at the MCG. Following a spectacular fireworks display, Geelong handed out at 127-point drubbing to the hapless Demons.

Saturday, 30 March, was a typical Melbourne autumn day. Twenty-two degrees celcius, cloudy with the occasional shower clearing to a reasonably sunny afternoon.[22] As well as being the first round of the 1996 AFL season, there was a Victorian state election and all those taking part in the game that day, whether as participants or spectators, voted at various polling booths around Melbourne. Premier Jeffrey Kennett was expected to defeat the Labor opposition led by John Brumby, and as the results filtered in that evening, this proved to be the case. After casting their votes, officials, players and supporters began making their way to Footscray for the game. Among the first to arrive at the Whitten Oval were the property stewards and trainers, who needed to be *in situ* well before the reserves arrived for their game at 11.15am. Casual and relaxed, many of these club stalwarts had seen dozens of Round 1 matches over the years. The mood was light, but it would become steadily more tense as the day went on.

Reserves coach Leon Harris would arrive around 9.00am, with his players following soon after. As they moved down into the dressing rooms, Greg Freemantle, the physical education advisor, worked with the injured or rested players while the others did their warm-ups, giving them a good training session in lieu of a full match.[23] Harris had a healthy number of senior listed players to select for the game against Hawthorn's reserves, coached by former Melbourne player Chris Connolly. The statisticians set themselves up in the coaches box for a day of recording kicks, marks, handballs and tackles and then collating the data at the end of each quarter for both the reserves and senior coaching staff. This mundane but necessary work kept them busy from 11.00am to 5.00pm.[24]

Most of the seniors and the remaining football staff arrived during the first half of the reserves game. While some went straight to work in the rooms, others lingered outside to watch the curtain raiser. Once the siren sounded for half-time, they too disappeared down into the bowels of the main stand to begin their preparations. As a smaller, underdeveloped suburban ground, the facilities at the Whitten Oval were not at the standard of the MCG or even the much-maligned Waverley. Still, they served their purpose. Behind the imposing presence of Tommy Couch at the entrance, players went through their pre-game routines and rituals. Amid the smell of liniment and the sound of tape being applied to ankles and shoulders, each man mentally and physically readied himself for the contest — some were on their own, silently contemplating the game, others with a more social disposition were up and about. The call would ring out for the next player on the tables for a liniment rub or strapping, and they would dutifully make their way to the likes of Kevin Elms or Jack Hancock, men who had been perfecting their craft for decades. Some players handled footballs, sharpening their actions and reactions as they internally repeated Nunan's instructions to run, handball, run, handball like a mantra.

Staff moved through the group, offering words of encouragement or instruction, particularly to the three debutants. Nunan's pre-game preparation would not involve worrying about the opposition (he preferred not to use taggers if possible), he just concentrated on his own players and their own game plan.[25] He was also not one for elaborate pre-game rituals — he let the players prepare before bringing them together ten minutes before they were to take the field. As was probably clear by now, Nunan was going to coach the team his own way: he did not rely on his assistant coach, Alan McConnell, on game day, sometimes leaving him in the coaches box when he came down to the interchange bench to give messages directly to the players.[26]

Across Melbourne, Fitzroy supporters observed their own familiar rituals: families gathered, listening to the Coodabeens as they prepared for the day ahead. Thermoses were filled and club colours donned.

As the players prepared, supporters slowly filtered into the Whitten Oval, arriving by car, by tram or from the nearby West Footscray station from the city — many crossing the Maribyrnong River from the east and entering the unfamiliar surrounds of the inner western suburbs. Some supporters stopped in at the Rising Sun Hotel on Geelong Road for a drink before entering the ground to watch the last quarters of the reserves amid building anticipation for the main game. Those who had purchased special memberships enjoyed reserved car parks outside the ground and a designated section of the E.J. Whitten Stand to sit in.[27] In between the action, supporters who had purchased the Round 1 *Football Record* for the princely sum of $2 read Gregg Hobbs' list of the League's top one hundred players (he had West Coast's Glen Jakovich as number one), Martin Flanagan's historical article on Tom Willis and H.C.A. Harrison and a column by Ross Oakley in which he looked forward to a year of centenary celebrations.[28]

There was cause for optimism among the faithful. With a new coach, a new system and some talented young players, they had every chance of confounding expectations. Several football pundits expressed modest optimism on their behalf. Geoff Poulter believed the Lions would be a vastly improved unit and noted that the coach had a 'firm and precise game plan'.[29] Rohan Connolly wrote that Nunan 'already has the Lions showing more system, competitiveness and potential than they had for at least the previous three years'.[30] Even Mike Sheahan saw positives, as Nunan ('a thinker and a winner') had the Lions playing to a system.[31] Gerard Healy thought the South Australian was 'a very impressive football academic with a hard edge' who would get the Lions playing to a 'well-drilled game plan based on supreme aerobic capacity'.[32] He believed that Lions supporters could look forward to a season of improvement.

As this was a Fitzroy home game, Dyson Hore-Lacy hosted the president's lunch. Held in the corporate area of the Whitten Oval (which offered a scenic view of the Melbourne skyline, if nothing else), the lunches provided the opportunity to host coteries and other invited guests, including representatives of the visiting team. Receptionist Fran Tascone and marketing officer John De Rango had likely spent considerable time organising, setting up and running the lunch and, among his many other commitments, Hore-Lacy was responsible for delivering a lively address for the attendees.[33] Fortunately there had been some good news that week, with South Australian electrical accessories company Clipsal agreeing to a one-year sponsorship deal for back-of-the-jumper naming worth a reported $100,000.[34] The other directors (who paid for their own lunches) were distributed around the tables, leading by example in purchasing raffle tickets and drinks to encourage the guests.[35]

If the diners had the chance, they might peer out over the oval to see bits and pieces of the reserves game. That day, it was a tight contest, with Hawthorn narrowly defeating Fitzroy by a single goal. Brett Chandler, Michael Brown, Frank Bizzotto, Peter Doyle and Jason Ramsey were among Fitzroy's best, while Brent Frewin, who had been picked up in the 1996 pre-season draft from South Mildura, led the Lions' scoring with two goals. With his primary task done for the day, Leon Harris stayed around to sit with the Fitzroy coaching staff for the senior game, offering any assistance he could to Nunan and McConnell.[36]

By 2.00pm it was time for the main game. Vice-captain Stephen Paxman led the side onto the ground in lieu of the injured Brad Boyd. On each jumper, Fitzroy's players had the special AFL centenary emblem on the front and the new sponsor Clipsal's name hurriedly sown on the back. By now, 10,000 spectators had moved through the turnstiles and into the ground, with those not at the Whitten Oval able to follow the action on Optus Vision or by tuning into Magic 693. Across town, Richmond was preparing to play Essendon at the MCG, while St Kilda was hosting North Melbourne at Waverley. On the ground, players soaked in the surrounds. After the last-minute run-throughs, trainers and other support staff departed from the field, Nunan made his way up to the coaches' box and the starting eighteen took their positions. At 2.10pm, the ball was bounced, Matthew Primus and Paul Dear rose to meet it and Fitzroy's 1996 season began.

...

It did not take Lions fans long to get excited about what Nunan had brought to their team. The Roys kicked with the wind in the first quarter and made full use of it, jumping the Hawks 'like a side-street mauler'.[37] Halfway through the opening quarter Fitzroy had put on five unanswered goals and were on top in most positions. The forward-line looked dangerous, with Molloy, Hawking, Cummings and Hogg shining early (both Hawking and Cummings had three first half goals each). Primus was commanding the ruck and Fitzroy's midfield was seeing much of the ball.[38] Seventeen minutes into the second quarter and a goal from the nineteen-year-old John Rombotis put the Lions up by thirty-five points. The small but dedicated band of Fitzroy supporters was in full voice.[39] 'We were playing great football up until half-time,' recalled Chris Johnson, whose towering mark over Hawthorn's Shannon Gibson encapsulated the flair and excitement about the Lions' game.[40] The enthusiasm was tempered by some late Hawthorn goals that drew the margin back. Nevertheless, the Fitzroy crowd was buoyant and cheered their team off wildly at the long break.[41]

Ken Judge, Hawthorn's new coach, needed to do something. At half-time he made a number of tactical moves, including placing Shane Crawford onto Rombotis (who had already amassed seventeen possessions) to curb his influence.[42] His changes had the desired effect. Starting the third quarter, Hawthorn kicked three goals to the non-scoring end and held Fitzroy goalless. There was a slight turning point when Anthony Mellington kicked a high ball across Hawthorn's goal in a desperate attempt to clear the area but instead it landed in the hands of Daniel Harford, who went back and kicked a goal to bring the margin down to ten points.[43] By three-quarter time Fitzroy's margin was cut down to three points with Hawthorn kicking with the breeze in the final term.⁴⁴

In the final quarter, Hawthorn's older hands, particularly Jason Dunstall and John Platten, closed out the game. Platten had been tireless all day and Dunstall finally broke Paxman's shackles and kicked several late but crucial goals, bringing his total to five. Fitzroy had been well led in the ruck by Primus, but, like many of his teammates, he tired in the second half. When he limped off in the last quarter, suffering from an ankle injury, Fitzroy's chances of winning the game left with him.⁴⁵ The game finished Fitzroy 11.5 (71) to Hawthorn 13.14 (92).

Fitzroy had been competitive until the final quarter, many of the young players had played well and Nunan's much-vaunted system showed what it could do. Primus had been excellent, with sixteen disposals and thirteen hit-outs. He was subsequently nominated for the Norwich Rising Star Award, and club officials hoped his injury was not serious.⁴⁶ Darren Holmes also earned praise from his coach and various pundits. The 25-year-old former Swan was imperious across half-back, marking strongly and — clearly taking Nunan's emphasis on handballing seriously — distributing twenty-five handballs throughout the game, which equalled the club record.⁴⁷

The result was much better than Round 1 the previous year when Fitzroy had lost to Essendon by seventy-four points and had not kicked so much as a point in the first half. Yet as a coach familiar with success, Nunan knew how to build a winning culture, and rewarding mediocrity was not the way. He believed that Fitzroy had a habit of being pleased if they played a good half or a good quarter of football. Nunan wanted to disabuse them of this notion: 'Today it was explained to them that it is just not acceptable.'⁴⁸ He dismissed the theory that the Lions were tired by the second half, saying that it was their state of mind that brought about their demise. He deflected the issue from one of fitness to that of work rate, not letting his young players off the hook.⁴⁹ Looking back with the perspective afforded by a long and successful career, Chris Johnson has sympathy for this view, noting that while the young Fitzroy side lacked full match fitness, they also lacked experience in being able to close out games and be mentally competitive for four quarters.[50] No matter what the issue was, Nunan was determined to change the way his team played, conceding that it would take weeks, if not months.[51]

After the game, players, staff and supporters headed back across the Maribyrnong to Northcote for the post-match function at the Fitzroy Club Hotel. A local band was employed for entertainment, and 'for those who enjoy some good food, good wine and a quieter surround', the upstairs dining room was open and available.[52] Election results came in, confirming Premier Kennett's victory, while Brisbane and Footscray played the Saturday night game at the Gabba. As was custom, players, officials and supporters mingled throughout the evening, reflecting on the day's game and no doubt trying to savour the memory of that glorious first half of football that promised so much.

...

By the afternoon of Saturday, 20 April, Fitzroy's early season optimism had well and truly faded. A 32-point defeat to former Fitzroy coach Robert Shaw's Adelaide in Round 2 was followed by a 51-point loss to Footscray. Despite the poor start, however, Mike Sheahan noticed that the Lions seemed 'more professional, positive and fulfilled than they have been for at least two years'.[53] Fitzroy were then defeated by a previously winless St Kilda by eighty-five points in what Nunan described as one of the most inept performances he had seen in his thirteen years of coaching. He was scathing about the large gap in quality between Fitzroy and the next best team in the competition and called out his players for picking up their wages without the will and the inner strength required to compete.[54] It was the lack of effort that frustrated him the most: 'You can have all the skills in the world,' he said, 'but if you won't have a go, there's not much there for us.'[55]

Nunan must have been wondering what he had signed up for. He had seen the talent and quality of some of his players, but he had also seen skill errors, lack of effort and his team being outplayed and out-muscled by larger and more experienced opponents. Nunan later admitted that his appreciation of the size and scope of the job at Fitzroy had increased since he applied for the job, and he believed that an AFL club list with forty-two players would have greater quality that Fitzroy's currently possessed.[56] He also might have underappreciated the level of pressure teams could apply to his players, denying them time and space to use their hands the way that he wanted. While he could take comfort that, for periods in a game, his game plan worked, he did not have enough players of sufficient skill and experience to execute it effectively for four quarters. 'If there was a midfield comprised of seven or eight Greg Williams,' one player recalled, the style would have worked perfectly.[57] Unfortunately, Fitzroy just did not have the cattle.

There were positives, however. Matthew Primus (who recovered quickly from his Round 1 injury) was the standout from the first couple of games, Martin Pike was dependable on half-back, John Rombotis was repaying the faith Nunan showed in him, Bamford was a revelation and Brett Chandler had been effective. Defence was as solid as it could be under the circumstances when they were losing so much ball in the centre. Boyd and Atkins were the prime movers on-ball, with the captain amassing over thirty possessions in Round 2 but being effectively tagged or injured the other games. If there was a specific issue troubling Nunan, it was an inability to find a forward set-up that worked. Molloy had kicked twelve goals and was potentially the answer, but around him there were too many question marks, particularly Jeff Hogg, whom Nunan would shortly drop. Although he tried Chris Johnson as a defender, he was forced to throw him forward on occasion as another option.

As dissatisfied as Nunan might have been with the state of his players, outside observers were taking note of what he was trying to accomplish. The *Herald Sun* noted that while the Lions looked 'a little scruffy' at times, they had a 'slick hand-pass operation with the third-highest number of effective handballs in the competition at 96 per game.'⁵⁸ In three of their first four games Fitzroy had out-handballed their opponents, spectacularly so in Round 1, with 159 handballs to 149 kicks, compared with Hawthorn's 197 kicks and 93 handballs. Yet they were still 0-4, sitting bottom of the ladder behind Melbourne and West Coast, both with one win to their credit. Confidence was beginning to ebb, as players began to expect a teammate error rather than demanding perfection. One journalist, who did not buy into the South Australian style, criticised their 'pathetic' possession game: 'They chip the ball around for two or three clean grabs but achieve nothing. They are not thrusting the ball forward, they are not decisive.'⁵⁹

As the season progressed, Nunan became frustrated by a difference between AFL and SANFL list management rules.⁶⁰ He had been successful with the South Australian system, where senior coaches could use an almost unlimited number of players in their reserves, giving senior coaches a good look at who they might want to add to their list in the future. At North Adelaide, he pushed out those who did not fit his system and tasked his talent scouts with finding him players who could ('turning over heads' was how he described the process).⁶¹ The AFL's draft system and list regulations inhibited this approach, frustrating Nunan throughout his time at the Lions.⁶² He would lament that there were better players in the SANFL or the WAFL than those at Fitzroy, but he had no way of bringing them to the club.⁶³ Instead, he continually cycled through the same shallow pool of players, dropping those he considered unable to play his system and to his standards, only to be forced to bring them back into the side a week or two later after their replacements had similarly been uninspiring.

In the early weeks of the season the interaction between Nunan and the board had been minimal. After several losses, however, Dyson Hore-Lacy and Colin Hobbs met with him to ask whether there could be anything that could improve the match-day performances. They were stunned to hear Nunan say that if they expected the club to win they should have hired a different coach. Nunan's vision for the team was development over two to three years, he could not and would not work to achieve instant results at the expense of longer-term improvement.⁶⁴ Later, the board asked Nunan to comment on the status on the club from his perspective as senior coach. He produced a page and a half memorandum outlining his dissatisfaction with the players on the club's list, the training venue, the social club, the management structure, the long-term planning and the business structure.⁶⁵ Sadly, there was little the board was able to do about the deficiencies Nunan identified and it was unclear how much he knew of the club's financial position.

In Round 5, the Lions travelled to Brisbane to play the Bears on the Sunday after Anzac Day. Nunan demanded a response from his players, wanting them to realise that they were 'at the bottom of the well' and needed to 'start to climb up the ladder, or at least, try to find the ladder'. Unless they could do that, he argued, they were kidding themselves.⁶⁶ Fitzroy started well and held a slender two point lead at the twelve-minute mark before Brisbane kicked away and put the result beyond doubt early.⁶⁷ Boyd and Atkins led Fitzroy's disposals with thirty-two and twenty-seven respectively, John Barker kicked three goals while Scott Bamford, Matthew Primus and Martin Pile were also effective.

The final score, Brisbane 24.14 (158) to Fitzroy 6.13 (49), was, in one sense, easier to accept than some previous losses. In the earlier rounds, Fitzroy had played teams they had a chance to beat. By Round 5, the Bears were sitting third on the ladder with three wins and one loss. While Mike Sheahan described the Lions as a 'dispirited rabble', they lost to the very in-form Bears in Brisbane, something much better teams than Fitzroy would also do that season.⁶⁸ Nunan did not make another post-game outburst. Instead, he believed that his players 'had a go', much more so than the week before.⁶⁹ By now, however, Fitzroy's on-field issues had taken a backseat to more pressing off-field concerns, particularly around the question of a merger. The Lions' abject performance against Brisbane elicited the exact same question in *The Age* and the *Herald Sun*: why would anyone want to merge with Fitzroy?⁷⁰ It is that question to which the attention of many was beginning to turn.

CHAPTER SEVEN

DEALS, RUMOURS AND ULTIMATUMS

'The only club we have a chance [to merge] with is Fitzroy and we aren't their preferred option. We haven't got enough to offer'

— Alan Piper, Brisbane Bears vice-president.[1]

While Michael Nunan struggled through the fixture with his young team, Dyson Hore-Lacy was wrestling with issues of greater consequence. After arriving at the decision to resume the search for a merger partner, the 'merger sub-committee' of Hore-Lacy, Findlay and Johnstone had been busy. The club had yet to give up on finding other sources of income to see it through 1996. Financial support from Bruno Grollo was still an open question, while John Birt was working on a potential $2 million sponsorship deal with the RACV.[2] Both options evaporated, however, and the search for an eleventh-hour rescue — which Fitzroy had benefitted from in previous years — became something of a forlorn hope.

The Fitzroy board was hoping, should these other options fall through, that the AFL Commission would accept the proposal advanced earlier in the year, for them to underwrite the club's season to buy time to find a merger partner. While this was initially greeted positively by the Commission, on 5 April, Oakley became the bearer of bad news. As had been made clear in the AFL's five-year strategic plan, the Commission did not want to become a banker for its clubs and Fitzroy's plan undermined this critical pillar of their strategy. The only way the AFL would accept a deal of this nature was if Fitzroy gave the League a guarantee that it would merge. While Hore-Lacy could offer assurances to Oakley that his board would try their best to finalise a merger, he could not offer an ironclad guarantee that a merger would be executed, as that decision ultimately needed the approval of the members and shareholders.[3] This left them at an impasse. As other financing options dried up, the inability of Fitzroy and the AFL to come to an accommodation placed additional pressure on the Lions. With cash-on-hand a delicate proposition, time was of the essence.

The main game for Fitzroy's merger sub-committee was to begin negotiations. Towards the end of 1995, the board had preliminary discussions with several clubs, but these were halted once it was believed that Nauru would provide an additional $500,000.[4] Fitzroy had many suitors, some serious, others simply seeking to acquire the AFL-endorsed merger incentives and other fringe benefits before casting the Lions into oblivion. Fitzroy's board had its own views for a prospective partner. The main preference, articulated clearly by almost every group the board discussed the matter with (including coteries, the cheer squad and the past players association) was that if Fitzroy was to merge, then it must do so with another Melbourne-based club. The only group for whom this was not a clear preference was the players, as they had slightly different priorities based on what was best for their football career.[5] This was not to say that there was no support among Fitzroy people for an interstate merger, as demonstrated in the debates throughout the year, but it was very much in the minority. Furthermore, as a merger would definitely entail a departure from the Whitten Oval, the board only wished to consider merging with clubs that played home games at the MCG. The newly improved Great Southern Stand, Hore-Lacy reflected, 'made watching football at other venues second-rate by comparison'.[6] Given these criteria, and the desire for an equal merger with a club that would not treat the venture as a corporate takeover, there were only a small number of viable candidates.

Despite these preferences, if the situation became dire, the subcommittee was prepared to compromise. A long-standing option had re-emerged earlier in the year in the form of the Brisbane Bears. As a merger partner, Brisbane fit very few of Fitzroy's criteria, but, given the Lions' predicament, it was still worthy of consideration. On 21 February, Noel Gordon, the Bears' burly, moustachioed president, called Hore-Lacy and let him know that he remained interested in a merger with Fitzroy. Gordon promised that the negotiations would not go public, and by March, discussions were underway.[7]

Brisbane's offer, which changed little throughout the year, was that the newly merged club would become the 'Brisbane Lions', with maroon, gold and blue as the club colours and a re-lyricised club song to the tune of 'La Marseillaise'. Brisbane knew Fitzroy wanted to preserve as much of its heritage as it could, and believed that if it retained significant Fitzroy accoutrements it might help soften the club to merging with a non-Victorian team. In fact, being a relatively new club gave Brisbane a significant advantage over older Victorian clubs: it could give away much of its identity to Fitzroy at comparatively little cost. Other potential suitors were more reluctant to dilute their heritage and identity, which were just as proud and longstanding as Fitzroy's.[8] In fact, grafting Fitzroy's history and heritage onto itself was an important part of what Brisbane wanted from a merger. Ross Fitzgerald, a Brisbane-based historian who had been granted access to the club to write a 'warts and all' book about their 1995 season, believed that Brisbane was a club 'trying to establish a tradition and a culture'.[9] Less charitably, when the club was still based on the Gold Coast, journalist Garry Linnell called it 'a fabricated club living in prefabricated surrounds and trying desperately to buy itself a soul and a tradition'.[10]

While its history was not as long and prestigious as others, Brisbane's past was worthy of respect. It had faced challenges no Victorian-based club would ever need to endure in its pioneering attempt to be Queensland's first VFL club. In 1986, Paul Cronin and Christopher Skase purchased a licence from the League to establish the club, and the Brisbane Bears were born. In their early years, Brisbane lacked a permanent home ground, played with a substandard list and had few supporters. Through the late eighties the Bears faced a series of financial issues and after the departure of Cronin and Skase, the club was sold to Gold Coast businessman Reuben Pelerman.[11] During this time, the League had adopted a more interventionist approach with the Bears, and the provision of priority draft picks and special recruiting zones helped the club acquire the likes of Michael Voss, Jason Akermanis, Clark Keating and Darryl White.

By the start of the nineties, Pelerman was losing significant money at the Bears and he agreed to release it from private ownership and revert to a traditional membership-based structure. Despite the perception in Victoria that Brisbane was living large on the AFL's largesse, it was barely operating at a break-even after private ownership ended. In a move to save about $400,000, Brisbane withdrew their reserves team (a part of the requirement for purchasing the licence back in 1986 was that they would need to pay for the cash-strapped Victorian clubs to send their reserves to Queensland to play). The club had no assets but, mercifully, no debt either — it operated very much hand-to-mouth.[12] Promisingly, the Bears made the finals for the first time in 1995 and finally showed some on-field form. Ross Fitzgerald declared that the Bears had now established themselves successfully in Queensland and cemented their place in the AFL.[13]

By early 1996, the Bears had persevered through the challenges of its early years and made for itself an admirable story of determination through trial of which the club should rightly be proud. Yet this did not compare to a century of history and tradition, with the rustedon support of generations of fans. A merger with Fitzroy offered the chance to bolster the club, give it a presence and a supporter base in Melbourne, as well as importing a gravitas it had previously lacked. Noel Gordon was particularly insistent on pursuing a merger. A former Victorian policeman who had moved to Queensland in the eighties to pursue business interests, Gordon had been president since December 1991, when the club reverted to a membership-based operation.[14] Brisbane and Fitzroy had informal discussions on and off for several years and early in the 1995 season, Gordon commented publicly about the possibility of Brisbane merging with Fitzroy. His remarks were met with unease by his vice-president, Alan Piper, who believed that the Bears had sufficiently solidified their position such that a merger with Fitzroy would no longer be beneficial. 'They don't have any players left,' Piper remarked, and while he thought they could 'garnish some sort of Melbourne base' from a merger, he would only consider giving up the Bears' name and colours if there were 'substantial financial benefits'.[15] This was before the Commission and the clubs agreed to provide a $6 million incentive package, which, as it had been designed to do, made the prospect of a merger more attractive.

Despite all Brisbane was offering, the unassailable fact remained that to accept this offer would result in Melbourne-based Fitzroy supporters losing the proximity to their club that they had enjoyed since 1883. This remained a significant impediment in the minds of most Fitzroy people, and they had expressed this view to the board in previous years and again through 1996. Alan Piper recognised their reservations. The tyranny of distance inherent in a potential Brisbane/Fitzroy merger did Brisbane officials no favours. At a Brisbane board meeting in June 1995, Piper declared that Fitzroy would not be interested in merging with Brisbane as the Bears did not have enough to offer, and no doubt feared that if they merged with Brisbane 'their history will be forgotten in a year or two'.[16] This assessment had not changed in ten months, although the level of Fitzroy's desperation had jumped markedly.

With Brisbane as their only suitor, Fitzroy had hoped that if the AFL Commission accepted their proposal to underwrite their season, they could find a partner more to their liking. When Oakley rejected the proposal on 5 April, it compelled the Fitzroy merger sub-committee to continue negotiating with the Bears. On 9 April, however, the AFL's solicitor, Jeff Browne, called Hore-Lacy with a counter-proposal: if Fitzroy handed back its licence, the Commission would grant a new licence until the end of the year to a new entity known as the Fitzroy Lions Pty Ltd (the club currently traded as the Fitzroy Football Club Pty Ltd). The AFL would own the entity and control its financial matters, although there would be Fitzroy representatives on the board. Fitzroy's sponsors and football operations would transfer over seamlessly, and its debt would stay with the old entity. At the end of 1996, this new entity would merge, with Fitzroy's directors providing input on the decision.[17]

The plan obviously suited the AFL, but it left Fitzroy's creditors with a significant haircut. The Commission indicated they would pay any debts that involved personal responsibility for the Fitzroy directors (mainly to the Australian Taxation Office), indemnify any debts accrued by the new entity and leave the old entity to wear its own.[18] As the old entity would have its single biggest asset (its AFL licence) taken away from it, the other creditors would be left to pick over a hollowed-out husk of a company. Indignant, Hore-Lacy rejected the idea and asked to see it in writing to ensure he understood exactly what was being proposed. The subsequent written version made it even clearer that the League wanted to cast the old organisation adrift.[19] With the $6 million merger incentive still on the table, the AFL was likely proposing a plan to ensure that the incentive package did not get swallowed up in debt repayment.

Meanwhile, as Fitzroy was negotiating with both Brisbane and AFL House, word leaked out that the Lions were again considering a merger. Reporting of this nature was not new; since 1986, Fitzroy had been linked with every other struggling team in the League, and the failed merger attempts, most notably in 1989 and 1994, only fuelled the speculation. Now, rumours began to spread again. On *The Footy Show* on 11 April, Eddie McGuire publicly speculated that Fitzroy had struck a deal with North Melbourne.[20] John Birt strongly denied these claims and scoffed at the notion that the club had recently held talks with North Melbourne, Melbourne, Brisbane, Footscray, Port Adelaide or anyone else, calling such assertions 'a load of codswallop'.[21] Birt's denials were genuine, but not particularly instructive. Hore-Lacy and the other directors had been keeping him away from the merger negotiations and he knew little (if anything) about the status or even the existence of merger negotiations. While this gave Birt plausible deniability, it also reinforced the belief within the media that Hore-Lacy was trying to hide the details of the negotiations to those within the club and, by extension, the members, supporters and general public and not fulfilling his obligations as a director.

Despite Birt's denials, the story was gaining traction. Several sources told *The Age* that Fitzroy and North were in negotiations, but others said Fitzroy and Melbourne were back in discussions. McGuire's assertion that Fitzroy and North Melbourne had already struck a deal was a surprise to North Melbourne president Ron Casey, who unequivocally denied the claim.[22] There was now blood in the water, however, and several weeks later, the *Herald Sun* reported that Fitzroy was in merger discussions with another club, believed to be Brisbane.[23] This new round of intense speculation, reporting, analysis and comment about a potential Fitzroy merger would only escalate over the following months.

How individual supporters reacted to the re-emergence of merger rumours depended on their personal dispositions. While some remained optimistic and defiant, others had succumbed to fatalism or realism. Kathy Doyle was of the latter inclination: 'I think most Fitzroy supporters knew, in our heart of hearts, that there'd be no more "fightbacks" and that this would be our last season in the AFL.'[24] For players and staff, particularly those who had been at the club for years, the public speculation was white noise. Alan McConnell became oblivious to it after a time.²⁵ Simon Hawking likened it to the boy who cried wolf; these issues had been hanging over the players' heads for a long time, he reflected, and while he acknowledged that these current stories seemed 'to be a bit more substantial', Hawking claimed they did not upset the players in any way.²⁶ Ever the professional, Stephen Paxman just concentrated on whether he was playing on the weekend, keeping the 'noise' away from his preparation, while Martin Pike was pragmatic: 'I let others worry about outside matters and just concentrated on playing football.'²⁷

Looming ominously at the end of April was Fitzroy's Annual General Meeting. Not only would the directors need to lay bare the state of the club's financial predicament, they would also expose themselves to questions about the future of the club, and no member or shareholder would fail to ask their elected directors whether merger negotiations were currently taking place and, if so, with whom. The meeting was originally scheduled for late March, but, with the ASC's approval, it pushed back to 29 April (the day after Fitzroy's Round 5 game against Brisbane at the Gabba) so that the financial reporting could be in order.²⁸ Merging had not been mentioned in the formal reports in the 1995 AGM, but now the growing media speculation made it an unavoidable topic.²⁹

As the rumours circulated, the Fitzroy directors deliberated about their response to the AFL's counter-proposal. Unacceptable as it was, the club still needed cash to make its payments throughout the year. On 14 April, the directors decided to put two new suggestions to Nauru, both of which involved Nauru advancing $500,000 to the club to see it through the year and the promise to pay them back out of the $6 million AFL merger inducement (something unavailable under the Commission's plan). These suggestions were sent to Nauru but no reply was forthcoming.³⁰ On 24 April, the directors received an updated proposal from the AFL, which was now functionally an ultimatum: if the proposal was not accepted by 5.00pm, Friday 26 April, it would be withdrawn, leaving Fitzroy with no financial guarantee from the League for the remainder of the season (and the Commission still able to invoke its financial solvency rule).[31]

This new proposal placed enormous pressure on the board — if they rejected it, they needed to be confident that they could secure a merger before the club's financial state became terminal. It helped ease their concerns that negotiations with Brisbane were well advanced, and once an agreement was signed, Fitzroy would have access to the $6 million inducement package. Still, the threat of pre-emptively running out of cash-on-hand was real. The club had met its player payments to mid-May, but their financial projections showed a progressively worse situation in June and July. The 'best advice available' suggested the directors that the club was not insolvent and could pay its debts if and when they were due. As a precaution, however, the board instructed Birt not to enter into any new contracts and determined the club would not incur any further debts.[32]

Ultimately, despite concerns about the club's short-term financial state, the board decided not to acquiesce to the AFL's 'dubious scheme' (as Hore-Lacy called it), even if it provided a fiduciary safety net for the club and its directors.[33] Merger discussions with Brisbane were sufficiently well advanced that the merger sub-committee believed a deal could be done soon. Whatever the drawbacks to a merger with Brisbane, it was preferable to the Commission's 'devious proposal'.[34] Accordingly, the 5:00pm deadline on Friday 26 April came and went without a response from Fitzroy. The directors had given up the chance for the AFL to underwrite their season, preferring instead to be the masters of their own fate. It was a calculated gamble. Fitzroy played Brisbane that Sunday none the wiser for the decision the directors had made.

...

As Fitzroy's directors grappled with this critical decision, officials from the Brisbane Bears were powering ahead, ensuing that the

'Brisbane Lions' would have the necessary institutional support from the AFL Commission, and importantly, the new club would be the beneficiary of all the promised incentives placed on the table the previous year. When the Leonda agreement's October 1995 deadline lapsed, there was no official indication that the whole package would remain available for a future merger. Seeking clarity, on Saturday, 27 April, Noel Gordon and his CEO, Andrew Ireland, met with Ross Oakley in Melbourne. The pair wanted to know if the $6 million was still on offer and whether, in general, the Commission would support a Fitzroy/Brisbane merger. Oakley told them neither he nor the Commission would become actively involved in the talks (no doubt recalling the acrimony and the ultimate failure of the 1989 Fitzroy/Footscray merger) and that clubs must work through the issues, such as jumper design, club names, logos and board composition, before presenting them to the Commission.[35] Despite the assertion that the AFL would not overtly support a Bears/Lions merger, there were allies in the Commission, particularly Terry O'Connor, the former West Coast chairman and strong advocate for non-Victorian clubs (a fact that Brisbane's officials were no doubt aware).[36]

By the Monday of the AGM, Brisbane had developed a robust merger agreement, with legal firm Blake Dawson Waldon working on their behalf for some months. During the negotiations, Brisbane had asked the Fitzroy representatives to disclose the club's debt, so that the full amount could be incorporated into the merger agreement and deducted from the $6 million to pay Fitzroy's creditors in full. While Oakley had assured Brisbane that the $6 million was still on the table, for the Bears, gaining the most of the incentive package was less important than the supporter base that would come along with Fitzroy; if they could also secure some financial return from the remaining incentive plus some additional players, that was a sufficient gain for engaging in the merger.[37]

That day, Gordon and Ireland met with Hore-Lacy at his chambers. They urged Hore-Lacy to sign the agreement, but he resisted, unwilling to commit to anything until after the AGM had passed. Ireland believed that Hore-Lacy did not wish to lie at the AGM if asked specific questions about Fitzroy's merger partners.[38] There was also the issue, as Hore-Lacy had been telling Oakley *ad nauseum*, that any merger proposal would need to be endorsed by a majority of members and shareholders, and he was yet to canvass their opinions about a potential merger with Brisbane. Many supporters no doubt wanted the board to continue fighting on alone, rejecting a merger entirely in the vain hope that the club could somehow remain as an independent entity. Hore-Lacy would need to build a consensus around a merger before signing anything. Regardless, Brisbane felt sufficiently confident in their advances that on 30 April they reserved, for two months, the name 'Brisbane Lions' with the ASC.[39]

That evening, Fitzroy members, shareholders, supporters as well as assorted media, gathered at the Fitzroy Town Hall. In *The Age*, Stephen Linnell described the meeting as 'possibly Fitzroy's most important in its illustrious, but recently troubled, history.' He speculated that the AFL would initiate crisis talks with Fitzroy if their financial position proved unsatisfactory (Oakley had hinted as much in the days beforehand).[40] Believing that Fitzroy was doomed, Mike Sheahan wrote that Dyson Hore-Lacy appeared to have no option but to publicly admit that the club had been and would continue to be negotiating a merger as one of the only remaining means for survival, with Brisbane believed to be the front runner.[41] Linnell must have been hearing the same things as Sheahan; he reported that Fitzroy had begun initial merger discussions with Brisbane ten days' previously and Hore-Lacy was going to seek a mandate from the members to continue down this path. When asked, Brisbane officials refused to confirm or deny that talks were taking place.[42] Some supporters believed the question of a merger would be put at the AGM. 'I've a horrible feeling it could be a sad night,' remarked member Robert Ellis.[43]

By the evening, media interest was at fever pitch. The meeting, due to start at 7.00pm, was delayed by an hour while organisers sorted out seating for the large crowd of over 1000.[44] John Birt had told the media that no cameras would be allowed inside and only print journalists — of whom there were many — would have access.[45] The town hall stage was bare, save for a Fitzroy jumper draped over the speaker's podium. For Hore-Lacy, this meeting needed to be about more than just reporting, there needed to be a show of resolve from the directors and the club to give confidence to members and supporters and to show to the general public that Fitzroy was not defeated (despite what the newspapers might be saying). It was no surprise, then, that he opened strongly: 'For those who have come to feed off our dead body, you are going to be hugely disappointed. Fitzroy lives! To those members of the press, and I am not referring to all of them, who have come along to witness Fitzroy's demise, I apologise.'[46]

Hore-Lacy's opening salvo electrified the crowd. Journalist Ron Reed wrote: 'The mob whistled and cheered as if some invisible full-forward ... had just performed the almost forgotten feat of kicking a winning goal.'[47] His address targeted the club's usual villains, the AFL and portions of the media, both to draw attention to the wrongs they had committed against the club (real or perceived) and, possibly, to distract from other areas. He blamed the AFL for denying the club revenue streams from playing games in Canberra and he attacked the media for concocting negative stories that drove away potential sponsors.[48] Patrick Smith looked cynically at this tactic (as well he might as one who belonged to one of the suspect groups in question). Hore-Lacy, he wrote, was at his best as a rabble-rouser, telling the members and supporters what they wanted to hear — that it was all the AFL and the media's fault.[49]

Eventually, however, he needed to address the elephant in the room. While the directors wanted the club to remain as a single entity, he told the meeting, the reality was that without an increase in revenue the continued existence of the club would be threatened and the board would be forced to examine merger options (indeed, they would be negligent in their duties if they failed to do so). In deliberately vague language, he announced that the board were looking at what was available, and had been for some time.[50] Hore-Lacy reassured members that they had made no arrangement with any other club, but he asked that no questions be put to him regarding specifics of any potential negotiations that may or may not be taking place (which many took as a tacit indication that indeed they were) because, not unreasonably, such discussions needed to remain confidential. He did note, when asked about preference for a merger, that there may be offers from interstate clubs better than those proposed by Victorian clubs, but the board's stated policy was to seek a merger with a Melbourne club first. Furthermore, he reiterated that the club would not merge without the approval of the members and the shareholders.[51] Despite his ambiguity and the obfuscation, the meaning of his words was clear — the Fitzroy board was actively looking for a merger partner. 'Now I've got some semblance of peace,' thought supporter Adam Muyt, 'no more rumour this, rumour that. Merging is now happening and so I can now start to work out what a merged Royboy gets to do on Saturdays in Melbourne during winter.'[52]

Board member John Stewart then presented the financial report, which, as Hore-Lacy later acknowledged, 'cast a fairly gloomy picture'.[53] For all the rhetoric and the theatrics of Hore-Lacy's address, there was no way Stewart could sugar-coat or spin the figures. The club's accumulated debt was $2.3 million, after recording an operating loss for 1995 of $263,834. Gate receipts and membership revenue were down and hotel revenue was meagre. Hore-Lacy acknowledged the obvious, that the club needed to generate significantly more revenue to compete with larger, more successful clubs. Yet he was confident Fitzroy would pass the AFL's financial solvency criterion, and, ever defiant, indicated that the club would take the AFL to court if it 'dared' appoint an administrator to run its affairs.[54]

Amid the cryptic pronouncements about mergers and the dire financial reporting, two positions on the board were spilled, one belonging to Hore-Lacy himself, the other to Robert Johnstone.

While the chairman was re-elected in a landslide, Johnstone faced a challenge from retired businessman Greg Basto, who had gained popularity with Fitzroy supporters as a result of a successful fundraising campaign in 1994. Basto had allegedly been campaigning for some time, and the other directors were either unaware of Basto's efforts or did not believe he was a serious challenger. Either way, they did not do enough to block him, resulting in Johnstone's narrow defeat. Basto claimed he supported Hore-Lacy and his aim was to get money for the club.[55] He also threatened to undertake a close analysis of Fitzroy's books, declaring, 'I'm in there to stir them up.'[56] Despite his enthusiasm, Basto's involvement in the club throughout the year was peripheral, his attempts at fundraising were quixotic and most of the key board meetings took place without him.

With all the drama of the evening, the actual intention of the members and shareholders was relatively unclear.[57] They had not been given an opportunity to vote on whether they would take the AFL's $6 million carrot for a merger — they had only been told that the directors, as per their legal requirements, had been looking into the matter. The question remained: should the club continue to fight on alone, or was it time to bow to the seemingly inevitable? On this, the supporters were divided. Some were still staunchly opposed to a merger and wanted the club to continue fighting; others recognised the reality and prepared themselves for a merger, although they were unsure how they would feel if it were Brisbane or another Melbourne club. One member summed up the situation succinctly: 'It's pretty pitiful one way or the other.'[58]

Addressing the media afterwards, John Birt thought Eddie McGuire's speculation on *The Footy Show* had a destabilising effect on the club, particularly on the field. Optimistically, he hoped that Dyson Hore-Lacy's comments had reassured the public that the club was 'very positive for the future' and that this would be reflected in the press reporting.[59] Patrick Smith looked more cynically on Hore-Lacy's performance. The 'showbiz QC' had been 'superficial and slick', and 'on the flimsiest of evidence, he had persuaded his members everything would be fine.'[60] Mike Sheahan was critical for different reasons, hoping that the show of defiance was only temporary, as he believed it remained in Fitzroy's best interest to seek out a merger to save its heritage and culture in some form.[61] Ron Reed wrote of the club: 'At least nobody will be able to say that they are going down without a whimper, however inevitable their fate might be. Count me among the traditionalists who are glad to see that.'[62] Despite Hore-Lacy's broadsides, the Lions still had some supporters in the media.

CHAPTER EIGHT

EXPLORING OTHER OPTIONS

'Relax, all your worries are over'

— Peter De Rauch, North Melbourne vice-president.[1]

Jarrod Molloy was born and bred Fitzroy. His father, Shane, was a powerfully-built back-pocket defender who played sixty-one games for the Lions in the late sixties and early seventies. Jarrod grew up barracking for his father's club (he ran onto the Junction Oval when 'Superboot' kicked one of his tons) and followed the Roys through the unfulfilled promise of the eighties. He dreamed of playing for the Lions and first got his chance in Round 2, 1994 in a win against Essendon at Princes Park.[2] His statistics from his debut season were modest: twenty games, eighteen goals and an average of just under twelve disposals per game. But he showed plenty of talent, being nominated for the Norwich Rising Star award in Round 5 after a four-goal game against Richmond.

Unfortunately, playing for the Lions was not conducive to seeing success. He won three of his first four games, and then only four more times by the end of the 1995 season. Having struggled under Bernie Quinlan, things were different in 1996. Nunan's approach suited the nineteen-year-old. 'We both like to win and to go hard,' Molloy recalled. There was mutual respect between the pair, and Molloy — still a young player — appreciated Nunan's advice and direction.[3] Nunan also made a crucial change to Molloy's game. Throughout his brief career, Molloy's coaches had played him as a forward. For Saturday's game against Richmond, Nunan placed him at full-back on Stephen Jurica. It was perhaps his most successful tactical move as Fitzroy's senior coach — Molloy played in defence for the remainder of the season and to some acclaim. Throughout the year he played on some of the game's biggest names, including Ablett, Dunstall, Lockett, Lyon, Sumich as well as up-and-comers such as Sav Rocca and Matthew Richardson. 'I'm pretty competitive,' he recalled, 'and the thrill of playing on such good players lifts you a bit.' It took him several weeks to learn how to play the position, and he threw himself into a weights program to develop his body to compete for strength with his opponents.[4]

Fitzroy's Round 6 game against Richmond would be at the Whitten Oval on the afternoon of Saturday, 4 May. With Molloy as his new full-back, Nunan gave Shane Clayton, Nick Carter and Brent Frewen their first games. For Carter, who was pick number twenty in the 1995 national draft, this was his opportunity to prove himself to the senior players. 'They are seeing you play for the first time,' he recalled, 'and probably thinking "okay, you're a young kid who got drafted high, but are you any good?"'[5] He and Clayton would become consistent starters for the Lions, while Frewen played only once more that season.[6] Nunan placed dutiful servant Brad Boyd in the backline to play on Matthew Richardson, with Stephen Paxman on Brendan Gale and Molloy on Jurica. Boyd was coming off a 32-possession game in Round 5. After injury had kept him out of Round 1, he had been trying to put together a good run of games: a heavy tag and he would struggle, but, given freedom, he could be highly effective.

As often happened that season, Fitzroy started strongly. Simon Atkins shut down Richmond's influential on-baller Chris Naish, forcing him to limp off at one point after a thumping tackle.[7] Fitzroy's defence was containing Richmond's forwards, Boyd, in particular, doing an excellent job on Richardson. Yet again, however, the Lions were let down by their forwards. Former Richmond captain Jeff Hogg proved ineffective as a full-forward target and was replaced by Simon Hawking who fared slightly better.[8] Nevertheless, the deficit was only twenty points going into the long break.

After half-time Fitzroy was threatening. Anthony McGregor kicked a goal from the boundary line to cut the margin to fourteen points and Chris Johnson took another spectacular mark, this time over Brendan Gale. Nunan thought they were playing pretty well … 'And then we lost Boyd.'[9] The captain had held Richardson well but came off with a hamstring injury ten minutes into the third quarter.[10] To fill the gap Nunan moved Molloy onto Richardson and Hogg onto Jurica.[11] While Molloy would play some good defensive games that season, it was too soon to expect he had learnt the craft of a body-on-body defender. Jurica was a soft introduction, but Richardson was a much harder proposition. Having kicked only two goals, Richardson now found himself in acres of space and put on another five, with Richmond's lead starting to blow out.[12] The Tigers' dominant and hardworking midfield surged over Fitzroy late in the third quarter and continued for most of the final term, Richmond kicking nine goals to two. Former Lion Paul Broderick was devastating in the middle for Richmond with thirty-nine possessions for the game.[13] In the end, the Tigers won comfortably, 23.16 (154) to 9.8 (62).

The Lions could not run out games, a trend that had not escaped Nunan's notice. 'We can do it for a half,' he said afterwards, 'and then seem to drop off … It's a combination of age and experience and perhaps a lack of ability.'[14] The opposition coach, Robert Walls, who had coached Fitzroy from 1981 to 1985, sympathised with his former club and believed Nunan was doing a 'terrific job' with his young players. He urged the club to give Nunan time to develop them properly: 'You're better off playing young kids who'll have a go than a few mercenaries who will just be there for the ride,' Walls remarked.[15] Boyd's hamstring kept him out for a week. Compounding Nunan's frustrations, Simon Atkins suffered a broken collarbone, and he missed the next three games. He could ill afford to lose these two, who were among Fitzroy's best until their respective injuries.

While injuries hurt Fitzroy badly this game, the general lack of depth in the squad was a factor that hampered the club all season. 'I don't have the couple of extra rovers or ruck-rovers,' Nunan lamented, 'We're unable to generate the same amount of power for the same period of time.'[16] Of his three first gamers, Nunan thought Clayton did quite well under the circumstances. Before the game, he had told the seventeen-year-old: 'Just play footy. You've got there because you've got ability. Just go out and play.'[17] His instructions were simple. Amid the anticipation, excitement and enjoyment of his first game, Nunan knew there was no point overloading the young man with directions. Clayton expected a fast and tough game, and while there was a temptation to be enthralled by playing on Wayne Campbell, he said afterwards: 'I just tried to play confidently, play my own game and just enjoy it.'[18] His sixteen disposals was a good return and the best of the three debutantes.

Despite having the difficult task of playing on Matthew Richardson for almost half the game, Molloy did creditably — his fifteen possessions were his best for the season to date. A player at the opposite end of both the ground and his football career was Jeff Hogg, who had seven kicks and one handball. Hogg played his first game for Richmond in 1986, and after a successful period at Punt Road was appointed captain in 1993. Then, in a difficult set of circumstances, the club traded him to Fitzroy. Richmond was trying to develop its list and plundered Michael Gale, Matthew Dundas and Paul Broderick from the ailing Lions. With the advent of Richardson as a key forward, Hogg became less critical to Richmond's structure, and, as he was out-of-contract, was offered in exchange. The deal came as a complete surprise to Hogg, who learned of it through Fitzroy, not Richmond.[19] Such was his resentment about how the Tigers handled his trade, he refused to return to Punt Road in any capacity for nearly a decade.[20]

Fitzroy's recruitment of Hogg was, in part, to replace Alastair Lynch in full forward. In this role he was less than successful: he kicked twenty-three goals in sixteen games in the 1994 season, and then eleven goals in ten games in 1995. Contemplating retirement at the end of 1995, Nunan arrived and convinced him to continue.[21] Unfortunately, their relationship soon soured: Hogg did not believe Nunan was giving him a fair go and Nunan went on *Talking Footy* early in the season and said Hogg 'hasn't put his hand up'. Nunan directed his criticism at Hogg as a goal-kicker: 'He was recruited as a full-forward,' Nunan explained, 'and was not kicking goals' (after playing the first six games he had kicked 5.7).[22] Nunan viewed him as a player trying to re-establish himself, a 'great trier' unfortunately plagued with back problems. After several weeks, Nunan looked at Fitzroy's future and realised Hogg was not part of it. He was dropped after the Richmond game and would not return to the senior side for many weeks.

...

Beyond the standard problems of out-of-form players and a lack of list depth, Nunan was facing problems he could not have imagined when he took the job in October 1995. The challenge of resurrecting Fitzroy as a competitive team was hard enough, but now he was dealing with the spectre of financial difficulties and a possible merger. He had been resolute at the AGM, describing his players as 'young boys on the front line'.[23] With merger in the front of many minds, it was not long before a reporter asked his thoughts. He was not aware of any discussions taking place at Fitzroy, he declared honestly, although he would be disappointed if the club merged and he was unable to finish the task of rebuilding. But, as he acknowledged, 'I'm not in control of that.'[24]

The man who was in some control, Dyson Hore-Lacy, had practically confirmed at the AGM that his club was seeking a merger. Ross Oakley should have been encouraged by Fitzroy's commitment. In that weekend's *Football Record*, Oakley unequivocally reiterated the AFL's position on the issue, presenting all the arguments he and the Commission had been making for years. One city could not support eleven teams operating at near professional levels of expenditure, Oakley wrote. The Commission's preference remained that clubs with weak supporter bases merge and retain as much of their tradition as possible rather than simply disappear after a long struggle.[25] After the article was published, Oakley denied it was 'pitched at Fitzroy'.[26] The *Football Record*'s editor must have disagreed because both photos used for the article featured Lions supporters.

Fitzroy did seem to be moving in Oakley's preferred direction, and the beginning of May brought events on at lightning speed. Until then, the only serious merger contender was Brisbane. The media had picked up their interest and many pundits declared them favourites. The *Herald Sun* speculated that the deal with Brisbane 'may well be close to a formality', with Mike Sheahan and Geoff Poulter pontificating over a hypothetical player list for the new Brisbane Lions.[27] While the newspapers socialised the football public to the idea of the 'Brisbane Lions', behind the scenes, Noel Gordon worked hard to make it happen. On Friday, 3 May, he and Andrew Ireland had again met with the AFL Commission. They presented the details of their merger proposal, and the Commission confirmed that they would provide $6.5 million to the merged club. All parties hoped to have the various merger documents signed by Friday, 10 May.[28]

On 9 May, Gordon, Ireland and Alan Piper met with the Commission again, this time specifically to discuss the issue of any football operations benefits the AFL would offer to a merged team.[29]

At the meeting between the clubs and the AFL Commission at Leonda on 19 June 1995, the Commission was prepared to offer a merged club a list of between forty-four and fifty players, depending on a seeding formula devised by AFL House, and an expanded salary cap to accommodate the additional players.[30] Based on the Leonda agreement, and their own preferences, Brisbane had included an enhanced player list as part of its merger agreement, but only asked for an increase of two players, bringing the total to forty-four. They were also prepared to cull their list and take a minimum of eight Fitzroy players, with the remainder going into the draft. Gordon wanted to minimise the perception of the Brisbane Lions becoming a 'super team' that would threaten the other clubs and thus invite opposition and a potential veto.[31] When put to the AFL Commission, the League's administrators confirmed that several details of the merger agreement were acceptable.[32]

On the other side of the negotiating table, Hore-Lacy needed to build support within the wider Fitzroy community for a merger. It was not necessarily a unanimous opinion among Fitzroy supporters that the club should merge, even in the face of all its troubles. Before the AGM, Frank Crea, a member since 1964, told a reporter, 'My attitude is, no merger at all. I wouldn't countenance it at all.'[33] He was far from the only one with this view. Others were resigned to a merger, but differed over the potential partner. 'I'd prefer to merge with a Melbourne club,' declared Robert Ellis, 'I would like to think we'd retain some identity.' Conversely, Lorraine Dellow preferred Brisbane: 'A Melbourne club would be a takeover rather than a merge.'[34] Given the lack of consensus, the board determined to begin building support by talking to the coterie groups after the AGM, both to give them greater insight into what was taking place and gauge their support for a potential merger.[35]

The first such meeting was at the Victorian Commercial Teachers' Association (VCTA) building on Hotham Street, Collingwood, with several influential supporters including Minister for Sport, Tom

Reynolds, in attendance. Hore-Lacy explained the issues and the situation. After hearing the report, everyone believed there was no alternative but merger, and if it was inevitable, most preferred another Melbourne club as a partner (although some, including Reynolds, favoured the Brisbane option).[36] Evidently, those present were informed that Fitzroy was not currently in negotiations with North Melbourne, despite some reporting to the contrary. The Fitzroy Foundation's Warren O'Neale attended this meeting, and later informed fellow Fitzroy Foundation governor, Bill Atherton, of what was taking place. If the board and the supporters were keen for Fitzroy to remain in Victoria, he must have thought, then surely the club should be talking to other Melbourne-based clubs. Atherton was a good friend of Peter De Rauch, the vice-president of North Melbourne and he called De Rauch to see if he could set up a meeting with representatives from Fitzroy. De Rauch agreed, Atherton told O'Neale, who informed Hore-Lacy.[37] Via this back-channel, Atherton set up a meeting between Hore-Lacy, De Rauch and North Melbourne president, Ron Casey, at O'Neale's home in Kooyong.[38]

...

When mergers were first placed on the VFL's agenda in the eighties, the intention was to combine two struggling Victorian clubs to form a much stronger entity. Based on their on-field form in 1996, North Melbourne might have seemed an odd match. The Kangaroos, captained by Wayne Carey, had played finals in 1993, 1994 and 1995 and, after Round 6, were second on the ladder. Not only that, but their list was deep — North had won the 1995 reserves grand final (and would win it again in 1996 by over one hundred points). The incentive for the Kangaroos to merge, therefore, was not for any short-term on-field benefit. Instead, a merger would address the club's structural issues: a lack of generational support and a lack of geographic support.

Founded in 1869, North Melbourne was one of Victoria's

oldest clubs. Yet it had only played in the VFL since 1925, after having competed in the VFA, where it won six premierships between 1903 and 1918. When North was eventually admitted into the VFL (alongside Hawthorn and Footscray), the club lacked many of the advantages accrued by the League's established clubs, particularly a well-developed supporter base. Their poor financial state prompted North to innovate. The most significant structural change came in 1986 when the then-president Bob Ansett floated the club and generated $3 million.[39] Despite this helpful injection, North still struggled against its historic handicaps: a small share of generational support, and an inner city heartland that gave it no room to expand its catchment area, both of which limited its ability to generate additional income.[40] In the climate of the late eighties, many radical suggestions were proposed to improve the club's lot: there were discussions about moving to Adelaide, Carlton offered themselves as a merger partner and, after Christopher Skase's empire collapsed, Brisbane approached them about a potential take-over.[41]

Faced with seemingly intractable problems, in the early nineties North's administration developed three options to increase its supporter base (which was seen as being the key to success): playing some games interstate, permanent relocation or a merger. Merging was appealing — rather than taking time to grow a new supporter base in another state, a merger would instantly give the club what it sought.[42] Accordingly, when Fitzroy was seeking a merger partner in 1994, North Melbourne expressed interest and began discussions. When the straight-dealing Ron Casey learned of Fitzroy's negotiations with Melbourne, however, he allegedly refused to have anything further to do with the Lions and the talks ended abruptly.[43] The AFL Commission meeting at Leonda in June 1995 and the $6 million merger incentive reignited North Melbourne's interest, as the club was looking to improve its facilities at Arden Street.[44] In September 1995, North Melbourne had presented a written proposal to Fitzroy to enter merger discussions, but despite some early contact the talks had led nowhere.⁴⁵ At the start of 1996, Hore-Lacy had reached out to Casey, but North Melbourne's president was seemingly still sour on Fitzroy.⁴⁶ Now with Atherton's intervention, merger discussions between the two clubs recommenced.

Despite discussions with Brisbane being well advanced, Fitzroy jumped at the chance to negotiate with a Melbourne-based club. A merger with North Melbourne offered many benefits to Fitzroy, not least of which was the ability to remain in Melbourne. In addition, North Melbourne shared a similar history, geography and culture with the Roys. The choice of North Melbourne, however, meant little unless the board could negotiate a favourable merger. Many feared that a merger with another traditional Melbourne-based club would be inequitable. The stronger club would want to retain as much of its heritage and identity as possible, thus subsuming the weaker club and making it unrecognisable. Collingwood, for instance, had continued informal merger discussions with Fitzroy in early 1996, with the Lions board ultimately rejecting their advances on the basis that the Magpies were too strong for any merger to be beneficial to Fitzroy.⁴⁷ An anonymous Collingwood source seemingly confirmed their priorities: 'We were prepared to give away some things,' the source said, 'but we were not prepared to give our heart and soul away.'⁴⁸ This was going to be a problem with almost any club Fitzroy negotiated with: the Lions could not help but be the weaker team, leaving it in a vulnerable negotiating position, and when it came down to negotiations, the stronger club would always want to preserve its 'heart and soul' over Fitzroy's.

Despite this potential problem, North Melbourne was an option well worth pursuing and negotiations began on the night of 5 May. Fortunately, both sides seemed to want a genuinely equal merger and discussions commenced in good faith. There was, of course, much to negotiate. Some details could be worked out between the representatives of the two clubs; others required legal expertise (mainly sorting out how two clubs with very different ownership and corporate structures would merge). Like any good corporate merger, North Melbourne wanted to know as much about Fitzroy's financial position as possible, and these details needed to be discussed. At the same time, other aspects of a potential merger, such as the exact nature of AFL's incentive package and what list and salary cap concessions the new club would receive, would need to be confirmed with AFL House directly.

Early discussions were positive, and both negotiating teams pushed forward clarifying many of the remaining known unknowns. On Thursday, 9 May, Casey and his CEO, Greg Miller, did what Gordon and Ireland had done and approached the Commission to clarify the merger incentives.[49] They were aware that at the Leonda meeting, the Commission had been prepared to offer a merged club a list of between forty-four and fifty players.[50] What AFL officials said to Casey and Miller on 9 May is unclear, but on 26 May, the Commission formally agreed that any club merging with Fitzroy could have an initial fifty-four player list, culled to a fifty-player list for the 1997 season and then incrementally reduced back to forty-two players by the start of the 2000 season.[51] It seems likely that this information was conveyed in some form to Casey and Miller during their earlier meeting. North Melbourne's representatives approved; not only was it largely in accord with the Leonda agreement, but it would help mitigate the disruption caused by combining two playing lists and the need to de-list so many erstwhile teammates. It was not good for the culture and morale of a playing group, North Melbourne officials reasoned, to lose too many players at once.[52] Currently in the middle of a successful on-field period, they did not want this jeopardised by any off-field disruptions.

The full ramifications of the decision to advocate for a 54-player list would only be apparent later in the year. For now, Fitzroy and North Melbourne continued their negotiations. On the afternoon of 9 May, they met again, with Fitzroy's finances as the main issue for discussion. After some hours, Fitzroy and North Melbourne had reached a handshake agreement for a merger. The new club would be the 'Fitzroy–North Melbourne Kangaroos' (they had arrived at the name using the principle that the team with the first name would lose their nickname and logo), the colours of both clubs would be used in approximately even proportions. They would compose an entirely new club song and, importantly, the number of board members from each team would be equal.[53] They arranged another meeting for the afternoon of Saturday, 11 May, where legal representatives from both clubs would hopefully determine the best approach to merging two corporate entities.

All this took place within a week. Brisbane would have been none the wiser, had they not been alerted to the discussion by a source within AFL House.[54] They still needed to hear the bad news directly from Fitzroy, however. Before entering into negotiations with North Melbourne, Fitzroy's representatives had arranged a meeting with Gordon, Ireland, Piper and their solicitors from Blake Dawson Waldron on Friday, 10 May — the date by which the Commission had hoped the Fitzroy/Brisbane merger would be formally concluded. As Fitzroy had not finalised the deal with North Melbourne, Hore-Lacy could not let Brisbane know that Fitzroy would most likely be rejecting their offer. Instead, they let Brisbane's representatives talk about sweeteners on top of their original proposal, including that the new club would play at least six games in Melbourne and the board would have two or three Fitzroy directors.[55] Fitzroy's directors politely heard them out and then let them know that they would inform the Bears of their decision on Monday, 13 May.[56]

...

While Fitzroy and North Melbourne negotiated, the AFL prepared for another tent-pole centenary celebration. As Round 7 coincided with the anniversary of the VFL's first ever round of football, the AFL decided to re-enact the exact fixtures played on 8 May 1897. It was a time,

Oakley told the *Football Record*, to 'look back or reflect on how our competition started, its development since then and its role as the national focus of Australian football'.[57] On this (99th) anniversary round, Essendon and Geelong would play on the exact date of their first league game (which placed it on a Wednesday night). On Friday night, Collingwood would host St Kilda at the MCG, with Melbourne playing Sydney (South Melbourne) at the same venue on Saturday afternoon and Carlton hosting Fitzroy at Princes Park. The eight remaining Johnny-come-lately clubs played each other over the rest of the weekend. Each foundation club would wear a 1890s-style heritage jersey, and as several Roys supporters pointed out, Fitzroy's maroon and yellow jumper made the players look conspicuously like the Brisbane Bears.[58]

In their 1897 fixture, Fitzroy defeated Carlton 6.13 (49) to 2.4 (16). Ninety-nine years later, Fitzroy had a difficult time replicating the result against the reigning premiers. Even a Carlton team without Stephen Kernahan, Peter Dean, Mil Hanna and Greg Williams were more than a match for the young Lions. Selecting his squad, Nunan shuffled the deck to compensate for losing Boyd and Atkins. He also needed to find a full-forward. Dropping Hogg and moving Molloy to defence left the forward line lacking. Anthony Mellington, a 21-year-old from Shepparton, had arrived at Fitzroy via the 1995 pre-season draft. He played six games in 1995 and the first three in 1996 in defence. Dropped to the reserves for Round 4 he kicked eight goals. Nunan brought him back for Round 5, but after only contributing one behind he was dropped. In Round 6 he kicked nine goals for the reserves, again making a case for inclusion in the senior team. Without Hogg and Molloy, Nunan selected him in the forward pocket.[59]

Those hoping for a decent footballing spectacle to match the gravitas of the heritage theme were sadly disappointed. A wet day made conditions at Princes Park slippery, frustrating Fitzroy's attempts to play a slick, possession-based game. Geoff Poulter, writing for the *Herald Sun*, saw what Fitzroy was trying to do, using handball to link up passages of play, but noted they had a tendency to 'fiddle', and their 'poor skill level was often exposed when they over-used the ball'.[60] There was no lack of effort, however. John Rombotis had twenty-nine disposals and played an excellent game in the centre, as did Darren Holmes on the ball, Martin Pike off half-back and Chris Johnson, who took another of the spectacular marks that were becoming his stock-in-trade.[61] For all their industry, however, it was the forward line where Fitzroy was weakest, lacking 'decent weaponry' (as one journalist described it).[62] The Lions were able to get the ball forward surprisingly often, but dropped marks and missed passes meant they could not turn territory into goals. Mellington exemplified Fitzroy's condition, kicking 2.4, but still showed potential as a forward target. Ultimately, Carlton won 18.17 (125) to 8.14 (62), and the Blues finished the re-enactment round second on the ladder. That they defeated Fitzroy by *only* ten goals was a positive indication for Nunan (and the margin only blew out late in the game). He could see his team developing, although reflecting upon the absence of Boyd and Atkins, he lamented that the lack of depth in his squad left him unable to cover injuries to senior players.[63]

One notable absentee from the re-enactment game was Dyson Hore-Lacy. Elaine Findlay had fulfilled his game-day commitments while he was at Warren O'Neale's house with representatives from North Melbourne and several lawyers putting the finishing touches on a Heads of Agreement — a non-binding document outlining the basic terms of a tentative partnership arrangement. By 4:00pm the two clubs had an agreement, with the only potential stumbling block being confirmation from the AFL that their $6 million was still available (which was later confirmed that evening by the AFL's solicitor, Jeff Browne).[64] Once the Heads of Agreement document was written up, Casey, De Rauch, O'Neale and Hore-Lacy signed it, with Findlay arriving later that evening to add her signature. 'Fitzroy Football Club (FFC) and North Melbourne Club (NMC) are desirous in merging their operations and wish to record the terms of the proposed merger,' the document read. It then outlined the agreed details, such as the new name, colours and the composition of the board.[65] After the signing and handshakes, the club officials opened a bottle of wine and listened to the last quarter of the game at Princes Park. Hore-Lacy recalled De Rauch saying: 'Relax, all your worries are over.'[66] Unfortunately for all concerned, he was incredibly far from the truth.

CHAPTER NINE

THE HIGH-WATER MARK

*'If only emotion were money,
Fitzroy would have been saved on Saturday'*

— Ron Reed, journalist.[1]

After the Heads of Agreement was signed, Dyson Hore-Lacy wanted Fitzroy and North Melbourne to make a joint public statement as soon as possible. Recent history had conditioned him to believe that once the League was aware of the agreement it would leak to the media within forty-eight hours. North Melbourne's officials resisted, however, concerned about how the announcement would affect their team's on-field charge towards a third premiership in seventy-two seasons.[2] Given that the agreement itself stipulated confidentiality (except to the AFL) and that no public announcements would be made unless both clubs concurred, Hore-Lacy was forced into silence, knowing full well that the chances of keeping the agreement quiet were minimal.[3] Events, however, moved much more quickly and more publicly than even he might have anticipated.

As far as the public knew, Brisbane was the front-runner for a merger with Fitzroy. While Brisbane had heard whispers that a new contender was in the race, they had heard nothing official from Fitzroy to make them believe that they were now out of the hunt. On Sunday morning, Noel Gordon called Hore-Lacy looking for reassurance. Hore-Lacy assured him that Brisbane was still in contention, but Gordon sensed it was not the case — Hore-Lacy seemed too relaxed, too comfortable. Alarm bells were ringing, and his suspicions were about to escalate.[4] As he discussed the potential Brisbane/Fitzroy merger with Hore-Lacy, thousands across Melbourne saw the headline 'Secret AFL merger talks: North Melbourne and Fitzroy tipped to form new club' on the front page of the *Sunday Age*.

The story's chief reporter, Rohan Connolly, wrote that the two clubs had been in detailed negotiations for several months and were 'poised to announce a historic merger'.[5] Connolly had an excellent source. Earlier in the week, a North Melbourne board member had approached the *Sunday Age* with details of the merger discussions. Unconvinced that a merger was in the best interest of his club, the board member presumably knew that once the negotiations were made public, it would stir up supporter antagonism and make it hard for Casey, De Rauch and Miller to finalise the deal.[6] Connolly was unaware of the Heads of Agreement struck the previous day, and some of his details were incorrect (for instance, he gave the name of the new club as the 'North Melbourne Lions'). Still, he outlined the prospective merger in detail, including a potential player list that notably featured only six Fitzroy players. Compromising the provenance of his information, he listed what North Melbourne planned to do with the $6 million incentive money.[7]

Connolly's story seemed genuine and authoritative, suggesting a seriousness about the prospect of a Fitzroy merger that had not been seen since 1989 (or, at least 1994), and it sparked a flood of discussion in the newspapers, on television and radio, as well as in pubs and homes across Melbourne. The prospect of a Fitzroy/North Melbourne merger found support from the *Sunday Age*, as it would enable the Lions to remain in Melbourne, allowing the 'diehard faithful who persevere each week' to 'feel their club has retained its link to the city and the people it once represented'. The prospect of an imminent merger also elicited sympathy from the newspaper, with an editorial lamenting that while history and tradition had a place in football, 'nothing speaks more these days than cold, hard cash'. As such, the 'hapless' club was heading for its 'final winter of discontent'.[8]

Richmond president Leon Daphne had an altogether different reaction. That Sunday, he used his president's lunch to criticise the potential merger, stating unequivocally that Richmond did not favour 'handouts' to clubs that could not 'cut it on their own'.[9] That the Tigers had needed VFL assistance in the late eighties before they dug themselves out of a financial black hole in 1990 with the Save Our Skins campaign (which raised $1 million in ten weeks) was seemingly neither here nor there.[10] Having arrived at financial safety, and having made the finals in 1995 for the first time since 1982, Daphne was determined to ensure that a merger did not compromise his club. This was despite Daphne, along with every other club president, having endorsed the AFL Commission's merger strategy and incentives package the previous year. 'We don't want the AFL to be making clubs stronger by merging through subsidies to make them stronger than the Richmond Football Club,' he declared bluntly and honestly.[11]

Meanwhile, with comment and speculation mounting, the senior officials at both Fitzroy and North Melbourne stuck to their agreement and refused to confirm whether they were, in fact, in merger discussions. Unfortunately, that did little to dampen the questions and conjecture. While there was always a healthy dose of fiction mixed into reporting about Fitzroy, Connolly's story was seemingly so comprehensive that it demanded confirmation or denial from the parties involved. That Sunday night, both Ron Casey and board member Mark Dawson said that their club was not involved in merger talks, but did not rule out discussions in the future. 'As far as

'I'm concerned the story has got no basis,' Casey said. One 'prominent North source' speculated that the source of the story had been Brisbane, who may have become disenchanted with Fitzroy after they cut merger talks with the Bears.[12] John Birt was typically plausible in his deniability, knowing nothing about any negotiations and telling journalists that Fitzroy had a board meeting that Thursday where they discussed nothing of the sort.[13]

Birt, however, was soon to be illuminated. On the morning of Monday, 13 May, following the signing of the Heads of Agreement and the publication of Connolly's article, Fitzroy's directors met at the Fitzroy Club Hotel, where Hore-Lacy informed Birt and the rest of the board about all that had transpired. The directors were unanimous that the North Melbourne deal was preferable to Brisbane's and they endorsed the course of action that Hore-Lacy and Findlay had set upon. Hore-Lacy told Birt that he could inform the staff of the board's intention to complete a merger, but to preserve some level of secrecy, he could not disclose the other club (although most could probably guess). Colin Hobbs was appointed to replace Robert Johnstone on the merger sub-committee, and the board authorised the sub-committee to finalise the North Melbourne merger.[14] With the board's approval, Hore-Lacy soon informed Brisbane's solicitor, David Dunn, that Fitzroy had decided not to merge with the Bears.[15]

Throughout the week, the newspapers were filled with articles and commentary about the prospective merger. On Wednesday morning the back page of the *Herald Sun* ran the headline: 'It's A Deal'. Possibly stung by their rival newspaper breaking the story on Sunday, the *Herald Sun* tried to fire back with its own exclusive, reporting that the Heads of Agreement (or 'in-principle agreement' as reported) had been signed the previous weekend.[16] Mike Sheahan seemingly wrote a piece on Fitzroy each day. He acknowledged that he had been a 'public tormentor' of the Lions over the past decade, but wrote that no-one was to blame for what had occurred, Fitzroy was simply 'a victim of the force of change'. He also retained his belief that a merger with Brisbane would better serve the Lions.[17] That evening, Brisbane officials publicly conceded defeat, disclosing that Fitzroy had formally advised them that their discussions were off and, more speculatively, declared a North Melbourne/Fitzroy merger to be a done deal. Greg Miller responded that same night, calling the suggestion that an agreement had been reached, or was even imminent, 'absolute bullshit'.[18]

Amid the inescapable volume of media coverage, Hore-Lacy once again implored North Melbourne's vice president, Peter De Rauch, that they should make a joint statement confirming the speculation. While the North Melbourne board would not be swayed on going public, Hore-Lacy managed to convince De Rauch that their respective players and staff deserved to know the whole truth about the negotiations.[19] Within his own club there was discontent over the secrecy and lack of information. When reporters had approached Michael Nunan for his thoughts on a potential merger, he revealed that neither the board nor the CEO had informed him about any merger negotiations, lamenting that if the rumours were true, it would be sad to have learned the details in the newspapers without first being informed by the club.[20] With North Melbourne's agreement, on Wednesday 15 May, Hore-Lacy talked to Nunan before then addressing the full complement of staff. He tried to ease their understandable concerns, informing them that the new club would select staff on merit and Fitzroy would meet all existing employment entitlements. Within the four walls of the club, Hore-Lacy later conceded, the staff were 'not entirely happy' with the merger.[21]

Across at Arden Street, the constant media speculation was starting to rattle North Melbourne. On Wednesday afternoon, the Kangaroos held a three-hour emergency board meeting. News of the meeting leaked to the media, who were soon camped outside. Unable to leave without confronting the press, Greg Miller finally admitted that North Melbourne was in negotiations with Fitzroy. As a result, North Melbourne's players were informed of the details that evening.

While Fitzroy officials had wanted to do likewise with their players, the club's training schedule forced Hore-Lacy to wait until Thursday night.[22] Several Kangaroos players were reportedly unimpressed with the prospect of playing for a merged club, a claim that North Melbourne officials denied. Parading Wayne Carey, Corey McKernan and John Longmire before the media at an impromptu press conference in the dressing rooms, Carey was asked whether he would play for a merged side.[23] He replied: 'I'm playing for North Melbourne now, and I'll be playing for North Melbourne for the rest of the year, and if something changes at the end of the year, so be it.'[24] In *The Age* the following day, Patrick Smith wrote that Carey had 'convinced no one that he would stay around if Fitzroy moved to Arden Street'.[25]

In the meantime, discontent grew among North Melbourne supporters, who began mulling over several unappealing aspects of the proposed merger. Not only would part of *their* club's heritage be lost, but the mere prospect of North Melbourne losing Wayne Carey was enough to raise the ire of many fans. It was, in fact, worse yet, as there was speculation Carey, McKernan and Wayne Schwass would be automatically out of contract if the Kangaroos merged, as they were contracted to play for 'North Melbourne', not 'Fitzroy–North Melbourne'.[26] Such a thought surely sent a shiver down the spine of every Kangaroos supporter. In later years, Greg Miller insisted that the response from the club's members and supporters at the time was overwhelmingly positive.[27] At the time, however, to calm fears he wrote to the members on behalf of board, reiterating that the directors were responsible for 'investigating all opportunities that may be available to secure the long term future of the Club', but they would not jeopardise the club's 'key assets': its members and players.[28]

With North Melbourne's players officially informed by their club, Fitzroy's turn came on Thursday evening. There were already reports that the players were becoming disenchanted with the growing media commotion, and Nunan criticised the media for the 'huge frenzy of activity' over the past week, which was no doubt distracting both his players and himself.[29] Brad Boyd, who was recovering from his hamstring injury and hoped to play that weekend, told reporters that the merger debate had destabilised the club, with players 'left out in the dark'. While he understood the need for the secrecy around the discussions, he noted: 'You wouldn't mind having a rough idea where you're headed.'[30] While he said the uncertainty was very stressful (especially if, occasionally, he and the players were unsure if they would be paid on time), morale among the players was still relatively high: 'We're such a young side,' he said, 'I don't think a lot of them feel really affected about it, they're just happy to be playing week to week.'[31]

On Thursday night, Dyson Hore-Lacy, David McMahon and Colin Hobbs travelled to the Coburg City Oval.[32] Before training, the players were asked to assemble for a meeting upstairs from the changerooms, joining the football department staff and the match committee. The president took them through the club's recent financial history and the rationale for the merger. He seemed embarrassed to tell them that the speculation was right and the merger was on. There would be jobs for some, he advised, but not all. The board was, however, working for an equal merger, and he reiterated what he had told the staff: personnel for the new club would be selected on merit.[33] After the bombshell, the players still needed to train. They ran three laps of the sandy oval before Nunan pulled them aside and said 'just train for half an hour, just play the footy'. There was no enthusiasm among the players, and it was unusually quiet — their minds were elsewhere.[34]

In time, many Fitzroy players embraced the prospect of a North Melbourne merger.[35] If a merger was their only course of action, then the benefits of North were far superior to that of Brisbane (despite assertions by Mike Sheahan and others that the players preferred the Bears option). Boyd was publicly in favour and looked forward to going from a wooden spoon team to playing in the finals (although this would also have been the case with Brisbane).[36] Some believed that the merged playing list would be large, giving them a better chance of securing a contact for 1997. Stephen Paxman, for instance, supported the North Melbourne option and believed he could get a spot in the merged team.[37] Many players liked the idea of remaining in Melbourne, and more than a few looked forward to the very enticing prospect of playing home games at the MCG.[38] There was, however, much to be done before that dream became a reality.

...

By Friday 17 May, several journalists had questioned how the public reporting and commentary was affecting the negotiations and the relationship between the two clubs. To Patrick Smith, history demonstrated once a merger plan was out in the open, it was doomed. From what he was hearing, by Wednesday afternoon the merger was collapsing by the hour.[39] Mike Sheahan also thought the merger was under threat; no doubt pleased that this kept Brisbane in the hunt.[40] Both journalists believed North Melbourne supporters were concerned, 'cool to angry' at the idea of losing Carey, Schwass, McKernan among others. Greg Miller did his best to manage the public relations angle, assuring his members that negotiations were only ten per cent complete. Smith found this hard to believe. 'There is no doubt it was significantly closer to clinching the deal last Friday,' he wrote, 'or Hore-Lacy would not have told the Bears to get lost.'[41] It was an astute observation. Sheahan also thought, spuriously, that Fitzroy supporters preferred a merger with Brisbane and suggested that preserving the name 'Lions' and the club colours 'seems to be a growing attraction'.[42] Supporter reaction later in the year suggested this was not necessarily the case.

Despite his earlier insistence on issuing a public statement about the Heads of Agreement, after a week of intense scrutiny, Hore-Lacy and the other Fitzroy directors now decided to say nothing publicly 'until the ink was dry on the agreement' (that being a final, legally binding agreement).[43] The long-established suspicion of the media continued to play a role. The board had often feared going public with their needs, principally for money, lest the unwanted publicity fuel the negative perception of the club. Hore-Lacy, in particular, was deeply distrustful of the media and its effect on the club. His philosophy was to give the press as little as he could, refusing to provide a running commentary on Fitzroy: 'It just aggravates the situation and makes another story,' he had remarked earlier in the year.[44] Now more than ever, he stuck to that philosophy. He received support from Patrick Smith, who considered it sensible that Fitzroy's negotiators keep their discussions secret until a deal was 'set in stone' (although he later remarked that keeping the players in the dark treated them with contempt).[45] He also praised Hore-Lacy, who had fought 'royally and belligerently' to give the Lions a future, but the club had been 'overwhelmed by circumstances — some beyond its control, others not'.[46]

The weekend's football provided a welcome distraction from off-field matters. On Saturday afternoon, North Melbourne dispatched Richmond at the MCG by 55 points, but it was Fitzroy that produced the result of the round. The Lions were back at the Whitten Oval, hosting Gerard Neesham's Fremantle. The Dockers were twelfth on the ladder, with three wins and four losses (although coming off a lamentable 96-point loss to Adelaide the week before). Neeshan, now in his second year, had been derided in the Melbourne football media for his so-called 'chip and draw' style of play, and the game offered a fascinating tactical duel against Nunan's South Australian skilful possession style. Nunan brought back Boyd, McCarthy and Cassidy. The midfield four of Rombotis, Primus, Johnson and Holmes remained from the previous game. Nick Carter joined Scott Bamford on the opposing wings, creating a partnership that would last for much of the season. Nunan placed Boyd at centre half-forward, Anthony Mellington at full-forward for the first time, along with Hawking, Barker, Dent and Dwyer. The back six — McCarthy, Pike, Clayton, Molloy, Bizotto and Paxman — was relatively settled, while Cassidy, Morton and McGregor were named on the bench.[47]

Merger talk was rife at the Whitten Oval; media crews hovered at the entrances to interrogate supporters, with most defiantly declaring they wanted to fight on alone. John Birt told reporters: 'People are getting agitated. They are backing the Fitzroy Football Club, nothing else.'[48] 24-year-old Naomi Thompson, a third-generation Lions supporter, handed out placards with slogans such as: 'AFL Help The Roy Boys – I'd Like To See That' and 'Let Fitzroy Cubs Become Lions'.[49] In a week where his public appearances had been rare, Dyson Hore-Lacy spoke at the president's lunch and revealed that eight clubs were interested in merging, six of them in the past few weeks and three making detailed proposals. Fielding questions from understandably curious supporters, he confirmed that North Melbourne was Fitzroy's preferred partner, and had been so for two years.[50] Then, at 2.10pm on Saturday 18 May, came the high-water mark of Fitzroy's fateful season.

The atmosphere at the Whitten Oval that afternoon was 'worth bottling', with supporters right behind the Lions from the first bounce.[51] The Lions made a strong start; Rombotis kicked an early goal after some slick handball work from half-back, but soon the game descended into a stalemate. Andrew Wills managed to kick the Dockers' first, and while Fitzroy struggled to break into their forward fifty, they nevertheless defended well. Unfortunately, Darren Holmes became an early casualty after being on the receiving end of Peter Mann's leading right elbow. He had been stepping back with the flight of the ball, trying to take a defensive mark on the wing, and was left concussed by the contact. Carried straight down the race on a stretcher, he took no further part in the game. Mann was reported and from then on received angry boos from the crowd.

After losing Holmes, the Lions conceded a goal to Kingsley Hunter and, as usual, looked to be struggling. Minutes later, when Matthew Primus kicked a clearing ball out of the defensive fifty, it seemed that Fremantle's Clive Waterhouse would take an easy mark on the wing. Waterhouse dropped the ball however, and after a scramble, Matthew Dent received a handball from Nick Carter and cleared the congestion. Kicking long into Fitzroy's forward fifty, Mellington strode out and marked confidently. He kicked from outside fifty, and the ball barely drifted through the goals. Fitzroy regained the lead at 2.1 to 2.0, and the game had turned. The Lions were suddenly stronger and more aggressive. Chris Johnson soon had a goal, with Mellington then getting his second from close range. A poor kick-in from Scott Chisholm gifted Rombotis his second, and Fitzroy went into quarter-time leading 5.3 to 2.1. Despite the early lead, Nunan's plans had slightly unravelled. Not only was Holmes out for the day, but Boyd went down with another hamstring injury. In hindsight, playing Boyd was a mistake, but an understandable one. He was the club's captain, and with his team struggling, he wanted to be out there with his teammates, not standing on the sidelines.

Nunan now had Cassidy and Morton off the bench, with Anthony McGregor as his remaining reserve. Yet despite the injuries, his team had established command of the game and kicking into the breeze did little to blunt their enthusiasm. The second quarter began in a stop-start fashion and was mainly played between the two fifty-metre arcs. Fremantle's Stephen O'Reilly kicked the first for the second quarter, and Fitzroy's coaches and supporters might have been forgiven for thinking that they were again throwing away a promising start. A boundary throw-in in Fitzroy's forward fifty left Mick Dwyer with ball in hand, running towards the goal, and the 27-year-old former Saint (who had been having a good quarter thus far) wobbled it through. Several minutes later, Brad Cassidy launched a long ball into the fifty. Mellington marked strongly and then kicked the goal from a set-shot. 'Fitzroy's work in close has been very impressive,' declared Terry Wheeler, the former Footscray player and coach now commentating for Channel Seven. 'Their hands are sharp, receiving the ball in clean takes and being prepared to give it on again.' Such plaudits were music to Nunan's ears.

After a prolonged arm-wrestle, in what was perhaps Fitzroy's most impressive passage of the day, Shane Clayton gathered the ball on the defensive fifty and handballed it to Matthew Dent, who kicked wide down the wing. The ball landed in space, and while Chris Johnson overran it, his trailing leg stopped it still, allowing Simon Hawking to swoop in and collect. He quickly fired off a handball to Scott Bamford, who took a bounce and then crafted a 90-degree kick to find Dwyer in space. Dwyer marked, ran on and kicked to the goal square, where an outstretched John Barker marked cleanly. Barker made no mistake from close range. It was as Nunan had wanted: run, handball, run, handball.

The players knew they were on top and sensed a rare win was in the offering. In the middle, Matthew Primus was impressive in the ruck, but it was the young centreline of Carter, Rombotis and Bamford who were a dynamic revelation. Having played only twenty-three senior games between them (Carter was eighteen, Rombotis nineteen and Bamford twenty-one), they were outclassing their better-credentialed opponents. Carter, in particular, was exciting. A product of Bendigo's Golden Square Football Club, his father, Dick, had played alongside a young Greg Williams. Carter was in awe of Diesel's work rate: 'He'd roll up to training an hour before everyone else and just kick goals by himself and would then be last to leave,' Carter recalled.[52] Nunan was impressed with young Carter — after making his debut in Round 6, he played every game for the rest of the season. Up forward, Anthony Mellington was the target Nunan had been looking for, converting Fitzroy's midfield dominance into scoreboard pressure. He had shown glimpses against Carlton, but this week he delivered, with strong marks and a mastery of the conditions, especially when kicking to the difficult Barkly Street end.[53] At half-time, the score was 8.3 to 3.5. The players went into the change rooms to thunderous applause from the meagre but passionate crowd.[54]

Fitzroy kicked with the wind in the third term. Confidence was up, and the Lions threatened to turn the game into an unlikely rout. Goals came from Johnson, Cassidy (twice in succession), Morton and Johnson again — with each, Fitzroy's confidence grew. As the margin increased the crowd became more vocal, and there was 'almost a sense of defiance', according to Dennis Commetti in the Channel Seven commentary box. Andrew Wills' goal with three minutes left in the third quarter was Fremantle's first for the second half. At the three-quarter time siren, there was a wave of anticipation among the overwhelmingly Fitzroy-inclined spectators. Moving into the huddle, Matthew Primus looked up at the crowd, and thought that it had doubled since the start of the game, as if word of an impending Fitzroy victory had spread across Melbourne and people had flocked to the ground to see it for themselves.[55] It was not just a trick of the eye, however, as hundreds of Roys *had* surged into the Whitten Oval. Adam Muyt had bumped into a friend who heard the half-time score on the radio and raced over from Ascot Vale with her two kids. 'Plenty of loaves and fishes to go around,' he remarked.[56]

If Fremantle were playing any other team but Fitzroy, they would have considered themselves down and out, but the final quarter started nervously for the unexpected leaders. Although the margin was fifty-one points at three-quarter time, quick goals to Brad Rowe, Kingsley Hunter, Tony Godden unsettled the Whitten Oval crowd. 'It's getting a little nervous here,' remarked Commetti, as Fitzroy could only manage a string of behinds. Improbable as it was, the chance of a victory seemed to be under threat, and John Birt turned away, unable to watch.[57] Then, following a scramble near the Fremantle goal, John McCarthy rushed the ball over, bringing the margin to thirty-five points. Coming out from goal, Jarrod Molloy found John Barker in the pocket, who in turn kicked down to the wing to Primus. The ruckman could not take the mark but gathered the ball off the ground and gave it to the pacier Bamford, who took off towards the forward fifty. A one-two with Simon Hawking allowed him to run into the fifty with time and space. After two bounces he kicked on his left to the top of the square where Mellington was waiting. He dropped the mark but it fell nicely, and he gathered, baulked his direct opponent and then snapped on his right as a Fremantle defender lunged across his legs in a desperate attempt at a smother. The ball sailed through the goals, Mellington had his fourth and Fitzroy supporters roared with delight. The situation had stabilised, and now it felt like the Roys were home with ten minutes left.

Both sides scored some late goals, but the match was decided. At the final siren, Fitzroy had won 16.11 (107) to 10.16 (76). A wave of jubilation swept over the crowd, evident for all to see. Ron Reed wrote:

> If only emotion were money, Fitzroy would have been saved on Saturday. If pride could be sold for a penny a pound and glee was made of gold, if tears of euphoria were legal tender, they could surely have raised a million dollars as the sweetest sound their long-suffering supporters have heard for a year, the final siren, wafted across the windswept Whitten Oval.[58]

While the AFL had spent millions on events to invest their centenary season with meaningfulness and a sense of history, none of it was 'more moving, more pleasurable to watch, than the Lions mustering the will to roar again — and their faithful revelling in it.'[59] The fans did not wait for the second siren — they burst onto the ground to mob the victorious players. Dyson Hore-Lacy said it was a 'fantastic reward for the people who have stuck by us through everything.'[60] Journalist Richard Hinds wrote that the Fitzroy fans 'celebrated as if they will never have a chance to celebrate again … And in their joy, they made you wonder what a heartless league it is that will not allow them to live to celebrate another day.'[61]

Fremantle had been unquestionably poor. They were possibly underprepared, overconfident and unready for the trip to Melbourne. But the victory was a testament to Fitzroy's coach, as well as to the work rate and talent of his players. Jake Niall wrote that Nunan 'finally saw the crisp passages of play he envisaged his players putting together when he took on one of football's toughest jobs.' It was 'exciting to see a young side mesh.'[62] The players had the most to celebrate. One fan recalled that they looked 'bloody happy' when they came off the ground.⁶³ 'There's nothing better than winning a game,' said Molloy, who had been imperious in defence.⁶⁴ Simon Hawking said it was a 'good feeling and it certainly beats losing every week, I can tell you'.⁶⁵ Eight of the Lions' twenty-one players had never experienced an AFL victory. Brad Cassidy was probably extra chuffed, having been delisted by Fremantle at the end of 1995.⁶⁶ Mellington's six goals were the best haul from a Fitzroy forward for some time. Along with his two Brownlow votes for the game, he received the match ball, which he kept for many years thereafter.⁶⁷

There were good performances all over the ground. One observer believed Martin Pike finished the game with close to a flawless display off the half-back line.⁶⁸ Nunan liked the work of Primus, Rombotis and particularly Carter, who 'controlled his side of the deck'.⁶⁹ The latter was nominated for the Norwich Rising Star award that round, and in just his third game his was a 'driving force' behind the Lions' win, with fourteen kicks, six marks and seventeen handballs.⁷⁰ Nunan considered Carter the 'quiet achiever', praising his attitude and humility, but most importantly, he did what he was told.⁷¹ The umpires considered Chris Johnson best-on-ground, with twenty-four disposals and three goals, three behinds, while Bamford, who had run himself ragged up and down the wing, received the single Brownlow vote. One player could not join in the celebrations. For Brad Boyd, carrying the burden of the captaincy was difficult enough, but to not be able to influence the contest to the best of his ability must have been torturous. One journalist noted that he 'cut a lonely figure as he left the Whitten Oval on Saturday night, preferring not to take part in the post-match revelry.'⁷²

Years later, Nunan stated that the win was a relief and a reward for the players who had worked hard to improve their skill levels.⁷³ At the time, however, he wanted to keep things in perspective. It was not 'some sort of grand final,' he declared, reminding them that successful teams won games week in, week out.⁷⁴ Sadly, he forbade the team from singing the club song in the rooms afterwards, promising the players that if they won the next week, they could sing it then.[75] But even he could not help but be swayed by the joy of the supporters: 'They are the passions of the people,' he conceded, 'and I always like to think this game and the clubs belong to people and not to corporate entities.' After all, he said, 'I don't think there are too many weeks in a coach's or a club's life where the events of this week take place.'[76]

For all the positivity the win produced at the club, the game was a stark reminder of the reasons Fitzroy was on its knees — the official attendance was only 5083, their lowest crowd of the year. 'No team can survive with such little paying support,' wrote journalist Greg Denham in *The Age*, 'even if it is high on emotion.'[77] But those were problems for another day. That evening, the club ignored Nunan and celebrated as if they had indeed won a grand final.[78] After celebrating at the final siren with everyone else, club receptionist Fran Tascone realised that the Fitzroy Club Hotel would likely receive an unexpected influx of supporters that evening and rushed across to Northcote to ensure it could accommodate the jubilant hoard that would soon bear down upon it.[79] Her concerns were vindicated: it was standing room only that night — the publican reported that as much beer was purchased that evening as in a normal week. So many fans travelled back to the hotel that the players could not find parking spots nearby and then needed to be escorted through the hotel to get to their post-match function.[80]

The faithful continued to celebrate long into the night. Not only had Fitzroy won its first game for the season, but with that win, it rose off the bottom of the ladder at the expense of Neil Balme's Melbourne (which had also recorded only one win in the season with, remarkably, a worse percentage). For a club in crisis, this was a blessed relief — they would have no better day in 1996.

CHAPTER TEN

SEALING THE DEAL

'I think the biggest hurdles have been climbed'

— Greg Miller, North Melbourne chief executive officer.[1]

With such a tight focus on the travails of a single AFL club, it is important to remember that in the broader sweep of Australian society, other events were transpiring that placed football in a proper perspective. On 28 April, 28-year-old Martin Bryant had murdered thirty-five people and injured a further twenty-three in a shooting spree at the former convict settlement turned museum of Port Arthur. The murders shocked the nation, with the recently elected Howard Government ushering in a raft of gun control legislation to restrict the availability of various high-powered weapons. Australians observed a minute's silence at 10.30am on 30 April; thousands poured onto the streets of Hobart, while in Melbourne the Stock Exchange shut and trams came to a halt.[2]

As the shock of the Port Arthur tragedy receded, Melbourne returned to a familiar rhythm. Premier Jeff Kennett fended off accusations of untoward involvement with the Crown Casino tender while his government established a five-member committee to help plan Federation Square.[3] Another set-piece of the AFL's centenary commemorations was the documentary, *100 Years Of Australian Football*, which premiered on Channel Seven and became the fourth most-viewed program that week behind *Blue Heelers*, *Better Homes and Gardens* and *The Footy Show*.[4] Finally, amid the negotiations with North Melbourne, his work as a barrister and his duties chairing the Fitzroy board, Dyson Hore-Lacy carved out some time in his busy schedule to write a letter. In his chambers, seven floors above Lonsdale Street, with his table a mess of legal briefs and piles of paper, he wrote to the members and shareholders of the Fitzroy Football Club, advising them that sometime in the coming months they would be asked 'to give their approval to a joint venture with the North Melbourne Football Club'.[5]

As the glow of Fitzroy's first win for the season began to fade, Fitzroy's board had returned to the more prosaic task of building support for a merger with North Melbourne. The notion, chiefly propagated by the newspapers, that the deal was a *fait accompli* was not the case. Beyond finalising negotiations with the Kangaroos, gaining the AFL Commission's endorsement and the tacit support from the other clubs, the Fitzroy board required formal approval from the club's members and shareholders. The move to secure their support was not before time. On 21 May, the AFL Commission officially endorsed Port Adelaide's entry into the AFL (subject to a decision by the clubs). While the Commission was prepared to run a seventeen-team league in 1997, retaining the number of clubs at sixteen had long been their preference.[6]

According to the club's Memorandum and Articles of Association, seventy-five per cent of members and shareholders needed to endorse a merger. Early meetings with key supporters and coteries had been promising, and convinced the board that a majority of Fitzroy people would indeed support a merger with North Melbourne.[7] In his letter, Hore-Lacy admitted that Fitzroy could no longer survive on its own despite the best efforts of the club and its supporters (it seemingly proved his point that he needed $4000 from the Fitzroy Past Players Association to cover the letter's postage and stationery) and after taking his usual swipes at the AFL he spelled out the case for a merger with the Kangaroos.[8] He argued it was 'far superior' to Brisbane's offer — only eight players in the new team, six games in Melbourne at different venues and two Fitzroy directors on the board — which he articulated to the members for the first time. He recognised that merging was not an ideal circumstance by any means, but it was the best they could achieve with their limited suite of options. He concluded by stating: 'Whatever we do, we are acting solely in what we believe are the best interests of our members/shareholders. I ask you for your continued support.'[9]

Some were not ready to even contemplate the relative merits of different proposals. Talk of Fitzroy's demise and a potential merger had been standard fare among Lions supporters for almost a decade, but now there seemed to be a certainty that perhaps was not there before. 'Fitzroy' as an independent club would be lost, and despite the pragmatism of a merger, some reacted angrily. 'It's not a merger, it's murder. It's the end of a football club,' pronounced John Blackman, a Fitzroy supporter of thirty-five years, 'I'm devastated.'[10] Paul Vassiliou told *The Age*, 'If Fitzroy can't play as Fitzroy, I'd rather see they didn't exist, rather than merge.'[11] Kathy Doyle was of a similar mind. 'I'd have preferred to see Fitzroy disappear altogether,' she recalled, 'and our history remain untainted, than be merged with another club.'[12] Others were more positive about the benefits of a North Melbourne merger. Shane Molloy, Jarrod's father, was happy for his son to play for the Kangaroos, where he would have access to specialist training and development. He was scathing of the way the club had neglected football department development of the past few years.[13] One Fitzroy supporter very keen on the merger with North Melbourne was 14-year-old father/son draft prospect Jonathan Brown, who relished the idea of playing alongside Wayne Carey.[14]

As usual, Fitzroy supporters directed much of their anger at the AFL. 'They can spend all their millions on the hooha that's gone on over the past couple of weeks, yet they won't help us out,' said one Lions' coterie group member. She believed the AFL was trying to remove Fitzroy from the competition while assisting Sydney and Brisbane to stay afloat, 'and I'm sick of it.'[15] Another believed that Fitzroy had been 'singled out' by the AFL Commission as the club to remove.[16] One supporter, who had his father's ashes scattered on Brunswick Street Oval, was angry, chiding the AFL Commission for forgetting it was 'a people's game'.[17] Others were resigned to the reality of the situation. Former president Leon Wiegard endorsed the proposed merger as a 'humane act'. He believed that Fitzroy supporters could not afford to have a team in the AFL, but 'they have to be respected because they are fanatics and they are so involved emotionally'.[18] The 63-year-old Norma Burnie, who had been supporting Fitzroy since she was twelve, was in favour of a merger if it meant Fitzroy did not go under: 'It seems the only option at the moment.'[19]

Some compared the North Melbourne deal with what Brisbane was offering. Geoff Lockwood, who had supported the Roys for four decades, preferred retaining the club colours to keeping the name 'Fitzroy'.[20] Others believed that remaining in Melbourne trumped any superficial appeal of colours, logos or club songs. Such arguments between Fitzroy supporters continued throughout the year and formed part of serious debate among fans as to what constituted their club's core identity. Both those supporting the North Melbourne merger and those in favour of Brisbane argued that their respective deal preserved the important aspects of Fitzroy, while often deriding the opposing option as little more than a take-over that would see Fitzroy all but disappear in a matter of years.[21] One supporter, Stuart Potter, expressed disbelief that the board would 'willingly sacrifice so much of Fitzroy's heritage and history' in a merger with the Kangaroos.[22] Potter was not alone in making this argument, with many both inside and outside the club (including Ross Oakley after the fact) criticising the North Melbourne deal, because it would allegedly leave only the faintest trace of Fitzroy on the North Melbourne jumper.

The Fitzroy board had considered this, but determined that North Melbourne was still their best partner. One Lions coterie member in favour of the North Melbourne merger argued that if the new club could just retain some of Fitzroy's heritage, then other supporters would eventually follow it.[23] The dilemma of deciding how much club identity would remain within a merged club, however, was at the heart of the merger issue in general. While for the AFL Commission and the administration, mergers were an economic necessity, for those with an emotional investment in a club, it was less clear cut. The now-famous image of Don Scott ripping a Velcro hawk from a Melbourne jumper during the acrimonious merger vote in September 1996 speaks to the powerful feelings that club identity engenders. One of the main reasons clubs had resisted the Commission's pleas to merge was the resistance to losing part of a club's character, even if it meant partial survival into the future. Fitzroy's board had determined that remaining in Melbourne and retaining the Fitzroy name was more important than the more visible Fitzroy presence in the outward club identifiers that Brisbane was offering. It was a trade-off that also satisfied many supporters.

Less happy were the North Melbourne supporters. They too would be sacrificing part of their identity and heritage, and many did not believe this was necessary given their strong on-field performance that season. It helped ease their concerns that the rumours of losing key players proved to be unfounded; helpfully, Wayne Carey publicly denied there had been a 'players' revolt': 'It was a load of rubbish really, so we thought we'd go and set it straight but ended up adding fuel to the fire.'[24] Furthermore, player agent Ricky Nixon stated that players contracted to North would be likely to remain so under a merger.[25]

Not all issues were smoothed over as easily. The announcement of the merged club's name — the Fitzroy–North Melbourne Kangaroos — caused a degree of consternation. Mike Sheahan thought the decision to go with this naming was sensible, as it would 'allay widespread suspicions of a North take-over'.[26] But why, North Melbourne supporters asked themselves, should they be relegated to second place if they were the stronger club? It was a question that continued to fester.

Trying to gain support for the merger required clear and balanced communications with an awareness that different audiences heard things differently. At one North Melbourne function, a Kangaroos board member, Mark Dawson, attempted to assuage the fears of his members. In 1997, he told them, 'Denis Pagan will be coach, Wayne Carey will be the captain, Corey McKernan and Wayne Schwass will be playing football in this side and the side that runs out on the MCG next year will still be the Kangaroos.'[27] All of this was true (as far as the details of the merger were concerned), but to Fitzroy, it created the unhelpful impression that their identity would become peripheral in the merged club. In a quirk of the fixture, Fitzroy's next opponent was North Melbourne on Friday, 24 May at the MCG. Aware of the growing tension between elements at the two clubs, Greg Miller used the president's lunch to praise Fitzroy's board and supporters for the strength and loyalty they had shown during the recent difficult years, declaring that North Melbourne was honoured Fitzroy had chosen it as a merger partner.[28]

For all the camaraderie at the president's lunch, there was still a competitive game to be played, and Denis Pagan and his team showed no mercy to the Lions. North was 'a finely tuned machine' and 'went into overdrive when it sniffed a percentage booster', winning 25.20 (170) to 9.11 (65).[29] If the match itself demonstrated one thing, it was that the incentive for North Melbourne to merge with Fitzroy was all off-field. On the field, the Kangaroos were a powerful unit, and few Fitzroy players would likely break into their current starting eighteen. Nunan was pleased with the endeavour, spirit and enthusiasm his players showed but lamented that they still lacked the necessary skill and quality, particularly when compared with the likes of Wayne Carey and Corey McKernan.[30]

After the game, journalists could not help but ask Nunan and Pagan about the merger speculation. Pagan believed that it had taken its toll on his players. Nunan concurred, lamenting that while the off-field drama should not affect the team, it was, nevertheless, having an impact.[31] The Lions also sustained two injuries that, while no-one was to know it at the time, spelled the end of two respective AFL careers. Frank Bizzotto suffered a dislocated shoulder, while Darren Holmes sustained a groin injury. Both had played their first senior games in 1991: Bizzotto for Fitzroy after being recruited from West Preston and Holmes for Sydney, having played his junior football in Albury. Bizzotto had only solidified himself in the seniors in 1995, the same season Holmes arrived in exchange for pick seventy-four in the national draft (used by Sydney to recruit Troy Luff). It was an inconspicuous end for the pair, and the first of many that year.

...

Following a break for State of Origin, on Saturday, 8 June, the Lions were defeated by Sydney at the Whitten Oval by seventy points. The win was a percentage booster for the Swans and elevated them from seventh to fifth. Elsewhere, Round 10 became infamous for the lights going out at Waverley during the match between St Kilda v Essendon — an unscheduled event in the AFL's centenary season but no less memorable. The following week, Fitzroy lost to Melbourne, coached by Nunan's former SANFL rival Neil Balme, by sixty-three points. Both games exhibited what had become a trend for Fitzroy: first-half competitiveness was undone by skill errors and fatigue in the second half. Dismissing the fatigue thesis, however, Nunan instead argued that some of his players were simply not 'up to scratch'.[32] Whatever the reason, the Lions had slumped to 1–10 for the season.

Merger speculation seemed to be another factor affecting the players. Writing for *The Age*, Greg Baum believed that the players were now playing for their individual, rather than collective, futures, concerned about where they would be playing in 1997. It was a reserves outlook, he wrote, that could 'at best produce reserves-standard football'.[33] Ruckman Brett Cook, who *was* a reserves player at that point, thought that after the potential merger with North Melbourne became public, players started to speculate about who would make the team. 'Whether most of us knew it or not,' he later recalled, 'I reckon many of us started to think a bit selfishly and it really eroded the team's performance out on the ground each week.'[34] After this latest defeat, and having endured weeks of media conjecture around the merger, Nunan spoke publicly and at length about the state of his team. He confirmed that the club's uncertain future was having a destructive effect on his players but he did not use this as an excuse for poor performances. Still, he conceded that Fitzroy had long ago lost its way and the team lacked the competitiveness required for the AFL (which was as nice as he could be about a 'very disappointing set of circumstances').[35] If some of the players were in a top-four side, he believed they would be 'completely different animals', and their development would be much quicker. 'It's extremely hard to retain positives in the environment we have at the moment,' he lamented.[36]

Privately, Nunan was becoming increasingly frustrated with Fitzroy's performances. He had seen what his team could do in their win against Fremantle. Now, three rounds later, he was concerned about his players' sliding form. He seemed to have returned to an earlier state of affairs, with an uncompetitive team and seemingly no way to motivate them. His solution was to use coercion. At training one evening the following week, Nunan informed his players via a memo that he would be fining them for mediocre performances. To justify it, he cited clauses 2.1 and 2.3 of their contracts: players must 'play football for the club to the best of his skill and ability' and 'obey all lawful and reasonable directions' from the club's hierarchy.[37] He argued that the usual method of disciplining poor performances — dropping players — was not an option in a club with such a limited pool of talent unless he wanted to unbalance the team. If a player disputed the fine, he could sit down with Nunan and watch a video of the game and if he was still not happy he could take the matter to the club's management.[38]

The players were incredulous, and they were not alone. The AFL's Director of Football Operations, Ian Collins, said Nunan's decision was 'fraught with danger'; AFLPA executive director Peter Allen denounced the approach, calling it 'completely inappropriate'.[39] Damien Smith, the manager and business advisor to several Fitzroy players, apparently had four calls from 'pretty stressed-out' clients the night before. He called it a 'classic example in negative motivation'. Whoever conceived it as a motivational technique 'probably graduated from the Attila the Hun school of people management'.[40] Outrageously, he even suggested that the action was just a ploy to stall the payment of players.[41] Nunan defended his approach, even in the face of possible legal action. The off-field turmoil was having a detrimental effect on the players, he believed, and he needed them to refocus on their football. He argued that a stricter adherence to his game-plan would produce results and avoid the second-half fade-outs that were keeping them from being competitive in more games.[42]

The weekend's game against Hawthorn at Waverley tested Nunan's motivational methods. Brad Boyd returned for only his seventh game of the season, but playing against Nunan was one of his former North Adelaide players, Nick Holland, who kicked 6.1 and proved to be the difference ('Why do they always do that to me?' Nunan asked rhetorically after the game, recalling the Jarman brothers' masterclass for Adelaide in Round 2).[43] Hawthorn won 17.12 (114) to 12.11 (83), but Nunan was pleased with the 'noticeable increase' in the Lions' competitiveness and work rate, hinting that he believed his punitive system had the desired effect. Happily for the players, no-one would receive fines.[44] Brett Chandler stood out, holding John Platten to fourteen disposals while accumulating twenty-three himself in his seventh game for the season. Nunan praised his performance, while one journalist wrote: 'If all Lions were as competitive as Chandler, Fitzroy would be a different team.'[45]

By the end of Round 12, Fitzroy sat in last place with its solitary win and a percentage of 55.7, six points adrift of Footscray in fifteenth. Carlton topped the ladder, followed by North Melbourne and the Brisbane Bears with Sydney lurking with intent in fourth. While the team played much of the 1996 season under a cloud of concern and uncertainty about the future, this was the last time Fitzroy would play without the immediacy of the club's dire financial position being so apparent. After this point, the club's players, staff, volunteers and supporters may have looked back on the first half of the season and considered themselves in relatively blissful ignorance compared to what was to come.

...

As Nunan and his players persevered through the season, Dyson Hore-Lacy was pushing ahead with securing support for the merger. On 20 May, he met with the club's major shareholders, who supported the board's decision to merge with North Melbourne. On the evening of 28 May he expanded his audience, meeting with any shareholder with 200 shares or more (approximately sixty people in total). 'We expect to put a vote to the members within a month,' he reportedly told them, explaining that there was no alternative to merger and North Melbourne was giving them a chance to live on in a meaningful way. 'We are too far down the track to change direction now,' he argued, 'there will be no 11th hour escape this time.'[46] The shareholders seemingly agreed, and voted to hand over their proxies to help secure the merger. Once Elaine Findlay finished the counting, the board had seventy per cent of the issued shareholdings and should the merger be put to a vote, they were convinced they would have the required seventy-five per cent of votes.[47]

Gaining the necessary support from within the club did not mean, however, that Hore-Lacy was having an easy time. Shepherding through a merger always promised to be difficult, but every week new hurdles and opponents arose to frustrate him. Rogue director Greg Basto was publicly criticising his fellow board members. Like 'rats deserting a sinking ship', he asserted, they had 'sold the club out' once the decision had been made to merge, giving up on marketing and other fund-raising activities.[48] He claimed he could raise $1 million by asking 1000 supporters to pledge $1000 each, and then asking 1000 businesses to donate $1000 each for a total of $2 million.[49] This plan was in the realms of fantasy — surely if raising $2 million were that easy, the other directors would have done so by now.

Hore-Lacy was also dealing with the media, treating it — as per usual — with suspicion, if not contempt. While both major newspapers in Melbourne ran articles that raised his hackles, on 30 May, *The Age* went too far for his liking. That day, Patrick Smith accused Hore-Lacy of poor leadership as Fitzroy's president and, in particular, of misleading the club's members.[50] While Fitzroy's chairman had weathered his fair share of criticism, this was out of order. He commenced court proceedings, alleging that Smith's article constituted defamation.[51] After a protracted legal battle, *The Age* relented and apologised on 20 December 2000, accepting that Hore-Lacy 'at all times acted with complete probity and propriety' in his actions regarding Fitzroy and its members and supporters.[52]

In Queensland, Noel Gordon was also making Hore-Lacy's life difficult. Brisbane's president did not believe that the Bears were truly out of the hunt. 'I've never conceded anything in my life,' he told *The Age*.[53] A merger with Fitzroy remained a priority; the Bears did not know if there would be another opportunity to merge with a Melbourne-based club and gain all the associated benefits. As such, Gordon began agitating through the media.[54] In a public letter to Hore-Lacy, released on 12 June, he alleged that 'private shareholders' of Fitzroy and North Melbourne were forcing the merger and denying ordinary members the right to express their views. He either suspected that the rank-and-file members were more supportive of the Brisbane merger than their directors were, or else he was just trying to create the appearance of impropriety to undermine Hore-Lacy. He further alleged that Fitzroy's president had provided his members with inaccurate information about the Bears' merger proposal. Hore-Lacy wrote an open letter of his own in response, rejecting Gordon's claims and condemning the 'concerted campaign' he appeared to be running in the press to advance his cause.[55]

Undeterred by the ongoing Hore-Lacy/Gordon fracas, on Thursday 13 June, Greg Miller confirmed during a radio interview that having completed a review into Fitzroy's finances, he knew exactly how much of the $6 million would remain after the Lions' debt was paid, and this did not present a problem for him or North Melbourne. Wading ever so slightly into the Brisbane/Fitzroy argument, he described Noel Gordon as 'a strange character'.[56] The following day, Hore-Lacy and Elaine Findlay met with North Melbourne officials at Arden Street, where they came to a final agreement concerning shareholding. Lawyers drew up a draft document recording the completed agreement, which was delivered to Hore-Lacy at his home that night.[57] In the background, the AFL Commission had confirmed the rules that would apply between Fitzroy and its potential merger partner, including the fifty-four player list at the time of the 1996 national draft and the $6.2 million financial package (on the basis that Fitzroy continued to operate during the 1996 season).[58] Everything was falling into place for the AFL's first merger to go ahead.

...

On the morning of Tuesday 18 June 1996, Fitzroy and North Melbourne were scheduled to sign a merger agreement at the offices of Corrs Chambers Westgarth. Following a meeting with representatives from Nauru, Hore-Lacy headed to his meeting with North Melbourne's representatives, but when he arrived he was informed that it was cancelled. Something was amiss. At this stage, the 67-year-old Ron

Casey, who had been hospitalised in May suffering chest pains, was recuperating in Queensland and, ever so slightly, during his absences the tenor of North Melbourne's negotiations had changed.[59] This soon became evident to Hore-Lacy and others on Fitzroy's board. Back at his chambers, he called Greg Miller, who told him there was something he needed to discuss. Sensing that there was a 'serious problem', Hore-Lacy's suspicions were confirmed at the re-scheduled meeting that afternoon.[60] Miller told the Fitzroy representatives that the name 'North Melbourne' was essential to its members, many of whom opposed the prominent placement of 'Fitzroy' in the new club's name. There had been strong views from the North Melbourne supporters against the merger; an anti-merger petition gathered 2000 signatures, and club legend Malcolm Blight publicly condemned the initial name proposal for giving Fitzroy primacy.[61]

Hore-Lacy told Miller to 'cut the crap' and give him the bottom line. Miller said to them that the merger would not proceed unless the club was called the 'North Melbourne–Fitzroy Kangaroos'.[62] Hore-Lacy felt like walking out. 'They had to have their name first,' he thought. 'They had to have the logo. They had to have the home ground and they would eventually have the coach, the captain and everything else which was important to them.'[63] The fears of many Fitzroy supporters hostile to the North Melbourne merger were being realised. Hore-Lacy, Findlay and others had negotiated a deal in good faith to create the 'Fitzroy–North Melbourne Kangaroos', and he told Miller that they would not alter it — to do so would signal that the merge was, as some feared, a take-over. He and Findlay left that meeting feeling 'extremely depressed', and considering that Brisbane's offer was starting to look more attractive.[64] Two days later, Fitzroy's board discussed North Melbourne's revised position. They flatly rejected the 'North Melbourne–Fitzroy Kangaroos', but threw around some alternatives, eventually deciding that the 'North–Fitzroy Kangaroos' was acceptable. They took this to the North Melbourne's representatives on Sunday 23 June, but Miller, De Rauch and Dawson would not give any ground. They did, however, agree to draw up a logo incorporating both a kangaroo and a lion.[65]

What had become apparent to Hore-Lacy and the other Fitzroy directors was that without any competition, North could throw its weight around without fear that Fitzroy would reject them and turn to another suitor. Bringing a second contender into the mix would strengthen Fitzroy's position. So, having been involved in a running brawl with Brisbane over the past several weeks, on Monday 24 June, Dyson Hore-Lacy called Brisbane's solicitor, David Dunn. He informed Dunn that he was considering recommending to the board that the choice between North Melbourne and Brisbane be put to the members, saying that if Brisbane were still interested in merging with Fitzroy, they should put forward their best offer.[66]

Brisbane officials were not stupid. By Tuesday, word of the disagreement between North and Fitzroy had leaked out, with *The Age* reporting the merger might have 'hit its most significant hurdle'.[67] In the *Herald Sun*, Mike Sheahan was also reporting (seemingly with some relish) that the name was causing issues and there was 'a growing view the merger is wobbly'.[68] Brisbane was cautious about being strung along by Fitzroy as a stalking horse to bring North Melbourne back to its original position.[69] Still, the re-engagement was an opportunity to get back in the game. Knowing that there was at least some support among the Fitzroy faithful, Brisbane stayed at the table, adhering to the poker maxim that all they needed was a chip and a chair to give themselves a chance of winning. The newspapers discovered Fitzroy's renewed interested in a Brisbane merger, and would later report that, after having been in contact with Fitzroy, Brisbane had checked with the ASC to see if the name 'Brisbane Lions' was still reserved.[70]

Yet North Melbourne remained Fitzroy's preferred merger partner, even with the recent turbulence. With their disagreement becoming a public issue, on Tuesday morning, 25 June, Hore-Lacy called the AFL's solicitor, Jeff Browne, to let him know that the deal was in jeopardy. Browne quickly arranged for dinner that evening between himself, Hore-Lacy and Peter De Rauch at Zio Joe's in East Melbourne to solve the name issue holding up the deal.[71] Over dinner, Hore-Lacy, De Rauch and Browne finally reached an agreement. The club's name would be the 'North–Fitzroy Kangaroos'; the logo would feature both a kangaroo and lion and a small gold lion would feature on the left breast of the jumper as a concession to Fitzroy for diluting the name. In all other respects, the agreement was the same as had been reached on 11 May. With the situation seemingly ameliorated, both De Rauch and Hore-Lacy signed the new deal.[72] On Thursday, 27 June, Greg Miller publicly stated that the two clubs had overcome all significant hurdles and an announcement on a merged club was perhaps only 'a week or so away'.[73]

top: Dyson Hore-Lacy looks out over the Whitten Oval (*The Age*/Nine Publishing FXB917876; photographer: Penny Stephens).

middle: The AFL Commission in 1996. Back row, left to right: Ron Evans, Graeme Samuel, Terry O'Connor, Colin Carter, Wayne Jackson. Front row: John Kennedy, Ross Oakley (*AFL Annual Report 1996*, p. 34, permission granted from AFL for use).

bottom: Fitzroy's board of directors during the club's AGM at the Fitzroy Town Hall, 29 April 1996. From left to right: Kevin Ryan, John Stewart, Robert Eales, Elaine Findlay, Dyson Hore-Lacy, John Petinella, Robert Johnstone, David McMahon and Colin Hobbs (*The Age*/Nine Publishing FXB918719; photographer: unidentified).

top: The Albion Charles Hotel, Northcote, formerly the Fitzroy Club Hotel, which, externally at least, remains similar to its appearance in 1996 (photo by author).

middle: An Ins and Outs Night at the Fitzroy Club Hotel. Shirley Hardy-Rix interviewing Jarrod Molloy and actors Kym Valentine and Ryan Moloney from *Neighbours* (photo provided by Jan Wright).

bottom: Fitzroy's trainers for the 1996 season. Front row, left to right: Mark Backway, Kevin Elms, Les Beasley, Arthur Aylward, Alec Gardner; middle row: Tom Couch, Ringo Hood, unidentified, Rob Robertson, Brian Taylor, Troy Hall; back row: Lance Upton, unidentified, Ian Cairncross, Jack Hancock, Tim Renwick (photo provided by Wilma Aylward).

top: Former player Eddie Hart (ninety-eight games for Fitzroy between 1941 and 1951), Fitzroy Supporters' Group member Jan Wright, former Premier John Cain junior and Nancye Cain (at one time the club's number one ticket holder) during a Fitzroy function in 1993 (photo provided by Jan Wright).

bottom: Three generations of Fitzroy supporters: Pat Leydon, with son David and grandson Sean, in 1994 (photo provided by Leydon family; photographer: Ward Leydon).

FITZROY FOOTBALL CLUB
AFL CENTENARY YEAR 1996

Back Row: Frank Bizzotto, Nick Carter, Brent Frewen, Simon Hawking, Jeff Hogg, Matthew Manfield, Matthew Primus, Brett Cook, Andrew Cavedon, Nigel Credlin, Jarrod Molloy, Marty Warry, Chris Johnson. *Second Row:* Brad Cassidy, Martin Pike, Jason Baldwin, Mark Zanotti, Jason Ramsey, John Barker, Greg Freemantle (Physical Education Advisor), Stephen Paxman (Vice Captain), Anthony Mellington, Shane Clayton, Brian McInnes, Mark Dwyer, Robert McMahon, Matthew McLellan. *Seated:* Peter Doyle, Darren Holmes, John McCarthy, Alan McConnell (Assistant Coach), Michael Nunan (AFL Coach), Brad Boyd (Captain), Leon Harris (AFL Reserves Coach), Nick Mitchell, Simon Atkins (Deputy Vice Captain), John Rombotis. *Front Row:* Scott Bamford, Stephen Zavalas, Danny Morton, Brett Chandler, Adam McCarthy, Daniel Ward, Leigh Picioane, Peter O'Brien, Wayne Lamb. *Absent:* Rowan Warfe, Matthew Dent, Peter Bird, Trent Cummings.

A relatively informal team photograph of the 1996 Fitzroy Lions, as appeared on a club poster that year. The photo includes all but four players from Fitzroy's list, as well as senior coach, Michael Nunan, assistant coach, Alan McConnell, reserves coach, Leon Harris, and physical fitness advisor, Greg Freemantle (photo by author).

top: Fitzroy's on-field leadership for the 1996 season, left to right: Brad Boyd (captain), Stephen Paxman (vice-captain) and Simon Atkins (deputy vice-captain) (photo provided by Jan Wright).

bottom left: Michael Nunan providing direction to his players during Fitzroy's Round 6 match against Richmond at the Whitten Oval, 4 May 1996 (AFL Photos: 25058).

bottom right: Alan McConnell during the 1996 season. A loyal servant of the club, he held several coaching positions at Fitzroy in the early nineties and was caretaker coach in 1995 and 1996 (AFL Photos: 25080).

top: Fitzroy players running onto the ground in their centenary jumpers and pants before the Round 7 re-enactment game against Carlton at Princes Park, 11 May 1996 (photo provided by Jan Wright).

bottom left: Fitzroy centreman John Rombotis about to distribute one of his twenty-nine disposals during the Round 7 match against Carlton (photo provided by Jan Wright).

bottom right: Chris Johnson flies for a spectacular mark over teammate Matthew Primus and Carlton's Matthew Allen as Darren Holmes watched on (photo provided by Jan Wright).

top: Matthew Primus in ruck against North Melbourne's Mark Roberts in Fitzroy's Round 9 game against the Kangaroos at the MCG, 24 May 1996. It was Fitzroy's first match at the MCG that season and a rare night fixture (photo provided by Jan Wright).

bottom: The 'sparrow-frail wingman' Scott Bamford during the Round 8 victory against Fremantle, 18 May 1996. Bamford also played every game of the 1996 season, and was awarded one Brownlow vote for his performance against the Dockers, showing impressive dash on the wing (AFL Photos: 25214).

top: Fitness advisor Greg Freemantle and veteran trainer Jack Hancock look on as players stretch in the rooms at the Whitten Oval. The senior trainers would be allocated numbers one to six (photo provided by Jan Wright).

bottom: Anthony Mellington comes off the ground after Fitzroy's Round 8 victory against Fremantle at the Whitten Oval, 18 May 1996. Mellington was among the best-on-ground with a six-goal performance (*The Age*/Nine Publishing FXB918720; photographer: Jim Hooper).

CHAPTER ELEVEN

A TOUGH DAY AT THE OFFICE

'I suspect they are insolvent'

— Michael Brennan, Fitzroy administrator.[1]

The island of Nauru is a minuscule dot in the vast expanse of the South Pacific Ocean, sitting to the north-east of Solomon Islands just south of the equator. Ringed by a beautiful coral reef, it has never been a tourist destination. Other South Pacific islands are easier to reach and offer more for visitors; in 1996, Nauru had several dilapidated hotels to accommodate guests and detritus left behind by the Japanese occupation in the Second World War as a chief tourist attraction. Still, to 9600 people, Nauru was home.

That this tiny Pacific island nation played a vital part in the saga of the Fitzroy Football Club is a quizzical detail, perplexing to those who cannot recall the country's heyday as a profligate investment baron. Nauru, the third smallest state in the world (only larger than the Vatican City and Monaco), was improbably wealthy in the early nineties due to the large quantities of phosphate buried in its twenty-one square-kilometre landmass. Much of its mining revenue was put into off-shore investments, including the purchase of several properties in Melbourne: Nauru House, the Southern Cross Hotel and the site of the Queen Victoria Hospital. Keen to make further inroads into Melbourne, in October 1994 the country decided to provide Fitzroy with a commercial long-term loan facility via the Nauru Insurance Corporation of $1.2 million. In return, Fitzroy would provide sponsorship opportunities for Nauruan businesses in Australia.[2] As part of the deal, Kinza Clodumar, an on-again/off-again member of the Nauruan Parliament, and personal financial advisor to the country's president, was elected to the board (for the sake of Fitzroy's company reporting, was described simply as a 'financier'). Fitzroy would also become heavily involved in the development of Australian rules football in Nauru. The club sent new coach Bernie Quinlan to the island to umpire the local grand final, a task previously undertaken by Gary Ablett Senior.[3]

The relationship had been progressing smoothly until the removal of President Bernard Dowiyogo from office on 22 November 1995, as a result of which Clodumur lost significant influence. Dowiyogo's successor, the 56-year-old Lagumot Harris, came to power facing a burgeoning fiscal crisis. Once the wealthiest per capita nation on earth, its dwindling revenue from its primary natural resource and a poor net foreign debt was making it difficult for the country to service several overseas loans. It also had a bloated public service, paid for by its boom in mining revenue. As a result, not only was Nauru's investment safety-net a shadow of what it could have been, but as the revenue from phosphate mining diminished, a cash-flow hole was growing ever wider. In February 1996, President Harris addressed the nation informing them that the decline in phosphate revenue and the resulting reliance on foreign borrowing had resulted in severe liquidity problems.[4] He passed his first budget in June, with an ominous pledge to enact harsh fiscal discipline and reform. Nauruans faced Kennett-esque rationalisation measures, including a user-pays medical system, increased charges for public services, privatisation, a wage freeze for two years, a halt to public service recruiting and a severe reduction in the overall number of public servants.[5]

At no other time have the internal affairs of a Pacific island nation been so important to the fate of an Australian rules football club. Fitzroy had struggled through negotiations with North Melbourne and weathered the public scrutiny, to the point where it looked as if the 'North–Fitzroy Kangaroos' would take the field in the 1997 AFL season. Yet, as always, financial issues threatened to foil the best-laid plans. By rejecting the AFL's proposal in April to underwrite their season, the club left itself exposed in a vulnerable cash position. The ASC became concerned, and shortly after the AGM they raided the club's auditors, KPMG, with a warrant for 'suspect trading whilst insolvent'.[6] Dyson Hore-Lacy had managed to smooth things over with the ASC, but lingering doubts remained about the club's financial position.[7]

Parlous as their situation was, with Fitzroy inching towards final merger agreement the AFL indicated that, if necessary, it would finance the club to allow Fitzroy and North Melbourne to complete the merger. With memberships closed for the season, the club was left with two main sources of income: gate receipts and the AFL dividend.[8] The club had approximately $100,000 of player payments due at the end of May. To pay these, Fitzroy requested an advance on their $300,000 dividend from the AFL, which they would ordinarily receive in late June. Before the AFL agreed to advance the money, they wanted a guarantee from the club that it would merge. Hore-Lacy reiterated his well-worn point, that he could not guarantee a merger without the approval of the members and shareholders. Still, the club needed the money, and the shareholders meeting on 28 May enabled the board to gain a sufficient number of proxies to convince AFL House of their intent.[9]

The story of Fitzroy's cash predicament inevitably leaked to the media, however, in addition to some dubious reporting about an AFL imposed deadline and a threat to appoint an administrator. In response, Hore-Lacy did the rounds on radio denying claims that the club would not pay it players: 'We will be able to meet payments … the AFL will not be taking over the club, we have got no deadline at all, and we will have finances for the rest of the year.'[10] Yet Hore-Lacy later conceded that Fitzroy was 'choking to death through lack of money'. The next AFL dividend could not come fast enough; there was a genuine risk that the club had run out of money and *would* find itself guilty of trading while insolvent.[11]

There was also the matter of resolving Fitzroy's debts. The repayment of all Fitzroy's creditors, not just Nauru, was a concern that hung over the merger negotiations, as the final amount would determine how much of the $6 million would remain for the merged club. While the Nauru Insurance Corporation was the club's one secured creditor, there was also a myriad of smaller unsecured creditors to whom the club owed money, not to mention the club's obligations to the Australian Taxation Office. The unsecured creditors ranged from players and staff to commercial vendors who provided any number of goods and services to the club in the course of its routine operations. Many had no emotional connection to Fitzroy beyond their business dealings and were hoping to recover whatever they could should the club be wound up. The total amount of Fitzroy's debt depended on who one asked and what future income or expenses they incorporated: the number could be as low as $2.5 million or as high as $4.5 million. Wherever the amount fell, it would consume a large portion of the merger incentive package and what was seemingly inescapable was that Nauru, as a secured creditor, would receive its $1.25 million, plus a little extra for interest. Acting on advice from accountants, Fitzroy's directors believed that they could pay Nauru $1 million immediately, and — given the apparent reneging on the $500,000 earlier in the year — this would constitute the equivalent of the club meeting its obligations in full.[12]

North Melbourne understandably wanted as much from the $6 million as possible and had determined that they would only allot $550,000 from the incentive package to go to Nauru. On Tuesday, 18 June, Hore-Lacy travelled to the offices of Baker & Mackenzie in the Rialto Building to meet with Graham Sherry, the solicitor acting for Nauru. Hore-Lacy put to Sherry that they could pay $550,000 after the merger, and he believed that they could get a further $200,000 from the AFL. Fitzroy's offer of anything less than 100 cents in the dollar puzzled Sherry, who nevertheless agreed to discuss the matter with John Stewart, one of Fitzroy's finance directors, and seek further direction from his client.[13] Nauru later informed Hore-Lacy that they would not settle for anything less than the full amount. With North Melbourne unwilling to go beyond $550,000, finding the additional money was a challenge for an already cash-strapped club.

Nauru's insistence on receiving complete payment was not merely a creditor looking for its debtor to honour its agreement: it was also a response to the country's ongoing financial predicament. On 28 June, the Finance Minister, Rueben Kun, told the *Nauru Bulletin* that the country's debts exceeded its assets, its financial position was 'extremely grave' and that the Bank of Nauru was in a 'serious state of insolvency'.[14] Nauru needed every cent it could get. During the year, the Government of Nauru had extracted an undertaking from the League that Fitzroy would let them know when their AFL dividend was due, forty-eight hours in advance. During the week beginning Monday 24 June, with the dividend due, the club duly informed Nauru. In return, Nauru issued an ultimatum to Fitzroy: repay the full $1.25 million before noon on Friday, 28 June, or else they would activate the default clause in their loan agreement and send in an administrator to recover the debt.[15]

It is important to understand what Nauru was threatening. An administrator is an independent official appointed to run a company in financial distress to determine the best course of action on behalf of the company's creditors. They are often appointed voluntarily by directors who hope for a corporate reconstruction to avoid liquidation.

Once in administration, the administrator assesses the company and then reports to the creditors within five business days. They would give creditors three options: terminate the administrator's appointment, wind up the company and appoint a liquidator or approve a 'deed of company arrangement' (a binding arrangement between the company and its creditors about how the company will pay its debts). While it was common that administration would be entered into voluntarily, secured creditors were also allowed to appoint an administrator to a company. Putting aside the veneer of football, the Fitzroy Football Club was a company limited by guarantee, subject to the same fiduciary and legal requirements as any other company. As a secured creditor, the Nauru Insurance Corporation had the means and the opportunity to appoint an administrator to manage the club's affairs if they had reason to believe their loan and the security were not all that secure.

Fitzroy's inquiries about paying less than the full amount of its $1.2 million debt, plus adverse media reporting on the financial health of the club and the country's fiscal predicament had likely prompted Nauru into this radical action. Nauru was undoubtedly aware of the general nature of the club's financial position and knew it needed to wait until Fitzroy received the latest AFL dividend to maximise their potential return. Dyson Hore-Lacy judged Nauru's ultimatum to be an empty threat — if Nauru moved against Fitzroy now, all they would find was a club with no money and few assets. If Nauru wanted to receive any sort of repayment, it needed to wait until Fitzroy merged and the $6 million had flowed into the coffers of the new club. However, Nauru could, if it followed through on its threat, use the administrator to execute a merger itself. To ensure this did not happen, Jeff Browne, the AFL's solicitor, took the equally radical step of informing the Government of Nauru's representatives that the $6 million incentive was now unavailable to Fitzroy.[16]

Ultimatum aside, Hore-Lacy still hoped to reach an amicable agreement with Nauru. He continued presenting debt repayment options, knowing that North Melbourne was limited in what they could offer. Finally, on Thursday, 27 June, they developed a scheme that Graham Sherry seemed to be happy with: they would pay $750,000 at the end of August, then $100,000 per year for the following two years with $50,000 in the third year. With Sherry's apparent endorsement, Hore-Lacy needed to ensure it was acceptable to North Melbourne. On Friday morning, Hore-Lacy unsuccessfully tried to get in touch with Peter De Rauch who was on his way to Perth in preparation for North Melbourne's game against Fremantle that weekend.[17]

...

On Friday, 28 June, those at the club were going about their work as usual. Glenn Warry was preparing to fly to Brisbane to watch Southport Football Club and scout among their younger players for possible recruits.[18] Greg Freemantle had been at the Fitzroy Club Hotel through the day, as had Alan McConnell, who had come in to do some work but had headed home to Research after lunch to clear some vegetation in the back acres of his property. On his way out the door, he saw a man sitting in the foyer. McConnell did not recognise him and thought little of it. Later in the afternoon, having just lit a bonfire, he received a call from the club, telling him that he had better return to work because the club had been placed into administration.[19]

The man McConnell had seen patiently waiting was Michael Brennan, Ernst & Young's National Director, Corporate Recovery. On Wednesday, 26 June, Sherry had approached Brennan about the potential Fitzroy administration, with Brennen eventually agreeing to undertake the task. Following a successful application, the Supreme Court of Victoria officially appointed Brennan as the administrator of the Fitzroy Football Club as at 12.45pm on Friday, 28 June 1996. His first act was to inform Fitzroy. Along with senior manager Mark Sheals and another manager, Greg Swann, Brennan drove to the Fitzroy Club Hotel. After serving the deed of appointment on the club's acting finance manager, Jocelyn Allen, he then waited for finance director John Stewart and the AFL's Director of Football Operations, Ian Collins, to arrive.[20] Part-time receptionist Melanie Gibb had gone down to the hotel's bar to place the staff orders for a late lunch. While there, Collins came in and asked for directions to the Fitzroy Football Club. Unaware of who he was or why he was there, she pointed him upstairs. When she returned to the office, she found it in a panic. By now, the staff knew what was going on.[21] Once Stewart arrived, he joined John Birt, Brennan, Sheals and Collins for a marathon five-hour meeting. At the same time, Swann, a former Australian rules player and current president of VFL side Williamstown, spoke with the staff and some of the players who had come in to the office.[22]

Pursuant with his responsibilities under the *Corporations Act*, it was Brennan's task to investigate the club's financial position and then report to the creditors within five business days. This early investigation would give him an idea of how much of his client's $1.25 million he could recover, and then give the unsecured creditors a sense of what might be left for them. His initial assessments were not promising. Placing the club's total debts at $4.5 million, he could see little cash on hand, no realisable assets and uncertainty about whether the club would collect from their trade debtors. Unless there was some money forthcoming, he said later that evening, the club would be unable to trade.[23] Ordinarily, an administrator in this position would probably look to liquidate the company to salvage whatever remained to pay its debts. Fitzroy, however, had one thing going for it — it retained its licence to play AFL football. This asset, valued at $4 million in the club accounts, was not liquid (i.e. it could not be sold for cash) but Brennan recognised very quickly that it was the key to accomplishing his task.

While no-one could purchase Fitzroy's AFL licence, there was one entity that would pay well over the $4 million for it. The AFL Commission would give Fitzroy (and a second club) $6 million to return their licence and arrange a merger — or at least that had been the case before the AFL withdrew the merger incentive package. Withdrawing the $6 million early in the week had been unsuccessful in preventing

Nauru from appointing Brennan, and it had nevertheless left the administrator with little room to manoeuvre. Beyond undertaking the typical administrator's task of investigating the club, getting the merger incentive back on the table and then merging the club to gain the $6 million became Brennan's primary objective. Assuming the creditors would uphold his appointment, Brennan could use the full power of the board to negotiate a merger, which he could justify if it enabled him to secure additional funds with which to recover the debts of Fitzroy's creditors.

All of a sudden, and to the shock and distress of those at the Fitzroy Club Hotel, Michael Brennan was now the Fitzroy Football Club, although his actions were largely governed by his obligations under Corporations Law. While he worked through the thorny issue of recovering Nauru's debt, he was also responsible for the more mundane task of running the club in lieu of the board of directors. While Brennan was an intelligent man, he was a career accountant and knew little about football administration, which was why Greg Swann was part of his team. As an experienced football man, Swann was to handle the ordinary affairs of the club while Brennan dealt with the higher-level issues.[24]

Meanwhile, Hore-Lacy had learnt of Brennan's presence at the Fitzroy Club Hotel. Stunned, he finally contacted De Rauch and put the repayment offer to him. De Rauch said it was too much, and that North would only provide $550,000. Furthermore, he had been talking to AFL Commissioner Graeme Samuel (who was also aware of Brennan's appointment). Samuel encouraged De Rauch to hold out against Nauru and not sign a merger agreement prematurely, guaranteeing that the North Melbourne/Fitzroy merger would go ahead at the end of the year. If North Melbourne held their nerve, Nauru would get nothing, and there would be an extra million dollars available for the newly merged club. Hore-Lacy told De Rauch that it was a 'huge mistake — and that if North Melbourne put their faith in the AFL, the whole thing would end up in disaster.'[25]

Finally, in the aftermath of their marathon discussion, Brennan and Collins convened a press conference at 6.00pm in a backroom of the Fitzroy Club Hotel. There, Brennan informed reporters that he suspected the club was insolvent, adding that there was 'no money in the bank and no realisable assets on hand'.[26] As expected, they were full of questions, only some of which Brennan was able to answer. Not privy to the backroom negotiations between the major players, reporters asked the obvious question: why had Nauru appointed an administrator? Brennan informed them that Fitzroy 'had committed a number of acts of default and the club had indicated rather unfairly they would pay all other creditors, but Nauruans were asked to accept something less than 50 cents in the dollar'.[27] Beginning his campaign to have the $6 million merger incentive reinstated, he declared that Fitzroy was open for merger offers from any club. Brennan said that his job was to maximise Fitzroy's one real asset, which was its licence to play AFL football, and wanted to come to an accommodation with the AFL, adding 'if the league decides not to help us, that will be the end of Fitzroy'.[28]

...

News travelled quickly across Melbourne. At 5.00pm, John Birt called Michael Nunan and pressed him to come into the office. Passing a growing media pack at the front door, Nunan soon learnt of the club's predicament, his mind no doubt racing as he considered the implications for his own future.[29] Glenn Warry abandoned his trip to Queensland and likewise headed back to the Fitzroy Club Hotel. Fitzroy Supporters' Group member Jan Wright raced into the office and found many of the staff in tears.[30] Alan McConnell called Greg Freemantle, telling him that the club was in a bit of strife.[31] One stunned supporter called up his equally upset mates, and amid their shock and despair, all they could say to each other was 'fuck'.[32]

Newspapers scrambled to put together reports for the front pages of their Saturday papers. Looking to Brad Boyd for comment,

Fitzroy's captain told the *Herald Sun* that he was shocked by the events. He knew the club was struggling with many of its payments, but he did not realise the full extent of Fitzroy's predicament until that day. 'There's no doubt it's just become extremely hard for the players,' he said. 'I just feel sorry for a lot of these young guys who have been put through this ordeal, it's just terrible. It seems to be getting worse now, it's pretty sad.'[33] *The Age* also called players for comment, many of whom knew nothing of what was going on or whether they should even turn up to the Whitten Oval the next day.[34] Simon Atkins heard from his golf partner that news of Brennan's appointment was all over the radio, and he rushed to his car to hear the latest developments.[35] John Rombotis heard on the television that night and became concerned when he heard Nunan say that while he *thought* Fitzroy would still play against Geelong on Saturday, he could not confirm it: if the coach did not know what was happening, how were the players to know?[36] Given the confusion, Glenn Warry became a little anxious, concerned that players would not show up for the game. He wanted to ring them all to check whether they would be at the Whitten Oval the following day, but Brad Boyd told him not to worry and assured him that Fitzroy would field a team.[37]

There would indeed be a game for Fitzroy on Saturday; the AFL had made sure of it. Collins had offered $100,000 to Brennan so that Fitzroy could play their match against Geelong. It was far too late to do anything but pay for the game to go ahead, and if Fitzroy did not play, it would be a breach of its licence agreement.[38] Collins made it clear, however, that there was no guarantee the AFL would extend this largesse forever.[39] There would need to be further discussion at AFL Commission-level about what the AFL would do to support Fitzroy for the remainder of the season, which, if the $100,000 for the Geelong game were any guide, would cost the League at least $1 million.

Driving home that Friday night, Hore-Lacy heard Brennan's 'extravagant' claims regarding the state of Fitzroy's finances. He immediately went on the radio to refute them, specifically the figure that was being thrown around as the club's debt, which he placed at no more than $2.7 million. Brennan, he argued, had projected what the club's debt would be at the end of the year and had ignored any future income, including AFL dividends.[40] He also refuted the suggestion that Fitzroy was insolvent, telling the media that as far as he knew, it had been solvent the day before.[41] It seemed all hell had broken loose, and Dyson Hore-Lacy was right in the middle of it. Talking to the *Herald Sun*, he was 'seemingly on the verge of tears', slamming the 'vindictive act' from Nauru in appointing the administrator. 'Fitzroy's been going for 113 years,' he said, 'and they're not likely to be bowled over by an administrator of a foreign country.'[42]

The following morning, the story dominated the front pages of both *The Age* and the *Herald Sun*, with subsequent pages full of reports, assessments and analyses. The *Herald Sun* noted that it was the first time in VFL/AFL history that an independent body had control of the ultimate destiny of a club.[43] Despite Hore-Lacy's clarifications, many journalists perpetuated Brennan's $4.5 million debt figure. They extrapolated what this would mean, primarily that no club would want to merge with Fitzroy and have the $6 million incentive eaten up by the $4.5 million debt and the $1 million AFL indemnity to complete the season. If Fitzroy were left to collapse, the League would save its $6 million for the next merger (at that stage, likely between Hawthorn and Melbourne).[44] In *The Age*, Anthony Mithen stated it was a 'safe bet' that Fitzroy would not be playing Essendon in Round 14 because he believed it unlikely the AFL would pay another $100,000 to 'put on another show for the living dead'.[45] There were also eulogies and jeremiads. In its editorial, *The Age* called it a sad and tragic day: 'No club deserves to die like this ... Vale Fitzroy. If not this week, then come September.'[46]

For Dyson Hore-Lacy, merger discussions had given way to crisis talks as the order of the day, as he and his board pondered whether Fitzroy would make it to the end of the season, much less find a merger partner to carry on the heritage of the club. On Saturday morning, Hore-Lacy called De Rauch, who was by now in Perth. De Rauch considered that the situation was a disaster.[47] Hore-Lacy, who still felt he had some control of events, wanted to finalise the merger quickly and announce it at the president's lunch before the game against Geelong. North was prevaricating, however, and Hore-Lacy believed they were following the AFL's advice to wait until the end of the year to merge.[48] It was a dangerous gambit.

With all that was going on, Fitzroy's players were still expected to take the field against Geelong that afternoon. On Thursday night, before chaos descended on the club, Nunan and the match committee selected the team for the weekend. Among the ins and outs, 21-year-old Jason Ramsey came in to play his first game. By Saturday morning, he did not know whether it was also to be his last game.[49] In Friday's *The Age*, Anthony Mithen suggested the game could be 'one of the biggest non-events of the year'.[50] Mithen's pronouncement obviously came before the shock of Brennan's appointment, after which the game took on significance neither he nor anyone else could have predicted.

Players arrived at the Whitten Oval as usual and went through their pre-game routines. Shunning his typical approach, Nunan wanted to address his players as soon as they arrived. Directing them straight to the coach's room, he talked to them for about twenty minutes, emphasising that their jobs were stable for the remainder of the season because their contracts were guaranteed by the AFL (although Nunan was not as sure about *his* remuneration). He admitted it was terrible preparation, but encouraged them to just think about the game and treat it like a grand final (appreciating that it might well be the club's last game).[51] Then Brad Boyd stepped up and encouraged the players to stick together, as it seemed like all they had was each other and the match committee.[52] He told his teammates that they were possibly the last team to pull on a Fitzroy jumper and spoke about the club's rich heritage, hoping to use the circumstances to find some extra motivation.[53] Alas, the events of the previous twenty-four hours destabilised, rather than inspired.

What could have been Fitzroy's final game drew a crowd of only 10,504, with the action during the game largely irrelevant compared to the gravity of the events taking place off the field. Playing the Cats would have been difficult in the best of circumstances — now the challenge was practically insurmountable. Geelong had played in three of the previous four grand finals and was an on-field powerhouse with experienced, skilful players. No-one posed as significant a threat as Gary Ablett. Jarrod Molloy contained him reasonably well, holding his own, rarely being out-bodied and keeping him to six goals. Elsewhere on the ground, Primus played well, Bamford was quick, and Johnson was 'occasionally spectacular'.[54] Yet Geelong's midfield was vastly superior to Fitzroy's; the mercurial Garry Hocking was too strong and creative for Brett Chandler and Martin Pike, who finished the game with thirty-five disposals and four goals.[55] Brad Boyd played at centre half-forward, carrying an enormous burden. A frustrated man, his emotions boiled over and several Geelong players told him to 'cool it'. Not taking kindly to receiving advice from players who had no comprehension of the difficulties he faced, Boyd retorted by giving them the finger, which was misinterpreted by field umpire David Ackland as being directed against him. Boyd was reported, adding insult to the ignominy of the situation.[56]

The final result was Fitzroy's largest loss to Geelong, their biggest loss for the season to date and the fourth-worst loss in their history: 6.3 (39) to 25.16 (166). Boyd called it 'a tough day at the office', and reportedly left the ground close to tears. Nunan could not find it in himself to berate his players; he simply acknowledged the circumstances. He believed that his players had 'genuinely tried their hearts out to have a go', and noted that they were playing against a side that had probably played more finals than his team had played games. Summing up how the events of the previous twenty-four hours had affected the players, he said: 'I guess the guys today had to carry 113 years of blood, sweat and tears and it's been a big chore for them.'[57] He knew that the team would turn up for its recovery session on Monday; he knew they would be paid until Thursday, but he knew little else about Fitzroy's future.[58] When asked about possible team changes for the next round, Nunan quipped: 'We're either all in or all out.'[59]

That night, Nunan, the players, with some wives and girlfriends, went out for a drink at Marianna's in North Fitzroy.[60] The night had been organised well in advance, intended to be a chance to gather the team together and try to get back on track for the remainder of the season. Now, it took the form of a wake. The players stuck together and had a good night, trying to forget about the mess that was the Fitzroy Football Club. Nunan let his hair down and took charge of festivities. In an act that was almost far too literal, he encouraged the players to sign their names on the wall at Marianna's, seemingly as the last Fitzroy team.[61] It was apparent to everyone now that the club as they knew it was finished, they just hoped they could play out the remainder of the season and then find clubs for 1997.[62] They ate, drank and sang along with the Jukebox long into the night — what else was there to do in such remarkable circumstances?

CHAPTER TWELVE

THE LONG WEEK

'I've always supported a merger for Fitzroy. I've also felt that the North option was a good option for Fitzroy, but things have changed'

— Kevin Rose, Collingwood president.[1]

Just like that, Fitzroy's fortunes had taken a dramatic and devastating turn. The club's financial state was now terminal and the reckoning, long foretold by those League administrators who wished to encourage the club towards a merger, was here. With no real assets and with minimal cash on hand, the Lions were finished as a professional football club in their own right. Any romantic hope of fighting on had completely evaporated — it was now merge or die. Fitzroy people — from Dyson Hore-Lacy and his board down to the lowliest supporter — were stunned. On Sunday, the Fitzroy Club Hotel was deathly quiet, save the sound of locals playing the poker machines.[2] Optimistically, Hore-Lacy still believed he could sign an agreement with North Melbourne to secure a merger and remove Brennan as the administrator. That Sunday, the board were still in discussions with the Kangaroos about a repayment scheme for Nauru. Convince Nauru that they could repay the $1 million, they reasoned, then Brennan would be satisfied and control of the club could return to its elected officials.[3]

There were, of course, any number of issues with this idealised course of events.[4] For one, North Melbourne appeared to be getting cold feet. Kangaroos officials, Hore-Lacy believed, were being enticed by the idea — allegedly championed by Graeme Samuel — that a merger could be concluded at the end of the year once Fitzroy had effectively been liquidated to repay its debt to Nauru.[5] There were also rumblings of discontent from other clubs, which would only become louder as the week progressed.

The chief problem, however, was Michael Brennan, whose appointment dramatically reshaped the landscape. His appointment had been a heavy blow to Dyson Hore-Lacy and his board, who now had no power to act on behalf of their club. Having worked so hard for so long, the matter was now, whether they wanted to acknowledge it or not, almost completely out of their hands.[6] Furthermore, there would be no single arbiter of the club's destiny. If there was to be a merger, it needed the endorsement of the AFL Commission, the support of other clubs (or at least the lack of a veto from them) and, crucially, a willing merger partner. Among the relevant parties there was broad in principle support for a Fitzroy merger, although each had different motivations behind their support.

Brennan's objectives remained unchanged from Friday afternoon: get the AFL's $6 million back on the table and finalise a merger to enable the best return for Fitzroy's creditors. As far as he was concerned, any and all options were on the table regarding Fitzroy's future. He publicly welcomed any club (not just North Melbourne) approaching him with merger proposals and even had discussions with representatives from Canberra about relocation.[7] Hore-Lacy declared that Brennan lacked the authority to negotiate with anyone, but the administrator thought differently.[8] Ian Collins weighed in, stating that Brennan *was* the Fitzroy Football Club, it was 'his obligation while the licence remains in place to act on behalf of all the creditors. If that means talking to clubs about a merger, he has that right whilst he has the licence.'[9] On hearing that Hore-Lacy still considered himself in charge of merger negotiation, Brennan retorted: 'I can't stop Dyson talking to people, and nor do I intend to, but any merger deal will have to be approved by the AFL and eventually approved by the creditors of the Fitzroy Football Club.'[10]

Brennan also continued to lobby for the reinstatement of the AFL's merger incentive package. For the AFL, having determined that Port Adelaide would be entering the AFL in 1997, there was no risk of having a fifteen-team league if Fitzroy collapsed. In addition, the early indications of the size of Fitzroy's debt suggested that the League could use its $6 million to better effect supporting a different merger later in the year. Many in and around the AFL knew that saving Fitzroy and endorsing its preferred merger with North Melbourne was far from inevitable. Throughout the weekend, AFL officials were equivocal on whether the $6 million would be reinstated. On Saturday night, Ian Collins informed the media that the 'goal posts have been moved' and the AFL needed to 'collate all the options, sit down and work through it' to come up with a 'balanced answer' to the question of whether the incentive package would be available to Fitzroy.[11]

To address this issue, and many others, the AFL Commission called an extraordinary meeting for Monday evening. Privately, AFL administrators were very uncomfortable with the notion of a manager from Ernst & Young running one of their football clubs and wanted the issue dealt with as soon as possible. Genuine empathy for Fitzroy's plight from some Commissioners, as well as the long-term commercial cost the League would incur if it lost thousands of supporters, also compelled the Commission to act quickly. Furthermore, while the League had indemnified the Lions to play against Geelong, the Commission were also uncomfortable with bankrolling the club indefinitely while a solution was found — financing Fitzroy's remaining games might not be worth the cost. Orchestrating a merger would therefore solve many problems, and the $6 million incentive could fund Fitzroy's remaining games (if, as expected, they put it back on the table). There was also the loss of prestige and credibility that would come if a VFL foundation club collapsed entirely during the AFL's centenary season.

Equally important to Fitzroy's fate were the intentions of the other clubs. Despite the consolidation of the League's management under the AFL Commission thanks to the Crawford Report in 1993, the Commission could not admit, expel, relocate or merge a club without consulting the clubs, and a two-thirds majority could veto the Commission if it decided to endorse a merger of which they did not approve. Simply creating an independent commission had not eradicated the intense parochialism of various clubs. If a North Melbourne/Fitzroy merger potentially created a 'super-team', the other clubs might be prepared to let Fitzroy sink into oblivion to avoid the obvious on-field threat.

All of this left Fitzroy, its officials, staff, players and supporters, decidedly not masters of their own fate. They were completely on the outside, unable to have any say in what would become of their club. They, like the rest of the football public, would be watching on as events unfolded. Adding insult to injury, on Sunday evening thieves tried to grab mementoes from the Fitzroy Club Hotel. The hotel manager, Carolyn Hall, heard the sound of glass breaking, and dashed upstairs to find several men unscrewing portraits of past Fitzroy players. The men had been drinking at the bar before deciding to purloin a piece of Fitzroy history. Hall later told the media that the attempted theft had 'added to the pain of the past few days'.[12] Brennan later ordered the removal of all memorabilia from the hotel to protect it.[13] Observers could not help but see it as a grim metaphor.

...

On Monday, the Fitzroy Club Hotel saw a stream of 'long suffering, disbelieving and dispossessed Fitzroy faithful' come to visit, seeking answers or just a sympathetic ear.[14] Volunteers were cleaning up after the attempted burglary, the 1962 team photo on the floor, trailing shards of glass. Some visitors were buying merchandise while it was still available — stubby holders for $8.50, boxer shorts for $29.95, ties for $30 — while others just needed a place to go.[15] Mary and Tom Greensill called in at midday. They had been in the crowd for the 1944 Grand Final, walking from the city to the Junction Oval due to a tram strike. Maree Szymasnki, Beverley Nopper and her mother, Ruby Foley, also came and sat glumly among the old photographs and memorabilia. 'They've wanted Fitzroy out for years,' said Foley bitterly, with no one in doubt about whom she was referring.[16]

Despite the despondent scene at the end of Saturday's match and the potential for it to have been Fitzroy's final game, their chances of playing out the season were much better than some feared. On Saturday morning, Hore-Lacy had been doing the rounds on radio and speaking with journalists, expressing his confidence that the North/Fitzroy merger would still go ahead and that Fitzroy would continue to play for the remainder of the season. On the latter point, he knew what AFL officials knew, that despite the cost of financing Fitzroy's final games, it would ultimately cost more if the Lions did *not* play. In addition to the loss of match-day revenue, due to the players' CBA, the AFL would be underwriting the player payments regardless.[17] He also knew Fitzroy's demise would damage the AFL's credibility, particularly in its celebratory centenary year.[18] Brennan also wanted the AFL to continue underwriting Fitzroy's games to give him more time to complete a merger (when asked about North Melbourne, he told journalists that they were in a 'very prominent position').[19]

In addition to merger discussions, Brennan continued to build a better picture of Fitzroy's financial position. The club was very asset poor indeed, and the peculiarities with the ownership of the Fitzroy Club Hotel confused him. He was unable to put an accurate amount on

Fitzroy's debt (although the $4.5 million figure was still being quoted in the media as gospel) but the bottom line was he needed the merger incentive money. 'If the AFL is serious about encouraging mergers,' he told reporters, 'they should say there is $6 million there — full stop.'[20] He also had many people coming to him with questions. Nunan's first words to him, for instance, were: 'Am I going to get paid?' Brennan was sympathetic, but could only reply: 'I've got no money with which to pay you.'[21]

The players were another consideration. That afternoon, amid sporadic rain, they arrived one by one at the Coburg City Oval wearing work clothes or club tracksuit tops, each with a 'haunted expression', for a 5.00pm meeting with Brennan. A pack of journalists waited outside, with Ron Reed commenting that most players were so anonymous that 'a group of seasoned professional football writers struggled to identify many of them'. A pair of shivering Fitzroy officials locked the gates to keep the media out, and 'the four rows of barbed wire topping the wire-netting made the place look like a concentration camp as the grey night closed in'.[22] Inside, Brennan presented a picture of the state of the club's finances and then Nunan told them that he would find new goals for the team if the AFL decided to keep them on life support for the final nine rounds. Most players wanted to play out the season, but some felt that they had been ignored in all the posturing over the club's future and its finances.[23]

Many players were still trying to comprehend what had happened. When Matthew Primus moved from Norwood to Fitzroy, he had expected the professionalism of the AFL to be a step up from the SANFL. The events since the previous Friday had left him bewildered; was this really happening in Australia's premier football competition?[24] The 24-year-old Matthew Dent had been putting together a good run of form over recent weeks. After his 33-disposal game against Sydney, Nunan described him as 'quite a hard man, a very honest performer', the type that most coaches wanted to accumulate at their clubs.[25] He was now likely hoping that other clubs would indeed be interested in him. Veteran Mick Dwyer just shrugged his shoulders and, 'with a world-weary sigh', was resigned to having his career shaped by forces much larger than himself. Anthony Mellington wanted to finish the season as Fitzroy's leading goalkicker, not least because it would help him attract the attention of potential clubs. Nick Carter, who had only played eight games in his career after coming into the side in Round 6, was just trying to put the drama out of his head and concentrate on establishing himself as an AFL player.[26]

Nunan took the opportunity to talk to the team, signalling his intention to resign if a Fitzroy/North Melbourne merger went ahead. He appreciated that in a merged club, Denis Pagan would undoubtedly be the senior coach, leaving no role for him.[27] Outside, he told the freezing pack of journalists that he was concerned about the players, the human element in what was unfolding, and lamented that they had been forgotten in the wider drama.[28] His players needed 'contact with the future', and wanted North Melbourne (if indeed the expected merger went through) and their football department to look after Fitzroy's players and 'give them a direction where they can have a new focus and a new beginning and play the last nine game for a real purpose.'[29]

Meanwhile, at 6.00pm, the AFL Commission gathered at AFL House for its extraordinary meeting. The purpose of the meeting was to consider three issues: the various options available to them after Brennan's appointment, whether the $6 million merger package would be reinstated and whether the AFL would financially support the Lions for the remainder of the season.[30] Since Friday, Ross Oakley had received several death threats of sufficient seriousness to warrant the intervention of the Victorian Police, about thirty of whom were called to the MCG in response. A 'massive' security operation was put in place for the meeting, including guards at the entrances and others who were dispersed through the Great Southern Stand where the meeting was held.[31]

The Commission's decision making would be guided by what was in the League's overall interests, not necessarily what was in

Fitzroy's best interests.³² It was clearly an option to cut Fitzroy adrift at that point and leave it to the creditors to dismember, but this was unappealing for reasons surmised by Dyson Hore-Lacy. Specifically, the five clubs scheduled to host Fitzroy stood to lose an estimated $2.9 million in revenue. In addition to the cost borne by the AFL in underwriting the players' CBA and the loss of prestige the AFL (and the Commission) would suffer in seeing the demise of Fitzroy, it was clear that the benefits of paying the Lions to play out the remainder of the season outweighed the costs.³³ Other issues, however, were less clear cut.

A merger between Fitzroy and another club (buttressed with $6 million from the AFL) would solve many problems — the complication of Brennan's involvement notwithstanding. The Commission, therefore, wanted some clarity about the state of the current merger discussions between Fitzroy and North Melbourne. Hore-Lacy was granted permission to address the Commission, and he presented the relevant facts about both the merger agreement and the repayment scheme with Nauru.³⁴ In closing, Hore-Lacy said that he held sufficient proxies to carry the vote on the proposed merger and requested that the Commission reinstate the merger package as Fitzroy could reach a settlement with Nauru within twenty-four hours and remove Brennan as the club's administrator.³⁵

Reading the room, Hore-Lacy believed that Graeme Samuel and Terry O'Connor (the champion of non-Victorian clubs) were hostile to Fitzroy and that Oakley was supportive; he could not read the others, including the chairman, John Kennedy.³⁶ Fitzroy's plan relied on North Melbourne's agreement, which remained shaky. After leaving the Commission meeting, Hore-Lacy tried to get in contact with Peter De Rauch to confirm their agreement. Fortuitously, just as Hore-Lacy was calling him, he arrived at the AFL House to meet with the Commission. The two men had a rushed conversation in the foyer and confirmed the arrangement and the repayment plan. Entering the Commission meeting, De Rauch confirmed the details of the merger negotiations, including how the $6 million would be spent ($550,000 for Nauru, $3 million for Fitzroy's other creditors and the remainder for a redevelopment of its Arden Street facilities).[37]

Having heard from Hore-Lacy and De Rauch, the Commission was satisfied that a merger agreement existed between Fitzroy and North Melbourne. The only issue to be resolved was the Nauru debt and, by extension, the removal of Brennan. After further discussion, the Commission agreed to reinstate the merger package and to make it available until 12.00pm on Friday 5 July, on the basis that both Fitzroy and North Melbourne could reach an agreement with the Nauru Insurance Corporation that would immediately terminate Brennan's appointment and finalise the merger agreement. If there was no merger by that time and/or Brennan's appointment had not been terminated, the Commission would retract the merger package for Fitzroy and withdraw all further support to the club, with the exception of financial support to allow it to play its Round 14 game.[38] If the clubs did merge, Fitzroy's operating costs for the remainder of the season would be deducted from the $6 million package.[39]

Crucially, the proposed player rules were explored. On 26 May that year the Commission had agreed that a merged club would have a 54-player list at the end of 1996, to be culled to fifty before the 1997 pre-season draft. After some discussion, the Commission amended these conditions, bringing the deal in line with the merger package presented to the clubs at Leonda in June 1995 — reducing the player list from fifty-four to fifty. Oakley agreed to discuss this change with North Melbourne.[40] Objectively, this was a minor adjustment, as under the 26 May decision, the merged club would need to reduce its playing list from fifty-four to fifty by the start of the 1997 season regardless. The Commission's new agreement would simply cut out the additional four players for the period between October 1996 and February 1997. However, North Melbourne, and Greg Miller in particular, had become strangely fixated on the 54-player list despite the club's obvious lack of need for such on-field incentives. Miller seemingly convinced himself that it had been agreed to at the Leonda meeting and any dilution of this position represented perfidy of the highest order. Despite being a minor matter, it was to become a heated and ultimately consequential issue throughout the week ahead.

As the Commission met, Brad Boyd faced the AFL Tribunal for the first time in his career to answer the charge of making an obscene gesture to a field umpire during Saturday's game. He conceded that his actions were an outworking of the trials he and his teammates were enduring. The stress of being the captain of Fitzroy was beginning to tell on him. All he wanted was to play football, not, as he said, 'Deal with all the politics and all the innuendo I've had to deal with in the past two years.'[41] Sensibly and mercifully, Boyd was cleared. The panel accepted his explanation that he gestured to Geelong's Martin McKinnon who was 'just saying a few things in relation to the situation of the club' and the field umpire just happened to be running past.[42]

Meanwhile, Fitzroy supporters across Melbourne waited anxiously for news of the Commission's deliberations. Knowing that Port Adelaide was entering the competition in 1997, there was no guarantee that the AFL would not simply leave the Lions to their fate. By now, Hore-Lacy had returned home, and, having said his piece to the Commission, sat watching the television waiting for the verdict. During the evening, former director Robert Johnstone arrived with a bottle of Scotch, and the pair had a quiet drink as they waited.[43] Finally, at 11:15pm the marathon Commission meeting concluded, having reached a decision on how to approach the unprecedented situation.[44] Sometime after the end of Channel Seven's *Talking Footy*, Oakley went on television to announce the Friday deadline for Fitzroy and North Melbourne to complete a merger, declaring: 'We've been given certain assurances by both clubs that they're very, very close to a deal. In fact, we assume they have a deal.'[45] Conditioned to think the worst of the AFL Commission, Fitzroy supporters breathed a sigh of relief that their club still clung to life, at least until Friday.[46]

...

Tuesday started positively. The football public arose to the headlines: 'Friday Lions' New D-Day' in *The Age* and 'Deadline — Merge By Friday Noon Or Die — AFL' in the *Herald Sun*.[47] Both Oakley and Brennan expressed confidence that a merger could be done by Friday, while Hore-Lacy and the Fitzroy board believed they had a solid merger agreement with North Melbourne and an acceptable debt repayment plan for Nauru.[48] Less pleased was Brisbane, which remained tenaciously in the discussion. That day, Noel Gordon denounced the Friday deadline, stating that Fitzroy had been 'handcuffed and blindfolded', with its members given no opportunity to have a say in what happened to the club.[49]

Despite the positivity, that morning North Melbourne held a board meeting. Ominously, Hore-Lacy was called shortly afterwards and told that North Melbourne officials wanted to see him, Elaine Findlay and Colin Hobbs that afternoon. Hore-Lacy immediately feared North Melbourne would back out of the deal. That afternoon, the meeting went ahead at Peter De Rauch's Brunswick offices. They discussed many of the details surrounding the merger and the repayment of Fitzroy's creditors, agreeing to meet again early in the evening at Mark Dawson's business in North Melbourne in preparation to meet representatives from Nauru and put the repayment plan to them.[50] So far, nothing was amiss.

During amicable discussions that evening, however, Miller pulled Hore-Lacy aside told him that North Melbourne wanted to reduce the number of Fitzroy representatives on the board of the new club and that Hore-Lacy would not be one of them.[51] Miller argued that recent events had 'tainted' Fitzroy's directors, due to the appearance of financial mismanagement; he offered four Fitzroy members on the new club's board, half the number previously agreed to.[52] After a pause, Fitzroy's president replied that while he did not mind retiring from football administration, 'there will be eight Fitzroy directors and there will be a Fitzroy vice-chairman.'[53] Internally he was 'seething', and relayed the situation to a shocked Findlay and Hobbs. 'I was floored,'

Hore-Lacy later wrote, 'I felt like I had been hit in the back of the head by a sledgehammer.'[54]

Meanwhile, with the merger seemingly certain, Nunan's decision to quit became public. He told the media that the AFL had effectively made the decision for him: 'They've finished me.' He was employed to do a specific job at Fitzroy, he said, and if the club merged than that job was finished. He knew little about the merger negotiations and was 'a bit lost for words' about the whole affair.[55] Nunan was not the only one in the dark. Unrest was fermenting among Fitzroy's players, several of whom were becoming openly frustrated with the lack of information from either the club's board (whom Brad Boyd believed had been 'a bit sketchy' on several details) or the AFL.[56] The AFLPA was also critical of Fitzroy's board for not keeping the players informed.[57] Many had families to support and mortgages to be paid, and, thus far, they had received no official and unequivocal indication from anyone about their short-term future. They just wanted answers.[58]

Soon, some players began to believe the only way they could express themselves with any force was to deny their labour. Rumours circulated about a potential boycott of Saturday's game against Essendon, and Ian Collins, in conjunction with the AFLPA, held a meeting after training at Coburg on Tuesday night. While the AFLPA CEO, Peter Allen, was unable to satisfy the players' questions on the proposed merger with North Melbourne and future payments, Collins could provide some clarity.[59] The AFL's Director of Football Operations reassured them that the AFL would guarantee their payments, regardless of the outcome of the merger discussions.[60] As he went through the details, Fitzroy's younger players just sat with hurt and confused looks on their faces, mouths agape, internally wondering, 'What the hell's going on here?'[61] Yet the concerns of those agitating for a strike had been assuaged, even if some of their teammates were incredulous at the whole notion. Jarrod Molloy understood their anxieties, but he had dreamed of playing for Fitzroy his entire life, and later reflected: 'There was no way I was going to forfeit the chance to wear my Fitzroy jumper.'[62] There was, of course, no telling how many more occasions he would be able to do so.

After one hour, Collins emerged from the meeting confident that the Lions would play on the weekend.[63] Privately, he had also given Brad Boyd an undertaking that he would keep him in the loop about any developments. With the potential revolt snuffed out, Collins hoped they could 'put some sanity back into a matter'.[64] Many players were happier once Collins had addressed them. Stephen Paxman was certainly relieved, with his wife due to give birth to their first child in little over a month's time.[65] Afterwards, Jarrod Molloy remarked pointedly that Collins had answered more questions than their own board.[66] For his part, Nunan likened the players to 'cattle in the pen', a commodity to be argued over, rather than individual people with their own insecurities and concerns. He was also critical that North Melbourne did not plan to release any of their support staff to work at the Lions once Nunan left, due to their understandable preoccupation with trying to win the premiership that season.[67]

Nunan's concern about North Melbourne's treatment of his players after the merger was touching, but premature. Given that the other clubs had the power to veto any proposed merger, the Commission agreed to convene a special meeting of the clubs on Thursday 4 July at 5.00pm to consider the proposed merger.[68] The potential outcome of this meeting was not looking good for Fitzroy. Resistance to the North Melbourne/Fitzroy merger among the clubs had been building for some time, with Leon Daphne leading the charge, fearful that the 'North–Fitzroy Kangaroos' would be a 'super club' and pose a significant on-field challenge.[69]

By Tuesday night, AFL House had informed the clubs of the specific merger details and the concessions the AFL would give to the new club. The notion that the North–Fitzroy Kangaroos would have upwards of fifty players on their list in 1997 was an instant concern. While most clubs continued to publicly express in-principle support for a merger, they were hesitant to endorse this specific deal.

Melbourne's president, Ian Ridley, expressed a common view: 'As we agreed at Leonda last year, all clubs should support a merger, however, I want to see what the ground rules are and ensure they haven't changed before making a decision.'[70] Unfortunately for North Melbourne, currently sitting on top of the AFL ladder, the optics of the merger were not favourable. It would be 'an absolute joke', Daphne told reporters, if clubs could not see it would be 'disastrous' to make North Melbourne stronger through a merger.[71] Melbourne's football manager, Richard Griffiths, thought it would be 'football suicide' for the other clubs to create the proposed 'super team'.[72] Wanting to give the clubs a chance to discuss the matter before they met with the AFL Commission at the MCG on Thursday evening, Daphne called a meeting of club presidents at Punt Road for Thursday afternoon.[73] For all the concerns about player revolts and the breakdown between Miller and Hore-Lacy, this issue was looming as the merger's biggest threat.

...

On Wednesday morning Hore-Lacy called Greg Miller to resolve their disagreement from the previous day. For Hore-Lacy the issue was parity on the board, for Miller it was ensuring no current Fitzroy directors would sit on it — neither could give the other a firm undertaking on either issue.[74] Hore-Lacy, Findlay and Hobbs now believed that North Melbourne officials were trying to maximise their position. Having to part with $3 million in debt repayment from their much-needed $6 million, they set about trying to extract as favourable a deal as they could with Fitzroy, knowing that it had a Friday deadline, the administrator was circling and there was no competition from other clubs (or so they thought).[75] They also likely believed that despite the grumbling, if it came to Friday and no merger was completed, they could convince the other clubs to support their proposal, as the alternative — letting Fitzroy die — was unacceptable to all parties.

The result, as Oakley would later note, was a 'touch of hubris' in how North Melbourne was going about business.[76]

With Hore-Lacy and Miller's issue still unresolved, the financial aspects of the merger also remained to be addressed. Fitzroy and North Melbourne representatives (with a gamut of lawyers in tow) met with Graham Sherry and other Nauru Insurance Corporation representatives in the offices of Baker & McKenzie to confirm that they would accept the debt repayment deal. Sherry indicated that Nauru would accept what Hore-Lacy was proposing, and while Fitzroy and North Melbourne could not secure a final agreement, everyone left the meeting 'well satisfied' that the issue of Nauru's debt was settled.[77]

Despite this, Hore-Lacy's concern remained. The great fear among many Fitzroy supporters, expressed also by several journalists, was that North Melbourne would merely absorb Fitzroy in a 'merger', take the $6 million package and remain, with little adjustment, the North Melbourne Kangaroos.[78] The longer the uncertainty with North played out, the more likely this outcome became in the minds of Fitzroy's directors. They needed options. It had just so happened that on that afternoon, finance director John Stewart called Hore-Lacy to tell him that he had been in touch with Brisbane's CEO, Andrew Ireland, who was still probing the prospect of a Brisbane/Fitzroy merger. Stewart had told him that the deal was practically done with North, but now Hore-Lacy, uncertain about Miller's commitment to their original agreement, asked Stewart to tell Ireland, 'the door is open half an inch'.[79] With this promising news, Gordon and Ireland flew to Melbourne that day and began lobbying club presidents in a bid to have Brisbane's offer heard at the Punt Road Oval meeting.[80] Brisbane believed they had negotiated a merger agreement in good faith back in April, one that was — at the time — acceptable to Fitzroy's board. This gave them a clear conscience in pursuing a merger with Brennan under the same terms. They had a significant advantage too, as one of their board members, Graeme Downie, was an insolvency expert — and would prove a valuable asset for the Bears.[81]

Arriving in Melbourne, Brisbane officials believed that gaining Brennan's support was the key to success. As he was obligated to prefer the deal that would give the creditors the best return, their offer allocated $3.9 million from the merger incentive package to the creditors, with an additional $300,000 earmarked for Brennan's fee as the administrator.[82] Bears officials met with Nauru's representatives, who indicated they would accept Brisbane's repayment scheme. Their offer also included fewer on-field concessions, including a 44-player list to placate the other clubs. The Bears felt this was a winning combination.[83] Brisbane then thrashed out the details with Brennan in Ernst & Young's 25th-floor conference room in the BHP Petroleum Building on Collins Street, giving him a good picture of what a Fitzroy/Brisbane merger would mean for Fitzroy's creditors.[84] By Thursday they were ready to make their case to the other key stakeholders: the AFL Commission and the other clubs.

As if the events of the week were not sufficiently convoluted, on Wednesday, Footscray threw themselves into the fray. Fitzroy's co-tenant at the Western Oval was not pleased with the prospect of the Lions reneging on their 20-year agreement, which would cost the Bulldogs financially (Footscray general manager Dennis Galimberti — the 'unguided missile' of the aborted 1989 Fitzroy/Footscray merger — said that the Bulldogs would stand to lose $1.3 million if Fitzroy reneged on the lease agreement).[85] Footscray president Peter Gordon declared that the club's directors were 'outraged at the duplicity of the Fitzroy Football Club and we feel we owe them no favours'.[86] Having issued a warning earlier in the year about what they would do if it looked like Fitzroy and North Melbourne would merge, on Wednesday, Footscray launched Supreme Court action against the two clubs and the AFL.[87]

Footscray was just the latest club to have objections to the proposed merger. Both major Melbourne newspapers reported tensions among other clubs and disquiet, according to Mike Sheahan, was growing 'by the hour'.[88] The playing list and fears of a 'super club' were the key issues, and North Melbourne were doing themselves no favours. On television Wednesday night, Miller announced that if they could not have fifty-four players then the deal was off. Fitzroy's directors had not been consulted on Miller's pronouncement, and its implications concerned them greatly.[89] With Miller sticking obstinately to his preferred list size, Dyson Hore-Lacy considered that North was now 'running its own race' and he could not understand Miller's insistence on this aspect of the deal, even in the face of clear opposition.[90] To Miller, it had become a matter of principle that the Commission and the other clubs should honour the spirit of the Leonda agreement. Furthermore, the North Melbourne board had made itself vulnerable by seeking a merger with Fitzroy. Miller assumed that, in doing so, North had the support of the AFL Commission, which had previously stated that a merger between two Melbourne-based clubs was its top strategic priority — a fact that seemingly galvanised Miller's resolve.[91]

Facing problems on several fronts, Ross Oakley hoped reason would trump parochialism.[92] There was much riding on the merger from the AFL's perspective and they needed to see it completed successfully and (if possible) amicably to pave the way for one or two future mergers. Oakley went on radio, suggesting that Thursday's meeting of club presidents at Punt Road was a referendum on the future of mergers. With a club on the brink of extinction, if this merger did not go ahead 'it's going to be pretty difficult to get two other clubs together if they know that the clubs are going to put them through this sort of situation'.[93] None of this boded well for Fitzroy's players, staff and supporters; those with significant stakes in the unfolding events but who were powerless to influence them. They were spectators in the decision that would affect them and generations of Roys to come. Thursday, 4 July, would bring matters to a head in the most dramatic fashion. 'All Fitzroy could do,' Oakley later wrote, 'was hope for the best.'[94]

CHAPTER THIRTEEN

ONE DAY IN JULY

'For strategic reasons, Ron'
— John Kennedy senior, AFL Commission chairman.

On the morning of 4 July, the Fitzroy Football Club's board of directors (with the exception of Greg Basto) gathered for a breakfast of toast and orange juice at the Victorian Commercial Teachers' Association building in Collingwood. The directors were at the end of a long journey. After years of dancing between merger negotiations and promises of financial salvation, the matter had been brought to a head with the appointment of an administrator. Providing Fitzroy with a final opportunity to merge before the club disappeared into oblivion, on Monday night the AFL Commission had endorsed the 'North–Fitzroy Kangaroos' in principle, and left it to the two clubs to get the deal done before midday on Friday. A merger with the Kangaroos remained Fitzroy's preference, even despite the recent turmoil caused by North Melbourne's officials. For due diligence, however, the directors again examined the Brisbane Bears' offer, sent through in its latest iteration the previous day. There were, they admitted, some attractive aspects of this deal, but ultimately it could not compare to the prospect of remaining in Melbourne — a factor that trumped almost everything else. To complete the merger, Fitzroy's officials needed a rapprochement with North Melbourne before the Commission's Friday deadline.[1]

In preparation for the merger to be completed on Friday, the AFL Commission had called a General Meeting of the Clubs at the MCG at 5.00pm that evening, where club presidents had the chance to veto the merger should that be their preference. Despite a decade of centralisation, the clubs still retained significant power when it came to decisions about their own. To allow the clubs to debate the issue in advance, Richmond's president, Leon Daphne, had organised a preparatory meeting at Punt Road Oval for 3.00pm. Dyson Hore-Lacy would attend as a courtesy, although he would not be able to vote on behalf of the Fitzroy Football Club.

As far as Hore-Lacy and the other board members were aware, the only purpose of the meeting was to give the presidents the opportunity to discuss the potential Fitzroy/North Melbourne merger. Right now, the signs did not look good that it would have the necessary support. During the morning, AFL solicitor Jeff Browne called Hore-Lacy and told him that, based on a recent straw poll, the merger would likely be vetoed if Greg Miller persisted with his demands for a 54-player list.[2] Daphne, who appeared to be leading the opposition, put it more bluntly the previous day. When asked what chance the merger had of being approved in its present form, he replied: 'None.'[3] For what it was worth, *The Age* condemned the clubs' concern about the extended playing list as 'churlish', questioning whether they were motivated by 'jealousy, naked self-interest or even schadenfreude'.[4] At best, their resistance seemed to be a negotiating position, a hard line so that the concessions in the merger agreement could be softened. Many clubs found it ridiculous that the team on the top of the ladder receive an expanded player list and extra allowances in the salary cap. A more reasonable outcome, many suggested, was for the new entity to have a 42-player list and the same salary cap as the other clubs.[5]

Greg Miller would have none of it, however, and stuck obstinately to his preferred list size. Miller was playing 'a most dangerous game of brinkmanship', Hore-Lacy subsequently wrote, yet despite his public defiance, he was becoming concerned.[6] When Hore-Lacy called him to relay Browne's information, the Fitzroy president detected a hint of anxiety in Miller's voice.[7] This could also have been due to the rumours that Brisbane was back in the hunt, and the complications that would create should it be true. While the public resistance from the other clubs worried Fitzroy's representatives slightly, when push came to shove, they probably believed that it was unlikely the other clubs would simply cast Fitzroy adrift. Instead, all parties would likely agree to reduced concessions for the new team and the agreement would be supported by the clubs. This reasoning would be completely undermined if there was another option for the clubs to consider. In the *Herald Sun*, Mike Sheahan, asked, 'Why is Fitzroy's fate simply a matter of a union with North Melbourne or oblivion?'[8] Few could doubt which other potential merger partner Sheahan had in mind for Fitzroy.

Brennan, meanwhile, had other responsibilities to attend to before he could address the merger question directly. As the administrator, he was legally obligated to meet with the creditors within five business days of administration commencing to give them the opportunity of either removing him or appointing another administrator. Brennan called this meeting for Thursday morning at the Fitzroy Town Hall.[9] Many creditors had no affiliation with Fitzroy beyond their commercial arrangements, although Michael Nunan, Glenn Warry and Jason Baldwin attended on behalf of the players and staff. As the creditors filed in, they passed the waiting media, which had become a permanent fixture nearby at every Fitzroy-related event. One supporter, who had been following the Roys since 1929, lamented his club's demise, but believed it was an inevitable result of the 'whims and fads of the capitalist system'.[10]

Inside, Brennan updated the creditors on the various merger offers, noting that the players and employees would be paid in full, and, with a small accommodation from Nauru, a modest dividend would remain for unsecured creditors.[11] When the formal vote was taken, the creditors determined to retain Brennan as the administrator — a tacit endorsement of his pursuit of a merger.[12] After less than half an hour, he emerged from the Fitzroy Town Hall informing the waiting media that he had two legs of his trifecta — a viable merger plan and the support of the club's creditors. All that remained, he said, was approval from the other AFL clubs.[13]

While Brennan was at the Fitzroy Town Hall, Footscray general manager Dennis Galimberti began a two-hour-long stint in the witness box at the Supreme Court. He sought an injunction against the North Melbourne/Fitzroy merger until the resolution of their claim for damages was resolved.[14] Lawyers for the AFL, North Melbourne and Fitzroy (and the administrator) accused Footscray of abusing the court process with an 'absurd' legal challenge in an attempt to jump the queue of Fitzroy's creditors. Julian Burnside QC, representing Footscray, said that they were not trying to stop the merger and the club would be happy for the newly merged entity to play their home games at the Whitten Oval. Much later in the day, Justice George Hampel dismissed their request for an injunction as Footscray could seek to recover its losses by a claim for damages.[15]

Back at the VCTA building, Ken Montgomery, a former North Melbourne CEO and current financial controller, arrived with the final settlement of the merger agreement. Having again given the Brisbane offer serious thought, Fitzroy's board remained committed to merging with North Melbourne. In an 'extremely emotional moment', the Fitzroy directors expressed their disappointment at the recent events, particularly Miller's interventions. Montgomery apologised on behalf of North Melbourne, and he said their directors were decent people just trying to get the best for their club. At 2.00pm, they signed the final agreement, which retained the provision for a 54-players list, offered Fitzroy's creditors $2.9 million from the incentive package and retained the original composition of the board of directors.[16] Once signed, Fitzroy had a formal merger document and an agreement to settle the Nauru debt. Hore-Lacy now needed to make his way to Punt Road Oval to learn whether the final piece of the puzzle, the endorsement from the other clubs, would be forthcoming.

Colin Hobbs drove Hore-Lacy to Punt Road and he arrived just before 3.00pm, slipping through a back entrance to avoid the media crowd.[17] He was followed not long after by Ross Oakley, in something of a surprise appearance. Apart from Footscray president Peter Gordon, who was still at the Supreme Court, the clubs (and Brennan) had assembled.[18] Daphne opened proceedings, and then Brennan addressed the meeting, updating them on the state of affairs with regards to Nauru.[19] Before the merger discussions began in earnest, Oakley took an informal vote on whether the clubs believed that the AFL should financially support Fitzroy to play out the season. He made the case that not only would it be embarrassing for the AFL in its centenary season, but the loss of fixtures would cost more than that required to bail out Fitzroy for the remainder of the year. With Oakley's strong support, the club presidents agreed unanimously. Oakley then left the meeting and headed back to the MCG.[20]

Then the real debate started. The North Melbourne/Fitzroy merger was put up for discussion, and, unsurprisingly, the other clubs baulked at North Melbourne's demand for a 54-player list. Miller reminded the meeting that they had all agreed to similar conditions the previous year, and whatever on-field advantages the merged club would have in the short-term would be diluted entirely in five years or so.[21] As reasonable as this latter suggestion was, it failed to penetrate the clubs' immediate self-interest. Even without the merger, North Melbourne was a formidable team that had made Preliminary Finals in 1994 and 1995 and was currently 10–3 in the 1996 season. Giving this team on-field concessions scared the other clubs sufficiently for them to withdraw into narrow parochialism. After debating for about half an hour, they took a poll. The club presidents voted down the North Melbourne/Fitzroy merger unanimously (14-1, North voted in favour and Brennan, on behalf of Fitzroy, did not vote).[22]

The meeting then took a sudden turn. Earlier, when running the gauntlet of reporters as he entered the Punt Road offices, Leon Daphne had been thoroughly unconvincing in his declaration that the meeting would only discuss the Fitzroy/North Melbourne merger. He clearly wanted a more agreeable Brisbane/Fitzroy merger on the agenda and, much to Hore-Lacy's surprise, such a proposal was now up for discussion.[23] Noel Gordon presented his offer, which included $3.9 million for Fitzroy's creditors and a 44-player list in 1997. North Melbourne officials rapidly reformulated their position, putting forward the same deal as Brisbane with regards to player concessions and matching the $3.9 million offer to the creditors, but Daphne refused to allow the meeting to consider it formally, deeming it unfair to Brisbane.[24] Outside the building, word spread among the assembled media that Brisbane's bid to merge with Fitzroy was gaining momentum.[25]

Meanwhile, at 4.00pm Ross Oakley had returned the MCG and made his way to Level 2 of the Great Southern Stand to the AFL House boardroom. As the club presidents were debating the Fitzroy/North Melbourne merger, the AFL Commission convened to discuss the matters at hand. The full Commission was in attendance for this historic meeting: the chairman, John Kennedy senior, Colin Carter, Ron Evans, Wayne Jackson, Ross Oakley, Terry O'Connor and Graeme Samuel, as well as Ian Collins and the AFL's Finance Manager, Kevin Lehmann. To begin proceedings, Oakley advised that he had addressed the meeting at Punt Road and not only was there now a Brisbane merger proposal, but it was likely North Melbourne would withdraw and revise its original proposal before presenting it for consideration.

A General Meeting of Clubs had been scheduled for 5:00pm, but as there were now two offers to consider, the Commissioners believed they needed time to evaluate both and deliberate on which to endorse and place before the clubs. Michael Brennan soon joined the meeting and advised that while a majority of club presidents had endorsed a merger in principle, they had overwhelmingly rejected North Melbourne's original offer.[26]

Back at Punt Road, St Kilda's president, Andrew Plympton, suggested that the matter should go to Brennan and the Commission, and once they had decided on a preference, it could be presented to the clubs for their veto. Most agreed to this proposal, and at 4.45pm the meeting concluded without any real resolution.[27] At 5.00pm, one representative for each club (with the exception of North Melbourne and Brisbane which had larger delegations), accompanied by a healthy number of reporters and cameras, made their way to the MCG.[28] As he walked through Yarra Park, Miller knew his bid was in trouble. The meeting had been disastrous, and with Brisbane firmly in contention he had little confidence that the Commission would continue to endorse the North Melbourne proposal. He held out hope that John Kennedy, being an honourable man, would exercise moral leadership of the Commission and see that it stuck to the position it had endorsed on Monday night, but this would likely not be enough.[29] The club representatives entered the AFL offices in the Great South Stand, aware that their responsibilities were far from over. The North Melbourne and Brisbane delegations were sequestered in separate offices while Dyson Hore-Lacy was left out in the foyer. The media loitered outside, waiting to hear how events unfolded.

At 5.10pm the Commission reconvened. Both the League's governing body, as well as its clubs, had originally faced a binary decision: reject or accept the North Melbourne merger, with rejection meaning Fitzroy's demise. Now, with another suitor in contention, discarding the North Melbourne option did not necessarily mean the end for Fitzroy. In debating the merger, the issue for the clubs was predominantly about on-field competitiveness; for the AFL, the implications of their decision were far more strategic. Before the Commissioners could deliberate properly, however, they needed both North Melbourne's revised offer and Brisbane's offer in writing.[30] Brennan knew that the Commission wanted a decision that night. While he technically had until noon the following day to pursue the best deal for Fitzroy's creditors, he was put on notice that Fitzroy's licence was terminable at will. Therefore, without the money or the time, he needed to conclude the matter that evening by gaining a merger that was acceptable to both the Commission and the clubs.[31] Dutifully, he left the boardroom and moved between the two contenders. The North Melbourne delegation wrote up their proposal, handicapped by a lack of legal and financial expertise on hand. Brisbane's offer was already a well-considered legal document, buttressed by Graeme Downie's expert advice.

The issue for Brennan was how large a slice of the $6 million would be available to pay off the club's creditors, as he was obliged to support the offer with the higher amount. Both clubs now effectively offered Brennan $3.9 million, which would cover the creditors plus Fitzroy's operating costs for the remainder of the season. Crucially, Downie had suggested that Brennan's fee sit outside this amount, decreasing what would be left over for the merged club at the end of the process but increasing the total available for creditors. As far as Brisbane could tell, North Melbourne's figure incorporated Brennan's fee, although both groups were in the dark about what the other was offering, as Brennan moved between the two trying to play them off against each other.[32]

Once Brennan collected the final proposals he took them to the Commission. Despite North Melbourne saying they would match Brisbane's offer, there were some differences between the two. Beyond shareholder technicalities for North Melbourne, the Brisbane proposal included salary cap increases whereas the North Melbourne proposal required none. Brisbane's offer included both an arrangement with the Fitzroy Club Hotel (which would prove problematic) and an agreement to pay Brennan's remuneration and costs; the North Melbourne proposal included neither.[33] Both clubs had made different arrangements with Nauru, and both had indicated they had Nauru's consent. Brennan was satisfied with both offers, and informed the Commission that Brisbane's deal was better for Fitzroy's creditors and was more likely to be approved by the clubs. He further indicated that he would accept either agreement, however, on the basis that he needed a merger for the $6 million, and if Fitzroy collapsed there would be very little left to repay anybody anything.[34]

As the Commission meeting continued and evening set in, outside the MCG, the assembled pack of media representatives kept the public updated with what little scraps of information were available. Reporting for Channel Ten, Peter Donegan advised, 'It does seem increasingly likely that a merger will take place, it's just a matter now of whether it is North Melbourne or whether it is Brisbane.'[35] One man who had no say in that decision was Dyson Hore-Lacy. No-one came to him to canvas his view or that of the other Fitzroy directors.[36] He called the other board members back at the VCTA to inform them of events and to ensure that they were still unanimous in their preference for North Melbourne. At some point, he told Oakley, but the CEO:

> did not seem to be interested at all. At this stage I may well have been an insect on the wall as far as anyone at AFL House was concerned. On that fateful evening, I do not recall ever feeling so irrelevant — nobody seemed at all interested in the views of the Fitzroy directors about the future of their club. It was quite obvious that the decision was going to be made solely on what the AFL considered to be in its best interests.[37]

It was a clear demonstration about the AFL's priorities.

Once the Commissioners received Brennan's recommendation, they debated the merits of both proposals, including their relative strategic benefits.³⁸ Brennan favoured Brisbane, and the other clubs were clearly against a North Melbourne merger. Both options would achieve the Commission's aim of reducing the number of clubs in Melbourne and make space for Port Adelaide. The only question was which club, North Melbourne or Brisbane, would receive the benefits of a merger? Given the Commission's aim of growing the game outside Victoria (as laid out in its five-year plan from August 1994), the choice was obvious.

The Commission revoked their endorsement of the Fitzroy/North Melbourne merger and resolved to accept the Brisbane offer. John Kennedy personally advised North Melbourne of the decision. Knowing it was all over, a 'shaken and disappointed' Ron Casey told Kennedy that North Melbourne would withdraw from any further discussion on the merger proposals.³⁹ Casey asked Kennedy why the Commission favoured Brisbane. 'For strategic reasons, Ron,' was his reply.⁴⁰ The North Melbourne delegation swept out of the AFL offices and passed Hore-Lacy, with Casey uttering the words 'we've lost' as he went by.⁴¹

The Commission's decision now needed to be put to the clubs to give them the chance to exercise their veto. This required some minor procedural dexterity. They convened a General Meeting of the Clubs at 6.20pm, and North's departure left fifteen clubs in attendance.⁴² Kennedy informed them that the original purpose of the meeting had been to let the clubs veto the first North Melbourne/Fitzroy merger. He then said that in light of subsequent events the Commission had revoked their original decision so there was no need for the clubs to consider it, and closed the meeting five minutes after it began.⁴³ Kennedy then gave notice of a further meeting to discuss the Commission's subsequent decision endorsing the Fitzroy/Brisbane merger. The clubs waived the period of requisite notice. Oakley then outlined the various aspects of the Fitzroy/Brisbane merger, including the 44-player list. He said that the Commission had reached its decision based on what it determined was best for the competition, what best fitted the AFL's strategic direction, that Brennan favoured it and that it preserved more of Fitzroy's tradition. He then gave the clubs the opportunity to veto the merger, but none did.[44] This merger, apparently, was much more palatable.

Nothing legal was signed, that would take another month to sort out, and the Commission still needed to nuance several issues. Still, the die was effectively cast. As the club representatives and the AFL Commission consigned Fitzroy to Queensland to join Gordon and his Brisbane team, Patrick Smith saw Hore-Lacy sitting outside the AFL offices in the Great Southern Stand, head cupped in his hands, 'a devastated man.'[45] After all of their efforts, Hore-Lacy thought, Fitzroy was finished.[46] He withdrew from the MCG and returned to a waiting Colin Hobbs, who drove the defeated president back to the other directors.[47] They subsequently went to the Office Inn Hotel on Wellington Street and watched Oakley, Daphne, Gordon and Brennan holding a press conference, 'gloating' at Brisbane's success. Gordon was throwing his head back and laughing, saying 'it's never over until the fat lady sings.'[48] 'It was a pretty dismal night, that night,' Colin Hobbs recalled years later. Pretty dismal indeed.[49]

CHAPTER FOURTEEN

A MIXED RESPONSE

'What are we going to do now?'

— Nicole, Fitzroy cheer squad member.[1]

Well away from the historic meetings at the MCG that Thursday evening, Michael Nunan was putting his players through a training session at the Coburg City Oval for the final time. They knew they would be paid for the remainder of the season regardless of how the merger discussions played out, but they retained a vested interest in the outcome. Some would undoubtedly be picked up by the newly merged club; others might find new clubs through the draft. Some probably realised that their chances of playing again in 1997 had diminished markedly since 28 June. Everyone was probably hungry for information, which, in the mid-nineties, was not at their fingertips. Brad Boyd had found himself with a friend in a high place. That afternoon he had met with Ian Collins, who filled him in on many of the recent developments in the merger talks, including that Brisbane was back in contention. During training, Boyd was able to share the news, making it sound as if Brisbane and North Melbourne were fighting over them (a scenario that he later thought was 'good for morale').[2]

The match committee still needed to select the team for Saturday's game against Essendon. Given the circumstances surrounding the Geelong game, it was unfair to punish anyone for their performances, but, until the very end, Nunan was a hard taskmaster. He made three changes to the team: Brett Chandler suffered a bruised rib the previous week and had not recovered, while Simon Hawking's two-possession game saw him dropped along with Adam McCarthy. The 24-year-old McCarthy had arrived at the Lions from North Melbourne at the end of 1994 as part of the trade for Matthew Armstrong. He had played thirteen games under Bernie Quinlan but could not find favour under Nunan. He was not to know it, but the previous week was his last game of AFL football. Coming in were John McCarthy, Danny Morton and Mick Dwyer, all of whom Nunan played forward in his ultimately futile quest to find a potent forward set-up.

At the end of the training session, the players were unable to enjoy their customary supper as their caterer was one of the club's numerous unsecured creditors. Most dispersed, but Boyd took several down to Fasta Pasta in Bell Street for a late meal.[3] While he was ordering his dinner, his mobile phone rang. Unable to get to his phone, Trent Cummings picked it up and answered with a blunt: 'Who's this?' It was Collins who, true to his word, was calling to tell Boyd the result of the AFL Commission meeting. The players went quiet as Boyd took the phone and listened to Collins give a run-down on the evening's events. As soon as he hung up, Boyd gave them the news. Several in the group instantly knew that they would not be playing for the Brisbane Lions the following season.[4] For Boyd, the announcement brought relief — with all the speculation and uncertainty of the previous days, weeks, months and even years, there was now a clear indication of Fitzroy's future. After letting the news sink in, the players began planning a 'farewell to Fitzroy' party after their final game.[5] Their coach did not have the same connections at AFL House, and Nunan only learnt of the news from an AFL employee when he phoned through the Lions' team for Saturday's game just after 7.00pm that evening.[6]

In the much warmer city of Brisbane, the Bears had also just finished up training, preparing to play ninth-placed Adelaide on Saturday night. Away from Melbourne, the Bears were not exposed to the gamut of media reporting on the merger issue, leaving their coach, John Northey, completely oblivious about what was happening at the MCG. For all he knew, Fitzroy and North Melbourne would soon be signing a merger agreement. Leaving the rooms, he ran into defender Darryl White, who told 'Swooper' that the merger had gone through. Assuming this referred to Fitzroy and North, Northey was stunned when White told him what had actually transpired.[7] He was in his first year as Brisbane's senior coach, and practically overnight his club had changed. Coaching a merged team in 1997 was not something he was expecting and even with the smaller merger package Brisbane had secured, there would be some dramatic changes to the club. Down in Melbourne, Andrew Ireland had tried to get in touch with the club back in Brisbane to give them the news before they saw it on television, eventually being able to tell them: 'Get ready — all hell is about to break loose.'[8]

Back at AFL House, those staff who had not already left the office helped set up a space to hold an impromptu press conference in one of the unused conference rooms. At the end of a long boardroom table, staff erected a media banner emblazoned with Coca-Cola branding and the gaggle of journalists and cameramen who had been patiently waiting around the Jolimont precinct since mid-afternoon packed into the modestly sized room. The North Melbourne delegation used it first, with Ron Casey and Greg Miller giving the waiting media their version of events while the final Commission proceedings were underway. Seeing Casey on television later that night, Hore-Lacy thought he looked 'terrible', while Trevor Grant wrote in the *Herald Sun* that his 'deeply-lined face showing the signs of a torrid few weeks, did his best not to show his anger'.[9]

Once the final Commission and club presidents' meetings finished, it was appropriate to make a formal announcement. For Oakley, this was a moment to savour. Ever since the Blue Report of 1985, it had been an article of faith among many Commissioners that mergers were a necessity if the League was to thrive. Some clubs had reluctantly come around to their way of thinking, driven by self-preservation rather than broader strategic thinking. Still, at the grassroots level, many supporters held Oakley and the Commission in contempt for what they were trying to do. Now, after years of being ridiculed and scorned by supporters, after the anger around the aborted Fitzroy/Footscray merger and the 'Up Yours Oakley' stickers, of being treated as if he was destroying the league he ran, he had a significant victory. Sitting down in the glare of cameras and surrounded by microphones and tape recorders, he allowed himself to enjoy the moment, for he had good news to proclaim.

'The Commission met this evening and approved a merger relationship with the Brisbane Football Club and the Fitzroy Football Club,' he declared, slightly faltering with his words as if to ensure he conveyed the gravitas of his pronouncement.[10] Sitting to his left, beaming like a Cheshire cat, was Noel Gordon. To his right was Michael Brennan, who legally represented Fitzroy and who was no doubt relieved that he now had a considerable sum of money to execute his responsibility as administrator. Leon Daphne, the face of the other clubs' opposition to the Fitzroy/North Melbourne merger, rounded out the quartet. As Oakley broke the news, it was telling that no actual Fitzroy person was representing the club. Marginalised all evening, Dyson Hore-Lacy had left the MCG a defeated man. It was a poignant sign, as if anyone was still in doubt, that what happened to Fitzroy was not of its choosing.

While the final details and agreements were to be worked out in the coming days, the merger was effectively finalised that night. During the press conference, in something of a Freudian slip, Oakley called the merger a 'corporate takeover', which more accurately described what would transpire. No new club would be created. Instead, the Brisbane Bears would officially become the 'Brisbane Bears — Fitzroy Football Club Limited' (subject to approval by the Bears members) and would trade as the 'Brisbane Lions Australian Football Club'. The Brisbane Lions were to respect the traditions of Fitzroy, incorporating much of Fitzroy's modern identity into the new club.[11] They would wear the existing Fitzroy jumper for away games for the first seven seasons, with the 'FFC' emblem replaced by the Fitzroy lion. There would be a new design for home games, and in seven years, the club would play all their games in predominantly Fitzroy colours (to be approved by the AFL). The club logo would use the Fitzroy lion 'in perpetuity' with three Fitzroy nominees appointed to the eleven-person board of the new club.[12]

On the vexed issue of on-field incentives, the Brisbane Lions would have an initial list of forty-four players in 1997 (with at least eight from Fitzroy as priority picks), reduced back to forty-two in 1998. They would have a $300,000 increase in their salary cap for 1997, eased off to $200,000 in 1998 and $100,000 in 1999. They would play eleven games at the Gabba and as many Victoria-based away games as possible, but no fewer than six at the MCG or Princes Park. After the merger, an appropriate entity would act as trustee of the Fitzroy memorabilia and also represent the interests of the Fitzroy members.[13]

In his contribution to the press conference, Michael Brennan went through some of the financial details. The Nauru Insurance Corporation had agreed to a settlement where they received ninety cents in the dollar. He said Fitzroy's staff and players would receive everything owed to them, and that evening the AFL wrote him a $400,000 cheque to meet Fitzroy's outstanding player payments. There would, he hoped, be a 'significant dividend' left for Fitzroy's unsecured creditors. Match expenses for Fitzroy's final games would come out of the $6 million merger package.[14] Noel Gordon indicated that once all the creditors had been satisfied the Brisbane Lions would have $2.5 million from the incentive package.[15] More than that, however, they had gained a measure of history and tradition by incorporating a 113-year-old Melbourne institution into their club and hoped to establish a supporter base of thousands of Fitzroy fans in Melbourne (which came with all manner of positive financial benefits). For Gordon and Ireland, this was reward for effort.

The question front of mind for journalists at the press conference, as well as thousands of football-interested members of the general public, was how did Brisbane, seemingly ruled out of contention some time ago, secure the long sought-after merger with Fitzroy? Significant credit was due to Gordon and his team, who doggedly stayed in the hunt long after their quest seemed a forlorn hope. Once the door reopened for them during the week, they took full advantage, lobbying both the other clubs to have their case heard and Brennan to show that a Brisbane deal would be favourable for Fitzroy's creditors. While Gordon attributed this latter tactic as the reason Brisbane emerged victoriously, he perhaps overstated his tactical brilliance.[16] Brennan eventually endorsed Brisbane over North Melbourne, yet he indicated to the Commission that either deal was acceptable. Tellingly, he supported the Brisbane deal in part because it was more likely to be endorsed by the other clubs — a much more important factor. As such, it is unclear what impact his preference had among Commissioners. After all, Brennan needed them more than they needed him.

The likely veto of any North Melbourne merger and the clear strategic benefits to the AFL of a Brisbane merger were just as influential in the Commission's thinking, if not more so, than Brennan's preference. Of all three factors, the opportunity to bolster the AFL's position in Queensland was likely the key issue. Indeed, at the press conference, Oakley declared that from the Commission's perspective a Fitzroy/Brisbane merger was the best outcome for the competition and fit into their strategic plan.[17]

North Melbourne officials offered another reason for the success of the Brisbane bid — the perfidy of the AFL Commission. As far as the Kangaroos were aware, the AFL's strategic plan had been to merge weaker Melbourne-based clubs to bolster their financial viability in the long-term. They had developed a negotiating position based on their interpretation of this aim and the Leonda agreement. Doing so exposed the board to criticism from inside and out, but they weathered the storm in part because they thought they had the endorsement of the Commission and the in-principle support of the clubs based on what all parties had seemingly agreed to in 1995. When the Commission was presented with two relatively equal proposals, however, they rejected their stated preference of a merger between Melbourne-based clubs and opted for the more attractive Queensland option. For North Melbourne, watching the Commission withdraw their support at the eleventh hour was galling. Many years later, Miller said of the AFL: 'They led us down the path, they promised us everything, they lied to us and at the end of the day they jilted us.'[18]

However, the idea that the Commission was free to choose between two options ignores the fact that the other clubs were openly hostile to North Melbourne, a scenario largely of North's own making. While the Commission can be accused of mixed-messaging when it came to the playing list (deciding one number in May and then revising it at the start of July), it was North Melbourne that pushed so hard for a list concession over and above what the other clubs had agreed to in 1995. Brisbane had been smart enough to appreciate that regardless of what had been agreed to previously, when the actual question was put before the other clubs they would never approve such a large expansion of a playing list. Dyson Hore-Lacy later called North Melbourne's insistence on the larger playing list 'stupidity', and argued that had they withdrawn it, the North Melbourne/Fitzroy merger would have gone ahead.[19] This would likely only have worked if done earlier, before discontent and resistance had time to grow. By Thursday, 4 July, when North Melbourne recalibrated its offer at the Punt Road meeting to match Brisbane, the other clubs were now fully antagonistic to a North Melbourne merger seemingly regardless of the list size.

Timing was not North Melbourne's friend. The Kangaroos had the misfortune of petitioning their competitors for an array of advantages right at a time when it was an on-field powerhouse. North Melbourne had made the finals for the previous three years and looked like an ominous proposition in 1996. Despite Brisbane's finals debut in 1995, the other clubs were clearly not concerned about the Bears to the same extent. To be sure, this was woefully short-sighted. As one reporter wrote the following day, 'A crucial long-term issue that will define the future of the competition into the next century came down to a matter of six or ten players who may not be around in five years' time.'[20] Still, making their decisions in this manner was the clubs' prerogative.

For their part, the clubs likely felt no remorse for going against the wishes of Fitzroy's board and kyboshing their preferred deal with North Melbourne. Disingenuously, during Oakley's press conference, Leon Daphne declared that the clubs were not prepared to let Fitzroy die 'without some opportunity to have a merger under satisfactory conditions'.[21] The conditions clearly needed to be satisfactory for them, not the Lions. Ultimately, however, they had the final say — not North Melbourne and certainly not Fitzroy. Daphne sat at the press conference no doubt satisfied that he had done his part to prevent a 'super team' from challenging Richmond's rise to glory. Greg Miller may well have had a wry smile five years later watching Richmond lose to the Brisbane Lions in the 2001 Preliminary Final by sixty-eight points.

It is also important to consider that Brisbane had re-entered the merger race not due to the Commission's intervention but due to North Melbourne's decision to change the number of Fitzroy representatives on the board of the merged club. The assumption from North Melbourne officials that they had no competition might have proved fatal. The Kangaroos may have hoped that despite the objections of the other clubs, the Commission would force the issue, preferring to see the Fitzroy/North Melbourne merger with the other clubs' complaints rather than have Fitzroy disappear completely. Opening the door for Brisbane destroyed this favourable calculus. Finally, it must be remembered that the North Melbourne-Fitzroy merger *did* have the Commission's support at the start of July, until it became clear that the other clubs would not countenance a Kangaroos merger. At that point, if the Commission wanted its merger, it would need to endorse an option that would be acceptable to the clubs.

Maladroit handling of the situation by North Melbourne, self-interested clubs, a dogged Brisbane Bears and the Commission's desire to strengthen the League in a non-traditional footballing state were the decisive factors in why the Brisbane bid succeeded (or rather, why the 'North–Fitzroy Kangaroos' failed).[22] Yet this outcome was not necessarily inevitable. If the Kangaroos had initially included a less generous list concession as part of their bid, it may have inclined more clubs to their cause and prevented the two-thirds veto. An unanswerable question remains whether the Commission would have still pushed the Brisbane merger if the clubs had not threatened to veto the North Melbourne option. The 'Brisbane Lions' would still have been the more strategically beneficial choice, but would Oakley, Samuel, O'Connor and the others have had the conviction to override the will of the clubs to achieve it? It is an interesting, if purely academic, question.

...

Across Melbourne, the AFL's most important constituency — the supporters — soon began hearing the news. Those who had expected to hear confirmation of a merger between Fitzroy and North Melbourne were shocked by the rapid and seemingly unexpected turn of events. None were more stunned than Fitzroy people. Their reactions that Thursday night were raw, but gave an early indication about where the fault lines would lie as fans came to terms with what had happened. As the Commission was sealing Fitzroy's fate, about 150 Lions supporters gathered for the regular Ins and Outs Night at the Fitzroy Club Hotel with John Blackman as the special guest.[23] Once they heard the news, many were angry and upset. Blackman could not bring himself to participate in the evening, citing bruised vocal cords. One of the Ins and Outs organisers, Shirley Hardy-Rix, spoke for many when she told a reporter:

> Everyone was resigned to merging with someone, but people are still pretty shocked ... A lot of people thought the Brisbane option would be OK, but I think deep down they would really have preferred North Melbourne so we could see them play more often. It's not really the jumper or the logo we want — because both have changed in the past — but it's pretty hard to support a team two states away. The disappointing thing is that it's come at the hands of the other clubs ... in my mind the other clubs have cut us adrift.[24]

Fitzroy had been in her family for as long as she could remember. Together with her husband, she sponsored one of the reserve players. She did not think that the popular Ins and Outs Nights would continue in 1997: 'When you've put your life and soul into the club, you go to the games and do all that, can you be bothered? I just don't know whether I can be.'[25]

In his press conference, Gordon wanted to assure the Lions supporters that 'the 113-year history of Fitzroy will be reflected as a combined team with Brisbane.'[26] Yet Gordon's jubilation over the merger decision spilled over to a fateful television appearance. After several celebratory drinks with Andrew Ireland and other Brisbane representatives, Gordon received a call from Channel 9 to appear on *The Footy Show* later that evening. As the show went to air, his general demeanour, plus some ill-advised remarks, failed to endear him to the Fitzroy fans he was, presumably, attempting to court as future Victoria-based Brisbane Lions members. When Billy Brownless put to him that Brisbane would play Fitzroy in Round 20, Gordon flippantly remarked, 'It's a chance to build a percentage.' Emboldened by his success that evening — in addition to a drink or two — Gordon tried to be funny in a room full of comedians. It did not work.

Oakley was disappointed with Gordon's performance; this was no way to build a supporter base in Melbourne.[27] Hore-Lacy agreed. Watching on, he believed that in the space of five minutes Gordon 'single-handily lost most of Fitzroy's supporters with what many thought were arrogant and insensitive comments.'[28] Those watching at the Fitzroy Club Hotel hurled invective at the television screen in response, while many watching from the comfort of their living rooms had the same reaction.[29] For supporter Paul Riding, it left a 'sour taste', and any sympathy for the Brisbane merger 'went down the drain'.[30] Andrew Roberts called it 'brazen arrogance', and thought Gordon would have tried to 'court and reassure' fans, not 'humiliate and ridicule a still proud club'.[31] Lyn Grentell, who belonged to a family of ten passionate Fitzroy supporters, penned a public letter to Gordon rejecting the merger on behalf of her family and rebuked him for his 'arrogance'.[32] Mike Sheahan was disappointed in Gordon, labelling him an 'ungracious winner'. The long-standing advocate for a Fitzroy/Brisbane merger must have been aghast at this kind of attitude from the victorious president, as it undermined many of the perceived benefits that a Brisbane merger would bring Fitzroy people.[33] Without the time to socialise Fitzroy supporters to a merger with Brisbane, Gordon had started his campaign to win hearts and minds very poorly indeed.

At the Fitzroy Club Hotel, Ins and Outs coordinator Jan Wright said that most fans were angry: 'A hundred of them were crying and I only spoke to one person who thought Brisbane would be all right.'[34] 71-year-old Jean Chaundy was more direct: 'I'm disgusted with the AFL.'[35] Wright articulated a popular view, that the League had an agenda to get rid of Fitzroy, enabled by the actions of the other clubs which had 'shafted one of their own'.[36] The prospect of merging with Brisbane, rather than a Melbourne-based club, was a point of particular consternation. Barrie Harvey had supported Fitzroy for forty-five years. He could have accepted a merger with North Melbourne, but upon hearing of the Brisbane deal he 'stormed to bed' and vowed never to support them again.[37]

...

Years later, Hore-Lacy reflected on the deal done that evening, describing it as 'one of the most cynical and insensitive acts ever perpetrated in the history of sport'. With little consultation with the Fitzroy members and supporters, the Commission 'obliterated' the club 'by the stroke of a corporately-driven pen'.[38] The chairman and his board were right to be angry; they had worked hard to secure a merger that made the best of a bad situation and, as of Monday night, they thought they had the Commission's blessing. By Thursday evening, everything they had worked for was in tatters.

Dyson Hore-Lacy had a miserable night's sleep but hit the radio the following morning.[39] He reiterated that Fitzroy had not been consulted in the decision, and suggested it might be still possible to force a merger with North Melbourne, as the AFL had given them the deadline of noon that day. Noel Gordon shut down that suggestion, stating that there was 'absolutely no hope' of Fitzroy merging with any other club apart from the Bears.[40] The Fitzroy directors could not take any legal action against the AFL (courtesy of the agreement Brennan had signed with the League), so instead they agitated for North Melbourne to do so. Citing section 52 of the *Trade Practices Act*, they alleged that the Commission had engaged in deceptive and misleading conduct. After consultation, North Melbourne declined to pursue this course of action.[41]

That Friday morning the merger dominated the papers; *The Age* ran with 'It's the Brisbane Lions' on its front page, accompanied by a large photo of a euphoric Noel Gordon.[42] Some sections of the media were jubilant. Mike Sheahan called it 'a triumph for planning, patience and persistence'. Fitzroy, he believed, would survive as 'a partner in a vibrant new force in Australian football'.[43] He continued to assert that the Brisbane merger was the Fitzroy supporters' preference, and that 'Dyson Hore-Lacy got this one wrong'.[44] Patrick Smith called it 'the most momentous day in 100 years of football'. He believed that the game was stronger for the events of the day; the 'bloated Melbourne market has shrunk,' he wrote, 'the frontier club Brisbane is stronger and richer and the history and tradition of the founding club lives on.'[45]

For the AFL, there were some housekeeping matters to attend to following the previous evening's events. The Commission convened at 8.00am, returning, many Fitzroy people likely thought, to the scene of the crime. They discussed some ancillary matters arising from the merger, including how they would put together the promised $6 million. The Commission also turned its attention to Melbourne and Hawthorn as the next merger, discussing the possible impact the Fitzroy/Brisbane merger might have had on the ongoing discussions, and — in a note of optimism in the afterglow of success — potential strategies to achieve a third merger. They also realised that given Fitzroy's sudden slide into administration, the AFL's financial solvency rule needed to be strengthened to improve the Commission's position about clubs experiencing financial difficulties.[46]

In Northcote, the Lions' players arrived at the Fitzroy Club Hotel to collect outstanding payments, made possible by the $400,000 cheque from the AFL. Noel Gordon also made his way there to address the club's small staff and tell them that their jobs were assured until the end of the season.[47] For the first time in years, there was certainty about the club's position and its future, albeit of the worst possible variety. The staff now knew they would need to look for new jobs for 1997, while the players began contemplating their options. From media reporting, they knew that Brisbane would take at least eight players, and those who missed out could try their luck in the draft. For some, this might be the time to retire.

With these considerations swirling around the team, there was still a game to be played that weekend. The match against Kevin Sheedy's Essendon at Princes Park that Saturday afternoon began the Fitzroy Lions' nine-game valediction to the AFL. In the *Herald Sun*, Geoff Poulter asked rhetorically: 'How could one expect the gallant young Lions to have their minds on the job after the events of the past week or so?'[48] For many, the opportunity to play football was probably a welcome distraction.

Saturday was shrouded in typical Melbourne winter's gloom, with the weather deteriorating as the afternoon wore on. The funereal atmosphere suited the occasion, and no doubt reflected the mood of many Fitzroy fans who had made their way to Princes Park. Not for the last time, the cheer squad's banner provided a commentary on events, reading: 'North Melbourne one day, Brisbane the next.' With the game starting in the driving rain, it seemed as far from Queensland as one could be.[49] While the contest itself was mostly unimportant, the certainty of the club's fate gave Fitzroy's final games significance and poignancy much more considerable than had two teams been merely playing for four premiership points. Rapturous applause from both Fitzroy and Essendon fans greeted the Lions when they ran onto the ground.[50] In a bold move, Nunan started Martin Pike at full-forward, and he repaid this opportunity with a goal in the second minute that 'detonated an explosion of Fitzroy feeling'.[51] Every Lions player on the field went to him, and they celebrated 'as if he had just hit home the winner at Euro '96'.[52] John Rombotis called it the best feeling of the year.[53]

In the first half, Fitzroy unleashed their pent-up emotion and attacked the contest ferociously, often at times getting in each other's way in their attempts to win the ball. It was a much stronger performance than the previous week; uncertainty had given way to resolve. At one point, Chris Johnson was awarded a free kick within the forward 50, the first such free kick, one Fitzroy wit joked, since the 1944 Grand Final.[54] The Lions even held a brief lead, thanks to more goals from Martin Pike and others. Simon Atkins returned to the middle of the ground and revelled in the wet and John Barker did well in defence with eight marks. Brad Boyd played on James Hird and held him to a modest afternoon by his high standards, while Matthew Primus enhanced his reputation as a promising young ruckman in an enthralling battle with Steven Alessio.[55] But Essendon were not the Baby Bombers anymore; they were a physically imposing side that would make a Preliminary Final that year. As had happened so often in the season, the young men of Fitzroy could not keep pace with their stronger opponents and dropped off considerably in the second half.

Essendon eventually proved too strong, defeating Fitzroy 7.10. (52) to 17.16 (118). Despite the result, the Lions were cheered off the field. Kevin Sheedy was one of those who applauded their effort: 'I think the Fitzroy players have been fantastic,' he said after the match.⁵⁶

Nunan was also pleased with his side's commitment and their work rate, telling reporters it was probably one of their better efforts for the season.⁵⁷ These were his final post-game remarks as Fitzroy's senior coach. Adding to the litany of issues facing the club, Nunan confirmed that he would indeed quit after that day's game. John Birt had been trying to convince Nunan to stay until the end of the season, but to no avail, conceding on Friday evening that he had 'virtually made his mind up'.⁵⁸ Nunan had the honour of leading his players off the ground. He had taken the job to build a team over three years, and now that opportunity was taken out from under him. 'It's a matter of principle and a matter of professionalism,' he said, 'my job has basically been torpedoed as far as I'm concerned and I'm left with no other option.'⁵⁹ Within minutes of walking into the Fitzroy changing rooms, he informed the players of his decision. Silence greeted the announcement.⁶⁰

Thanking the players and the staff, Nunan headed out the door, but returned and said, 'Oh look, I've got just to do one more thing.' Shortly after his appointment, he had been given a Fitzroy centenary bomber jacket. The club's doorman, Tommy Couch, had taken a fancy to it, and said to Nunan: 'Coaches come and go; I really like that jacket and if you don't fulfil your commitments for any particular reason can I have it?' Nunan said he could. Recalling his promise, he took off his jacket and handed it to Couch. 'There you are, Tommy,' he said, 'there's that jacket you wanted.' And with that, he was gone.⁶¹

...

'I went to Fitzroy to build a club,' Nunan said many years after his departure from the Lions.⁶² Circumstances outside his control did not allow that to happen. He was unaware of the severity of the club's financial problems when he was appointed, and he was completely unaware of any merger discussions; like so many at Fitzroy, the media became his primary source of information about what was taking place. When the negotiations with North Melbourne became public, he said, 'I've got no idea about it, I'd probably be the most innocent person you'd come across.'[63] He was later angry when he learned that the board had been actively seeking a merger since January and had not informed him.[64] Had he known how precarious the club's position was at the end of 1995, he might not have taken the job. He had accepted the opportunity because he thought the club was being supported by the AFL — as early as the pre-season, he began to realise this was not the case.[65]

Within the club, he lived up to his reputation as a perfectionist and a hard taskmaster. He won many players over with his commitment to transforming them into a team that could win matches and play an attacking style. 'He had a good philosophy,' reflected Chris Johnson, 'we just weren't good enough to execute it.'[66] John Rombotis found his leaving difficult, as Nunan had placed a lot of faith in the nineteen-year-old midfielder.[67] Martin Pike also acknowledged that Nunan was good to him, and appreciated that he had invested his time and energy into the club as if it was 'going to go on forever.'[68] Matthew Primus knew that he wanted to 'throw everything into the way he wanted to coach' and understood why he felt unable to continue.[69] Some players were critical of his decision to leave, however, and those who had not prospered under his coaching just shrugged their shoulders at his departure and asked: 'Who's the next guy?'[70]

It is difficult to provide an assessment of Michael Nunan as Fitzroy coach, both due to the conditions he was forced to work under and the depleted team he inherited. After one of the early games of the season, Gareth Andrews wrote in the *Sunday Age* that Nunan could be the greatest genius of all time 'and I guarantee the result would still be the same.'[71] In the *Herald Sun*, Trevor Grant summed him up succinctly as a 'good coach in a dud job'.[72] All observers acknowledged that he had taken on a hard assignment, Mike Sheahan called it the 'toughest coaching job in memory, perhaps in AFL history'.[73] He had also decided to adopt a long-term approach to rebuilding the side, one that was unlikely to produce wins in the short-term and which was never allowed to come to fruition. His team tried to play his way, in most of their matches they out-handballed their opposition by the percentage of disposals if not outright. By the end of May, Fitzroy had the highest number of handballs per game of any team.[74] Commentators could see Fitzroy's run and handball style, even if it was often not executed with precision.[75] The win against Fremantle gave the media a chance to acknowledge the work he had done with a thin list at a resource-poor club. Patrick Smith called his performance at Fitzroy 'extraordinary', as it showed 'the effectiveness of his teaching and the raw ability of his young team'.[76]

Notwithstanding his record at Fitzroy, Michael Nunan offered much as a well-credentialed SANFL coach. Despite rumours (and possibly his aspirations) that he might coach again at another club, the 66-point loss to Essendon was his last contribution to the AFL. He left Fitzroy nine weeks before the club itself departed from the League. His exit drew to a close a most challenging and remarkable week; Matthew Primus told the media after the game: 'I don't think any other club in AFL/VFL history has had to go through what we went through this week.'[77] With the high drama over, the aftermath would linger for days and weeks — if not years. No-one connected with Fitzroy would be left unaffected: players, the staff and supporters now needed to come to terms with what had happened and begin the slow and arduous process of working out what to do next.

CHAPTER FIFTEEN

SELLING THE MERGER

'It hurts me to know Fitzroy is no longer going in its own right but this is a new era, a new beginning so get behind it'

— Kevin Murray, Fitzroy legend.[1]

The decision to merge the Fitzroy Lions and the Brisbane Bears had been made, endorsed and would soon be a legal reality. Now, its advocates needed to win over the constituency that would make it truly succeed: the supporters. The merger had little legitimacy in the eyes of Fitzroy's directors, but if enough club members supported it then that would justify and endorse the Commission's controversial decision. Ambitiously, Noel Gordon hoped to attract up to 8000 Fitzroy supporters to increase the club's overall membership to 20,000 within two years.[2] This task, however, could not be done through boardroom negotiation. Brisbane had acquired Fitzroy — its history and heritage, its colours and eventually, some of its players — but

Fitzroy's really valuable asset, its supporters, were free-thinking agents and would not automatically transfer their allegiances to the Brisbane Lions. 'Supporters aren't stock,' Martin Flanagan wrote days after the merger, 'they can't be bought. They can only be won.'[3]

Yet this was a difficult time for Fitzroy fans, and many could not bring themselves to contemplate supporting the new club just yet. One supporter likened it to 'your husband dying and someone saying to you at the graveside, "Ah, you're going to re-marry"'.[4] Fitzroy people were mourning the loss of their club, in many cases expressing a grief that would only become more acute as the season neared its end. Shortly after the merger, Barry Dickins wrote a powerful article for *The Age* that finished: 'Never was a love-force so shabbily looked after. It's too late now for a last-second resurrection. Some will not cry for Fitzroy. Others will never stop. I'm one of them.'[5]

The open issue was whether the same people who felt angry and/or despondent upon hearing the news of the merger would come to support the Brisbane Lions in 1997 and beyond. In his memoirs, Ross Oakley described the public response as 'mixed'.[6] This may have been the case over the longer-term, but a survey of those at Princes Park for Fitzroy's game against Essendon suggested that the AFL-endorsed Brisbane Lions would struggle for support. At the game, Martin Flanagan had moved among the Fitzroy faithful, taking their temperature. He saw little evidence of widespread support for the Brisbane option, 'not in the signs held up around the ground, not in what was said to me, not in the long impromptu oration delivered to the media by a Fitzroy supporter at the end of the match.'[7] Many were adamant that North Melbourne was the better option and coterie member Shane Harrop believed that among the coteries 'it's all North Melbourne'.[8] Brisbane's problem, Flanagan thought, was that for all Fitzroy's troubles, it was a genuine club with close ties between their players and supporters. Moving the club to Queensland would sever the bonds that had developed over the years. For fans that loved Fitzroy because it resembled a local footy club, it just would not be the same.[9]

Despite the criticism, the merger had advocates, and even Dyson Hore-Lacy acknowledged that many supporters had approached him encouraging a deal with Brisbane.[10] Bruce Ferrall, a supporter of fifty years, believed that the Brisbane merger was 'so obviously' the preference of the supporters and, seemingly, the players.[11] Another supporter, Alan Harrison, considered it the best thing that could have been done.[12] Several supporters *did* favour Brisbane because the club's colours would remain largely intact.[13] There was also a lingering perception that the North Melbourne merger would have been a 'takeover'; one supporter wrote: 'I am sure those supporters who are whinging are more happy to watch the Lions eight times in Melbourne compared to nil.'[14] This argument was made by Brisbane officials, who suggested that without the merger with Brisbane, Fitzroy's history, colour and emblem would have been 'engulfed' by a rival Melbourne-based club.[15] Like all Fitzroy supporters, Sam Lord and his family were shattered by the merger, but had been preparing for the eventuality for some time and, seeing the advantages Brisbane offered, were keen to throw themselves into the Brisbane Lions.[16]

While the Brisbane option had some support, it seemed to be in the minority, with many fans either antagonistic or agnostic. Mere days after the merger, letters from Fitzroy supporters began pouring into the major newspapers. Those who took the time to write to newspapers were clearly a self-selected group, the most passionate and aggrieved. If there was a great silent majority of Fitzroy supporters who were in favour of the Brisbane option, however, they were being very silent indeed. The hostility towards Brisbane was possibly more than its advocates (particularly Mike Sheahan) might have predicated. At that early stage, many supporters could not disentangle their feelings of loss for Fitzroy with a decision about who they would follow in 1997. While the arguments for Brisbane may have been compelling, many Roys were simply not in the emotional state to hear or accept them. It was particularly so when it appeared the AFL (long the villains for Fitzroy) had orchestrated the merger against their will, making the 'Brisbane Lions' a symbol of the League's perfidy.

Many labelled the merger a 'disgrace', and one supporter declared that there was no chance he would follow the Brisbane Lions or the AFL ever again, as the merger had shown football 'for what it is', a game that valued 'greed, selfishness and the almighty dollar' above all else.[17] Another fan wrote: 'I will be giving away football. My heart bleeds'.[18] Henry Landini condemned the 'AFL-endorsed Brisbane', declaring that any 'self-respecting Fitzroy supporter should see through this charade and remain a supporter of a Melbourne team'.[19] Fitzroy member Daniel Zavattiero called Brisbane 'an undesired partner', adding, 'I cannot understand how any Fitzroy supporter will embrace it given the disgusting circumstance that brought it about.'[20] Kevin Campbell, vice-president of the Fitzroy coterie The Pride, said that until the AFL Commission handed Fitzroy over to Brisbane, a merger with the Bears would have been accepted by many supporters (although North Melbourne remained the preferred option). But he believed that the manner in which the merger was achieved, more than the choice of merger partner, had 'embittered a lot of people'. For that reason he predicted many fans would switch their allegiances to North Melbourne.[21]

Opprobrium towards Ross Oakley, AFL Commission and the other AFL clubs was virulent. Tom Balaam, a Fitzroy member and shareholder, was 'absolutely disgusted' with the AFL and the other clubs, who 'must have found it hard last Friday to wash the Fitzroy blood from their hands'. He would not be supporting the Brisbane Lions.[22] Another disgruntled supporter called the merger 'the most foul act ever in football.'[23] Keith Lofthouse 'solemnly' swore that he had attended his last AFL match: 'For me, no Fitzroy means no football.' While he did not blame Oakley entirely, he was convinced that part of Oakley's 'vision' for the League was seeing Fitzroy's demise, adding: 'Football has lost its soul, Mr Oakley.'[24] Merv Wilson called the decision to vote against the North Melbourne/Fitzroy merger 'the most disgraceful act in the 100-year history of the VFL/AFL'; to him the 'merger' was 'a takeover in every sense' and he would not be buying a membership for the Brisbane Lions.[25] Mike Sheahan came in for a share of criticism.[26] Arthur Paul wrote: 'Well Mr Sheahan, you and the AFL get what you wanted — a Brisbane Lions merger. What do we Fitzroy members get? Virtually nothing. We are dumped with a club we dislike and our wishes for the North merger were not even heard.'[27]

Few correspondents seemed to indicate they would follow the new club, a fact evident to Jarrod Molloy, who sensed that the club's supporters 'weren't too keen on the idea of Brisbane'.[28] One Fitzroy member, Peter Allen, argued that the League's assumption that Fitzroy members would automatically follow Brisbane was 'seriously misguided', noting, 'Fitzroy people have for 113 years supported a Melbourne-based club named Fitzroy. Our ability to do this ends in nine weeks.' He added that he would more likely support Carlton than Brisbane, 'and hell will freeze over before either occurs'.[29] It seemed the elements of the merger designed to appeal to Fitzroy fans (the nickname, logo and club colours) were not as instantly persuasive as its advocates might have hoped. 'The colours are only window dressing,' one fan wrote, 'The soul of the club has been destroyed. A part of the fabric of football has been torn and it will never be mended.'[30] Julian Agius asked: 'Does the Brisbane board expect Fitzroy supporters to follow television football simply because of the inclusion of the Lion name and a splash of blue on the Bears jumper? The spirit of the Fitzroy Football Club died last week more than 10 years after the life support was switched off. It will take more than token concessions to convince most Fitzroy supporters otherwise.'[31] Noel Gordon, it seemed, had work to do.

...

While the Fitzroy fans aired their frustrations, the players and staff were adjusting to their new situation. John Birt nominally remained the CEO, but Brennan's deputy, Greg Swann, managed the day-to-day running of the club with Birt's assistance. Despite all that had happened, Fitzroy was essentially still in the position it had been for much of the season: cash and asset poor. While the club's running costs for its final games was covered out of the $6 million, this did not mean it was suddenly flush with funds. The AFL guaranteed the players' salaries, while Brennan had guaranteed that the staff would get paid. Beyond that, the club still operated hand-to-mouth.

Despite winning the contest to merge with Fitzroy, Brisbane could do little to assist. Once the Commission had endorsed the merger, they made it very clear to Brisbane that for the sake of the integrity of the competition they were not to have any involvement in Fitzroy's football operations. On the request of the players, however, Brisbane was able to secure Waverley Park as a new training venue.[32] Gordon, Ireland, Scott Clayton (the former Fitzroy player turned Bears' recruitment manager) and several other officials also met with the players on the morning of Sunday, 7 July, to keep them informed. They tried to start a dialogue, but many of the younger players felt intimidated, given the perceived disparity between the two clubs (certainly in ladder position).[33] Finally, Jeff Hogg raised the question on every players' mind: can they find out straight away which of them would be going to Brisbane?[34] Unable to give a direct answer, the Bears' representatives discussed the timeframe on when the decision would be announced. Concerning the need to find a caretaker coach, Gordon promised the players and staff that by 5:00pm Monday 8 July someone would be appointed.[35] Despite the importance of finding a coach, Brad Boyd knew that the eight players was the burning question; as soon as they knew who the eight were, everyone could start planning their futures.[36]

Despite Brisbane's assurances, by Sunday night it was clear that no-one wanted the job as Fitzroy's caretaker coach. This was understandable: if Nunan's job was difficult, the task set for his successor was diabolical. Fitzroy had struggled all season and were unlikely to win any of their remaining eight games, as the players began thinking about their futures at the expense of playing for the team. In addition, the new coach would be unemployed come the end of the season. Former Fitzroy coach Rod Austin was approached, but he turned it down. Alan McConnell was another candidate, but the

39-year-old assistant coach had serious reservations. 'If you stand in front of a playing group you have to believe you can make a difference,' he later reflected. He could not see how, standing before the Fitzroy Lions, with eight games left of professional football, he could make any difference at all. He was not going to accept the position, but then Brad Boyd called him and asked him to take the job. 'We need somebody who will look after us,' Boyd said, 'nobody else cares.'[37]

Ultimately, McConnell was moved by the human consequences of the merger on Fitzroy's players and he accepted the offer. On Monday afternoon, Brennan appointed him as caretaker coach, with reserves coach Leon Harris doubling as his assistant. Harris had played junior football with McConnell, and was happy to support his friend during what they both knew was going to be a difficult time.[38] McConnell was a popular choice among the players, many of whom had come up through the club with him. He was known and respected as a 'players' coach', someone who was a good communicator and excellent with young players.[39] He was under no illusions about his role: 'I'm a short-term coach,' he declared, 'in a short-term club.' Publicly, his aim was to have Fitzroy 'going out in style with our heads up and some dignity.'[40]

Yet he understood that an individual mentality would inevitably start to creep into the players as they all looked towards 1997. This was frustrating for a man who had spent six years at Fitzroy building up the club as development coach and then reserves coach. 'In the end,' he thought, 'that team thing I was looking to build up will all be going somewhere else.'[41] Taking charge of training shortly after his appointment, he told the players: 'I see it as my duty to ensure that this group of people, all of whom have some future in football at some level, have a positive eight weeks together'. His biggest challenge was to make sure the players and football staff looked after each other.[42] Privately, he let it be known that he was not beholden to the players, even though they had asked for him. 'If I was going to be the coach, I was going to be the boss,' he recalled, telling the players: 'If you burn me, I'll burn you. If you play on your own you won't play in my team. We must play together.'[43]

McConnell's first task would be West Coast in Perth on Friday night, just four days after his appointment. He was positive heading into the game, the players had trained well and the resolution of the merger discussions had allowed the team to go about its business under less scrutiny and with fewer meetings to attend.[44] Furthermore, it was likely a pleasant reprieve for the players and football staff to escape Melbourne for a time and just concentrate on playing football. McConnell made minimal changes to the team, bringing in Rowan Warfe (who was never a favourite of Nunan's) and Brett Chandler who had fully recovered from injury. Both men had only played eight times that season, yet they went on to play all the remaining games.[45] The match itself was as expected, Fitzroy suffering a 68-point loss. Three minutes into the second quarter John Rombotis took one of the marks of the season over Paul Symmons, Daniel Metropolis and Ashley McIntosh, and went on to kick the Lions' second goal.[46] Tragically, Brad Boyd went down early with a suspected hamstring injury, another cruel blown in a season that had already given him too much grief. After the game, West Coast invited the Fitzroy players and staff into their rooms for a farewell, and the Eagles' coach, Mick Malthouse, gave a memorable speech to mark the occasion.[47]

...

Back in Melbourne, Roys supporters continued to sort out where they stood in relation to the merger. By Saturday 13 July, the *Herald Sun*'s letters editor, David Aldridge, commented on the correspondence they had received on this issue. The volume of mail was 'massive, language often intemperate and emotions verging on the ballistic. While correspondents covered most possible views almost all agreed that no credit could accrue to the AFL and in particular to "Ross the Boss" Oakley. The majority view held Fitzroy and its supporters were pawns in a game to allow the AFL to achieve its long-time aim of giving Brisbane a Melbourne base.'[48]

In addition to writing ill-tempered missives, many supporters attended public demonstrations. Rabble-rouser Greg Basto had called a meeting of supporters at the Fitzroy Town Hall on the evening of Tuesday, 9 July.[49] A crowd of approximately 400 showed up to plan their opposition to the Brisbane merger, including with a potential street march from the steps of Parliament House to the MCG. Two supporters, Shane Harrop and Janene Howells (a Lions supporter of thirty-two years who was married to Ross Oakley's brother-in-law) were becoming active and prominent in organising anti-merger activities. For Howells, the Brisbane merger spelt the death of Fitzroy. Neither believed the 'Brisbane Lions' would have a true Victorian identity and they refused to support an interstate club. As with many Fitzroy supporters, they felt North Melbourne had the better offer, and, believing that there was a strong groundswell of support from disenchanted Fitzroy supporters anxious to renew negotiations with North Melbourne, they optimistically believed the Brisbane/Fitzroy merger could yet be overturned.[50]

More supporters' rallies soon followed. Dyson Hore-Lacy spoke at one organised by Harrop, Howells and Shirley Hardy-Rix. At the rally, Greg Miller announced that North Melbourne sought permission from the League to incorporate Fitzroy's golden Lion logo on the Roos' guernsey for away and pre-season games. The idea was to perpetuate Fitzroy's legacy and give fans an alternative team to support in Melbourne. Colin Hobbs and Jan Wright also addressed the crowd. When Hore-Lacy spoke he was heckled by 'an abusive handful' of the 200-plus in attendance. Not giving up, he told the meeting that the Fitzroy/Brisbane merger could still face a legal challenge.[51] The idea was quixotic, but it gave Hore-Lacy something to cling to well after the decisive moment had passed.

Brisbane, meanwhile, was confidently moving ahead. On the night of 18 July, Gordon unveiled the 'Brisbane Lions' jumper at a special information evening to about 600 Bears members in Queensland.[52] Many were not happy with the design; when the jumper was unveiled, one supporter yelled: 'That's a Fitzroy jumper!'[53] Brisbane media manager Peter Blucher said that many members 'feel a little hard done by in terms of the lion logo as opposed to the bear ... The guernsey is Fitzroy's, the name is Fitzroy's and the song is Fitzroy's'. While he said it was understandable that they were aggrieved, 'there has to be a bit of give and take'. Brisbane's board had already ratified the design but it remained to be signed off by the AFL.[54] The Bears had scrapped plans for an additional (and more Fitzroy looking) home-and-away jumper, reneging on part of the merger agreement decided just days before. But they took the opportunity to denounce North Melbourne's plan to put a lion on their away and pre-season jumper, calling it ridiculous and correctly asserting that the AFL would never approve.[55] They also revealed the new theme song, which was to use the tune of 'La Marseillaise' and that the best and fairest award would be named after Roger Merrett and a yet-to-be-determined Fitzroy person selected by Fitzroy members.[56]

...

In Round 16, Fitzroy prepared to play Collingwood at their ancestral fortress of Victoria Park. 'Smith Street will lose a little of its soul when the Roys are no more,' wrote Stephen Rielly in *The Age*. 'Sentiment is for the terraces, though, and this final parting will only deliver loss fifteen for the Lions for 1996, and defeat 131 against the black and white neighbour and foe.'[57] The location only heightened the sense that it was the end of an era for suburban football. McConnell had to do without Brad Boyd, who was unable to recover from the abductor muscle injury he sustained in the first quarter against West Coast.[58]

For all the wistfulness about playing one final game against the old Smith Street rivals at Victoria Park, the day was made infamous by the Fitzroy cheer squad. Throughout the merger discussions, supporters had been vocal but lacked any formal mechanism to express their views on what was happening to their club. The anger and frustration felt by so many letter writers and talkback callers found expression in what must be the most notorious banner in VFL/AFL history. The cheer squad spoke for many when they composed their statement during the week. Now, on Sunday afternoon, it was raised at Victoria Park for all to see.

> Seduced by North
>
> Raped by Brisbane
>
> F****d by the AFL

It was a brazen and powerful declaration from a marginalised constituency with little power to change the fate of their football club; one cheer squad official said the banner was the only way they could get their word across.[59]

John Birt distanced the club from the sentiments and the cheer squad confirmed it had not been approved by club officials. In his memoirs, Ross Oakley mentioned this incident, and seemed to suggest it represented only the 'hardcore' who said 'it's not our club any more' and 'showed their contempt for all [the merger] stood for'.[60] The AFL initially wanted to take action, but they found it difficult as the club had not approved the banner and, in any event, it was hard to see how any punishment would be significant compared to what had already transpired. As one journalist asked: 'How do you fine a club which has nothing left but pride?'[61] The AFL eventually decided to ignore the inflammatory remarks, satisfied, at least, that the club had no knowledge of the cheer squad's intent.[62]

The banner was only the most obvious demonstration of Fitzroy supporters' feelings; all around Victoria Park, there was a frisson of discontent. By now, Harrop and Howells had formed the Victorian Football Protection League, and were selling black armbands for 20 cents each as a 'mark of respect for the death of Fitzroy'. They also planned to have anti-Brisbane placards behind the goals at both ends of the ground.[63]

With the theatrics in the crowd as an external distraction, there was still a game to be played. Collingwood came in full of confidence, having defeated North Melbourne the previous week by over ten goals. With recruiting staff from other clubs watching on, Fitzroy turned in one of its better performances of the year.⁶⁴ The Lions fought hard in the first half and deserved to be in front, going harder at the ball and putting their bodies on the line. Primus dominated Damian Monkhorst and then Mark Richardson, Pike seemed to be everywhere and had twenty-three possessions by half-time, Atkins and Morton offered good support and Bamford and Rombotis provided powerful running. But, as had been the case for much of the season, Fitzroy's forwards let them down. McCarthy and Hawking missed set shots and Johnson had a certain goal smothered on the line. Had it not been so, Fitzroy would certainly have been in front at half-time.⁶⁵ At the long break, Collingwood coach Tony Shaw gave his players a spray and made some positional changes, including placing Nathan Buckley into the midfield from defence. In the third quarter, Collingwood set up a match-winning lead, kicking six goals to one with fluent, skilful ball movement. Fitzroy managed to equal the Pies' three goals in the final quarter and finished the game well, yet victory had eluded them once again. The final score was Fitzroy 10.16 (76) to Collingwood 17.14 (116).⁶⁶

As with the game against Essendon, the Fitzroy players were given a standing ovation by the Collingwood supporters as they left the ground. Compared to the 'torrent of spit and sarcasm' Leon Harris remembered receiving during his playing days, this was a much more pleasant experience.⁶⁷ There was genuine feeling within the Collingwood Football Club over Fitzroy's demise — Tony Shaw in particular was saddened that Magpie/Lions clashes would be a thing of the past.⁶⁸ He praised Fitzroy's spirited performance, noting that if they had kicked straight early 'we were going to be in heaps (of trouble) at quarter-time'.⁶⁹ The Magpies threw an 'old-fashioned' after-match function for Fitzroy and players, officials, wives and girlfriends ate from large plates of sandwiches from pristine white tablecloths on trestle tables in the Collingwood gymnasium. Club legend Bob Rose gave a brief welcoming speech where he acknowledged the long and healthy rivalry between the neighbouring clubs. The traditional 'beer and sandwich chat with the opposition' had since died with the requirement for players to attend corporate and coterie functions after games. One journalist observed, 'The after-match get-together equates to Fitzroy — everyone misses it but no-one was prepared to fight to save tradition.'[70]

...

The cheer squad's banner against Collingwood and the deluge of angry correspondence from Fitzroy people made it unmistakably clear that Brisbane still needed to win over large sections of the Fitzroy supporter base prior to the 1997 season.[71] There was, of course, a group that would never accept the merger in any form and would either follow a completely different club or cease following the AFL entirely. Noel Gordon was not going to waste his time chasing them. Instead, his target was the large number of fans who, while they mourned the loss of Fitzroy as a club in its own right, could be convinced to support Brisbane provided there was sufficient Fitzroy identity represented in the new club. He made statements in the media extoling Fitzroy's culture and history, saying 'you have to pay the due deference to the people who have heritage on their side', striking a more diplomatic chord after his ill-fated remarks on *The Footy Show*.[72]

Together with Andrew Ireland, he met with three coterie groups on Monday 22 July. The outcome of these meetings was less than positive for the Brisbane hierarchy, with two of the three declining to commit themselves to the Brisbane Lions.[73] Looking beyond the coteries, on 16 July, Ireland and Birt wrote a letter to invite Fitzroy members to a 'Members' Forum' at the Dallas Brooks Hall, East Melbourne, on the evening of 24 July to provide them with the 'background and rationale' behind the merger decision and its ramifications. The letter was optimistic in tone, speaking up the benefits of the Brisbane merger and letting them know that the people of Brisbane wished to extend 'a warm hand of friendship and "football-ship" to the members of

Fitzroy'.[74] Gordon knew it would be a tough meeting, but expressed his enthusiasm for it, telling the media he looked forward to addressing Fitzroy supporters so he could 'tell them the truth as to where we are coming from and what we are proposing'.[75] He would deal with any problems or misgivings among Fitzroy people and was very confident that once the full details of the merger were put to the supporters there would be 'a lot of very satisfied and happy Fitzroy people'.[76]

Some 2000 Fitzroy supporters came to the Dallas Brooks Hall meeting on Wednesday, 24 July at 7.30pm. *The Age* predicted it would be 'fiery, with substantial pockets of Fitzroy's support threatening to voice their displeasure over the pending merger' — and they were right.[77] The Bears administration had a tip-off that there would be trouble and employed additional security for the evening.[78] Almost immediately Gordon and Ireland were faced with a chorus of booing and opposition, with Ireland likening it to having bouncers bowled at his throat.[79] Unperturbed, Gordon unveiled the Brisbane Lions' new jumper and song, having arranged for Jim Keays of The Masters Apprentices to sing a rendition.[80] He believed that there was a sufficient amount of Fitzroy represented in the jumper and song that the Lions supporters would see that 'it is going to be a merged club rather than an individual takeover.'[81] More persuasively, the Bears had gained endorsements from past Fitzroy greats, including Laurie Serafini, Garry Wilson, Bernie Quinlan, George Coates, Matt Rendell, Leon Harris and Bill Stephen.[82] Dyson Hore-Lacy did not attend but Colin Hobbs did, and when Gordon asserted that some Fitzroy directors were in favour of the Brisbane deal, Hobbs grabbed the microphone and stated 'either name the directors or withdraw the allegation because it is nothing but a bloody lie'. There was no response.[83]

Despite the animosity, the raucous crowd seemed to be evenly divided between those in favour of a merger with Brisbane and those who preferred North Melbourne.[84] To win over those still unconvinced or hostile, Brisbane unveiled its greatest asset: club legend Kevin 'Bulldog' Murray. While Gordon and Ireland were being shouted down, Murray garnered much more sympathy from the Fitzroy members and brought with him a significant amount of influence and gravitas. 'It hurts me to know Fitzroy is no longer going in its own right,' he told the crowd, 'but this is a new era, a new beginning so get behind it ... We are fortunate we have got this offer to go to Brisbane. They have given us a lot of concessions. What more can you ask for than our jumper, the lions and theme song?'[85] Murray became a champion of the merger, one the Brisbane administration sorely needed. If *he* was not able to convince Fitzroy supporters to give the Brisbane Lions a fair go, no-one was.

The outcome of the meeting was mixed, although Gordon came away confidently predicting more than 3500 Fitzroy members would sign up to the Brisbane Lions in 1997 (having lowered his expectation from the 8000 he proffered on the night of the merger).[86] Deidre Worn of the Ladies Auxiliary was one of those members who remained unswayed. Calling it the worst night she had ever been to, she screamed herself 'absolutely stupid'. 'They insulted us,' she recalled, 'they treated us like we were dirt.'[87] Another supporter, Jeff Sayers, went with an open mind, but was not impressed.[88] Gordon had opened the door for Fitzroy supporters to follow the Brisbane Lions, but it remained to be seen how many would walk through.

In the midst of the rancorous debate, some important measures were quietly finalised as the merger process moved towards completion. The AFL Commission had agreed in principle to the Fitzroy/Brisbane merger on the night of 4 July, but it still needed to approve the finalised merger once all the details were sorted. This was done when the Commission met in Perth on Sunday, 21 July, with the Commission resolving to 'recognise, accept, adopt and implement the Brisbane/Fitzroy merger'.[89] There could be no ambiguity about the League's decision.

Brennan's obligations as the administrator were also far from finished. Regardless of whatever the AFL Commission, the Brisbane Bears and the other clubs had decided, he was legally required to hold a second meeting of creditors where *they* could decide the club's future. Their options, however, were limited: they could return the club to the control of the directors, put the club into liquidation or accept a 'deed of company arrangement' which was, in essence, the merger agreement. Since 4 July, the substance of the Fitzroy/Brisbane merger as endorsed by the AFL Commission and the other clubs had been written up as a formal legal document. The basic truth of the matter was that accepting the merger was the only option that would realistically give the creditors any return. The arrangement document outlined how the creditors would be paid and what steps Brisbane would take (in line with the Commission agreement) to change its identity to incorporate Fitzroy. It also indicated that Brisbane would make an offer to purchase the lease for the Fitzroy Club Hotel. The Fitzroy Football Club itself would not be liquidated, with the merger incentive package used to pay the club's creditors. The club would continue, albeit under administration, with no licence to compete in the AFL, and with Brennan intent on maximising the return for the club's unsecured creditors (over 120 in total).[90]

All of this information was presented at the second creditors' meeting, held on 25 July, the day after the Dallas Brooks Hall event.[91] Despite impassioned attempts by Dyson Hore-Lacy, Colin Hobbs and Peter De Rauch to contest Brennan's claims that the merger with Brisbane was the best outcome, the creditors endorsed the proposal that Brennan argued would see them gain between 40 to 57 cents in the dollar (the variance largely rested on whether Brennan could determine that the Fitzroy Club Hotel belonged to the club or not).[92] After the meeting, Brennan publicly declared that the merger with Brisbane was now a 'done deal'.[93] The Fitzroy directors and North Melbourne made noises about Supreme Court action, but the game had been played and lost. Having accepted Brennan's deal, the creditors left the building with little comment, although one person, reflecting on the message from the cheer squad at the Collingwood game, remarked: 'I think the banner said it all.'[94]

CHAPTER SIXTEEN

CUSTODIANS OF THE JUMPER

'The players have been through hell this year'

— John Birt, Fitzroy chief executive officer.[1]

On Monday, 1 July, at the start of the most significant week in Fitzroy's history, Michael Nunan spoke to the media about how his players were being treated amid the drama that was taking place around them. He believed they had been forgotten, and described them as the 'real wreckage' of the club's plight.[2] By the end of the month, Nunan had gone, yet his players remained tethered to the club for its remaining games of the season until they too would be cast adrift. To some extent, the players could not be forgotten in all that was taking place. They remained the living embodiment of the club, continuing to run out onto the ground each weekend to play their part in the club's drawn out and public departure from the League. Yet the story of the individual players themselves was often lost, with the 'human side' of the merger being represented by the heartbroken supporters.

The situation the players found themselves in was different to that of the supporters, as they did not necessarily have the same deep and lifelong emotional connection to the club. The players' concerns at that time were still personal, but in a different way. Fitzroy had given them the opportunity to play AFL football. Now, there was no guarantee this would continue into 1997.

With the exception of those willing to call time on their football careers, the aim of every player was to be recruited by another club. The most direct route was to be selected by Brisbane, yet given the disparity between the quality of Fitzroy's playing list and that of Brisbane's, it was unlikely there would be any more than eight players going north. The Bears had until 18 October, seven days before the national draft, to finalise their choices. Formally, any players unhappy about being nominated by Brisbane were able to approach the AFL Appeals Board, but in practice they would merely indicate to Brisbane's officials that they were uninterested. The remainder not selected for the new Lions would be delisted and could nominate for the national draft.[3]

Once the Bears' football department had processed the shock of their new situation, they set to work drawing up lists and approaching players. The decision on who Brisbane would select was primarily in the hands of the Bears' senior coach, John Northey and the recruiting manager, Scott Clayton, with input from Andrew Ireland and Alastair Lynch.[4] As per the instructions from AFL House, Brisbane maintained a clear separation between the football operations of their club and those of Fitzroy.[5] Thus, in deciding on their player selections, Brisbane's interactions with Fitzroy's football staff was limited: neither McConnell nor Warry were approached about their thoughts on the playing list or whether any players had any specific issues of which they should be aware.[6] Nunan offered his assessment, but only for a price (an offer that Brisbane declined).[7]

While Fitzroy's list was weak, some names stood out, Brad Boyd being perhaps first and foremost. He had expressed interest in playing for Brisbane, but, with typical modesty, was unconvinced that he would be chosen.[8] Wherever he ended up in 1997, however, he desperately did not want to play for another lowly club — his five years with the Roys had been enough. 'I've been thrashed so many times,' he said at the start of August, 'when you really put everything into it and you've just been thrashed, there's nothing worse.'[9] He had been tremendously loyal to Fitzroy, turning down several offers to leave, but he was ready to move on and few could begrudge him that wish.[10] Injuries were the main concern about his suitability for being selected, yet despite his disrupted season, he was undoubtedly a talented and valuable player.

Among the team, Boyd thought there were about three or four lay-down misères to go to Brisbane: Chris Johnson, Jarrod Molloy, John Barker and Matthew Primus were obvious candidates.[11] All four were young, gifted and had years of quality football ahead of them. Each had been nominated for the AFL Rising Star award in their debut seasons and their names continually appeared on hypothetical playing lists of potential merged clubs. Moving to Brisbane would see them join a club that was clearly on the rise — the Bears were on track to play finals that year and there was no reason to suggest the new-look Brisbane Lions would not challenge for a premiership in due course. The downside (for some) was the move away from Melbourne, a factor that had seen many players prefer North Melbourne as their merger partner. For others, however, it would be liberation. 'I'd be happy to go,' declared Jarrod Molloy, 'I'm not much of a surfer, but I like the warmer weather; the cold weather here is not to my liking.'[12] Molloy also recognised that the Bears were heading towards greater things and Brisbane's officials hoped that the addition of several quality players would only enhance their prospects after the merger.

Another player keen to leave Melbourne was twenty-year-old Chris Johnson. He had arrived at Fitzroy as a promising Under 18s player. In the 1993 TAC Cup Grand Final, he produced a seven-goal/best-on-ground performance. Fitzroy coach Robert Shaw had gone to the game to watch Johnson's teammate, Jarrod Molloy, but he was impressed with Johnson and selected him with Fitzroy's first pick in the 1993 national draft.[13] Since his senior AFL debut in Round 2, 1994, Johnson's star had continued to rise, and in 1996 he was called up to the Victorian State of Origin team's extended squad. 'He's an exciting prospect,' remarked Victoria's chairman of selectors, Gerard Healy.[14]

Played forward or on the ball, Johnson's talent was evident: he was fast, skilful and had a spectacular vertical leap. He was also reluctant to do any defensive work, and his set-shot kicking often left much to be desired. In 1996, he had continued to improve and evolve as a player. After a series of punishing training sessions he was confident kicking on both his right and left foot and he also began playing in defence (which, if nothing else, exposed that his defensive game required work).[15] In fact, he found playing in defence enjoyable, as he could be part of constructing attacks, rather than waiting to be on the end of balls as they entered the forward line.[16] He also moved forward when necessary, and by Round 10 he had kicked ten goals.

There was also another dimension of Johnson as a player and as a man. His father, Lloyd Johnson, was of the Gunditjamara people, the traditional owners of southwestern Victoria. As a young man, Chris proudly watched his father play for their local team, Jacana, and then the indigenous-based Fitzroy Stars, and saw a growing number of Aboriginal players in the AFL. He drew inspiration from these role models, aware that football had not always been welcoming to those of indigenous heritage.[17] Drafted in October 1993, he found himself playing League football when the plight of indigenous players was gaining greater status and claims of racial vilification on the field were being taken more seriously. That year, Nicky Winmar and Gilbert McAdam had played in the infamous Victoria Park game against Collingwood. In the 1995 season, Damien Monkhorst racially vilified Michael Long during the Anzac Day game and Johnson was involved in lobbying the AFL for the drafting of the racial vilification rules. He was proud to be indigenous, and wanted to ensure that he was publicly identified as such.[18]

In several respects, Johnson stood out among the forty-two players of Fitzroy's list. He certainly had not escaped Brisbane's notice. Shortly after the merger was announced, Bears' recruiting manager, Scott Clayton, met with Johnson about a move to Queensland. Keen to continue his promising career, he quickly confirmed that he was interested in playing for the Brisbane Lions (unlike some of his teammates, he could not wait to leave Melbourne) and negotiations commenced over the contract details.[19] Through the media, Johnson's manager, John Riordan, tried to get the best deal for his client, declaring: 'He is not going to play for the peanut money up there.'[20] In hindsight, Johnson acknowledged that he probably should have waited until the end of the season before beginning these discussions, but he was still only a young man, and was happy to go along with his agent or others advising him.[21]

Someone who was less enthusiastic about Brisbane was Matthew Primus. Shortly after the merger was agreed, he had been publicly positive about potentially moving north, describing Brisbane as a 'fantastic club to go to', with 'a bright future for the next 10 years or so and fantastic facilities'.[22] He shortly reconsidered his position, however. Brisbane already had strong ruck stocks (Matthew Clarke and Clarke Keating) and he did not want to play for Brisbane's reserves team in the QAFL where his football would likely atrophy.[23] His management reportedly began preparing legal options to avoid playing for the Bears, while he faced the prospect of standing out of football for a year or returning to the SANFL.[24] On 12 July, the AFLPA indicated that it would not support Primus in his fight to avoid moving to Brisbane, as they were loath to back any Lion threatening to break ranks after the AFL had guaranteed player payments for Fitzroy.[25] The public stand-off continued, as behind the scenes, the Bears worked to determine how to manage the situation to best advantage.

Another key prospect, John Barker, was also hesitant about moving to Queensland. Several weeks after the merger was decided, Scott Clayton invited the 21-year-old to his hotel in Melbourne's CBD. There, he informed Barker that he was to be one of Brisbane's selected players. Barker, the grandson of Fitzroy forward Claude Curtin, was unsure whether to be happy or not. Given his family connection to the club, his sense of melancholy about Fitzroy's fate was more acute than most other players. There was also something about the situation that did not sit well with him. Among his teammates he knew that there were those who did not want to go to Brisbane, with the move interstate and the likelihood of struggling to break into the senior team as compelling detractions. Nevertheless, he was glad that he was considered of a sufficiently high ability to warrant selection by the Bears.[26]

Very soon, the playing group had figured out the likely candidates to be recruited by Brisbane. 'They weren't named officially until the end of the season,' Brett Cook noted, '[but] you had a pretty good idea who they'd be.'[27] The fate of the majority remained uncertain. As the season neared its end, McConnell identified three main groups among the players. First, he suspected that some who had accepted Brisbane's offer had already put the cue in the rack to avoid getting injured (which would affect their contracts). Second, there were probably fifteen or so who knew they would not get a contract anywhere, and so their minds moved from performances on the field to wider personal issues.[28] The 27-year-old Simon Atkins, for instance, was not confident Brisbane would want him, but jokingly told people: 'My body doesn't agree with the sun anyway.'[29] The 29-year-old John McCarthy was very unsure about his future, but hopeful he could continue playing somewhere.[30] Back-up ruckman Brett Cook thought his AFL career was 'pretty much finished'. Apart from four games at the start of the season, he had been playing consistently in the reserves and did not think he would generate much interest.[31] After a troubled couple of years at Fitzroy, Jeff Hogg, who would be turning thirty in October, decided not to nominate for the draft and planned to retire. Working against many of Fitzroy's players who wanted to keep their AFL careers alive was the stigma of losing week after week. Jason Baldwin believed that with all the negative media around Fitzroy, people forget that there were some talented footballers in the team.³² Matthew Dent concurred. In his three seasons with the Roys, he thought he had demonstrated that he could play, but 'nobody notices you when you're losing'.³³

The third group comprised the remainder of the list, mainly the younger players, who had no idea about what was going on or what would happen next.³⁴ Approaching this group (and eventually the staff too) about their future arrangements was the responsibility of Brisbane's Victorian manager, Kinnear Beatson. For several years the Bears had maintained a small office in Melbourne to manage its football operations when the team had played in Victoria. Beatson had usually spent his time on recruiting duties, as well as managing match logistics in Victoria and looking after the Melbourne-based members. Now, not only would his role change dramatically in 1997, but he became something akin to the Bears' permanent representative in Melbourne during Fitzroy's awkward final months as an AFL club.

The process took place over the final months of the home and away season and into September and produced mixed results. Rowan Warfe was initially told he was not selected, but then Bears officials approached him and asked if he would be interested if Brisbane could not secure their initial eight picks. 'I didn't want to go interstate,' he recalled, 'particularly given I wasn't in that initial crop of eight.' He decided that he would go back into the draft and hope for the best.³⁵ John Rombotis took one look at Brisbane's centre line and decided he would try his luck with the new Port Adelaide team instead.³⁶ In talking to Fitzroy's players, Beatson did not sugar-coat the fact that many would struggle to earn their spot at Brisbane. When he met eighteen-year-old Nick Carter at the end of the season, he said: 'We know you played seventeen games, but your last half dozen games were no good and you're not just going to walk into this side.'³⁷ 'Some guys opted to say no to the offer,' reflected Carter, who, unlike some of his teammates, was keen to continue his career in Queensland.³⁸

The prospect of moving interstate was a serious issue for 22-year-old Scott Bamford. The 'sparrow-frail wingman' (183 centimetres and seventy kilograms according to the *Football Record*) could kick accurately on both his left and right foot and had suited Michael Nunan's style of play perfectly.[39] His particular physical qualities invited a variety of colourful descriptions: he was 'super quick', Stephen Paxman recalled, but he 'would get blown over in a windstorm'; Martin Flanagan likened him to the Man from Snowy River's horse, 'undersized but just the sort that won't say die'.[40] Fitzroy selected him in the first round of the 1995 AFL national draft with pick number four, taking him from Nunan's former club, North Adelaide. McConnell had the task of helping him relocate from Adelaide and had enormous difficulty finding him a place to live, because, as a Fitzroy player, real estate agents were sceptical about the security of his income. Ultimately, McConnell had to threaten an agent with the notion that his objections were illegal.[41] Now, Bamford was looking at the prospect of having to move again.

Despite being 'literally a kid' (according to McConnell) he was married with two children.[42] On 20 May, his wife, Anne, had given birth to their second daughter, Katelin, twelve weeks premature. Naturally she required much care and attention: 'She was touch and go for a while,' Bamford recalled, 'you can't explain what that feels like, or what goes through your mind.'[43] With both of their families in Adelaide, he found himself providing near full-time care to their eldest daughter, Emma, giving Anne as much support as he could and worrying about Katelin. Football was the only thing they had, both financially and as a support network, since they moved to Melbourne. It also gave Bamford some time and space. 'It was a relief to think about something else,' he reflected. 'You thought of Katelin so much, to go to training or play … it helped you feel better.'[44] There would obviously be issues if the Bamford family needed to uproot again and move to Brisbane.

Bamford's circumstances were particularly acute, yet they illustrate the complex personal issues affecting players in the aftermath of the merger that were often hidden from public view. At that time, even the best AFL clubs were not structured to provide comprehensive player welfare support, certainly not to the degree of modern, professional clubs. The Fitzroy Supporters Group had offered valuable player welfare support, but the demands on the players following the merger increased as the club's attention on player welfare fell by the wayside: Fitzroy lacked the resources, Brisbane was unable to intervene in Fitzroy's football operations, and the AFL did not seem to care. 'The players were just hung out to dry,' recalled Glenn Warry, who called on the services of the Victorian Institute of Sport and their career wellbeing program to fill the gap.[45] Marty Warry had been recruited through the 1994 national draft and had only begun playing regular senior football from Round 18. He thought that the players had often been forgotten as the club lurched from one drama to another that year. 'The club had bigger issues than to worry about some young kid trying to make his way in footy,' he said years later.[46]

...

In Round 17, Fitzroy travelled to Adelaide. With only six games left to impress potential clubs, the players did themselves few favours against the Crows. It was not at all clear that Adelaide had lost seven of their previous eight games; in front of a crowd of 31,880, they very quickly put Fitzroy to the sword. The game was effectively over at half-time, with Adelaide taking a 106-point lead into the long break. Fitzroy was 'aimless' and its midfield was a shambles. The usually dominant Primus struggled in the ruck and the Lions were poor with their execution.[47] Fitzroy clawed back some respectability in the second half and outscored the Crows 8.8 to 7.7, but this was too little too late. Adelaide had clearly put the cue in the rack at half-time and were tiring due to their effort in the first half.[48] The Crows ran out ninety-nine-point victors, 26.10 (166) to 9.13 (67). McConnell invoked the spirit of his immediate predecessor, lamenting that when the 'heat was on, we were pathetic'.[49]

Simon Hawking's four goals were one of the only positives from the game, although he picked up a hamstring injury that ruled him out for the following week.⁵⁰ Despite this, his longer-term future was looking more promising, with the 23-year-old being mentioned as one of the likely candidates for selection by Brisbane.⁵¹ Recruited from Fitzroy's Under 19s side as a left-footed defender, he showed plenty of promise in 1993 during his first year (accumulating a Brownlow vote for the Round 22 victory over Melbourne), but the transition to senior football was difficult and he contemplated walking away from the club. Glenn Warry and reserves coach Ross Thornton encouraged him to continue with AFL football, and he played all twenty-two games in 1994, earning a Rising Star nomination alongside Molloy, Johnson and Barker.

Hawking developed so well that Richmond had tried to recruit him at the end of 1994, seeking a quality key position defender (something they had lacked for years). Despite an enticing offer, Hawking stayed, but only once Fitzroy matched Richmond's bid.⁵² He continued to develop as a defender, but by the end of 1995 the team, still trying to find a replacement for Alastair Lynch, needed more options up forward and Hawking found himself named in the forward line. His 1996 season had been modest. Starting most games up forward, he had kicked 14.13 by the time the Adelaide game ended and was being talked about as a potential Brisbane recruit. 'It might surprise some to see a player like Hawking ... considered a certain Brisbane pick-up,' Alastair Lynch wrote in the *Courier-Mail* in early August 1996. 'What people need to remember is that some players find it difficult to produce their best in a difficult environment, but have the potential to adapt to better surroundings. The Fitzroy players have been through hell in the last twelve months and, given a more stable Brisbane environment and better players around them, some of the young Lions will step up to the next level.'⁵³

Many around Fitzroy hoped that the players would be given an opportunity to thrive in new environments. Hawking, however, was becoming increasingly strung out and emotionally exhausted as the season headed towards its conclusion. Confident that he would likely be playing somewhere in 1997, he did not bother talking directly with other clubs and was content to wait until he heard from his manager. 'I couldn't wait to get to the end of that season and just get away from it all,' he admitted, recalling that he was quite happy not to think about football for a while.[54]

Returning to the Whitten Oval for a bottom-of-the-ladder dogfight against aggrieved co-tenant Footscray, McConnell made a number of changes in response to the lamentable game in Adelaide. By now, Fitzroy had moved its training to Waverley Park, which was a distinct improvement from the Coburg City Oval. Unfortunately, on the Thursday night before the Footscray game the property van containing guernseys, footballs and gear broke down on the way to training. It was poor preparation for a game that, under ordinary circumstances, Fitzroy had a chance of winning. McConnell's plans were further upset when he received a phone call early on gameday concerning Stephen Paxman.

Paxman was another player with a good chance of being recruited for the 1997 season. Playing in a poor squad always makes defenders look worse than they are, particularly if a midfield is being overrun. History would prove Paxman to be a formidable defender. Clean cut, physically imposing with a professional mentality to the way he approached his football, he took the game seriously. He arrived at Fitzroy in the late eighties from the club's metropolitan zone (covering Bulleen, Templestowe, Doncaster and Donvale), a long-standing incubator of Fitzroy talent. By 1996, the 25-year-old was the club's vice-captain and the Adelaide game had been his ninety-eighth in Fitzroy colours. Until this round Paxman had played every game of the season, but some things are more important than football. That morning, Paxman's wife, Sharon, had gone into labour with their first child, ruling him out for the game.[55]

Without Paxman, Hawking or Molloy (who had also suffered a hamstring injury against Adelaide), McConnell shuffled his team around and called up the nineteen-year-old Marty Warry for his first game of the season. This proved to be a blessing for Warry, a Fitzroy supporter growing up, who went on to play each of Fitzroy's final AFL games.[56] Conditions were poor at the Whitten Oval; one observer wrote that 'the muddy surface was swathed with sand across the centre and wing to soak up the moisture'.[57] A scrappy game ensued. Fitzroy players worked hard to get their hands on the ball and break out of congestion, but they did themselves no favours with poor disposal around the ground and missed shots on goal. The main problem remained the inability to convert opportunities in the forward line: playing at full-forward, Anthony Mellington was beaten by Tony Campbell and the Lions' centre-half forward, John McCarthy, was well held by Chris Grant. Even when the forwards did get their hands on the ball they were inaccurate. McConnell brought on Jeff Hogg in the second half to provide the missing forward target, but he only managed two possessions in a disappointing performance. Marty Warry's first goal in League football, twenty-two minutes into the final quarter, put the Lions within fifteen points, but Fitzroy's determination in the contest could not compensate for poor skills. Footscray just scraped over the line 8.12 (60) to 6.9 (45).[58] This was Fitzroy's narrowest losing margin for the season, and as one journalist noted, a win 'could so easily have been a tonic for the terminally-ill club'.[59]

Despite the doom and gloom around the club, there was some news worth celebrating. That morning, Sharon Paxman gave birth to a daughter, Georgina.[60] As Sharon happened to be the granddaughter of Fitzroy premiership captain Fred Hughson, their daughter was the living embodiment of the notion that the heritage of the Fitzroy Football Club would live on, regardless of what happened at the end of the season.

…

For a player in the midst of such a tumultuous time at a lowly club, 23-year-old Martin Pike was having a very good year, on the field at least. After Round 8 Ted Hopkins, football writer and former Carlton premiership player, considered him alongside Guy McKenna as the best performing regular half-back flanker of the AFL season so far.[61] He had always showed promise as a footballer. The South Australian had impressed as a teenager for Norwood, before being selected by Melbourne with pick number nine in the 1992 national draft. While the Demons intended Pike to play on the half-back line, he was the third tall forward (alongside Garry Lyon and David Schwarz) in a Melbourne team that made the Preliminary Final in 1994.[62]

Yet his nascent career was jeopardised by his off-field notoriety. Mike Sheahan described Pike as someone who 'found himself in a man's world before his time'.[63] Once he started playing AFL football and earning a footballer's salary, he 'acquired a taste for the good life', which saw him traded from Melbourne to Fitzroy (although allegedly the Demons were so determined to get rid of him they would have delisted him anyway).[64] He reached a nadir in December 1995. He had spent a particular night at the Tunnel nightclub celebrating the selection of his friend, Test cricketer and Victorian paceman Damien Fleming, for the Australian squad in the Boxing Day Test. Stumbling out of the venue, he tried to drive home, being prevented by his intoxicated state and the close watch of a policeman.[65] This was his third drink-driving offense: while living in South Australia he was convicted twice for driving under the influence, the first occasion when he was only seventeen.

In July 1996, amid the chaos of what was happening to Fitzroy, Pike went before the Magistrates Court, pleaded guilty and was given a six-month jail term. The sentence was subsequently reduced to a community-based intensive corrections order. He was also banned from driving for five years and fined $1000. Nunan appeared as a character witness, telling the magistrate that Pike had 'resurrected his life' since the start of the year, becoming responsible and organised and had taken on a leadership role at the club.[66] He had certainly stepped up as a player in 1996. Initially apprehensive about his career after moving to the Lions, Nunan's arrival proved beneficial for him. The South Australian knew Pike's strengths from his SANFL days, particularly his ability to run off half-back, and he came to admire

Pike and what he was able to achieve. 'He was basically extremely tough,' Nunan said years later. 'It didn't matter what he'd got himself into. He didn't try to walk away or hide. He didn't lie.'[67]

In Round 18, Pike had a 23-possession game where he had also laid four tackles. He was the fifth-highest possession winner on a poor day at the Whitten Oval. Conditions would not be much better the next Saturday as Fitzroy played its final game at the ground, lining up against St Kilda. Pike played in his customary half-back flank role, new father Stephen Paxman was named in the side and Marty Warry's performance against the Bulldogs had earned him another senior game. Nunan had described Fitzroy's earlier match against the Saints as the most inept performance he had seen in thirteen years of coaching. The Lions hoped to give a better account of themselves in their fourth-last game in the AFL.

The state of the Whitten Oval had degraded all season, and was now labelled as being in 'third-world condition'.[68] As a result, both teams struggled to play fluid and attractive football. Fitzroy could often put a chain of handballs together, but their disposal by foot was poor, particularly when searching for a leading forward. St Kilda cruised through the game and when Fitzroy managed a goal, the Saints were able to reply within minutes. Fitzroy's dependable players could not carry the rest of the team. Simon Atkins began in 'a blaze of glory' but was tagged out of the game by Dean Anderson after half-time. Matthew Primus used his strength in the ruck but gave away six free kicks. Brad Boyd was matched with Robert Harvey and 'while beaten overall, did some constructive things with the ball'.[69] Fitzroy managed only a single point in the final quarter, the game ending with a 53-point victory to St Kilda, 13.10 (88) to 5.5 (35).[70]

McConnell was disappointed in his team's inability to convert from hard work up the ground. 'Our skill level came home to haunt us pretty strongly today,' he said.[71] Like other coaches had done since the merger was announced, St Kilda's coach, Stan Alves, gave credit to Fitzroy for managing to play in the adverse conditions.[72] Pike was impressive again. In recent weeks he had realised that tight defensive efforts on his opponent were unlikely to prevent a Fitzroy defeat and decided to play loose on his man and 'just get as much ball as I could'.[73] McConnell eventually admonished Pike for his loose checking, although he was pleased that he was still willing to be competitive and win the ball in close.[74] That day he had thirty-seven disposals, including twenty-six kicks. While many clubs, including Brisbane, were wary of recruiting him due to his off-field reputation, Adelaide and Port Adelaide became increasingly interested in bringing the South Australian back home. He certainly wanted to continue his career. 'You play AFL football to experience finals and win grand finals,' he said later that year, 'and at Fitzroy I haven't seen that action.'[75] Nunan was right, Pike was not one to lie: calling his time at Fitzroy a 'waste' from a professional perspective, he wanted to go to a club that would not accept losing.

...

In ordinary circumstances, Fitzroy might have won several of its final games, particularly in Round 16 against Collingwood. Yet these were not ordinary circumstances. Effectiveness suffered as players ceased fighting for a spot on the list or trying to have success as a team, and ambiguity about the future pervaded the playing group. McConnell tried to motivate the players, but Brett Cook believed he was 'pushing shit uphill', as most had gone into self-preservation mode.[76] 'I suppose every player got a bit selfish,' Brett Chandler reflected, with many thinking the same thing as John Rombotis: 'I've got to survive ... I've got to get on a list.'[77] Simon Hawking conceded that this attitude seemed perfectly logical: 'Until we heard otherwise,' he noted, 'everyone was out of a job next year.'[78] Some, however, resisted the temptation to start playing selfishly: Stephen Paxman took pride in playing for the team, as he did his whole career.[79] Marty Warry, who was just beginning to play regular senior football, did not feel as if the players were becoming overly selfish. Despite the adverse circumstances, he still enjoyed playing League football, as any nineteen-year-old would if they had dreamed of playing in the AFL all their life.[80]

Despite all this, off the field the players stuck together.[81] 'All we had was each other,' noted Chris Johnson at the end of the year, 'we became very close as a result of everything that went on.'[82] Brad Boyd echoed these sentiments: 'We all get along so well,' he said in early August. 'That's all we've got now, each other as players. We are a really tight-knit club. It will hit us all when we run out for the last time in a Fitzroy jumper.'[83] And despite the temptation to devolve to individualism, there was a unifying impulse about their predicament, one that became more evident and resonant the closer Fitzroy came to its final AFL game. The Lions players, whether they liked it or not, were now no longer just players — they were representing the club at this historic moment in time, and had a duty to the supporters and to the club's history. For some, such thinking was likely too maudlin. Leon Harris was past the stage of being emotional. 'Let's just get on with it and get it over as quickly as possible,' he thought after the merger was announced.[84] Yet Alan McConnell believed that his players had become custodians of the jumper, a responsibility probably too weighty to be placed on the shoulders of Fitzroy's young players, who continued to wrestle with their own personal and professional challenges as the season neared its end.[85]

CHAPTER SEVENTEEN

THE LONG GOODBYE

'I suppose in those long years I've been around the club I've been happy, but to see it end this way is devastating'

— Frank Bizzotto, Fitzroy defender.[1]

On Monday, 12 August, clubs, journalists and supporters reflected on the weekend of bruising football just passed and looked ahead to September. Sydney had moved to the top of the ladder with a strong win over Richmond, which also pushed the Tigers down to ninth. Not for the first time that season, North Melbourne and Brisbane had a spirited duel, with the Bears emerging victorious and moving up to third behind the Kangaroos in second. With West Coast sitting in fourth, Victorians faced the terrifying prospect of three interstate games in the first week of the finals (in 1995, all nine finals had been played in Melbourne). Attributing the negativity to 'parochial media', AFL spokesman Tony Peek reported that AFL officials were elated at the prospect, particularly the idea of finals at the SCG and the Gabba.² As usual, Mike Sheahan was cosmopolitan about the issue. 'Remember,' he wrote in the *Herald Sun*, 'the "A" in AFL stands for "Australian",' adding that while the previous years had seen interstate finals and even two interstate premierships, the volume of finals being played outside Victoria meant that 'it is 1996 that promises to change the face of football for Victorians forever'.³

Many other themes that had defined the Oakley era were also alive and well that week. Ross Oakley questioned the viability of the Whitten Oval as an AFL venue. While encouraging Footscray to maintain the venue as a training and administrative base, he believed that the ground's surface and stadium precinct fell short of League standards.⁴ The Tasmanian Football League continued to work on its bid to have a Tasmanian team enter the AFL, announcing that week that such a club would return eighty to ninety per cent of its profits to its ailing local clubs.⁵ The AFL's next potential merger, between Hawthorn and Melbourne, was gathering steam. Hawks president Brian Coleman believed that without a merger the club could eventually find itself in a dire financial situation, stating 'we don't want to become another Fitzroy'.⁶ On Wednesday, an emotional Coleman announced that Hawthorn would be seeking a merger with Melbourne.⁷ While the Melbourne board had yet to declare its hand, on Monday night, a group of Demons greats, including Ron Barassi, endorsed moves towards a merger.⁸ Not all past players were as enamoured with the prospect. Former Hawthorn premiership captain Don Scott launched Operation Payback, a fundraising venture aimed at generating $1.7 million to thwart the proposed merger. Oakley dismissed the anti-merger advocates as the ranting and raving from 'people on the fringes', while Coleman declared: 'To avoid extinction, or a Fitzroy-style slide into a cycle of debt, uncompetitiveness and ultimately a takeover, we must merge and merge very soon.'⁹

Fitzroy was well past such concerns. By mid-August, the club had all but disintegrated. Dyson Hore-Lacy and his board were powerless, while Michael Nunan, in whom many held high hopes at the start of the season, was gone. Supporters took sides on the question of endorsing the merger and supporting the Brisbane Lions, and while all fans mourned the demise of their club, many lashed out at a variety of targets, some justified, others not. In the face of growing tensions among the wider club community, John Birt conceded that 'the cracks are showing a bit' and before Fitzroy's Round 18 match against Footscray he made an impassioned plea for the club to 'finish the season with the great dignity and pride which Fitzroy has had over its 113-year history'.[10]

As he had done since coming to Fitzroy, Birt tried to remain positive about the situation. Yet while he was still nominally the CEO, he had no money and little power — Ernst & Young manager, Greg Swann, effectively ran the affairs of the club on behalf of the administrator and if he needed anything, he went to the AFL via Ian Collins.[11] Swann and his team had established themselves in the upstairs boardroom at the Fitzroy Club Hotel, working with Birt, Susan Cornish and the accounts staff to enact the deed of company arrangement. Despite the circumstances, the Ernst & Young team and the Fitzroy staff got along well — the outsiders were commendably compassionate about the fate of the club, led by Swann who was himself a football person and appreciated the difficulty of the situation.[12]

Downstairs, every piece of club memorabilia had been stored away to prevent it from being stolen. A historical committee had been established the previous year to select items for the AFL's centenary exhibition, 'Hidden Treasures, a visual history of Australian football'.[13] Since Brennan's appointment in late June, the committee had been cataloguing the club's memorabilia to determine what belonged to Fitzroy (and hence what could be sold off to pay the club's creditors) and what had been lent by supporters. Brennan decided not to liquidate this treasure trove, but still, storing away the physical history of the club was another sad reminder of what was being discarded.[14] Receptionist Fran Tascone had an especially difficult job, receiving calls and visits from distraught members and supporters. 'I've never heard so many crying members before in my life,' she recalled, with people offering to re-mortgage their houses or children wanting to give their pocket money to help the club. She offered a sympathetic ear and shoulder to cry on, but ultimately had the unenviable task of telling them that there was nothing that could be done to save Fitzroy.[15]

The football department kept to itself, determined to do the best they could, but feeling increasingly isolated, with no help from the AFL and Brisbane looking to take whatever it could from the club and discard the rest. 'It wasn't a pleasant time,' recalled fitness advisor Greg Freemantle, who was also acting as the club's runner with the departure of David Hookes.[16] The match committee had not met formally in weeks; before each round, Alan McConnell determined the team and informed people after the fact. For McConnell, the club had been reduced to himself, the football department and the players.[17] 'The end couldn't come quick enough,' reflected Leon Harris, who, in addition to his full-time job, was still coaching the reserves, assisting McConnell and participating in a growing number of Fitzroy functions to mark the end of the club's life in the AFL.[18]

The year had taken its toll on everyone at Fitzroy; although just in his first year of AFL football, Matthew Primus was surely correct when told the *Herald Sun*, 'In your footy career you're not going to come up against anything that is going to be as hard as this year has been.'[19] By now the players likely knew (or at least suspected) who would be going to Brisbane, with the remainder trying to sort out what they would be doing in 1997. They had dragged themselves through their remaining games since Round 14, contesting as best they could with a team that was coming apart. Now, they entered the final three games, each significant well beyond the chance to gain four premiership points. With the initial shock of the merger having passed, Fitzroy supporters readied themselves for these final, emotional games, as their club slowly said goodbye to the AFL.

...

As notoriously foreshadowed on *The Footy Show*, Fitzroy's final AFL 'home' game came in Round 20, when it hosted Brisbane at Princes Park. Those of a humorous disposition commented that it was little more than an intra-club match (one wit suggested that Fitzroy could forfeit and save the Bears the travel time).[20] Lions fans did not see the funny side, with many still viewing Brisbane negatively as the club taking Fitzroy away from Victoria against its wishes. For the players, this was their chance to audition for the remaining places on Brisbane's list. It would also be Stephen Paxman's 100th game — a milestone most of his teammates could only dream about at that stage.

It was a sad sight at Princes Park that Saturday afternoon. Fitzroy's third last AFL game drew a crowd of just 6469. While rain and wind made conditions unpleasant, the seeming abandonment of the club by all but the most hardy and dedicated spoke volumes about why Fitzroy had ended up as it had. Waiting for the start of the game, Martin Flanagan was struck by the silence, like a pall had descended over the ground.[21] This funeral atmosphere was shattered when Brisbane ran onto the ground, as angry boos from the Fitzroy fans reverberated around the stadium. So aggressive was this treatment that Brisbane's coach, John Northey, rebuked the supporters after the game. Signs were held aloft declaring 'BRISBANE NO!' and 'WE ARE VICTORIAN' — those fans making their position on the merger abundantly clear. Worse was the treatment of Brad Boyd. That morning it was reported that he had accepted a lucrative four-year deal with the Brisbane Lions. Many supporters viewed this as treason and abused him throughout the game. 'Fitzroy's disintegrating,' lamented one supporter in the outer.[22]

Away from the tension in the stands the game played out predictably. The Lions started well, as they had done for much of the season, and showed some fight in the first quarter. But Brisbane, which would make a Preliminary Final that season, was far too strong. The

21-year-old Michael Voss dominated the centre of the ground and was well on his way to a Brownlow Medal.[23] Fitzroy tried to keep pace in the first half but completely capitulated in the second as its young players failed to run with their more mature opposition. McConnell acknowledged that his midfield was 'slaughtered' from half-time on, admitting that the team lost cohesion as several of his players went 'kick-chasing' in the second half to display their wares to Brisbane.[24]

Individually, Matthew Primus fought hard around the ground, showcasing why he was such sought-after property. Martin Pike played on future teammate Darryl White and the two had a 'spirited duel'. Pike picked up twenty-five possessions roaming across halfback but 'let himself down' with sometimes errant disposals, while White had a relatively quiet day, nursing a sore knee at the end of the game alongside worry about being reported for kicking Fitzroy's Matthew Manfield.[25] Despite the poor second half, Fitzroy did manage 100 points; John McCarthy kicked four and young Marty Warry, in his third game, kicked three. The latter had proved a late surprise for the Lions, and could have been the forward target Nunan had been looking for had he played him earlier in the season. Brisbane won comfortably, 29.13 (187) to 14.16 (100) and despite all the anger directed at him, Noel Gordon had been right — it was a percentage booster.

Fitzroy fans invaded the ground after the game and Boyd hastily made for the dressing rooms, more than slightly concerned for his safety.[26] McConnell had felt anger in the crowd and denounced the treatment of Boyd (and others) as a 'disgrace'.[27] Boyd later called it the worst day of his life.[28] A large group of fans gathered around the entrance to the Lions' race after the game and stayed for many minutes, chanting and clapping. Boyd understood the fans' reaction, but pleaded, 'We can't do anything about it. We've just got to play, and I wish people would understand that. It's out of our hands.'[29] Patrick Smith wrote that the game was always going to be difficult, but 'those in the outer made it much worse than it should have been.'[30] Another journalist noted: 'Brisbane's principal reason for merging with Fitzroy was to establish a Melbourne supporter base. If Saturday's spectator turnout was any indication, this could be a long time coming.[31]

It had been an ugly game, both with respect to the scoreboard and the behaviour of some in the crowd. Yet even in this highly charged environment, the emotion of Fitzroy's fate could still be expressed gracefully. Media personality and long-time Fitzroy supporter John Blackman had attended the president's lunch. Inspired by a song played at his daughter's school-leaving ceremony, he choked up as he addressed the room:

Adieu my dear Fitzroy, adieu

For 40 years I've loved you

Although it's time for us to part

You'll always be here in my heart

Farewell old Roy Boys, fare thee well

The times you've made my great heart swell

I'll cherish always the maroon and blue

Adieu, my dear Fitzroy, adieu.[32]

...

When the players arrived at the Coburg City Oval for training the following Tuesday night, they were met with a message pinned to the notice board: 'Meeting 5pm.' Alan McConnell berated his players for the easy goals they conceded against Brisbane. There were still two games to play, he reminded them, yet finding motivation to keep playing was a challenge. 'We all want to get it over with,' recalled John Rombotis, who was on track to play every game that season.[33] Of these difficult final games, Round 21 against Richmond, the final AFL game in Victoria, was going to be the biggest. While the fixture had not been Fitzroy's friend in recent years, playing their final game in Melbourne at the MCG was fortuitous, allowing tens of thousands of supporters to attend.

Everyone knew it would be an event — Victoria's chance to say goodbye to Fitzroy. Writing for *The Sunday Age*, Jake Niall rejected the assertion that the club would live on in the Brisbane Lions: 'Fitzroy dies next week and this week is the last chance for most supporters to see it alive, in the flesh.'[34] The AFL decided that it would mark the occasion with a series of events before the game. They organised a lunch in the Great Southern Stand's Legends Room for Fitzroy greats, followed by a motorcade, with all living captains and best and fairest winners invited to take part. There would also be a function at the Fitzroy Town Hall that evening. Events, big and small, were held throughout the week to mark the occasion. At training on Thursday night, 53-year-old Norm Brown, who played in the Fitzroy side that beat Richmond at the MCG in 1970 in front of Queen Elizabeth II, came to talk to the players in the hopes of inspiring them for Sunday.[35] Ever the professional, Stephen Paxman was frustrated that the build-up was distracting from the game itself; 'Yes we were done after ninety-six,' he recalled, 'but we were still playing a game of footy.'[36]

Richmond v Fitzroy was the only game in Melbourne that Sunday, giving the match the space its historical significance deserved. That morning, Fitzroy people readied themselves to see 'the last rites administered' (as one fan described it).[37] The McLaughlin brothers, Simon and Evan, had grown up as fanatical Fitzroy supporters, wearing their Lions jumpers so often that their mother could only wash them if she physically pinned her boys down and removed them herself. Although they would be flying to Perth the following week for Fitzroy's final AFL game, it in no way lessened the gravity of that day's game. Like thousands of Roys supporters, they made their way to the MCG, meeting the rest of their family and friends outside Gate 12 before taking their seats near the boundary line in the Ponsford Stand.[38] Around them, thousands of fellow supporters slowly filled the

MCG, many, one observer noted, 'in conspicuously new scarves and beanies'.[39] Some, however, could not bring themselves to attend at all: 'Nothing could be more galling to the true Fitzroy-lover than an AFL-endorsed "crocodile tearfest",' wrote Mark Dees.[40] Another supporter stated: 'I could not go and say goodbye ... I was very depressed, it was all pain and suffering going to those last games.'[41] One fan simply wanted the season to finish 'so we could move on'.[42]

Before the game, possibly the greatest ever assemblage of Fitzroy champions gathered for the past players' function. Even Perth-based Ron Alexander, John Duckworth and Ian McCulloch flew in for the occasion. Only two living best and fairest recipients could not attend: Johnny Murphy was coaching Box Hill and Scott McIvor's wife was about to have a baby.[43] Past players mingled and no doubt reflected on better times, and as the function wound down, Bill Stephen led a rendition of the club song, followed by three cheers. The former captains and best and fairest winners were then ushered down to take part in the motorcade at 1.30pm. Names such as Alan Ruthven, Kevin Murray and Bernie Quinlan (Brownlow medallists all) as well as the likes of Garry Wilson, Warwick Irwin and Matt Rendell were a reminder of the club's pedigree. As Bernie Quinlan went around the ground he saw supporters 'howling in the crowd', while some booed Gary Pert and Paul Roos for their perceived disloyalty.[44] The scoreboard played a video outlining Fitzroy's history, with footage of on-field highlights from the seventies and eighties. An eerie hush then fell over the crowd, almost like a minute's silence. And then the disembodied voice from the scoreboard said the words 'a new dawn', no doubt espousing the AFL encouraged message; 'Tell that to the Fitzroy fans,' one journalist wrote.[45]

With all the ceremonies and the emotion, the match itself was somewhat lost — football had 'become almost incidental at that stage', Greg Freemantle lamented.[46] That morning the players arrived for only their second game at the MCG that year. Jarrod Molloy, who was still recovering from his hamstring injury, was determined to play. McConnell brought him back in, along with Simon Hawking.[47] Emotion was high in the dressing rooms. By now Chris Johnson knew he would be playing for the Brisbane Lions in 1997, but many of his teammates were still in limbo: 'They probably didn't think they were ever going to run on the MCG with an AFL jumper on,' he thought.[48] Simon Atkins told his teammates the atmosphere was similar to that of a final (he had played in several with Footscray).[49] On a whiteboard, McConnell simply wrote: WE MUST WIN.[50] Fitzroy's reserves, which were actually in a good run of form, had won the curtain raiser, 19.21 (135) to 11.9 (75). It gave some hope that the seniors too could produce something remarkable for the supporters.

At approximately 2.00pm, Brad Boyd led his team out onto the MCG where they were greeted by a guard of honour of former players, more than 400 children dressed in the Fitzroy uniforms and the roar of 48,884 spectators (the largest crowd at a Lions game for some time).[51] The players broke through the banner, followed by the children, 'like a colourful, human streamer' as one observer described it.[52] Alan Ruthven tossed the coin — the 1950 Brownlow Medallist finding the demise of his former club difficult to take.[53] Conspicuously absent from the MCG that day were the members of the AFL Commission, who were in Adelaide to watch the Crows play Collingwood. 'Who said people return to the scene of the crime?' asked Patrick Smith.[54]

Fitzroy's champions returned to the stands and watched helplessly as the modern incarnation of 'the club we hold so dear' was mauled in a spectacle unbefitting the history and gravitas of the occasion. A wave of emotion swept across the crowd at the first bounce, but it dissipated in minutes.[55] Fitzroy were flat ('revved up but mentally drained' was how Rombotis described it) and Richmond, looking for a big percentage to help make the finals, demolished them with little sympathy.[56] Matthew Richardson ran riot and even with his erratic kicking, managed to pile on the goals. He went through four direct opponents: Boyd, Mellington, Paxman and Molloy, none of whom could stop him.[57]

Fitzroy was barely there. Richmond's midfield carved them up and sent ball after ball towards Richardson and Brendon Gale. The Lions only managed five goals for the match, three to Warry, one each to Boyd and Barker. On one of the saddest days in League history, Fitzroy completely capitulated. The final score of 28.19 (187) to 5.6 (36) was the club's second worst loss in its history — an ignominious way to say goodbye. The match may have been 'a mere footnote to the greater historical marker of Fitzroy's last game in Melbourne', but the loss still stung.[58] Martin Pike, who continued his good form with a 27-disposal game, called it 'a disgrace'.[59] Many of the players and staff felt like imposters, unable to bear the weight of the responsibility with which they were charged. Fitzroy had won three games in two seasons and the chances of a good contest, much less a Lions victory, were slim, yet thousands of Roys supporters came to the match anyway.[60] 'Just watching the team and the colours for the last time in the flesh,' declared Adam Muyt, 'was enough of a reason to be there.'[61]

Alan McConnell found the whole experience 'pretty soul-destroying'.[62] After the siren, he strode out onto the ground to be with his players. In the stands, supporters were in tears. Past players sobbed. McConnell sought out Brad Boyd. They both knew that they would be expected to do a lap of honour around the ground, and almost to a man each player hated the idea. Stephen Paxman, for instance, took every game seriously — a lap of honour after a 151-point loss just did not sit right with him (although he understood the wider reasons for doing it).[63] Boyd told McConnell that they just had to get off the ground quickly, but McConnell reminded him that there was no choice: almost 50,000 people had turned up to watch the Fitzroy jumper run around on the MCG one last time, and 'we happened to be the idiots in the jumpers'.[64] There was a brief standoff, and then the players reluctantly agreed to run the Great Southern Stand boundary before heading down the race.[65] Despite advocating for it, McConnell considered the lap of honour the worst thing the players had to endure that day.[66] 'It was just terrible,' McConnell said, 'it was terrible to put them through that, they were humiliated.'[67]

But the gesture, however painful and embarrassing for the players, had purpose. Thousands of fans sobbed as the team passed by. For Richmond coach Robert Walls, it was not until he saw the team doing their final lap that the reality of losing Fitzroy to the competition 'hit home'.[68] Mercifully for the players they never finished the lap, with scores of supporters streaming on to the ground to share the moment.[69] McConnell was briefly concerned for the safety of his players, but it was actually the supporters who needed to worry.[70] The AFL had increased security specifically for the game, and as sixteen-year-old Hayley Sanders ran onto the field she was tackled to the ground by a security guard. She managed to struggle free and ran to Martin Pike, hugging him for protection.[71] Soon, hundreds of Roys supporters were running out to take part, overwhelming the security guards and culminating at the players' race. Many fans were chanting insults at Ross Oakley, while one fan set a Fitzroy jumper alight. Another, Maureen Neill, laid a simple wreath in the club's blue, gold and maroon colours in the centre circle.[72]

Surrounded by fans, the players made their way to the race as the MCG scoreboard declared: 'So long Fitzroy and thanks for the memories.'[73] Players and staff were shielded from the media after the game for about an hour, most mourned privately and quietly. Boyd was left feeling numb. McConnell told his players to take their time to regroup and several, including Boyd and Paxman, shed a few tears.[74] The caretaker coach had, one reporter wrote, 'the wrung-out expression of a man who had lost far more than a football team'.[75] More than thirty minutes after the siren sounded, some players could not even contemplate the showers. The eerie stillness was only broken by the sound of supporters trying to gain entry into the rooms, held back by police and MCG security. Ground staff briefed Tom Couch and asked Glenn Warry if he could venture outside to calm the increasingly hostile fans. He declined.[76]

Out on the ground, supporters continued to grieve. Hundreds of fans steadfastly remained at the top of the race and sung the club song over and over. They continued to sing, chant and clap for the best part of forty minutes after the final siren. Simon McLaughlin was too numb to run out onto the ground to join them. Instead, amid scores of grown adults weeping around him, he steeled himself to go through this experience again in one week's time.[77] Among the tearful supporters was the club's number one ticket holder, Tom Reynolds, who cried at the football for the first time in his life.[78] Dave Beaumont was also in tears: 'I was devastated. My football club was dead … It was a miserable day, everything was crap, it was just one of the worst days of my life.'[79] Kevin Murray declared it 'the end of suburban football as we have known it'. He was wearing his old jumper, a pair of footy socks from his playing days, and, as always, his 1969 Brownlow Medal.[80] Eventually, thousands of Fitzroy supporters spilled out of the MCG into Yarra Park, many in tears, most never to see their club play an AFL game in person again. Many felt angry, others were distraught, while some just felt hollow and numb. Joy Paine had shed a tear during the game. Afterwards she spoke for many, lamenting: 'It's been a sad, sad day.'[81]

While no one doubted that the game had been emotional for every Fitzroy fan at the ground that day, the number of supporters in the crowd was a point of consternation. 'One fancies more Fitzroy supporters turned up than for the past decade,' wrote Patrick Smith.[82] Where had all this support been, he asked, 'It must hurt those who battled the long, lone fight for survival.'[83] Here, Smith and Dyson Hore-Lacy were in accord. Fitzroy's president was critical, if not saddened — he too saw the influx of supporters 'brandishing new items of merchandise such as scarves and flags' and reflected, 'I could not help thinking that if these people had been as supportive during the previous few years, we might not have been in the predicament we were.'[84] One supporter wrote to the *Herald Sun*: 'If only all the Fitzroy supporters at the MCG on Sunday had memberships, we might have survived. I am as guilty as anyone.'[85] A merchandise vendor noted that they were now selling Fitzroy gear 'by the truckload'. 'If they'd had this sort of support during the year,' he commented, 'they would never have folded.'[86]

That evening the City of Yarra hosted a reception for the club at the Fitzroy Town Hall. Bernie Quinlan had never seen so many people with tears in their eyes. The hall was packed out, Brad Boyd and Bill Stephen were the two guest speakers. After the official dinner, Boyd continued on to the Fitzroy Club Hotel to meet more supporters. As with the town hall, the hotel was packed and the atmosphere was 'like that of a premiership'. Pleasantly (especially in light of his treatment at the Brisbane game), Boyd found the supporters very warm towards the players and through all the adversity they still maintained their passion for Fitzroy. He ended up at the Napier Hotel for several beers before heading home at 1:00am, feeling 'totally drained'.[87] Fortunately, there was only one final match before it was all over.

CHAPTER EIGHTEEN

A TOUCH OF SADNESS

'We've done what we needed to do, we get off, we move on'

— Leon Harris, Fitzroy reserves coach.[1]

In the final week of August 1996, their Royal Highnesses, the Prince and Princess of Wales were formally divorced, US President Bill Clinton was re-nominated as the Democratic Party's candidate for the November presidential elections, and somewhere in Afghanistan, Osama bin Laden declared a holy war on the United States, issuing the 'Declaration of Jihad Against the Americans Occupying the Land of the Two Holiest Sites'. In Australia, the Fitzroy Football Club, its players, the remaining staff and thousands of supporters were preparing for the club's final week as a member of the league it had helped to create in 1896. On Sunday, 1 September at 2.10pm, Fitzroy would play Fremantle at Subiaco Oval and then never play another AFL game again. People believed that Fitzroy would never be seen again in any form: there seemed no hope of a resurrection.

'Tomorrow, Fitzroy disappears,' wrote journalist Ross Brundrett in the *Herald Sun* that Saturday. 'They go north to merge, but the reality is they will disappear into the ether.'[2] Never before or since would a game between the teams 14th and 16th on the ladder carry so much historical significance.

But this was no abstract historical event; for thousands of Fitzroy supporters, it was an occasion with deep personal significance. 'The merger means the end of football for me,' declared Roys supporter Justin Calverley, whose uncles Des and Bruce had played for the club in the thirties and forties, 'I will never barrack for another team.'[3] One young supporter decided to travel to Perth for the game. Her grandfather had died the previous year, and the loss of Fitzroy invoked similar feelings, describing it in terms that would be used by many other supporters to articulate how it felt: like a death in the family.[4] Barry Dickins had composed a eulogy for Fitzroy: 'We were the blushing maiden on her wedding night, embarrassed about not knowing how to undress. In the end we were raped and left for dead in Brisbane ... I have screamed for Fitzroy in the outer ever since Mum had me. Now Fitzroy has been had. And beheaded as well. We will never run on again, in any way, shape or form.'[5]

In that weekend's *Football Record*, Ross Oakley acknowledged that for Fitzroy supporters there would be 'a touch of sadness' as the club made its last appearance in the AFL.[6] In his view, however, Fitzroy people could be comforted knowing that the club's colours and the Lions name would be preserved in its merger with Brisbane. Whether he actually believed this or not, he needed to sell the idea of continuity and preservation of heritage to help convince Fitzroy people to support the merged club. Contra to Oakley's subdued expectations, Fitzroy's final week in the League was very emotive indeed, and while many supporters did choose to support the Brisbane Lions in 1997 and beyond, that in no way lessened their anguish. Geoff Slattery, editor of the *Football Record*, read the mood slightly better than the League's CEO, writing that Fitzroy supporters would 'weep and gnash their teeth with the fury of their loss'.[7] Faced with the prospect of seeing their team play its last AFL game, supporters, those who had given years of their lives and much emotional investment, reacted accordingly.

Their grief was not helped by the fixture. For some time, the football world had looked ahead to Fitzroy's final match against Fremantle in Perth. The idea of this game being so far away from Melbourne was dispiriting. It was 'hard to imagine a more lonely or tragic demise,' wrote Patrick Smith in early June.[8] Many supporters, particularly older men and women who had been following the Roys for decades, would miss out on seeing their club's final League game. Surely, many suggested, the fixture could be adjusted to give Fitzroy a more fitting end? These pleas fell on deaf ears. On 4 June the AFL ruled out moving the game to Melbourne.[9] It would be unfair on Fremantle, administrators argued, not only would it cost the Dockers money, but it might affect their chances of playing finals. Options were posited, such as switching Rounds 21 and 22, so that Fremantle would not lose its home game.[10] Fitzroy officials undertook a mountain of work to try to convince the League to move the game.[11] The Dockers' general manager David Hatt eventually called their Round 22 home fixture 'non-negotiable', and the AFL was unwilling to intervene for the sake of Lions supporters.[12] Ross Oakley called it 'dull impartiality' that consigned Fitzroy to play its final game in Perth. He later admitted that the League could have handled the whole situation better, but 'a draw is a tough thing to unpick'.[13]

Mike Sheahan, ever one to antagonise the Lions, had heard from Tony Peek, the AFL's communications manager, that all the discussion about the issue seemed to come from non-Fitzroy people, leading him to ask: 'Do all the Fitzroy people care when and where they are when the final siren blows for them? It seems not.'[14] Come 1 September, a great many people cared. Jan Wright considered it 'absolutely disgraceful', while Fran Tascone called it 'gut-wrenching' and was particularly devastated for those older supporters who could not make it to Perth.[15] Simon Hawking concurred: 'That was a real insult to everyone,' and to Glenn Warry it was traumatic, 'because the players and fans didn't want to be playing their final game on the other side of the earth.'[16] Expressing an alternate view, Stephen Paxman actually preferred that their final game was away from Melbourne, as it sheltered the players a little and allowed them to be surrounded by an intimate group of family, club officials and a small number of loyal supporters.[17]

As he did the week before, Alan McConnell gave his players a spray on Monday night for their performance against the Tigers. Few had played well, although Matthew Primus could hold his head up, having dominated Richmond's Justin Charles in the ruck.[18] McConnell emphasised the importance of maintaining their focus for the final game, although he probably knew this would be tough.[19] Winding up the club's football operations provided many distractions, some emotional and poignant, others cold and corporate (such as the sight of a termination notice sitting on McConnell's desk when he arrived for work on Wednesday morning).[20] As had been the case during dramatic or important times of the year, Fitzroy received significant coverage in the media that week. In addition to post mortems of Sunday's disastrous game against Richmond, the major newspapers ran all manner of articles on the Lions, reflecting on the club's history and the human cost of its imminent departure from the League.

Thursday night was the team's final training session at the Coburg City Oval, with several hundred supporters watching on. Some fans cried, others joined in kick-to-kick with the players and grabbed autographs. 'I haven't stopped crying since they started training,' said Bruce Lynch, a heartbroken 31-year-old supporter who was there with his six-year-old son, Ryan. 'We're human beings, we all have our emotions and if you let them show that's what footy's all about.'[21] It was the biggest crowd Brad Boyd had ever seen at a Fitzroy training session. One fan had laid a wreath in the centre of the ground. While it was a touching gesture, it made training difficult, and after a brief debate about the appropriateness of relocating it, the wreath was respectfully moved to the side of the ground once training commenced in earnest.[22] Throughout the evening the players were in good spirits, with Danny Morton up to his usual pranks. Boyd tried to enjoy his last training run. It was 'sad in a way', but he chose not to dwell on it.[23] John McCarthy brought along framing borders for the team to sign, giving those who wanted the option of having their final jumper framed and surrounded by the signatures of Fitzroy's last AFL team.[24]

Later that evening there was a Last Supper at Marianna's, which the club's hierarchy had organised to thank the staff for all their efforts over the years. More than one hundred people attended: players, trainers, stewards, timekeepers and administration staff. Timekeeper Arch Parsons had been at the club longer than most players had been alive. Kevin Elms was in tears, wondering what he would do in 1997 without Fitzroy. McConnell, who had been with Fitzroy on and off since the Under 19s, was also very emotional, and many of the players realised what a fighter he had been for the club and how much he cared for his players. The gathering brought home the fact that this diverse group, bound together in service of the club, would soon go their separate ways, disbanding and dispersing a core part of the modern Fitzroy Football Club. Brad Boyd reflected that people like property steward Glen Ford and doorman Tommy Couch represented 'the true spirit of Fitzroy'.[25]

That same evening the Fitzroy Supporters' Group held the final Ins and Outs Night, changing their venue to the Fitzroy Town Hall to accommodate a crowd of over six hundred. Boyd was the guest speaker, supported by Fitzroy greats such as Garry Wilson, Mick Conlan and Grant Lawrie. The usual camaraderie and revelry of an Ins and Outs Night was replaced with a sense of melancholy, and co-organiser Jan Wright said it was the saddest night in her life. The weekly function had been such a joyous focal point for Fitzroy supporters, successful beyond anything the organisers could have imagined. 'It's tragic to think that all this is going to end,' she lamented.[26] By now, the 25-year-old Boyd was feeling particularly drained. Without a president and a full-time coach, he had become Fitzroy's figurehead, and his propensity to accept every function and speaking invitation (lest he disappoint the already heartbroken supporters), as well as copious media requests, was taking its toll. Mercifully it was soon coming to an end, but he, like everyone connected with the club, was not free from the emotional impact of all that was taking place. 'It feels like I'm losing something from my life', he reflected.[27]

...

For the final time, McConnell selected his team. It was a significant decision, not just historically but also financially. The remainder of the players' contracts would be paid out at whatever rate they received in their final game: if they played seniors, their payout would be base salary for seniors, if they played in the reserves, it was much less.[28] One omission struck a particularly sour note for some who had been with the Lions for several years. Jason Baldwin had played 125 games for the Lions since 1989, including each game since Round 17, but McConnell decided to omit him from the team for Round 22. The 26-year-old veteran was the club's longest-serving player, and this, in addition to the way he had been treated by Nunan, left a bad taste in his mouth.[29]

For Fitzroy's final AFL team, McConnell selected Primus, Atkins, Dent and Bamford in the middle, with Barker and Carter on either wing. Hawking, Warry, Rombotis, McCarthy, Boyd and Johnson were in the forward line, with Warfe, Pike, Clayton, Molloy, Chandler and Paxman in defence. Doyle, Morton and Hogg were on the bench.[30] Some knew they would be playing for Brisbane next season, while others were confident they would find another club. Some feared that this would be their final senior game at AFL level, while others knew it for a fact. Several, stung by their performance the previous Sunday, were genuinely looking forward to the game. Boyd, Molloy, Primus and Rombotis met at property steward Glen Ford's home at Tullamarine before they headed to the airport. They were enthusiastic, and Rombotis thought they were an outside chance to win. 'Remember,' he noted, 'we did beat Freo earlier in the season.'[31] On their flight from Melbourne, Ansett Australia staff inscribed their boarding passes with the words 'Fitzroy Forever'.[32]

The team was joined by thousands of Fitzroy supporters, desperate to travel to Perth any way they could. Those who remained in Melbourne could watch the game on Channel Seven, the official broadcaster making the sensible decision to show this game live, rather than a delayed broadcast of Richmond v North Melbourne at the MCG (where the Tigers were fighting for a spot in the finals). Some Roys would watch at home with family and friends, others would venture out to be with fellow supporters at the Fitzroy Club Hotel or any number of other pubs in and around Fitzroy. An informal picnic was organised at the Brunswick Street Oval for Sunday lunchtime, where fans could partake in an 'El-Cheapo' sausage sizzle before the main event.[33] It was, Adam Muyt recalled, such a beautiful day: 'No clouds, or wind, seductive light glowing over everything, the first real hint of spring warmth. Like the day was created just to confound whatever sombre spirits were hovering around.'[34] From there, Muyt and others moved to the nearby Tramway Hotel. A crowd at the Fitzroy Club Hotel grew, while other supporters moved into their living rooms. Tuning into Channel Seven's coverage of the game, they once again cursed Ross Oakley and the AFL for the fact that they were so far away from their beloved club at such a poignant time.

Across in Western Australia, 22,515 people had made their way to Subiaco Oval. Emotions were high among the travelling Fitzroy fans. One banner, held aloft by three ageing male supporters, read: 'Born 1883 — Murdered 1996.'[35] One 51 year-old, Irene Smith, had flown from Dubai via Singapore. 'I had to get through this game,' she recalled, 'because it's like a death and I wasn't as upset over the death of my mother as I am over this.'[36] Two club trainers, Troy Hall and Tim Renwick, had paid for their own flights to Perth, determined to be part of the final game. When they arrived, Glen Warry told them that the club had employed local trainers and they would not be needed. Unimpressed, the pair argued their case, and after some debate, it was decided that they would work the second half.[37]

The AFL administration had made Round 21 its send-off for Fitzroy, and, 'with its customary sensitivity' (wrote Martin Flanagan) was not prepared to waste any more resources this week.[38] But Fremantle proved unexpectedly generous, contributing a reported $10,000 to the occasion to ensure Fitzroy's last AFL game was treated with due respect (probably indicating the influence of Ron Alexander, one of Fremantle's directors and a former Fitzroy captain and best and fairest).[39] They arranged a function room for Fitzroy coterie members and sponsors and brought Kevin Murray, Bernie Quinlan, Ron Alexander and Haydn Bunton Junior out onto the ground before the game to unfurl the 1944 VFL Premiership flag.[40] The Dockers players would also wear black armbands in solidarity.[41] Fremantle's treatment of Fitzroy was much appreciated at the time and has been long remembered. It was 'quite telling', recalled supporter Rick Lang, who had flown to Perth for the game, 'that a club only a few years old could read the situation better than the AFL.'[42]

As it approached 12:10pm local time (or 2.10pm in Melbourne), Alan McConnell, Leon Harris and Greg Swann made their way to the coaches box as support staff for both clubs and the interchange players vacated the field. As the starting eighteen for both sides took their positions, the Channel Seven commentary team of Drew Morphett, Kevin Bartlett, Ross Glendinning and Dwayne Lamb made the final remarks. In the middle of the ground, Matthew Primus readied himself for the opening ruck contest, with Simon Atkins positioned centrally and Scott Bamford and Matthew Dent as the pincers, ready to move in from either side. At the appropriate time, 28-year-old field umpire, Stephen McBurney, held the ball aloft, and once he had received the confirmatory blast of the siren, paused, before slowly walking in for the first bounce. Fitzroy supporters at Subiaco, in Melbourne and all across the country, braced themselves for an emotional few hours.

...

The game began in blistering fashion: Fremantle had two goals before the ball had entered Fitzroy's forward fifty. A rebounding end-to-end tussle then ensued, with both sides inaccurate in front of goal. With six minutes of playing time left for the first quarter, a rampaging Rowan Warfe received a handball from a static John McCarthy on the wing and he charged forward. Kicking from over sixty metres out, Marty Warry could not get on the end of it and it rolled through for a behind, making the score 2.5 to 0.4. Fremantle's full-back, Andrew McGovern, kicked to himself and then ran out from defence. In his enthusiasm, he was penalised for running 'a country mile' (according to Kevin Bartlett). Simon Hawking was the nearest Lions player, and he was given the free kick, about forty metres out on a bad angle for a left-footer. Undaunted, Hawking's shot sailed through, and the large travelling Fitzroy faithful cheered loudly. Shortly thereafter, Chris Johnson hit the post twice (once on each for balance), and had he scored either, the two teams would have been practically level with approximately three minutes of the quarter remaining. When the two teams played in May, Fitzroy had taken these opportunities. Now, with so much having happened since, they were wayward. Fremantle then kicked away, ending the quarter 4.6 (30) to 1.6 (12).

The Roys had given a good account of themselves thus far in a fast, tough game. Once the second quarter began, however, Fremantle took control. Playing at their home ground, and without any of the emotional baggage shouldered by Fitzroy's players, the Dockers attacked their goals frequently and accurately. By the time the Lions had their second goal — a crumbing effort from Marty Warry at close range — it was 8.6 to 2.7. Fitzroy got another from McCarthy before the quarter was out, but by half-time the Dockers were forty-six points in front.

Despite their desire to win this final game, the Fitzroy players had little left to give after an emotionally draining season. It had been difficult for the team to concentrate, Jarrod Molloy believed, and there seemed a feeling of emptiness about the pre-match preparation.[43] Primus knew it would be good to have a win in their final game, but conceded, 'I think we were just drained by the time we got there.'[44] After the game, John McCarthy told boundary-rider Dwayne Lamb: 'Thursday nights you've got functions, Tuesday nights you've got functions, you're saying goodbye to people, you've got a lot of emotional people around the club, it's just been very hard for these young blokes to keep focussed on a simple game of footy.'[45] 'We lost our momentum two or three weeks ago,' McConnell conceded after the match. 'There's just been too much baggage we've been carrying, and it's just been too much.'[46]

Fremantle began the third quarter as they had played most of the second: fast, direct and with purpose. Warry managed a second goal from close range, bringing the margin back to forty-six points. The nineteen-year-old was having a good game, probably the best of his career. At the contest, Fitzroy could be aggressive, but they often lacked the ability to run with opponents or swarm a ball-carrier. Fremantle players would often find themselves in acres of space, and occasionally ran too far into empty territory. Despite their exhaustion, Fitzroy fought hard where they could and the game became feisty at times, McCarthy and Johnson being the main perpetrators. There were, however, still moments of levity. As Kingsley Hunter was taking a set-shot for goal a male streaker ran onto the ground to the cheers of the crowd. Undeterred by the glancing display of male nudity in front of him, Hunter kicked his third, bringing the score to 13.7 (85) to 4.9 (33).

Halfway through the quarter, Primus managed a huge goal, snapping the ball around his body from forty metres out, but it was still a 52-point margin. He had done well but was beginning to tire in the ruck up against the combined power of Matthew Burton and Jeff White. A quick Clive Waterhouse double took the Dockers over 100 points, with Fitzroy still languishing on thirty-nine. John McCarthy, who had been animated that quarter, missed a set shot after getting on the end of a Simon Atkins kick. Then, a flurry of late Fremantle goals brought the three-quarter-time score to 20.8 (128) to 5.10 (40). Fitzroy's defence had broken down, and lumbering Fremantle forward Waterhouse could not quite believe how many marks inside fifty he was taking.

Watching on from the stands, many Fitzroy fans were overcome with what was taking place, each reacting to the game and the experience in their own way. 'It was excruciating,' recalled Simon McLaughlin, who was at the game with his brother, Evan. 'I had never felt so lonely in all my life.'[47] A supporter sitting beside Martin Flanagan would weep for much of the final quarter, 'not like someone indulging emotion but rather like someone who is one the edge of an emotion that is beyond control.'[48] Jan Wright just sobbed and sobbed: 'It was terrible, really terrible.'[49] Other fans were more aggressive. A group behind the goals showed customary displeasure at the umpiring, with one remarking, 'Congratulations, you've crucified us now for 113 years.' They were not swayed by Oakley's arguments, standing by a banner that read: 'The BRISBANE LIONS — NOT FOR THESE BOYS. Thanks for the memories, FITZROY.'[50] Back in Victoria, fans at the Fitzroy Club Hotel cheered and barracked passionately, many with tears in their eyes.[51]

Out in the three-quarter-time huddle, McConnell challenged his exhausted players to win the final quarter. It might have seemed a perfunctory aim, but when one quarter of AFL football was all that was left, it mattered a great deal. Spurred on, the Lions hoped to start strongly, but after a turnover, Gavin Mitchell added another goal to Fremantle's total and it looked like the final quarter would be more of the same for the Lions. Fremantle held the ball in their forward half but started to become wayward in their goalkicking. Then, after the ball had been locked in the Dockers' half for some time, Matthew Dent got a clearing kick away, which Brett Chandler chased and gave to Simon Atkins. Atkins launched it long into Fitzroy's forward line and allowed Warry to take a mark over the top of Stephen O'Reilly. Kicking the goal, Fitzroy went on a roll. McCarthy kicked one from a set shot that only barely snuck past the near goalpost. As 'Fitzroy' chants began to echo around Subiaco, the Lions surged the ball forward. Bamford drove the ball deep into the forward line, and after a chain of handballs in congestion it came to Martin Pike (who McConnell had moved into the middle for the final quarter), who kicked a good goal just in from the boundary line, about thirty-five metres out. 'The Lions giving a good roar,' Morphett declared, with Fitzroy now having kicked three goals to one that quarter.

Fremantle steadied somewhat, and with a couple of goals they were back in front for the quarter. Then, from a centre bounce, Rombotis cleared to Hawking, who just managed to mark at centre half forward. He went back and sent it deep to Warry, who could not take the mark but was infringed against and awarded a free kick. The nineteen-year-old kicked his fourth and almost had a fifth moments later when he tried to kick the ball over his head after he was spoiled from taking a mark just out from the goals. Seemingly realising this was their last role of the dice, some of Fitzroy's players began to put on a show — although a little too much for McConnell. 'We had a couple of blokes trying to kick the last one and one bloke tried to take the mark of the year and shouldn't have been up there,' he said, 'I couldn't help myself in sending the necessary message.'[52]

With about five minutes remaining, Andrew Wills for Fremantle kicked an errant ball deep into his forward line, which was easily cleaned up by John Barker. He sent the ball wide to Jeff Hogg, whom McConnell had brought on for his final game in the AFL. The former Richmond captain paused, before driving the ball long down the line. McCarthy and Warfe rose but neither could take a clean mark.

Fortunately the industrious Chandler swooped at the fall of the ball. He fended off an opponent and then fired a handball to Danny Morton in space. Morton saw Boyd leading out from the forward fifty and hit him on the chest with a well-weighted pass. Too far out to score, the captain sent the ball across the ground to Atkins, who marked inside fifty. Atkins wasted no time: off a short run-up he launched it right on the fifty-metre line and watched it sail through the goal at an unstoppable height. It was Fitzroy's fifth goal of the quarter and their final in the AFL.

The Lions had put up a good fight that quarter and had outscored the Dockers, but, thanks to several late Fremantle goals, only just. With only minutes left, Fitzroy had kicked 5.1 to 4.4 in the final term. If the Dockers snuck a late goal they would win all four quarters. Nearing the final siren, the ball rebounded from Fitzroy's forward line and Fremantle worked it well down their right wing, culminating in a mark for Kingsley Hunter inside his forward fifty. With seconds left in the game, he went back and kicked from about forty metres out on a slight angle. The ball drifted to the left for a minor score and the siren sounded only seconds later. 'Go the Lions,' shouted Kevin Bartlett, with his co-commentator, Drew Morphett declaring it: 'The end of an era, the end of an age'. Fitzroy had won its final quarter. It was the smallest possible victory Fitzroy could achieve that day, but with all the club had lost that year, it was a victory that could never be taken away. The final score was 24.13 (157) to 10.11 (71).

...

The Fitzroy players were bereft. Many dropped to the ground, some wept. John Barker, a grandson of Fitzroy, struggled to keep composed. Simon Hawking was far more emotional than he thought he would be. 'Up until then it was the emotion building up to it and the reality was at arm's length,' he recalled, but when the siren went, however, the reality of the situation full sunk in.[53] With the cameras showing distraught Fitzroy players and supporters, the broadcaster soon cut away to an advertisement, *The Age* noting: 'Perhaps we're not meant to see just how painful death can be.'[54]

Out in the middle of the ground, Alan McConnell asked Leon Harris, 'What do we do now?' Without hesitating, Harris said: 'Mate, we've done what we needed to do, we get off, we move on.'[55] Like the Richmond game, though, the significance of the occasion demanded acknowledgement after the match. The Fitzroy club song was played, and then, in a poignant touch, Fremantle arranged for Sara Macliver, member of the West Australian Opera Company and one of Australia's best operatic voices, to sing Robert Burns' 'Auld Lang Syne'. Finally, after Fitzroy's long, draining and at times sordid farewell, there was a touch of dignity about proceedings. Standing on the roof of the Town & Country stand on the southern side of the ground, microphone in hand and in a slight breeze, she sang a requiem to mourn Fitzroy's passing, her angelic voice unaccompanied yet undaunted. It was an understated moment, yet very powerful. 'Not since Ted Whitten went around for the last time at the MCG has an audience been so taken by an overwhelming sense of emotion,' wrote one reporter. 'Part of football went with EJ that day, another part went with Fitzroy here.'[56]

The players came off the ground through a guard of honour provided by Fremantle and to a standing ovation from the crowd. Jarrod Molloy left the field 'like a man who has just witnessed a serious accident, looking pale and distraught'.[57] For some players, the full significance of the occasion only hit them as they were leaving the ground for the final time as Fitzroy players.[58] Seeing all the distressed Fitzroy faces in the crowd, it occurred to Brett Chandler, really for the first time, how important the club was to its supporters and what its departure from the AFL really meant to them. That scene, as well as the end of the Richmond game, remains in his mind.[59] As had been the case the previous week, while Alan McConnell recognised the symbolic importance of the guard of honour and the recognition of seeing the Fitzroy jumpers depart from an AFL ground one final time, he personally felt that it was recognition he did not deserve, having coached the club only eleven times for eleven loses.[60] He was, nevertheless, a great servant of the club in its difficult final years and deserved recognition for stepping up and taking on the caretaker role, which everyone knew had only one, painful outcome.

In the rooms the players and staff spent five minutes together in silence. McConnell eventually called the players together but no-one could think of what to say or do. Some wanted to sing the club song and others did not, so everyone sat and looked at each other.[61] McConnell himself tried to make a speech, but he was too choked up with emotion.[62] Jarrod Molloy and John Barker had both had good games — Barker led the Lions' disposals with twenty-three, while Molloy, as he had done so well since Round 6, had been solid in defence. As both had a strong familial connection to the club, the moments after the game were particularly poignant. In the rooms, Molloy came across Kevin Elms, who had been with the club so long that he had worked with Jarrod's father, Shane. Elms was in the trainers' room, emptying water bottles, as he had done hundreds of times before. The pair hugged and cried as the Fitzroy club song played in the background.[63] Elsewhere, Barker was ushered into the doctors' room, where his mother and aunt were waiting. In an emotional moment the trio embraced each other, each having their lives shaped and, to some extent, defined by Fitzroy. Barker had always known what football meant to people, but that moment was as powerful an evocation as he could witness about what Fitzroy meant to those that loved it.[64]

After the game, the players and staff joined hundreds of Fitzroy supporters, heading to the ironically named Brisbane Hotel on Beaufort Street, owned by former Fitzroy player Ian McCulloch (a West Australian who had moved over to Victoria to play sixty games for the Roys in the seventies).[65] Supporters, players and officials mingled and spilled out onto the street. Even 'Big' Ron Alexander blew off an official Fremantle function to come down to the hotel and take part in the Irish wake.[66] Fitzroy people blocked the road outside the hotel, with supporters sitting on the gutters. Fran Tascone was amazed at the sheer number of people who had flocked to the venue.[67] The fans mixed with the players, one supporter noticing how very casual and relaxed it was, as if a huge weight had suddenly lifted off everyone's shoulders.[68]

...

Most of Fitzroy's staff and players arrived back in Melbourne at 12:10am on Monday morning. A small band of diehard fans, loyal wives and girlfriends applauded as they filed into Melbourne Airport. Stephen Paxman did not know what to say, telling the waiting media, 'it feels like a part of me has just been ripped out'.[69] Rowan Warfe was happy that it was all over; 'It was a long, long year,' he said, 'and I think everyone was just relieved at the end that it finished.'[70] McConnell later described the final games as like 'going to a state funeral eight weeks in a row — it was hard work'.[71] He admitted that the team had lost its momentum three weeks beforehand, and in the final weeks there was 'a lot of emotional baggage we have been carrying'.[72]

One player definitely relieved was Brad Boyd. He was not in a talkative mood when he arrived at Tullamarine: 'I've had enough' he said, before making a quick exit.[73] It is easy to understand his reticence — he had carried the weight of being 'the stoic, public face of a dying team' since July, after the president's authority had been usurped by an administrator and the coach had quit.[74] Boyd stood out beyond others that year, reflected Alan McConnell, he was playing under duress with a bad back while shouldering an immense responsibility as captain.[75] 'You could tell he had the weight of the world on his shoulders,' thought Marty Warry, and many other teammates agreed.[76] For those paying close attention to Fitzroy during the club's final days in the AFL, Boyd had won many admirers by the way he conducted himself. 'What he did that year was sensational,' reflected Glenn Warry.[77] Indeed, what he had achieved at a struggling football club was outstanding by any measure. Geoff Slattery summed up the feelings of many:

> I will long remember his stoicism under enormous pressure during the latter days of the Fitzroy FC. A captain to the end, capable of grace under constant assault. Never was a task too great, never a question too silly. Never did he forget that he was representing a club of great history, culture, and passion. May his career prosper.[78]

No AFL captain has had to play under that level of stress and responsibility. Even by Round 4, one commentator observed that he played 'as though his burden was becoming too great for a man of his tender years'.[79] Exhausted, and no doubt greatly relieved that his ordeal was over, he had every right to seek quiet and solitude. Years later, Boyd would poignantly sum up that early morning airport arrival: 'We came home, but the club didn't.'[80]

CHAPTER NINETEEN

LOOSE ENDS

*'I've never gotten over losing my club.
I laid awake at night thinking about it'*

— Kevin Elms, Fitzroy trainer.[1]

With the removal of Fitzroy completed, the AFL surged into finals without missing a step. Sydney finished atop the ladder, aided by 114 goals from Coleman Medallist, Tony Lockett. North Melbourne, Brisbane and West Coast finished second, third and fourth, with Carlton, Essendon, Geelong and Hawthorn rounding out the top eight. Richmond, whose Round 21 intensity against Fitzroy was inspired by the vain hope of boosting their percentage to squeak into the finals, finished ninth. Fitzroy ended its final AFL season with one win, twenty-one losses and a percentage of 49.47. Anthony Mellington was the club's leading goalkicker, finishing the season on 22.26 across eighteen games. Fitzroy's reserve side had fared better, finishing tenth in the twelve-team league with a 7–15 record. Andrew Cavedon, who was on Fitzroy's senior list but never played a senior game that season, kicked thirty-nine goals for the season. Mellington, who played four games in the reserves, still managed twenty-seven goals.

While the dust settled on Fitzroy, Ross Oakley's centenary celebrations continued at pace. On the Monday evening after the conclusion of Round 22, a double event was held at the Princess Theatre. Not only would the All-Australian team be announced, but so too would a special VFL/AFL Team of the Century. Fitzroy had more luck with the latter, with the centenary team including Kevin Murray and Haydn Bunton Senior as players and Norm Smith (captain/coach at Fitzroy from 1949 to 1951, until he moved on to his legendary career at Melbourne).

Meanwhile, the other potential merger, the 'Melbourne Hawks', was building towards a climax. Arguments for and against were being made in public and in private, while familiar voices offered their views. Does merger spell the death of football clubs, asked Mike Sheahan, 'Or can it mean their rebirth and resurrection as a super power?' Sheahan, naturally, still took the latter view.[2] The matter even reached Victorian Parliament, with the state Treasurer, Alan Stockdale, responding to a question of the economic impact of the AFL's merger policy by endorsing the approach and encouraging the Melbourne/Hawthorn merger.[3] Unfortunately for the devotees of economic rationalism, prospects of a second AFL merger in 1996 were dashed on the night of 16 September, when the members of both met separately to vote on the proposal and Hawthorn members voted the merger down.[4] While disappointed, Oakley remained committed to the belief that mergers would take place in the next few years. 'It is difficult to see this number of clubs surviving,' he remarked, 'and if clubs don't merge they run the risk of going out of business like Fitzroy, which would be a disaster.'[5]

Meanwhile, Fitzroy's merger partner was still playing football. Brisbane had finished the season in third, behind North Melbourne in second. Under the MacIntyre Final Eight System, they did not play each other in the qualifying finals. Both teams won in the first week and once Brisbane had seen off Carlton in a semi-final at the Gabba, the two merger contenders met at the MCG on Saturday 21 September to play for a place in the grand final Unlike the contest in the AFL's boardrooms, North Melbourne emerged victorious, defeating Brisbane 17.12 (114) to 11.10 (76). The Brisbane Bears' final game garnered nothing of the emotion that Fitzroy's farewell received. Dyson Hore-Lacy later wrote that no-one thought of farewelling the Bears, as 'few believed that what happened constituted a true merger between the clubs'.[6]

The other preliminary final was won by Sydney, with a memorable point kicked after the siren by Tony Lockett. All year, Sydney had been an example for Fitzroy supporters about how the AFL Commission imposed restrictions on *their* club that it actively flouted for others. On 26 September *The Age* reported Sydney's accumulated debt by October 1995 was almost $2.5 million, which he noted was $100,000 more than Fitzroy's at the same time. Furthermore, audited accounts filed with the ASC questioned the club's ability to continue to operate without substantial input from both the AFL and the club's major corporate sponsors. The Swans' operating losses in 1994 and 1995 were $1 million, despite an increase in AFL funding. In 1996, the AFL injected $725,000 into the Swans, in addition to financial assistance of more the $1 million the previous year.[7] Patrick Smith opined that Dyson Hore-Lacy must have wept at seeing the figure: 'Clearly, the AFL was never going to let his club live. They had more than $2 million for Sydney and nothing but disdain for the Lions.'[8] It displayed the stark reality of the situation: Sydney was strategically important to the AFL, Fitzroy was not.

During grand final week the usual traditions were observed. Monday night James Hird and Michael Voss won the Brownlow Medal (tied with Corey McKiernan who was ineligible due to suspension). Martin Pike polled best for Fitzroy, with two best-on-ground performances against Adelaide in Round 2 and Collingwood in Round 16. On Saturday, 28 September, North Melbourne and Sydney contested the 1996 grand final. Paul Roos had played 269 games for

Fitzroy and accrued a gamut of individual awards, while John Blakey had played 135 games — both were appearing in their first AFL grand final. The other AFL clubs must surely have felt themselves vindicated in their decision to reject Fitzroy's merger with North Melbourne, given that the Kangaroos went on to win comfortably, 19.17 (131) to 13.10 (88). As the North Melbourne players celebrated on the MCG turf with a special gold centenary premiership cup, the 1996 AFL Centenary season came to a close.

...

Back at the Fitzroy Club Hotel, Fitzroy's remaining staff were waiting until their employment expired on 31 October, either helping to wind up the affairs of the club or simply treading water to ensure they were not found in breach of their contracts. The football department had little to do: Freemantle, for instance, spent his days in the gym, swimming, running or having lunches with McConnell. Greg Swann and his Ernst & Young team worked on the administration issues, supported by John Birt, Glenn Warry and the other office staff, while Kinnear Beatson, Brisbane's Victorian manager, had moved in to determine which staff and volunteers would transition over to the Brisbane Lions in 1997.[9] Beatson's task was inherently fraught with emotion, given all that had happened that year. While some Fitzroy people were keen to continue with the merged club, others wanted nothing to do with it. Beatson did not enjoy his time at the Fitzroy Club Hotel — 'It had a real stench of death about it,' he recalled — and at times the interactions with Fitzroy staff was tense.[10] A sense that Brisbane were just taking what they wanted and were liquidating the rest only reinforced the perception that the merger had been little more than a hostile takeover.[11]

As this played out, Alan McConnell and twenty-four players left the country for an end of season trip to Bali (McConnell was 'conned' into going with them as something of a chaperone).[12] They stayed at the Ocean Blue Resort at Kuta Beach from 7 to 15 September — t-shirts were made up proclaiming: 'Lions '96 — the Nightmare is Over'.[13] Two women from Williamstown, Melissa Cracknell and Donna Biderman, were also staying at the resort, and later made allegations concerning the Fitzroy players. The pair claimed they were subjected to 'the most appalling and disgusting human behaviour' they had ever seen, and presented a litany of grievances, each more sordid than the next, until one player was said to have strangled a rooster.[14] Once their allegations reached Australia, John Birt issued a statement saying that the suggestions of misconduct involving more than one player were unsubstantiated, certainly 'no worse than what goes on in any end-of-season trip', although he apologised for any offence 'that may have been caused unintentionally by the players'.[15] Most players contend that there was little substance to the story, and no more eventful than any other post-season football trip (which does not excuse any poor behaviour but does contextualise it). By November the AFL seemed to agree, and after an investigation the League decided against taking any action over the alleged 'end-of-season rampage'.[16]

Upon their return to Australia, the club held its Best and Fairest award evening at the Fitzroy Town Hall. Promoted as a traditional footy pie-night, Adam Muyt noted sardonically that there was 'no [money] left for much else'.[17] In a relaxed, informal and even cheerful atmosphere, hundreds of fans jammed into the venue to watch a seemingly endless stream of awards presented by coterie and support groups and finally the club. Pike was the overwhelming crowd favourite and received an increasingly rowdy reception for each award he won. By the time he received the main award, 'The wear and tear of a big night had clearly taken its toll.'[18] Pike received a standing ovation in an 'emotional finale' when he narrowly beat Matthew Primus, polling 299 votes, with Primus getting 291 and Bamford on 255.[19] Accepting the award, Pike thanked the club doctors for providing him with Panadols for his Sunday morning recovery.[20]

By now, the Brisbane Bears had announced their initial selections from Fitzroy's list. Brad Boyd and Chris Johnson had already been reported, and on 8 September, Scott Clayton announced that Jarrod

top: Scenes at the Whitten Oval following Fitzroy's Round 13 defeat to Geelong, 29 June 1996. Given the predicament the club found itself in, supporters were unsure whether it was to be the final time they ever saw their club play a game (*The Age*/Nine Publishing FXB918723; photographer: Vince Caligiuri).

bottom: The recently installed administrator of the Fitzroy Football Club, Michael Brennan (left), at the Fitzroy Club Hotel with AFL's Director of Football Operation, Ian Collins, 28 June 1996 (*The Age*/Nine Publishing FXB918721; photographer: Jason South).

top: Brisbane President Noel Gordon (left) and Fitzroy administrator Michael Brennan shake hands following the historic AFL Commission meeting on the night of 4 July 1996 (Newspix NP1111387; photographer: Mark Smith).

middle: North Melbourne's President Ron Casey (left), CEO Greg Miller (centre) and board member Mark Dawson address the media having withdrawn from the race to merge with Fitzroy, 4 July 1996 (*The Age*/ Nine Publishing FXB918724; photographer, Joe Armao).

bottom: Michael Nunan departs the field following the Round 14 defeat to Essendon at Princes Park. It was his final game as Fitzroy's senior coach (Newspix NP1114943; photographer David Geraghty).

top: Fitzroy's infamous banner from the Round 16 game against Collingwood at Victoria Park, 21 July 1996 (*The Age*/Nine Publishing FXB918725; photographer Joe Armao).

bottom: Fitzroy supporters at Princes Park for the Round 20 game against the Brisbane Bears making their feelings known about the merger, 17 August 1996 (Newspix: NP1111388; photographer: Andrew Brownbill).

top: Waiting outside the MCG, Evan McLaughlin was one of thousands of Lions supporters who attended the Lions' Round 21 game and made it Fitzroy's largest crowd since Round 10, 1993 (photo provided by Simon McLaughlin; photographer: Simon McLaughlin).

bottom: Fitzroy's 1996 best and fairest, Martin Pike, during the Round 21 game against Richmond where he finished with twenty-seven disposals. John Rombotis is seen in the background (AFL Photos, 25031).

top: Standing on the MCG after the game against Richmond, Alan McConnell (right) tells Brad Boyd that the players need to run a lap of honour following Fitzroy's 151-point loss (*AFL Annual Report 1996*, p. 28, permission granted from AFL for use).

bottom: Fitzroy's players acknowledging the crowd during their reluctant 'lap of honour' in front of the Great Southern Stand (*The Age*/Nine Publishing FXJ236179; photographer: Jason South).

top: Hundreds of Fitzroy supporters congregating on the MCG turf in front of the players' race after the game against Richmond. One banner expresses a widespread sentiment (*The Age*/Nine Publishing FXJ290682; photographer Joe Armo).

bottom: Fitzroy legends Bill Stephen (left) and Bernie Quinlan (right) at the Fitzroy Town Hall before the dinner thrown by the City of Yarra to commemorate Fitzroy's final AFL game in Melbourne, 25 August 1996. Earlier that day they shared a car during the pre-game motorcade around the MCG (Newspix: NPX67277; photographer: Craig Hughes).

top: Fitzroy greats Garry Wilson (left), Mick Conlan (centre) and Leon Harris (right) at the Fitzroy Town Hall for the 1996 season's final Ins and Outs Night, 29 August 1996 (photograph provided by Jan Wright).

bottom: After the Round 22 game against Fremantle at Subiaco, Fitzroy's players leave the field for the final time as an AFL team, 1 September 1996 (AAP Image/Sport the Library).

top: Chris Johnson receiving his premiership medal following the 2001 AFL Grand Final, 29 September 2001 (AFL Photos, 28246).

bottom: Fitzroy's senior men's team celebrating its 2018 VAFA Premier C Grand Final victory, 15 September 2018 (photo provided by the Fitzroy Football Club; photographer: Phyllis Queally).

Molloy, Scott Bamford and Nick Carter had also agreed to terms.[21] Other discussions were taking place behind the scenes, but one player who knew categorically that he would not be going to Queensland was Martin Pike. Despite his outstanding season, Pike had been informally advised that Brisbane, evidently concerned about his off-field antics, were not interested in him.[22] 'You get a bad headline for 10 seconds of playing up,' he noted, 'it's a shame that 10 seconds can affect your whole life.'[23] He looked back to his home state of South Australia, still hoping the Crows, Port Adelaide or even his old club of Norwood might be inclined towards him.[24]

By early October, Brisbane announced Simon Hawking, John Barker and Shane Clayton would round out their minimum allotment of eight Fitzroy players.[25] While the merger agreement allowed Brisbane an expanded salary cap to fit in their new players, it was not unlimited. The cap, in addition to some players rejecting Brisbane's offer, prohibited them from selecting every player they might have wanted.[26] They had also worked out a deal with Primus: not wanting to play for the Lions in 1997, they would nevertheless select him, but immediately trade him to Port Adelaide as an uncontracted player for picks three and twenty-six in the national draft.[27] This invoked howls of indignation from Victorian clubs, who throughout the year had resisted giving the new South Australian club concessions that were, in their eyes, too generous. Port Adelaide had circumvented the restrictive rules about recruiting, with their selection, by proxy, of Fitzroy's talented, young ruckman — sticking it to the Victorian clubs who had worked so hard to achieve the Fitzroy/Brisbane merger.[28]

With Brisbane's selections locked in by 18 October, those who had not made the cut tried their luck in the national draft on 25 October. Of the twenty-seven Fitzroy players that nominated, eleven (John Rombotis, Rowan Warfe, Matthew Dent, Matthew Manfield, Martin Pike, Marty Warry, Robert McMahon, Trent Cummings, Jason Baldwin, Brad Cassidy and Brent Frewen) found new homes.[29] North Melbourne's selection of Pike surprised Malcolm Blight, Adelaide's new coach, who believed that the Crows were the only club prepared to gamble on him and his $100,000 asking price. When asked, Denis Pagan said that Pike (a 'Glen Archer type' who could play all over the ground) was a best and fairest winner and 'perhaps the most talented player in the draft'. While North was aware of his 'shortcomings', Pagan believed they could offer a 'strong program' at a 'caring club', and how he responded to that was 'up to him'.[30]

Glenn Warry was happy to see so many of his players given a chance at clubs with stable environments, where they could 'have a good crack at their future'. Warry was surprised, however, that Brett Chandler and Brett Cook were not picked up, and he said that both of them, along with Stephen Paxman should be among the first picked in the pre-season draft in February 1997.[31] Paxman's non-nomination to the draft raised eyebrows, and the League quickly sought to investigate, as there was a strong belief (which turned out to be correct) that Port Adelaide were interested in him. Had he nominated, he would have almost certainly been selected in the first round. As it was, he nominated for the pre-season draft (where Port Adelaide had the first pick) and he was selected by the Power.[32] Along with Paxman, Cook, Chandler, Anthony Mellington and Nigel Credlin all found new clubs. Finally, Jason Ramsey was selected by Richmond in the 1997 rookie draft.

As it transpired, only fifteen of Fitzroy's forty-two players on the 1996 list were not signed for other clubs the following year. Some, like Jeff Hogg and Mick Dwyer, had already decided to retire. For others, like Simon Atkins and Darren Holmes, non-selection in the draft forced their hand. In total, eleven players had nominated for the draft and had been passed over.[33] Frank Bizzotto's twelve-week injury made him an unpalatable prospect for other clubs, as did Nick Mitchell's prolonged knee injury — although both continued to play at lower levels for some time.[34] John McCarthy looked around for a club, but with no avenues available he returned to Tasmania to be player/coach at North Hobart.[35] Danny Morton went back to North Adelaide in 1997, but returned to the AFL via the 1997 national draft to re-join Primus, Rombotis and Paxman at Port Adelaide.

Jason Baldwin, the only player on Fitzroy's list who started playing for the Lions in the eighties, left the club on bad terms. He had not seen eye-to-eye with Nunan, had only played eleven games that season and had been dropped for the final game against Fremantle. He was twenty-six years old, and, having played 125 games still considered himself 'a half-reasonable AFL footballer', aimed to bring up his 200th game at his new club Richmond. He noted that there were certain people at the club who 'didn't think I was up to it' and he planned to let them know once he reached his milestone.[36] Unfortunately for Baldwin, he only played two senior games with Richmond before announcing his retirement at the end of the 1997 season.[37] A loyal servant of Fitzroy, who stuck with the club when many of his teammates fled to higher ground, he deserved a better end to his career.

While the players were sorting out their future, several legal and financial matters remained to be finalised. Throughout September and October, Michael Brennan attended to Fitzroy's affairs, still responsible for ensuring that the club's unsecured creditors received as large a return as possible. A lingering issue for the administrator was the ownership of the Fitzroy Club Hotel lease, and he launched legal action, looking for a ruling as to whether the hotel belonged to the football club. If so, Brennan argued that it could be sold and Fitzroy's creditors would be the beneficiaries.[38] Eventually the matter was settled by the Supreme Court, which found that the hotel was not owned by the Fitzroy Football Club but rather, as Fitzroy's board had intended, by a separate company controlled by several club directors.[39]

At midnight on 31 October, the last day of the footballing year, Fitzroy's licence to compete in the AFL ended and the Brisbane Lions formally came into existence.[40] Brennan spent the day signing cheques to the value of almost $1 million from the AFL's merger package, constituting the final payments to Fitzroy's players.[41] By the end of the year, full payments had been made to all priority creditors, players had received full payment for the 1996 football season, as had all support staff, and outstanding and current superannuation contributions had been paid to ensure that all players, past and present, had received their correct entitlements.⁴² By the time the over 120 unsecured creditors were paid out the following year, they received just 27 cents in the dollar, significantly less than the amount (between 40 to 57 cents in the dollar) forecast by Brennan in July 1996. The final dividend was lower, Brennan advised, due to a higher than expected level of legal claims and several unrecorded but important claims by former employees.⁴³

By the time of Brisbane's AGM on 25 February 1997, the final hurdle was cleared to complete the merger, when Brisbane's members voted overwhelmingly to change the club's name to the 'Brisbane Bears – Fitzroy Football Club Limited', trading as the Brisbane Lions.⁴⁴ As had been argued throughout the year, what transpired was not strictly a merger: the Brisbane Bears had changed aspects of their club identity to incorporate the Fitzroy Lions, they had been given concessions from the AFL Commission, as well as their $6 million lump sum payment, of which, after distributions, only about $1 million remained for the club to use.⁴⁵ In most other respects, the Brisbane Bears of 1996 would differ little from the Brisbane Lions of 1997, albeit, Brisbane officials hoped, with several thousand Fitzroy supporters swelling the number of club members in Victoria. Only time would tell how successful the merger arrangement would be.

...

Fitzroy's players, staff and volunteers emerged from the momentous year in a variety of states. Few at the club were untouched by the events of 1996, with the senior staff and board members, in particular, under significant stress throughout the period and devastated in the aftermath. Alan McConnell, as the breadwinner with a young family, had wanted to shield them from the stresses of his job: 'There was a lot of angst at work, I didn't need to create more angst at home.'⁴⁶ In the years afterwards, he and Boyd talked about what had happened and the toll it had taken. 'We both felt we were probably looking after a group of people,' he reflected, 'but not necessarily ourselves.'[47] 'It really hurt me,' reflected trainer Lance Upton, 'the last two years were very hard.'[48] Kevin Elms was devasted by what happened in 1996. 'It destroyed me', he said years later, 'the stress of it all hurt my health. I had a bad skin cancer. I was touch and go. It slowed my recovery too. I've never gotten over losing my club. I laid awake at night thinking about it.'[49]

Few had suffered the slings and arrows of 1996 as severely as Dyson Hore-Lacy. Being Fitzroy's president had been a difficult and costly responsibility; by 1996, it had practically become his full-time job and he paid both a personal and professional price. His marriage broke down that year, and he would live apart from his wife and three children. Despite the pleas of his colleagues to drop his involvement with the Lions, he deferred or turned down legal work because of the time Fitzroy demanded of him, costing him untold thousands of dollars.[50] After one particular game, a supporter watched him walk to his car at the Whitten Oval: 'It was in fading light, and he was stooped over with both hands in his pockets ... He looked like he was walking to his grave. He had the weight of the world on his shoulders.'[51] Mike Sheahan wrote that he 'gave of himself physically, spiritually and financially for his footy club for a long time. The fight took a heavy toll.'[52]

At the time, it was hard for supporters to truly appreciate the immense volume of work he and the board had done behind the scenes over many years to try to save Fitzroy, and when the club went into administration he was subject to some questioning and criticism. On 6 July, as Fitzroy played Essendon days after the merger, many Fitzroy supporters told Martin Flanagan that Hore-Lacy 'had a lot to answer for.'[53] Looking back, it is difficult to sustain any specific charge against him. As *The Age* was forced to acknowledge, at all times he acted with complete probity and propriety.[54] His book, *Fitzroy* (published in 2000), was an account of his time at the Lions, allowing him to articulate the difficulty of managing a financially stricken club in the face of an often hostile media and an (at best) indifferent AFL administration. The 'quixotic defender of underdogs' had more than lived up to his reputation. He concluded *Fitzroy* with the words: 'I regret what happened in the end but as for the journey, I was proud to be part of the struggle.'[55] He had vowed to retire from football administration after 1996 but remained involved with Fitzroy for many years. In fact, all the board members (with the exception of Greg Basto) stayed with Fitzroy well into the new millennium. As difficult as the fight had been in those final years, they could not abandon the club, and looked for whatever ways they could to rebuild it from the ashes.

For his part, there was speculation that Alan McConnell would fill the vacant senior coach position at North Ballarat, but on 14 November 1996 he was announced as Geelong's development coach.[56] He was later the head AFL coach for the Australian Institute of Sport before joining the Greater Western Sydney Giants. Other staff and volunteers went their separate ways. The trauma and emotion of Fitzroy's final weeks had a big influence on Glenn Warry, who moved out of club administration and into player welfare and development.[57] Leon Harris, who was only ever part-time at Fitzroy, took over the role as coach of the Vic Country Under 16s and Under 18s for the national carnival.[58] Greg Freemantle hoped to work for another club, but was unsuccessful and returned to his job as a secondary school PE teacher.[59] John Birt, along with marketing officer John De Rango, receptionist Fran Tascone and his secretary, Sandra Hounslow, found jobs with the Brisbane Lions' Melbourne office.

The volunteers and part-time employees also went their separate ways. Property stewards John and Glen Ford were so disenchanted that they were lost to the AFL for good.[60] Many of the statisticians were taken by Melbourne, but it seemed that few trainers were willing to work elsewhere, except at Brisbane.[61] Stalwarts Kevin Elms and Lance Upton decided to work for the new Lions. Upton was initially 'pretty dirty' on the merger, but after meeting with Kinnear Beatson and seeing the Brisbane Lions jumper (which contained more 'Fitzroy' than he was expecting), his attitude softened.[62] Similarly, Elms was convinced to go with Brisbane because they took the Fitzroy song and the Lions name; they recognised the honour board and there was a 'Fitzroy look' to the jumper.[63]

With many players finding new clubs, McConnell hoped they would improve in more professional and competitive environments, where there was a cost to poor performances and the rewards for winning were far greater.[64] For those easily getting senior games at Fitzroy, being at a new club in a truly high-performance environment where there was competition for the starting eighteen was something of a shock. Nick Carter found that the mentality and habits cultivated at Fitzroy were insufficient to make it at other clubs: he was not just going to walk into the senior team each week as he had done at Fitzroy, and officials at his new clubs told that in no uncertain terms.[65]

The fortunes of those who went on to other clubs varied, as is the case with all who aspire to play professional football. Some were cruelled by injuries, others fell out of favour with their new coaches, some failed to adjust to the demands required in more competitive teams, while a handful went on to have substantial careers well into the 2000s. Matthew Primus and Stephen Paxman, for instance, both played over one hundred games for Port Adelaide, while Rowan Warfe and Matthew Dent had modest post-Fitzroy careers for Sydney and the Western Bulldogs respectively.

Some found that their prospects had been cut short, either because they had shouldered too heavy a burden while playing at a young age or were poorly developed at the club with limited facilities. Both Nunan and McConnell thought that many young players were getting senior games too early, both before they had earned them and before their bodies were ready.[66] For years Glenn Warry had also expressed reservations about bringing young players into a club that was not a high-performance environment and playing young men prematurely.[67] Many players also recognised the cost of their time at Fitzroy. John Rombotis, for instance, believed that as a nineteen-year-old with a still-developing body he should not have been playing in the centre so much, although it gave him the opportunity to play on some of the greatest midfielders of the era.[68] Nick Carter felt the effects from his seventeen games that season: he was tired some weeks, and thoroughly demoralised when his opponents had better statistics.[69] He struggled to play many senior games after 1996, a common story among his cohort of young Lions.

As players dispersed at the end of 1996, the men who comprised Fitzroy's final AFL side went down in history. 'It's a bond,' Brad Boyd said in 1997, 'what we went through together. You can never break that.'[70] The club left an indelible imprint on many. Stephen Paxman had met his wife at a Fitzroy club function. As Sharon was the granddaughter of Fitzroy premiership captain Fred Hughson, Fitzroy would always be a part of his life.[71] For Matthew Primus, the club was his entry into the AFL system, but being at the Lions was not just about personal ambition — he looked back on the club fondly: 'It was just a really good footy club, it had a really good soul to it.'[72] Simon Hawking expressed a similar sentiment, 'I'm immensely proud to have played for the club,' he stated, noting that Fitzroy had allowed him to realise his dream of playing AFL football.[73] Marty Warry's eight games for Fitzroy were the sum total for his AFL career, despite being picked up by Collingwood for 1997. Contemplating whether he would have played more games if he had been drafted by another club, he nevertheless would not have exchanged his time playing for the club he barracked for as a boy: 'I was privileged to have worn the jumper.'[74]

...

The end of the year brought another era to a close, as Ross Oakley stepped down as the AFL's CEO. The 54-year-old had spent a decade in the VFL/AFL hot seat, and felt the time was right to depart and hand over to a successor. While the likes of Ian Collins or Jeff Browne were considered possible replacements, in a nod to the League's national ambitions, the Commission looked beyond the Victorian heartland and appointed former South Australian footballer and administrator Wayne Jackson. On Monday, 16 December 1996, a black-tie event was held to farewell Oakley (Dyson Hore-Lacy was conspicuous by his absence).[75] The man who many saw as the architect of Fitzroy's demise said goodbye to the League he had transformed.

Taking an objective view, Oakley achieved everything he needed to, and more, to usher the VFL into the twenty-first century, avoiding the type of serious friction that rugby league experienced during the Super League war in the mid-nineties. Few Fitzroy people could probably bring themselves to admit it, but with Oakley as CEO, the Commission had made significant achievements. It had nationalised the competition (a necessary step to ensure its survival) and implemented important equalisation measures, such as the salary cap and the national draft, to break the stranglehold on success held by the top clubs (between 1967 and 1989, only five different clubs won premierships). Crucially, Oakley signed increasingly large sponsorship and broadcast deals that would, in time, secure the League's financial future. His final such deals were the most impressive: in 1992, he signed a deal with Channel Seven to be the AFL's broadcaster, worth $17 million per year for six years, a total of $102 million, and in 1994 he signed a seven-year, $30 million deal with Coca-Cola to be the AFL's major corporate sponsor. The AFL was on the verge of being a financial powerhouse.

But football is not an objective business activity and the black-tied well-wishers at Oakley's farewell dinner were not the game's most important constituency. He had prosecuted an agenda, firmly believing it was in the League's long-term best interest, but to do so, he had detached himself from many aspects of the game that were deeply personal to supporters (those people, he wrote, who 'wear their birthright on their sleeves and will fight to the death to hold on to what has always been theirs').[76] While he understood their concerns, they could not be allowed to interfere with several necessary (but deeply unpopular) decisions required to save and grow the League. As a result, he was often in conflict with supporters, many of whom may well have uttered the words of Laurie Holden, the coach from David Williamson's *The Club*: 'I love football and I love this Club and it's a bit hard for me to understand someone who holds both of them in contempt.'[77] Oakley did not hold football in contempt, he just had the misfortune of managing the difficult transformation of a game with so much emotion invested in it by those who loved it.

His time as CEO came at a cost beyond simply being lampooned and reviled in public debates. 'I had death threats,' he reflected years later, 'I had guards on my home for about eight weeks, my kids had to be escorted to school. I must say, at that time you wonder whether it's all going to be worth it.'[78] Was there any sympathy from Fitzroy supporters? Certainly not initially, and probably not even with hindsight. Even in 2013, none of Barry Dickins' anger over what had happened to Fitzroy had dissipated: 'I miss seeing Fitzroy play,' he wrote, 'and hope that Ross Oakley roasts in hell as we speak for what he's done to the poor old Royboys.'[79] Many supporters held Oakley personally responsible for what happened to Fitzroy, and as CEO at the time, he bears responsibility for what happened on his watch, the good and the bad.

In less prosperous times, Oakley had accepted the received wisdom of 'economic rationalism' and advocated mergers as the only expedient to 'save' the League's weaker clubs without working with clubs to explore alternative means to raise revenue or grow supporter bases. He encouraged, cajoled and, according to Fitzroy people at least, eventually coerced the Lions into a position where a merger was its only option. Certainly there were other factors forcing the Lions down this path and, as Oakley continually points out, it was the club's creditors who ultimately called an end to Fitzroy's time in the League.[80]

Still, that he celebrated the merger at the time and has defended it ever since leaves little doubt that this was his preferred outcome for Fitzroy, and as the League's CEO, his preferences mattered. For strategic reasons, Oakley wanted Fitzroy to merge, and while he argued that the League lacked the money to save the club, it was clear that he also lacked the will. For this reason, even twenty-five years after 1996, the anger of the Fitzroy faithful towards him has not abated, and probably never will. This is just something he must live with. The passion of the fans, he acknowledged, was what made football great — 'It's also what makes the game a bugger to manage.'[81]

CHAPTER TWENTY

DEATH IS NOT THE END

'When you're standing at the crossroads that you cannot comprehend, just remember that death is not the end'

— Bob Dylan.

On the morning of Saturday, 29 September 2001, the Essendon Football Club was on the hunt for immortality. Denied the opportunity to contest the 1999 AFL Grand Final due to one of the most compelling Preliminary Finals in recent memory, in 2000, the Bombers swept almost all before them. In order to solidify their legacy as one of the League's great dynasties, however, Kevin Sheedy's third great Essendon side needed more than one premiership to its name. Standing in their way was the Brisbane Lions. Vanquished finalists in 1999 and 2000, Leigh Matthews' team had won fifteen consecutive games in 2001 beginning with a 28-point victory in Round 10 over the same side they faced that afternoon. For Brisbane, be it the Bears or the Lions, this was a historic day. One of the AFL Commission's long-term goals was to see the game thriving in the northern states. Sydney had made the grand final in 1996, but were unable to overcome a powerful North Melbourne side. Now, the Brisbane Lions had the chance to take the AFL premiership cup north of the Murray River for the first time.

Of the twenty-two players Brisbane's match committee selected for the game, only one, Chris Johnson, was from the 'Fitzroy Eight'. Few others had thrived in Queensland. Scott Bamford managed two seasons before finishing his career at Geelong in 1999. Nick Carter played five games for Brisbane in 1997 and 1998, only to be traded to Melbourne where he played even fewer games. 'I remember winning the reserves best and fairest in both years at Brisbane,' he recalled, 'so my form at that level was fine, but I just never managed to break into that senior side regularly and be a consistent contributor.'[1] Like Carter, Shane Clayton played five games in two seasons with Brisbane. Delisted by the Lions at the end of 1998, he was drafted by North Melbourne and played ninety-nine games for the Kangaroos, including in their 1999 Premiership team.

Unbeknownst at the time, Simon Hawking had played his last AFL game in 1996. Unable to break into the senior team in 1997, he was traded to Sydney with Brent Green for pick 31 (used to select young Western Australian midfielder Simon Black). Hawking could not get a game at Sydney or at his next club, Collingwood, and retired permanently at the end of 2000. John Barker had one year with Brisbane before he went to Hawthorn (as part of the trade for Brad Scott). While the demise of Fitzroy left him feeling disillusioned and detached from football for several years, he nevertheless went on to play 113 games for the Hawks.[2] Jarrod Molloy initially settled well in Queensland, but a knee reconstruction and scaphoid problems affected his first few seasons. He was the Lions' leading goalkicker in 1999, but his 2000 season was his last with Brisbane. 'I enjoyed it for a while,' he said at the end of that year, 'but I got to a stage where I needed a bit more structure off the field.' That would come from a move back to Melbourne. He was traded to Collingwood for defender Mal Michael, and remained with the Magpies until he retired in 2003.[3]

Johnson, however, had not only stayed in Brisbane but had lived up to the potential he had demonstrated at Fitzroy. By grand final day in 2001, he had played ninety-four games for the new Lions and polled eleven votes in the 2001 Brownlow count. Ironically, he was initially desperate to return to Victoria and, in his own words, 'the first one who wanted to jump ship'.[4] Joining Johnson at Brisbane was Martin Pike, who had won a premiership with North Melbourne before moving to Brisbane at the end of 2000. The former wild-man had been reforming himself since his early days, and would have the distinction of playing in six grand finals in seven years, winning four. Running onto the ground at the 2001 Grand Final, Johnson and Pike were side by side, marvelling at how far they had come from the dark days of 1996.[5]

Brisbane's eighth player from Fitzroy was the tragic figure of Brad Boyd. Arriving at his new club, he asked not to be considered for a leadership role, opting instead to concentrate on his own game after an injury-plagued year.[6] Unfortunately, injury continued to disrupt his football, and he finished at Brisbane in 1999. By rights, Boyd should have been part of the Brisbane Lions premiership years, but as one journalist noted, while Boyd had the ability to be a superstar, 'he didn't have the body.' Reluctant to discuss his playing career, particularly his final two years as captain of the club, he told a reporter years later: 'Don't be feeling sorry for me, who wants to hear my story anyway?'[7] He was probably the most poignant figure in Fitzroy's demise, the young captain carrying the impossible burden. Had he been playing that Saturday afternoon in September 2001, it would have been one of the most emotional sights in football. Sadly, it was not to be.

...

It may have come as a surprise for many that grand final day, but for all the talk of the demise of Fitzroy in 1996, to invoke Mark Twain, reports of the club's death were greatly exaggerated. By 1998, Michael Brennan had fulfilled his obligations in enacting the deed of arrangement between Fitzroy and the Brisbane Bears, the Fitzroy Football Club came out of administration and held its 113th AGM on 22 July that year at the Fitzroy Bowling Club.[8] At that stage, Fitzroy was a club without a team. It remained as a public company, never liquidated, but without a licence to compete in the AFL. Among its 733 shareholder-members, seventy-two per cent did not follow the Brisbane Lions and seventy-eight per cent did not follow any other AFL club.[9] At the AGM, they voted to continue the club and, building on the work done by Dyson Hore-Lacy and the other directors since the merger, Fitzroy developed a partnership with the Coburg Football Club in the VFL.[10] The Coburg–Fitzroy Lions existed for just over one year (August 1999 to the end of 2000) until Coburg entered into an affiliation with the Richmond Football Club for the 2001 season. At that point, the Fitzroy connection was abandoned.

By 2001, Dyson Hore-Lacy was still the club's president, despite having wanted to leave football after the bruising events of 1996.[11] Under his leadership the board continued to seek ways to be involved in football. Back in 1998, they began a sponsorship agreement with VAFA E Grade club the Fitzroy Reds and the Fitzroy Junior Football Club (which the Fitzroy Lions had helped establish in 1993), which played in the Yarra District League.[12] The Reds were formerly the University Reds Football Club, affiliated with the University of Melbourne. In 1997, they disassociated from the university and became the Fitzroy Reds, with support from the Fitzroy Football Club and the Fitzroy Foundation. By 2001, Melbourne University was looking to cut all ties with the Reds, and Fitzroy's secretary, Bill Atherton, suggested that the Roys become their major sponsor. This caused some concern among certain directors, who still thought Fitzroy should be associated with the game at its higher levels. Nevertheless, a majority of the board decided to embark upon the relationship.[13] Fitzroy had thus positioned itself as a vessel for supporting grassroots football, maintained a shop in Mordialloc selling merchandise, and a museum, both of which generated funds to support the two clubs.

The relationship between the Fitzroy board and the Brisbane Lions was complex. They recognised that Brisbane had made efforts to engage with its Victorian supporters and the Fitzroy heritage, largely due to the intervention of Leigh Matthews. Brisbane wanted to add the initials 'BB/FFC' to the back of their jumper from 2002 and petitioned the AFL to be referred to as the 'Lions' on the scoreboard when playing in Melbourne, rather than 'Brisbane' or the 'Brisbane Lions'.[14] Brisbane had not, however, removed the ongoing $1.25 million debenture, implemented by the AFL and Brisbane to ensure that Fitzroy did not act up following the merger. This arrangement continued to be a point of contention, and one former board member, David McMahon, refused to attend the Brisbane Lions-organised Fitzroy Team of the Century dinner in Melbourne on 3 May 2001 (for which McMahon had been nominated for a position in the team).[15] On 3 September 2001, the debenture was finally removed, much to the relief of the Fitzroy board, and with the Brisbane Lions making the 2001 Grand Final, there was a rapprochement of sorts. During grand final week, Dyson Hore-Lacy wrote to Graeme Downie, Brisbane's president, congratulating the Lions for reaching the grand final, thanking the club for its genuine efforts to embrace Fitzroy supporters and wishing them luck.[16]

...

How did the Fitzroy supporters feel about the game? The answer depended on the decisions made in the aftermath of 1996, when one supporter, speaking for thousands of broken-hearted fans, asked: 'I have lost my football club, what do I do?'[17] Each supporter was unique. 'Every Fitzroy person dealt with the merger differently, has dealt with the post-merger differently and has a different emotional connection with different parts of the club,' noted club stalwart Arthur Wilson many years later. 'That's the beauty of it and that's the hard part as well, because you can't tap into everyone's immediate emotional connection.'[18]

Supporters faced three broad options and based on their own preferences and predispositions they decided which suited them: they could support the Brisbane Lions, they could support another Victorian club or they could stop following the AFL altogether. Brisbane offered a modicum of continuity, but it was both interstate and the symbol of Fitzroy's AFL-endorsed demise. Following another Victorian club, particularly North Melbourne, was a difficult choice, as they had been barracking against such clubs their entire lives. Lastly, those who could not choose always had the option of swearing off the game altogether. As terrifying as this prospect might have seemed, many followed through, determining that AFL without Fitzroy was simply not worth following.

Of the other Victorian clubs, North Melbourne made a big push to court disenfranchised Fitzroy supporters. In Round 21, 1996, it had invited Fitzroy members to attend its game against Geelong.[19] Noel Gordon accused North Melbourne of 'trying to drive a wedge between Fitzroy and Brisbane' and 'pinch another club's members'.[20] Always one to call out hypocrisy, Patrick Smith claimed Gordon had some cheek in criticising North for attempting to lure disillusioned Fitzroy supporters to Arden Street. North Melbourne, Smith believed, had 'every right to grab as many members as it can. North has learned the hard way that in the AFL, it's every club for itself — unless, of course, you have the blessing of the AFL Commission. Then you just name your price.'[21] The match might not have been the advertisement North Melbourne was hoping for, with Geelong victorious 16.13 (109) to 14.12 (96). Supporter Wade Britnell was unconvinced: 'As hard as you can try, you just can't change your team when you've barracked for them all your life.' He began supporting the Brisbane Lions in 1997.[22] North Melbourne *was* able to entice many Fitzroy supporters, however, and several formed the 'North–Fitzroy Pride' coterie, led by Kevin Campbell.[23]

Those who refused to give the game away but who could not bring themselves to barrack for the Kangaroos or the Hawks or any of the other tribal rivals pondered the merits of supporting Brisbane. At the end of the 1996 season, John Birt wrote to the club's members and supporters. Acknowledging the 'emotion and pain' following the merger, he encouraged Fitzroy people to support Brisbane and be part of 'a new and financially strong club' with an 'exciting future in the AFL'. Like others, he argued that the colours and jumper were a compelling reason to support the new Lions, and it was 'a right and a duty' of Fitzroy people to carry on the club's heritage as part of the Brisbane Lions.[24] For many, this argument was compelling. 26-year-old Graeme Tatti believed the colours made Brisbane more palatable: 'It's like our flag, our country ... And we get Alastair Lynch back.'[25] Trainer Lance Upton eventually found himself pleased that Fitzroy had merged with Brisbane rather than North Melbourne, as he felt there was much more Fitzroy represented in the new club than would have been the case with the Kangaroos. 'We would have just had a lion on their shorts,' he believed, 'that's all.'[26] Skott Dean found he could not barrack against the Fitzroy colours, plus, Kevin Murray's endorsement was persuasive: 'If it's good enough for him, it's good enough for me.'[27]

There was a perfectly valid debate to be had about the degree to which simply adding colours and a logo made the Brisbane Lions a spiritual successor to the Fitzroy Lions. Brad Boyd argued that Fitzroy was continuing, 'but in a different form'.[28] For others, it was not so simple. One supporter argued that if the colours were so important, he could follow the Adelaide Crows, as the difference was negligible: 'It is the Fitzroy name that gave the club its life and identity.'[29] For many, the attachment to a sense of place mattered more than symbols. 'The moment we lost the name Fitzroy,' Barry Dickins lamented, 'we lost our immortal soul as well as the rapid forfeiture of our history.'[30] Rick Lang, who did decide to follow Brisbane, nevertheless found the dearth of coverage in the *Herald Sun* a sad reminder that he follows an interstate club.[31] Supporter Gary Coomber declared that he could not support Brisbane for that reason: 'They're the Brisbane Lions.

The colours are very nice, but they could be maroon and blue and the Gorillas, but they're still Brisbane … I'm a Victorian and I'll always be a Victorian.'[32]

Despite these objections, hundreds of Fitzroy supporters decided to sign up as Brisbane Lions members in 1997. By May of that year, the new Lions had 3300 members in Melbourne, over 3200 more than the Brisbane Bears had in Victoria the previous year.[33] Fitzroy supporter Alan Munro was not going to barrack for another Victorian club. He thought about North Melbourne, 'but I've always barracked against them and everyone else.'[34] Ken Bailey expressed a similar sentiment: 'To me, for the older people, when you're brought up with Fitzroy football, you can't barrack for the other clubs here.'[35] He decided to support the Brisbane Lions. Still, many Roys probably supported Brisbane not because they were enthralled and enamoured with the new entity, but because after a period of grieving, they decided that they wanted to continue following AFL and supporting a team. Given that they had spent their lives barracking against every other club, particularly those in Melbourne, the Brisbane Lions seemed like a satisfactory alternative; it was not Fitzroy, but it was better than nothing. Over time, genuine affection and loyalty to the new Lions would grow, complementing, but never replacing, the love for the old Roys.

The Brisbane/Fitzroy marriage took time to truly develop, and it was not until the premiership years that many Fitzroy supporters truly embraced the new club. The Brisbane Lions reaching the 2001 AFL Grand Final brought those who had chosen the merged club to the cusp of glory, a place Fitzroy had rarely ventured. Peta Phillips, the daughter of Lions Auxiliary and Fitzroy Life Member Alvie Phillips, had been heartbroken in 1996. She was not enthusiastic about North Melbourne, and, after a time, decided to follow the Brisbane Lions as there was some semblance of Fitzroy there to cling to. The reward came on 29 September 2001. 'I got used to losing at a very young age,' she said.[36] For the first time in fifty-one years she was going to watch her team in a grand final. Interviewed in Grand Final week, Dot Thompson, another Ladies Auxiliary stalwart and Life Member, had no regrets about following Brisbane. Clen Denning, who played in Fitzroy's 1944 premiership side, similarly declared: 'Brisbane is my team, there's no doubt about that.'[37]

There had been no stronger Fitzroy advocate for the merger than Kevin Murray, and during Grand Final week he urged Roys who had not done so already to embrace the Brisbane Lions.[38] 'We were all so divided back in 1996,' he said during the week, 'and I think a Lions win on Saturday will show that Fitzroy is not dead and buried. It lives on in the Brisbane Lions.'[39] If they had not already decided to follow the Brisbane Lions, adopting the Queensland team was unlikely to occur overnight. Still, the opportunity was ripe for hearts to be softened. At the grand final parade, Martin Flanagan saw a supporter who epitomised the old Fitzroy, 'a quiet, kindly man with a passion for books, social causes and a struggling football club'. Flanagan had met him infrequently during Fitzroy's final years, seeing 'the long pain of that slow death upon his face'. That day, Flanagan asked whether the passion was back. 'Not quite,' the man said, still draped in his ancient Fitzroy scarf, 'but it's coming.'[40]

Taking the field on the last Saturday in September, the Brisbane Lions were triumphant, defeating Essendon 15.18 (108) to 12.10 (82). It was a victory built on the Brisbane Bears, eleven players had belonged to Brisbane before the merger, plus Alastair Lynch, who had joined in 1994. Six others were drafted by the club from the 1997 national draft onwards, and three, including Martin Pike, had been traded in. Still, there was enough Fitzroy on the field to make the connection meaningful. Chris Johnson was the direct link, alongside Pike and Lynch who had more circuitous routes. Nineteen-year-old Jonathan Brown, the Lions' father/son selection from the 1999 national draft, and 21-year-old Luke Power, who had grown up barracking for Fitzroy, were a fusion of Fitzroy heritage and the modern Brisbane Lions reality. They had just achieved something that had eluded their childhood heroes and that had been beyond the ability of generations of Fitzroy players.

Fitzroy people who had not embraced Brisbane were nonplussed by the result. One old Royboy, not affiliated with Brisbane, attended the game as a journalist. When asked whether he would be supporting the Lions, his response was to stand up and yell: 'Die you Queensland scum!'[41] For others, the premiership mattered a great deal. 'It was an unbelievable feeling,' recalled Sam Lord, who had been supporting the Brisbane Lions since 1997, 'something I thought I'd never experience.'[42] Kevin Elms, who was still strapping ankles after all these years, kissed the ground and cried, 'I was just so proud to be involved.'[43] Kevin Murray stood in the stands, wearing a Fitzroy scarf and his 1969 Brownlow Medal, as proud as anyone at seeing what his new club had achieved.[44] As the celebrations continued into the night, one fan ended up at the Napier Hotel, with a crowd of supporters singing Fitzroy songs and celebrating in Fitzroy's heartland: 'That whole time was marvellous, it's a good as footy gets'. Another recalled, 'It wasn't Fitzroy that day, but there was enough Fitzroy there for us old Royboys to enjoy.'[45] A premiership was not compensation for losing their club, but it was still something special.

The premiership cup was taken to Brunswick Street Oval the following Sunday and presented to 6000 waiting fans. One woman, Eunice Mushet, was fighting back tears as she held a 1903 Fitzroy membership ticket. She watched the Roys with her father and grandfather, waiting for a premiership since 1944. Now, with her own Lions-supporting grandchildren, she savoured this emotional and poignant moment. Reflecting on what it meant to cheer on Brisbane, a city that was geographically and culturally so distant from Fitzroy, she said: 'You don't really go over to Brisbane. Behind it all, it is still Fitzroy to us.'[46] For Eunice, death was not the end, and the AFL Premiership Cup was at Brunswick Street Oval to prove it.

CONCLUSION

COUNTING THE COST

How much is a football club worth? A balance sheet will show a club's assets and liabilities, a monetary calculation of its value. This is important and only a fool would believe otherwise. As Fitzroy discovered, it can be fatal. It does not, however, reflect the real value of a football club. As this book has made abundantly clear, for many people, the significance of a football club goes well beyond the boundaries of light entertainment on a weekend. When asked for his highlight of the 1996 season, Alan McConnell remarked that the events of that year were an enduring reminder of how important football is to people's lives.[1] 'For the keen supporter,' academics John Cash and Joy Damousi wrote, 'the club occupies the position of being, at once, a social institution and an object of fantasy with which they identify.'[2] Even the AFL's annual report from 1996 noted that 'because of the emotion involved, it is almost impossible to discuss football in economic terms.'[3] And as Ross Oakley himself wrote in his 2014 memoirs, 'some things in football run deeper than money'.[4]

Yet football clubs cannot exist on the goodwill of those that love them. Clubs inevitably incur expenses in the course of conducting football operations, requiring income. Depending on the scale of operations, revenue may only need to come from memberships, sponsorships and donations. Alternatively, clubs could branch out into all sorts of commercial endeavours, such as merchandise, poker machines or partnerships with government to share the cost of capital expenditure. Pressure on clubs to generate revenue was not an invention of the eighties. At Fitzroy's 14th AGM in April 1897, the financial report indicated that due to a decrease in gate receipts the club's financial condition was 'not flourishing'.[5] Despite that, the committee presented a balanced result, with income and expenses roughly equal at £386 1s 6d, the equivalent of just under $35,000 in 1996. These numbers, even when adjusted for inflation, are small compared to the increasing costs associated with football in 1996, much less in today's terms. But all things are relative; it provides no peace of mind to have small expenses if income is even lower. Nevertheless, one year later, after 'careful management on the part of the office-bearers' and the 'liberality of leading citizens', Fitzroy was able to wipe off the debit balance and secure a credit of £23.[6]

For much of the twentieth century, the costs associated with running football clubs were so modest that officials and administrators did not need to consider undermining the nature of the club to ensure it remained a viable financial entity. The notable exception was University Football Club, which bowed out of the VFL at the end of the 1914 season, unable to maintain its amateur, university-based ethos and field a competitive team, replete with the necessary expenditure on player payments.[7] Fitzroy was always a club with a small membership base and a constrained geographical catchment area from which to gain supporters. Still, for decades this did not negatively affect its ability to generate necessary income — within the scope of the VFL, all clubs were similarly limited — although it likely affected its on-field performance.

By the late seventies, however, financial pressures on clubs were becoming more acute. The traditional arrangement of a humble club secretary overseeing modest income and expenses season-by-season began to change when the costs of running a club, particularly player payments, rose exponentially. As writer Elliot Cartledge noted, player payments from 1972 to 1980 increased by 1826 per cent, seven-and-a-half times the rate of inflation, while income sources struggled to keep up.[8] This increase was unsustainable without radical changes. Consequently, the eighties saw a dramatic transformation in the VFL, leading to the push for the national competition and, crucially, a reduction of clubs in Melbourne. This financial crisis forced weaker clubs to either make hard choices or have hard decisions thrust upon them. The exemplar was South Melbourne, which moved to Sydney at the end of the 1981 season. Despite at times fierce resistance by supporters to keep the club in Melbourne, the financial realities of the situation were too great.

The University and South Melbourne examples beg the question: how much of the soul of a club could administrators and officials part with for financial gain, long-term advantage or even just to stay in the top-flight league? At the end of 1996, Footscray changed its name to the Western Bulldogs and moved its home ground from the Western Oval — decisions made to assist the club financially. 'As a supporter everyone feels ruffled,' remarked Irene Chatfield, the Footscray fan at the epicentre of the 1989 Fightback campaign, 'but we'll still be the Bulldogs.'[9] Brisbane decided that it could dispense with ten years of 'Bears' history and identity in the pursuit of becoming the 'Lions'. It was a calculating move and compared with the impact of losing a 113-year-old club, seemingly insignificant, but the 'Bears' meant something to those who had supported the club since its inception. Theirs was a difficult journey, one not discarded lightly.

Fitzroy was just as complicit in these calculations. 'Fitzroy Football Club can never be in Brisbane,' remarked a character in Peter Temple's 1999 book *Black Tide*. 'Nobody can take the Lions to Brisbane ...

Because Fitzroy Football Club can only be in Fitzroy.'[10] While a fine sentiment, the club's physical connection with its suburb had long since ceased. Retaining the name 'Fitzroy' was important, but geographical connections were a luxury the club could not afford. As its financial state became increasingly dire, successive administrations looked for ways to remain in the VFL/AFL and retain the Fitzroy name while being prepared to move increasingly further from its roots. They were willing to play games in Tasmania; they were willing to play games in Canberra. They were ready to merge with Footscray in 1989 to form the 'Fitzroy Bulldogs' or North Melbourne in 1996 to be the 'North-Fitzroy Kangaroos'. The name was the one aspect with which the club was loathed to part. Even after the merger with Brisbane was decided, club legend Bill Stephen argued that the new club needed to include 'Fitzroy': 'They have got to offer us the name because if they don't, then it will only be the Brisbane Football Club and that's not a true merge.'[11] By the end, Fitzroy people were willing to do anything and give away much of the club's identity if it meant retaining the name 'Fitzroy' in the Australian Football League.

The League administration sat over the top of these dilemmas. Like their clubs, the VFL/AFL had expenses to pay and needed to generate income to meet them. Administrators also had a broader role of balancing the need to run a competition with the clubs and the heritage of the League against the opportunities inherent in branching away from being a suburban competition based solely in Melbourne and Geelong. While there was (and remains) much affection for the bygone era of the VFL, it was a patently unsustainable model for a football league looking to become thoroughly professional. The crisis period in the eighties helped to push along many necessary initiatives aimed at strengthening the competition financially. In that context, drastic action to save the League, predominantly through nationalisation, was fully justified.

It also seemed prudent to ensure that clubs were financially healthy without requiring VFL/AFL assistance (a conclusion reached without the precognition of knowing an explosion of broadcast revenue was only years away). During much of the eighties and early nineties, the VFL itself lacked sufficient spare cash to prop up weaker Melbourne-based clubs: the Commission used surpluses to pay down the League's own debt and support the strategically important clubs in Sydney and Brisbane. The approach was laid out in the five-year plan presented in August 1994. The AFL would be a generator of income, but not a banker to the clubs — they needed to be financially stable on their own. The plan was also unashamedly pro-merger. In the minds of those who ran the AFL, mergers were the best way forward for struggling clubs, because the alternative was letting them disappear. Whether through a lack of means or a lack of will, the AFL was not disposed to consider extraordinary steps to keep a struggling Melbourne-based club in the competition.

In the case of Fitzroy, by 1996, a merger had become the only way in which the club, even in a diminished form, could remain in the AFL. The club's board had flirted with this option for years, and by the start of 1996 had become resigned to it as a last resort. Fitzroy's inability to find a way to generate revenue through the eighties and early nineties had proved fatal. While there were many factors affecting this, Fitzroy people maintain that the Commission deliberately rejected proposals (such as playing home games outside Victoria) to ensure that a merger was its only option. Certainly, League administrators denied the club various revenue-raising initiatives over the years, either on technicalities or seemingly on the whims of the Commission. The argument at AFL House likely went that since mergers were both inevitable and necessary, it did no good to prolong Fitzroy's life when it could, like South Melbourne, take the plunge with a radical transformation and presumably, reap the benefits. Few senior officials thought that mergers were not inevitable and that, if given the right support, a struggling club such as Fitzroy could be shepherded through its difficult times to have a place in the modern AFL. The League was not as powerful and paternal as it would become, and mergers were the order of the day. While one can lament the Commission's insistence on mergers, as was seen in the VFA and during the establishment of the National Rugby League, expulsion or financial ruin was a much more severe fate that could befall an unwanted club.

Part of the tragedy of Fitzroy is that the AFL Commission's merger policy did not last much longer than 1996. Shortly after the 1996 Grand Final (and the failure of Melbourne and Hawthorn to agree to a merger proposal), the Commission decided to withdraw its $6 million incentive package for several reasons. First, they realised that it was a de facto guarantee of a club's debt and there was a view that future directors would manage a club's affairs confident that if insolvency occurred, a merger, albeit under administration, would free directors from their financial responsibility for the club's debt. Second, the Commission was concerned that too much of the incentive package might be used to pay off an insolvent club's debt, rather than being put towards a newly merged club, and thus not represent a good investment by the AFL (which, it must be remembered, was not as cash rich as it would subsequently become) and $6 million could be put to better use.[12]

Finally, the Commission realised that the emotion of the merger issue was too powerful to overcome. From the confines of AFL House, mergers probably seemed rational and straightforward, and some club boards explored them as per their fiduciary obligations. Supporters, however, were passionately against them. The $6 million inducement was aimed at boards, not members, and it meant very little to the rank-and-file, those who, time and again, fought to preserve their clubs no matter the cost. 'It was clear,' the AFL noted at the end of 1996, 'that regardless of the considered opinions of the clubs' boards, the chance of receiving adequate member support is minimal.'[13] While Oakley had argued that supporters would eventually support a merger rather than see their club die, the failed 'Melbourne Hawks' venture suggested the opposite: many members would not endorse a merger if there was even the slightest hope that their club could continue in its own right. 'If that is what they want, so be it,' Oakley's successor, Wayne Jackson, remarked in October 1996, 'the AFL cannot buy a merger for $6 million.'[14] It was a powerful realisation from AFL House, and one not before time. The Commission retained the view that mergers were the preferred path for Melbourne clubs with small supporter bases, although it would only consider financial assistance on a case-by-case basis and would need to be satisfied that a merger proposal had strong support from the members of the clubs involved.[15] As history showed, the AFL's merger policy ultimately disappeared with Ross Oakley.

To add insult to Fitzroy's injury, the catastrophe predicted to befall Melbourne's weaker clubs never came. A rising tide of broadcast revenue floated all boats. In 1998, Channel Seven concluded a broadcast deal for AFL football at $40 million per year to 2001 (up from $17 million per year as negotiated in 1992). In 2001, Foxtel, Channel Nine and Channel Ten secured the rights at $100 million per year for five years. The influx of money helped both the League and its clubs and incentivised the retention of clubs in the League; it was in the AFL's best interest to have as many games as possible to maximise the potential advertising revenue to the broadcaster. There was also an acceptance from the AFL Commission that many of the methods Fitzroy had sought to pioneer were now appropriate if poorer clubs were to continue. Playing home games in other states, for instance, was a viable, lucrative and indeed necessary for some clubs. So too, it seemed, was gaming revenue. Whatever the moral issues involved, in time, it may have become the means for Fitzroy to reach financial security, as it was for other clubs. Had Fitzroy hung on long enough, the new environment and its revenue from the Fitzroy Club Hotel it might have made it to safety. As supporter Rick Lang lamented, 'it didn't need to be inevitable.'[16]

...

At the turn of the century, it seemed that everyone in and around the AFL could breathe a sigh of relief. It was not that the old problem of needing to generate income to cover expenses had vanished, but there was now an AFL Commission that was committed to helping clubs, rather than coaxing them into mergers. The League dividend became inequitably distributed, favouring the poorer clubs, while growing broadcast revenue ushered in a period of prosperity. With the AFL headed towards financial security, a diminishing risk of clubs becoming insolvent and three Brisbane Lions premierships seeming to vindicate the 1996 merger, few, it seemed, wished to dwell too heavily on the 'merger era' and the full cost of Fitzroy's departure. Besides, the action on the field always engrossed the attention of those who still had teams to support. As writer and Geelong supporter John Harms wrote: 'When players run out onto the footy field you don't think about how they were drafted, how much they earn, who sponsors them. Footy is too engaging for that.'[17] Indeed, most football supporters quickly moved on from 1996, focussing on what lay in store for their own clubs, leaving Fitzroy to recede further into the past with each season.

But we ignore the events of 1996 at our peril. The significance of the merger, and issues it raised, are too important to be forgotten. The Fitzroy Football Club, its officials, players and supporters, were the casualty of the larger tale of an amateur, suburban football league evolving into a modern, professional and national competition. Those running the League argued that for this transformation to be successful, both the central administration and the individual clubs needed to adopt a corporate mentality in the way they conducted their affairs. The fate of Fitzroy was a stark demonstration of this change. Following the merger announcement, Glenn Warry remarked that if the players had not realised it before, they were undoubtedly now aware that football was not a sport but a business.[18] Many supporters, whether writing to newspapers, calling radio stations or merely expressing their views privately to one another, echoed these sentiments.

In creating the modern AFL, Oakley and the Commission had changed the League irrevocably. They had not merely turned a suburban football league into a national competition, but, as Elliot Cartledge argued in *Footy's Revolution*, by turning to commercialisation to save the League, the competition had become enslaved to the commercial forces providing the income necessary to keep it afloat.[19] For some, this was a price worth paying. Others ardently disagreed. No matter one's opinion, the change was paradigmatic and likely irreversible. In the week before Fitzroy's final AFL game, Patrick Smith took the opportunity to pontificate on the broader implications of Fitzroy's demise. 'It is a watershed weekend and it is also the vision of Ross Oakley and his Commission,' he wrote. 'Football for thousands upon thousands of people will never be the same again. You better have got it right, Ross.'[20]

The steady commercialisation of the game has also commodified the passions and investment of supporters in their football clubs. The sense of belonging to a club can be passed down generations, and become deeply entrenched in how individuals and families understand themselves, their sense of identity and their personal stories. AFL clubs benefit from the generational support of thousands of people who commit themselves financially and emotionally to their clubs and who would not extricate themselves under almost any circumstances. This is a significant advantage for the AFL as it seeks to operate within a contested sporting and entertainment market. Yet if the commercialisation of the League was both inevitable and necessary, how far down the path of corporatisation and commercialisation does the AFL still need to go before the adverse effects become too great for its constituency to bear? This remains an open question. As officials constantly look for new ways to raise revenue and grow the game, the loyalty and emotional attachment of supporters with their clubs should never be taken for granted.

Of course, the implications of 1996 are not merely abstract or academic. Reasonable people can differ over the merits of the AFL's transformation into a national brand and whether the benefits have outweighed the costs, but few would suggest that the loss of Fitzroy to the League was not a profoundly sad event. In 2003, one of the chief architects of the AFL's merger policy, Graeme Samuel, remarked that 'you can't talk about mergers, you can't talk about teams disappearing, you can't talk about rationalising … without really understanding that it has a major impact on supporters, on club directors, on players right across the board'.[21] He also called the notion that Victoria could not support eleven clubs a 'myth' that he regretted perpetuating. His revelation was welcome, yet the damage had already been done. The greatest legacy of 1996 is the scars still born by Fitzroy people to this day, as what was once a community united around the love of a football club fractured, never truly to be made whole again. While most supporters have come to terms with what happened in 1996, much sadness, anger, disillusionment and grief still remains. Like the three supporters at the Prince of Prussia in Peter Temple's Jack Irish books, many Roys are still 'nursing glasses of beer and old grievances'.[22]

This book has offered ample testimony of the merger's personal impact upon supporters. Kathy Doyle, for instance, had developed a large and diverse group of Fitzroy friends. The thought of 1996 being Fitzroy's final year and that 'the thing that had brought us all together was about to be ripped away from us' made her profoundly sad.[23] Skott Dean loved the Roys. 'I just wish I could bottle how I feel about Fitzroy,' he said during an extensive discussion about his memories of the club. He embraced the Brisbane Lions, but it never quite replicated the sense of belonging or the passion and joy of being a Royboy.[24] Stuart Winstanley also spoke in powerful terms as he recalled his feelings after Fitzroy's final game in Melbourne. 'My soul was defeated,' he lamented. Like Dean, the Brisbane Lions did not entirely fill the void.[25] Jan Wright still feels Fitzroy's absence from the AFL, particularly on those two occasions where supporter excitement is at its most palpable: the start of each new season and grand final day.[26] Finally, each weekend for many years, William Oliver and his father would go to the football to watch Fitzroy. This allowed them to share their mutual love for the club and bond in a way that was, at times, difficult outside the context of sport. After 1996, they never attended another AFL game together, his father heartbroken at what became of the Roys. 'It was more than just a club they destroyed,' Oliver reflected, 'and they couldn't care less.'[27]

On 7 July 1996, in the aftermath of the merger agreement, the *Sunday Age* ran two articles about Fitzroy on the same page. One, the paper's editorial, interpreted the merger rationally, while the other struck a much more emotional tone as it explored the meaning of the week's events. The editorial noted: 'It was a merger that had to happen, if not like this. Struggling at the bottom of the ladder, short of sufficient (and affluent) supporters and hopelessly in debt, Fitzroy could not survive alone. But the acceptance of reality took an unconscionable time to reach its inevitable conclusion.'[28] The other article, written by the editor of the *Sunday Age*'s 'Agenda' section, Ken Merrigan, offered an impassioned eulogy for his club: 'We've lost an inheritance, a sense of being the connection between the past and the future.' The supporters had lost their birthright, he wrote, 'A ticket to part of what it is to live in Melbourne — that great, running, partisan discourse on what happened last weekend and what will happen in the weekends ahead.'[29] The passing down of generations was broken, with memories and allegiances now carried by a faithful remnant. One day there will be no-one left who can say they saw the Fitzroy Football Club take the field in Australian football's highest competition. That day, Australian rules football will have lost something special.

EPILOGUE

On the afternoon of 14 July 2018, Melbourne produced a perfect winter's afternoon. The sun was out, few clouds were in the sky, and a lack of breeze kept the temperature reasonably warm. My wife and I had recently travelled down from Canberra to let family and friends meet our three-month-old son, Joel, for the first time. Amid the endless gatherings, lunches and coffees, I took the opportunity to take him to the Brunswick Street Oval to see Fitzroy. That day the Roys were playing Peninsula Old Boys in the VAFA's Premier C division, and Joel became the fourth generation of Westerman to come to this ground to watch the club. He did little actual spectating, however, as he was largely unaware of what was happening on the field in front of him and cared very little, alternating between periods of sleep, agitation and contentment. My mother purchased a small, handmade Fitzroy beanie to keep his head warm. Moving around the ground, he received a good share of favourable comments, with many hoping that this visit would be the first of many. If the Roys replicate their performance that day — a convincing 123-point victory — I will certainly be keen for him and any future siblings to return.

I love coming to this ground. The beautiful, heritage-registered grandstand lets one see the Melbourne skyline over the rows of terraced houses, a view that epitomises inner-city suburban football. It is easy to imagine Brunswick Street Oval in its heyday hosting VFL games, with crowds pouring in on foot from across the suburb, or alighting from a W-class tram stopping outside the ground. It has also grown to have a special personal resonance. I came here the week my father died, just to watch a match and get away from things for a while. Dad and I came to watch Fitzroy as often as we could. Perversely, Dad appreciated the lower standard of non-professional football, as he believed it made the game less predictable and, as a result, more enjoyable. He loved the local flavour to game days, that you could go out and hear the coach's address at the quarter time huddle or squeeze into the rooms after a win and sing the club song with gusto. If you were lucky, you might see Kevin Murray in the crowd. Bulldog was always happy to have a photo with a fan and show them the 1969 Brownlow Medal still worn around his neck.

Kevin Murray's presence at Brunswick Street Oval is a reminder that the current VAFA club is a continuation of the Fitzroy that Murray played 333 games for between 1955 and 1974. The story of how the club returned to competitive football is a tale worthy of more space than an epilogue will allow. In the years following the merger, the Fitzroy Football Club continued to support the Fitzroy Reds. This partnership drew in many old Fitzroy supporters who were keen to follow a local football team. The Reds had been successful in lower leagues, winning the D1 division premiership as recently as 2005, but by 2008, the club was in financial trouble, struggling to service a debt of $20,000. As it happened, Fitzroy had a spare $20,000 from the sale of the lease on the Fitzroy Club Hotel. To help the Reds avoid financial ruin, Fitzroy's secretary, Bill Atherton, suggested a formal merger between the two entities, brining Fitzroy's financial weight to the Reds' football operations.[1] On 8 December 2008, the Fitzroy Football Club directors unanimously agreed to a merger, which was also agreed to by the Reds. 'This club's been in the big time and had her throat cut,' Atherton remarked at the time, 'but she lived on and now she's back.'[2]

On 18 April 2009, the newly-merged Fitzroy Reds played its first competitive game in the VAFA's D1 section (the league's fourth division). Hosting Prahran (a club with a similar trajectory to the Roys) at Brunswick Street Oval, Fitzroy, captained by Jim O'Reilly, won a solid victory, 16.12 (108) to 8.9 (57). The Roys finished fourth that season, but made the grand final. On an unseasonably hot and very blustery September day, they were defeated by Rupertswood, 12.80 (90) to 9.11 (65). Still, Fitzroy was back as a footballing entity in its own right, consolidating itself in the VAFA and building a new chapter of the club's storied history. Fitzroy is now the only Australian rules football club that has been a member of the VFA, VFL, AFL and the VAFA.

Few people have done as much work to bring the Fitzroy Football Club to where it is today as Bill Atherton, who became the club's secretary in 1998 after it came out of administration. He accepted the role, offered to him by Elaine Findlay, primarily to ensure that the AFL and the Brisbane Lions adhered to the terms of the merger agreement.[3] He is proud of where the club has ended up, and will remind anyone who will listen that Fitzroy did not die in 1996 but lives on as a prosperous amateur club. The club provides a blue-ribbon senior competition to the young men and women of Fitzroy and the surrounding districts at the club's original home ground, almost exactly what the club was doing in 1884. Fitzroy is still in business, but at a level that does more good for the suburb and for those that love traditional football.

'It's a great little community,' reflected David Leydon, the old Fitzroy supporter who was elected as the club's vice president in 2019.[4] He re-engaged in the club following its exit from the AFL, and has followed its journey into amateur football. Many old Roys have come out of the woodwork to follow the club, attracted by the prospect of seeing the Fitzroy jumper running around Brunswick Street Oval again. 'It's just the most beautiful thing to see,' declared Leydon, who is just as committed to the VAFA club as he is to the Brisbane Lions.[5] Elaine Findlay, who remained as a board member until 2010, agreed: 'It's wonderful that young people are playing at Brunswick Street Oval.'[6] But Fitzroy is more than just a bastion for old Royboys. Those who supported the University Reds still follow the club in its current form, and the connection with the Fitzroy Junior Football Club has seen many locals (both players and their parents) come to support the club too. They may barrack for other AFL clubs, but their local team is Fitzroy. A notable example is club president, the Collingwood-supporting Joan Eddy, who likely had little idea that when she dropped off her five-year-old son for Auskick at Fitzroy in 1997, she was setting on a path to be involved with Fitzroy for years to come.[7]

For some people, however, Fitzroy *did* die on 1 September 1996. Regardless of the continuation of the corporate entity known as the Fitzroy Football Club, its departure from the AFL signalled the end of many supporters' engagement with the club. Many football supporters have a singular focus on the AFL, and in the absence of Fitzroy, they might follow the Brisbane Lions, North Melbourne, the Western Bulldogs or perhaps no-one. They may not know about the club's resurrection in the VAFA, or if they do, they do not necessarily consider it to be the same club as the one that played in the VFL and AFL. This is perfectly fine. Enjoying football (and sport in general) is as much an individual activity as it is a collective project.

Still, the Fitzroy Football Club (incorporating the Fitzroy Reds) *is* a continuation, in both spirit and reality, of the club that was founded at a Brunswick Street hotel in September 1883. After three seasons in the third division (Premier C) the Roys looked like they could challenge for that elusive premiership. Dad and I went to the preliminary final in 2012 against Mazenod at the Trevor Barker Oval in Sandringham. Mazenod had proved to be a prickly foe over the years. Sitting in one of the pockets, there was one passage of play that sticks in my mind. At one stage, Fitzroy's Luke Ablett was bringing the ball out of defence and he kicked it long down the left wing. From our vantage point, it looked as if he had kicked into complete empty space. Momentarily I chastised him for such a poor disposal, and then, right as the ball dipped to head height, a Fitzroy player drifted into my vision and the ball floated effortlessly onto his chest. It was perhaps the best pass I have ever seen. Ablett, an AFL premiership player, was clearly more talented than most players on the field, and that small, innocuous piece of play proved it for me. That is part of the beauty of football at the amateur level, it allowed skilful players to really show how capable they were, like league football had been in the days before players professionalised and they were 'sports scienced' *ad absurdum*. Raw and natural talent still shines through in the AFL, but perhaps not as markedly as in the lower leagues.

Defeating Mazenod, Fitzroy went on to play the grand final against Parkdale (I could not attend due to a wedding) but the Roys lost 13.10 (88) to 15.16 (106). After several seasons in Premier B division, the end came in 2017 and the Roys were ignominiously relegated back to Premier C division on percentage. Meanwhile, in 2015 the club initiated a partnership with the Australian Catholic University to field a women's team in the Victorian Women's Football League, under the name Fitzroy–ACU. By 2019, the Fitzroy Football Club had seniors and reserves for both the mens and womens teams, plus thirds, Under 23s and Under 19s — it was now a robust, thriving and thoroughly modern community club.

Yet there was still one prize that had alluded a Fitzroy senior mens team for decades. Bereft of glory for so many years, in 2018 Fitzroy fought its way into the Premier C Grand Final after a powerful season. Expecting to face minor premiers Williamstown CYMS, they instead took the field against Old Geelong, who had stunned the CYs in the Preliminary Final by one point. The grand final, played at the Trevor Barker Oval on 15 September 2018, was a day to remember for Fitzroy, with its reserve team also making their grand final (and also against Old Geelong). The reserves started the day well, with a 6.6 (42) to 4.9 (33) victory. Then came the main event. Fitzroy's seniors charged out the gate strongly, and in front of a large crowd they put on eight goals without reply in the first quarter. From then on it was a masterclass of skill and precision in difficult conditions. By the final siren, Fitzroy had won 16.11 (107) to 5.7 (37). Roys stalwart and former club captain Rory Angiolella was best on ground. He sat in a long and proud line, that stretched back through Boyd and Roos, Murphy and Murray, Gale, Hughson and Bunton, right back to Patrick McShane. Fitzroy faithful who had never seen a premiership in their lives celebrated just as hard as any AFL supporter would have done if their club had won a grand final. On ABC Radio, Coodabeen Champion Jeff Richardson, declared: 'This proves to everyone who doesn't already know. Fitzroy lives!'[8]

BIBLIOGRAPHY

Interviews and Correspondence

Bill Atherton, 10 September 2019
John Barker, 14 August 2019
Kinnear Beatson, 11 November 2019
Brett Chandler, 10 July 2018
Rob Clancy, 12 November 2019
Rohan Connolly, 1 October 2018
Mark Dawson, 8 October 2019
Skott Dean, 11 January 2020
Kathy Doyle, 29 July 2020
Elaine Findlay, 12 November 2019
Greg Freemantle, 12 August 2019
Fran Gazzola, 1 May 2020
Melanie Gibb, 18 February 2020
Leon Harris, 17 June 2020
Simon Hawking, 14 April 2020
Colin Hobbs, 12 August 2019
Andrew Ireland, 23 January 2019
Chris Johnson, 11 May 2020
Rick Lang, 2 March 2020
David Leydon, 19 September 2019
Sam Lord, 21 February 2020
Tony Mazoski, 18 January 2020
John McCarthy, 8 January 2019
Alan McConnell, 10 August 2018
Simon McLaughlin, 26 September 2020
Greg Miller, 30 January 2019
Nick Mitchell, 24 September 2019
William Oliver, 11 November 2019
Stephen Paxman, 10 July 2018
Matthew Primus, 26 September 2019
Tim Renwick, 14 May 2019

John Rombotis, 13 July 2018
Greg Swann, 14 January 2019
Lance Upton, 29 June 2020
Glenn Warry, 15 November 2018
Marty Warry, 18 January 2020
Stuart Winstanley, 12 November 2019
Jan Wright, 3 December 2018

Primary Records

AFL Commission Minutes
Australian Football League, *Annual Report 1996*
The Deed of Arrangement between Fitzroy and the Brisbane Bears – August 4th 1996
Fitzroy Football Club, *1993 Annual Report and Audited Financial Statements*
Fitzroy Football Club, *1994 Annual Report and Audited Financial Statements*
Fitzroy Football Club, *1995 Annual Report and Audited Financial Statements*
North Melbourne Football Club, *1996 Annual Report and Balance Sheet*
North Melbourne Football Club, *1997 Annual Report and Balance Sheet*
North Melbourne Football Club, *1998 Annual Report and Balance Sheet*
Skott Dean papers
Victorian Parliamentary Debates

Books

Brown, Jonathan with Adam McNicol. *Life and Football*. Melbourne: Michael Joseph, 2015.

Button, James. *Comeback: The Fall and Rise of Geelong*. Carlton: Melbourne University Press, 2016.

Cartledge, Elliot. *Footy's Glory Days: The Greatest Era of the Greatest Game*. Richmond: Hardie Grant, 2013.

Cartledge, Elliot. *Footy's Revolution: The Inside Story of the AFL*. Richmond: Hardie Grant Books, 2018.

Carter, Pete. *Fitzroy's Fabulous Century: The 100 Greatest Victories 1897-1996*. Perth: Mr Smudge Books, 2020.

Cash, John and Joy Damousi. *Footy Passions*. Sydney: UNSW Press, 2009.

Coventry, James. *Time and Space: The Tactics That Shaped Australian Rules – and the Players and Coaches Who Mastered Them*. Sydney: Harper Collins, 2015.

Craig, Neil and Michael Nunan. *Heart Rate Training For Horses*. Adelaide: Performance Matters, 1998.

Davison, Graeme. *The Rise and Fall of Marvellous Melbourne*, second edition. Carlton: Melbourne University Press, 2004.

Donald, Chris. *Fitzroy: For the Love of the Jumper: 100 Players Who Made the 'Lions' Roar*. Essendon: Pennon Publishing, 2002.

Donald, Christ. *Kevin Murray: Heart of the Lion*. Essendon: Pennon Publishing, 2005.

Fitzgerald, Ross. *The Footy Club: Inside the Brisbane Bears*. St. Lucia: University of Queensland Press, 1996.

Haigh, Gideon. *Silent Revolutions: Writings on Cricket History*. Melbourne: Blank Inc., 2006.

Harms, John. *Play On: A Sporting Omnibus*. Fitzroy North: Malarkey Publications, 2015.

Holmesby, Russell. *The Death of Fitzroy Football Club: The Story of Fitzroy's Demise in the Words of the Men & Women Who Lost Their Club*. Melbourne: Hardie Grant Books, 2020.

Hore-Lacy, Dyson. *Fitzroy*. Fitzroy: Lion Publications, 2000.

Linnell, Garry, *Football Ltd: The Inside Story of the AFL*. Sydney: Pan Macmillan, 1995.

Lynch, Alastair with Peter Blucher. *Taking Nothing For Granted: From Chronic Fatigue to the MCG*. Sydney: Harper Collins, 2005.

McCalman, Janet. *Struggletown: Public and Private Life in Richmond 1900-1965*. Carlton: Melbourne University Press, 1984.

Mueller, Andrew. *Carn: The Game, and the Country That Play It*. Sydney: HarperCollins Publishers, 2019.

Muyt, Adam. *Maroon and Blue: Recollections and Tales of the Fitzroy Football Club*. Carlton North: Vulgar Press, 2006.

Nixon, Peter. *An Active Journey: The Peter Nixon Story*. Ballan: Connor Court Publishing, 2012.

Oakley, Ross with Jonathan Green and Geoff Slattery. *The Phoenix Rises: The amazing story of the salvation of Australian Football*. Richmond: Slattery Media Group, 2014.

Parkinson, Tony. *Jeff: The Rise and Fall of a Political Phenomenon*. Melbourne: Viking, 2000.
Robertson, Jill. *Gertrude Street Fitzroy*. Fitzroy: Fitzroy Historical Society, 2008.
Roos, Paul. *Beyond 300: An Autobiography*. Milsons Point: Random House, 1997.
Ryan, Peter. *Side By Side: A Season With Collingwood*. Melbourne: Slattery Media Group, 2009.
Temple, Peter. *Bad Debts*. Sydney: HarperCollins, 1996.
Temple, Peter. *Black Tide*. Melbourne: The Text Publishing Company, 2012.
Williams, Ken. *For Club and Country*. Melbourne: Melbourne Cricket Club, 2000.
Wilson, Lorraine. *Carn the Lions*, second edition. Melbourne: Cardigan Street, 1996.

Articles

Australian Dictionary of Biography entries.
Bradshaw, Sue. 'John McMahon: a Talk for the Fitzroy History Society', *The Fitzroy History Society*, April 2005.
Mendes, Philip. 'The Death of Fitzroy Football Club: A Personal Reflection', *ASSH Bulletin*, No. 25, December 1996, pp. 37–41.

Newspapers/Periodicals

The Advertiser
The Age
The Argus
The Australasian
The Australian
The Bendigo Advertiser
The Canberra Times
The Courier Mail
Daily Telegraph
Financial Review
Fitzroy City Press
The Football Record
The Guardian
The Herald
The Herald Sun
Inside Football
Jewish Herald
Leader
The Mercury
Mercury and Weekly Courier
Punch
The Register
Sportsman
The Sunday Mail
The Sydney Morning Herald
The Weekend Australian
Williamstown Chronicle

ENDNOTES

Prologue

1. 'D. Morgan, Caterer, Pastrycook, Confectioner, etc.', *Fitzroy City Press*, 14 April 1883; 'D. Morgan, Caterer, 83 & 85 Gertrude Street, Fitzroy', *Jewish Herald*, 3 October 1884.
2. 'Complimentary Banquet to the North Fitzroy Cricket Club', *Mercury and Weekly Courier*, 11 August 1883.
3. 'Ex-Cn McMahon's Banquet', *Fitzroy City Press*, 18 August 1883; 'Mr M'Mahon's Banquet', *Herald*, 18 August 1883.
4. 'Fitzroy Football Club', *Fitzroy City Press*, 4 October 1884.
5. Graeme Davison, *The Rise and Fall of Marvellous Melbourne*, second edition, Carlton: Melbourne University Press, 2004, pp. 11–12.
6. Ibid., p. 286.
7. A.R., 'Fitzroy', *Age*, 1 June 1935.
8. 'Football', *Mercury and Weekly Courier*, 22 September 1883; 'Football', *Fitzroy City Press*, 22 September 1883.
9. 'Football Meeting', *Argus*, 28 September 1883; Advertisement, 'John McMahon', *Mercury and Weekly Courier*, 22 September 1883.
10. A.R., 'Fitzroy', *Age*, 1 June 1935; 'Mr. J.H. Simpson', *Age*, 9 December 1935.
11. 'Football', *Fitzroy City Press*, 6 October 1883.
12. 'Football', *Fitzroy City Press*, 13 October 1883.
13. Gideon Haigh, *Silent Revolutions: Writings on Cricket History*, Melbourne: Blank Inc., 2006, p. 242; Ken Williams, *For Club and Country*. Melbourne: Melbourne Cricket Club, 2000, p. 71.
14. 'Old Boy', 'Football: Fitzroy's Fighting Forces', *Australasian*, 1 June 1940.
15. Chris Donald, *Fitzroy: For the Love of the Jumper: 100 Players Who Made the 'Lions' Roar*. Essendon: Pennon Publishing, 2002, p. 20.
16. 'Metropolitan Licensing Court', *Argus*, 3 June 1886.
17. 'University v. Fitzroy', *Australasian*, 9 May 1885; 'Football', *Fitzroy City Press*, 17 April 1886.
18. Haigh, *Silent Revolutions*, p. 242.
19. John Ritchie, 'Worrall, John (1861-1937)', *Australian Dictionary of Biography*, National Centre of Biography, ANU, http://adb.anu.edu.au/biography/worrall-john-9192/text16235, published in hard copy 1990, accessed 26 October 2019.
20. 'Old Boy', 'Football: Fitzroy's Fighting Forces', *The Australasian*, 1 June 1940.
21. 'Geelong v Fitzroy', *Sportsman*, 13 August 1884.
22. 'Victorian Football Association', *Leader*, 3 May 1884.
23. 'Sporting Notes. Football', *Fitzroy City Press*, 3 May 1884.
24. Ibid.; 'Sporting Notes. Football', *Mercury and Weekly Courier*, 3 May 1884.
25. 'Fitzroy Football Club. Silver Jubilee', *Fitzroy City Press*, 18 September 1908.

MERGER 347

26 'Football', *Williamstown Chronicle*, 10 May 1884.
27 'Fitzroy v Geelong', *Leader*, 24 May 1884.
28 'Geelong v. Fitzroy', *Sportsman*, 13 August 1884.
29 Ibid.
30 'Fitzroy Football Club. Silver Jubilee', *Fitzroy City Press*, 18 September 1908.
31 Peter Pindar, 'The Football Season of 1884', *Australasian*, 4 October 1884.
32 'Football. South Melbourne v Fitzroy', *Weekly Times*, 4 October 1884; 'Fitzroy Football Club', *Fitzroy City Press*, 4 October 1884.
33 'Fitzroy Football Club', *Fitzroy City Press*, 4 October 1884.
34 Sue Bradshaw, 'John McMahon: a Talk for the Fitzroy History Society', *The Fitzroy History Society*, April 2005.
35 'Mr. J.H. Simpson', *Age*, 9 December 1935; 'Old Boy', 'Football: Fitzroy's Fighting Forces', *Australasian*, 1 June 1940.
36 Ritchie, 'Worrall, John (1861-1937)', *ADB*, accessed 26 October 2019.
37 'Moonee Valley Races', *Punch*, 28 July 1904; 'Church and organ', *Punch*, 9 June 1910.
38 Haigh, *Silent Revolutions*, p. 243.

Introduction

1 Patrick Smith, 'Ten thousand witness the death of a club', *Age*, 1 July 1996.
2 Andrew Mueller, *Carn: The Game, and the Country That Play It*, Sydney: HarperCollins Publishers, 2019, p. 293.
3 Gary Tippet, 'Wounded Lions roar in vain', *Sunday Age*, 30 June 1996.
4 Michael Lovett, 'Player pay fears as the end looms', *Sunday Age*, 30 June 1996.
5 Adam Muyt, *Maroon and Blue: Recollections and Tales of the Fitzroy Football Club*, Carlton North: Vulgar Press, 2006, p. 192.
6 Martin Flanagan, 'Defiant to the end', *Age*, 1 July 1996.
7 Michael Lovett, 'Player pay fears as the end looms', *Sunday Age*, 30 June 1996.
8 Gary Tippet, 'Wounded Lions roar in vain', *Sunday Age*, 30 June 1996.
9 Melissa Fyfe, 'Lions fans in mourning', *Age*, 1 July 1996.
10 Michael Lovett, 'No Roar Lions', *Inside Football*, Vol. 26, No. 20, 3 July 1996.
11 Correspondence, Kathy Doyle, 29 July 2020.
12 Martin Flanagan, 'Defiant to the end', *Age*, 1 July 1996; Melissa Fyfe, 'Lions fans in mourning', *Age*, 1 July 1996.
13 Stephen Howell, 'Lamentable Lions', *Sunday Age*, 30 June 1996.
14 Ashley Browne, 'The last of the Lions', *Age*, 2 May 1997.
15 Russell Jackson, 'What becomes of the broken hearted: the footy stalwarts who kept Fitzroy alive', *Guardian*, 25 August 2016.
16 Interview, Greg Swann, 14 January 2019.
17 Chloe Saltau, 'The last Roy Boyd', *Age*, 2 September 2006; Muyt, *Maroon & Blue*, p. 220.
18 Interview, Alan McConnell, 10 August 2018.
19 Peter Ryan, *Side By Side: A Season With Collingwood*, Melbourne: Slattery Media Group, 2009, p. 261.
20 AFL, *Annual Report 1996*, p. 4.
21 Interview, Alan McConnell, 10 August 2018.
22 Ashley Browne, 'The moment that began Fitzroy's long, slow death', AFL website, 25 June 2016, https://www.afl.com.au/news/46466/the-moment-that-began-fitzroys-long-slow-death.

23. Mike Sheahan, 'Bears Steal Prize', *Herald Sun*, 5 July 1996.
24. Dyson Hore-Lacy, *Fitzroy*, Fitzroy: Lion Publications, 2000, p. 221.
25. Greg Hobbs, 'Big, Big Stories', *Football Record Almanac*, August 1996.
26. Ashley Browne, 'The last of the Lions', *Age*, 2 May 1997.
27. Muyt, *Maroon & Blue*, p. 16.

Chapter One

1. Simon Hawking, 'Marriage breakdown began with the powers that were', *Age*, 18 July 1999.
2. Gabrielle Murphy, 'A Fitzroy family through and through', Brisbane Lions website, https://www.lions.com.au/news/2018-06-15/leydon-fitzroy, accessed 31 October 2019; Jack Banister and Kasey Symons, interview with David Leydon, *The People's Game: An AFL Podcast*, podcast audio, 31 August 2019.
3. Interview, David Leydon, 19 September 2019.
4. '"Best Game of All". Conan Doyle's Praise of Australian Football', *Register*, 6 October 1920.
5. Elliot Cartledge, *Footy's Glory Days: The Greatest Era of the Greatest Game*, Richmond: Hardie Grant, 2013, p. 225.
6. John Cash and Joy Damousi, *Footy Passions*, Sydney: UNSW Press, 2009, p. 20.
7. Pete Carter, *Fitzroy's Fabulous Century: The 100 Greatest Victories 1897-1996*, Perth: Mr Smudge Books, 2020, p. 341.
8. Rohan Connolly, 'Fitzroy's five best home and away wins from 1970-96', *Age*, 30 December 2015.
9. Cash and Damousi, *Footy Passions*, p. 19.
10. Philip Mendes, 'The Death of Fitzroy Football Club: A Personal Reflection', *ASSH Bulletin*, No. 25, December 1996, p. 43.
11. Janet McCalman, *Struggletown: Public and Private Life in Richmond 1900-1965*, Carlton: Melbourne University Press, 1984, p. 141.
12. Muyt, *Maroon & Blue*, p. 141.
13. Interview, Skott Dean, 11 January 2020.
14. 'Fitzroy Football Club', *Fitzroy City Press*, 14 April 1892.
15. Muyt, *Maroon & Blue*, p. 21.
16. Ibid., p. 18.
17. Interview, Stuart Winstanley, 12 November 2019.
18. Muyt, *Maroon & Blue*, p. 23.
19. Simon Ferguson, 'Family Lives For AFL Poor Cousin', *Herald Sun*, 2 July 1996.
20. Jon Anderson, 'Short Pants: Luke Power (Brisbane Lions)', *Herald Sun*, 14 June 2000; Marika Dobbin, The Boys From Old Fitzroy, *Age*, 16 August 2008.
21. Mike Colman, 'Disenchanted Fitzroy fans returning to the fold', *Courier-Mail*, 15 September 1999.
22. Marika Dobbin, The Boys From Old Fitzroy, *Age*, 16 August 2008.
23. Interview, Sam Lord, 21 February 2020.
24. Muyt, *Maroon & Blue*, p. 148
25. Ibid., p. 147.
26. Mendes, 'The Death of Fitzroy Football Club', p. 38.
27. Ed Bannon, 'Family kept the faith from start to finish', *Herald Sun*, 26 August 1996.
28. Interview, Rob Clancy, 12 November 2019.
29. Cartledge, *Footy's Glory Days*, p. 215.
30. Muyt, *Maroon & Blue*, pp. 137–8.
31. Ibid., pp. 181–5.
32. Martin Flanagan, 'The club they hold so dear', *Age*, 20 May 1996.
33. Muyt, *Maroon & Blue*, pp. 80, 100.
34. Ibid., p. 93.
35. Jonathan Brown with Adam McNicol. *Life and Football*, Melbourne: Michael Joseph, 2015, p. 31.

36 Rod Nicholson, 'Doc's down, ordering Macs', *Sunday Mail*, 5 May 1996.
37 D.M. Andrews, *Victorian Parliamentary Debates*, Legislative Assembly, 1 September 2015, p. 2930.
38 Mendes, 'Death of Fitzroy Football Club', p. 41.
39 Muyt, *Maroon & Blue*, p. 202.
40 Mike Sheahan, 'Merge or bust', *Sunday Age*, 18 July 1993.
41 Stephen Linnell and Ashley Browne, 'Fitzroy's future again at risk', *Age*, 5 February 1994; Stephen Linnell, 'AFL plan dooms Lions'. *Age*, 23 August 1994.
42 Stephen Linnell, 'AFL's $4 merger plan – Crunch time for Fitzroy', *Age*, 14 June 1995.
43 Interview, Skott Dean, 11 January 2020.
44 Alastair Lynch with Peter Blucher, *Taking Nothing For Granted: From Chronic Fatigue to the MCG*, Sydney: Harper Collins, 2005, p. 75.
45 Lynch, *Taking Nothing For Granted*, p. v; Interview, Glenn Warry, 15 November 2018.
46 Gareth Andrews, 'Fitzroy in the throes of death', *Sunday Age*, 21 April 1996.
47 Paul Roos, *Beyond 300: An Autobiography*, Milsons Point: Random House, 1997, pp. 217–31.
48 Glenn McFarlane, 'The No. 1, worn by Fitzroy legends Kevin Murray and Paul Roos, voted fifth greatest number', *Herald Sun*, 19 July 2014.
49 Mike Sheahan, 'Lions' Roar Fades To a Death Rattle', *Herald Sun*, 29 June 1996.
50 James Button, 'The lionhearts of Fitzroy', *Age*, 6 July 1996; Roos, *Beyond 300*, p. 210.
51 Interview, Brett Chandler, 10 July 2018.
52 Interview, Rob Clancy, 12 November 2019.
53 Tony de Bolfo, 'Off-Field Woes Affect On-Field Performances', *Herald Sun*, 1 July 1996; Interview, Skott Dean, 11 January 2020.
54 Barry Dickins, 'Last rites for the Royboys', *Age*, 6 July 1996.
55 The average attendance for home games at Princes Park in 1992 and 1993 had been 14,625, compared to 10,771 for homes games at the Western Oval in 1994 and 1995
56 Muyt, *Maroon & Blue*, p. 201.
57 'Club membership reach new high', *Football Record*, 5–7 July 1996.
58 Martin Flanagan, 'The club they hold so dear', *Age*, 20 May 1996.
59 Data based on AFL Tables.
60 Martin Flanagan, 'The End', *Age*, 2 September 1996.
61 Gabrielle Murphy, 'A Fitzroy family through and through', Brisbane Lions website, https://www.lions.com.au/news/2018-06-15/leydon-fitzroy, accessed 31 October 2019; Jack Banister and Kasey Symons, interview with David Leydon, *The People's Game: An AFL Podcast*, podcast audio, 31 August 2019.
62 Interview, Alan McConnell, 10 August 2018.

Chapter Two

1 Richard Hinds, 'The Lion tamer', *Sunday Age*, 3 March 1996.
2 Joyce Brown, 'Lions barking up the right tree with Nunan …', *Inside Football*, Vol. 26, No. 4, 13 March 1996.
3 Stephen Rielly, 'Two days to go … and the coach is going bananas', *Age*, 7 February 1996.
4 Andrew Bain and Andrew Maher, 'A Lion in a Blues camp?', *Sunday Age*, 22 October 1995; Rohan Connolly, 'New coach Michael Nunan rolls up his sleeves and – The rebuilding begins', *Sunday Age*, 29 October 1995.

5. Stephen Rielly, 'Two days to go ... and the coach is going bananas', *Age*, 7 February 1996; Mal Brown, 'In the Jaws of a Lion', *Inside Football*, Vol. 26, No. 13, 15 May 1996; Interview, Glenn Warry, 15 November 2018.
6. Interview, Tim Renwick, 14 May 2019.
7. Anthony Mithen, 'Lions need discipline, says Nunan', *Age*, 12 October 1995.
8. Interview, Alan McConnell, 10 August 2018; Richard Hinds, 'The Lion tamer', *Sunday Age*, 3 March 1996, p. 7; Rohan Connolly, 'New coach Michael Nunan rolls up his sleeves and – The rebuilding begins', *Sunday Age*, 29 October 1995.
9. Interview, Greg Freemantle, 12 August 2019.
10. Hore-Lacy, *Fitzroy*, pp. 138–9; Elliot Cartledge, *Footy's Revolution: The Inside Story of the AFL*, Richmond: Hardie Grant Books, 2018, p. 127; Interview, Colin Hobbs, 12 August 2019.
11. Patrick Smith, 'Nunan's $65,000 is lowest pay of AFL coaches', *Age*, 14 October 1995.
12. Ibid.
13. Anthony Mithen, 'Lions need discipline, says Nunan', *Age*, 12 October 1995; Rohan Connolly, 'New coach Michael Nunan rolls up his sleeves and – The rebuilding begins', *Sunday Age*, 29 October 1995; Hore-Lacy, *Fitzroy*, p. 139.
14. Richard Hinds, 'The Lion Tamer', *Sunday Age*, 3 March 1996.
15. James Coventry, *Time and Space: The Tactics That Shaped Australian Rules – and the Players and Coaches Who Mastered Them*, Sydney: HarperCollins, 2015, pp. 178–81; Peter Cornwall, 'Legendary Sturt coach Jack Oatey a football visionary who changed the game', *Advertiser*, 23 November 2013.
16. 'Under The Hammer', *Football Record*, 29–31 March 1996.
17. Stephen Rielly, 'Two days to go ... and the coach is going bananas', *Age*, 7 February 1996.
18. Richard Hinds, 'The Lion Tamer', *Sunday Age*, 3 March 1996.
19. Interview, Brett Chandler, 10 July 2018; Interview, Stephen Paxman, 10 July 2018; Interview, John Rombotis, 13 July 2018; Interview, Chris Johnson, 11 May 2020.
20. Interview, Stephen Paxman, 10 July 2018; Jon Anderson, 'A Day in the Sun', *Herald Sun*, 16 May 2009.
21. Dwayne Russell, 'Pssst', *Sunday Age*, 14 August 2005.
22. Interview, Brett Chandler, 10 July 2018.
23. Andrew Maher and Andrew Bain, 'The Wrap – Club By Club', *Sunday Age*, 15 October 1995.
24. Interview, Colin Hobbs, 12 August 2019.
25. Hore-Lacy, *Fitzroy*, p. 139.
26. Anthony Mithen, 'Lions need discipline, say Nunan', *Age*, 12 October 1995.
27. Muyt, *Maroon & Blue*, p. 218.
28. Ibid., p. 219.
29. Interview, Simon Hawking, 14 April 2020.
30. Muyt, *Maroon & Blue*, p. 215.
31. Rohan Connolly and Linda Pearce, 'The Queue Starts Here', *Sunday Age*, 10 September 1995.
32. Ibid.
33. Gerard Healy, 'The Burning Question', *Herald Sun*, 22 March 1996.
34. Jake Niall, 'Crows should not get carried away with win', *Sunday Age*, 28 July 1996.
35. Interview, John McCarthy, 8 January 2019.
36. Bryce Lewis, 'Simon says: Lions Are No Easybeats', *Inside Football*, Vol. 26, No. 1, 21 February 1996.

37. Muyt, *Maroon & Blue*, p. 219; Interview, John Barker, 14 August 2019.
38. Richard Hinds, 'The Lion Tamer', *Sunday Age*, 3 March 1996.
39. Interview, Greg Freemantle, 12 August 2019.
40. Greg Denham, 'Baldwin sees end to dark days', *Age*, 13 December 1996.
41. Joyce Brown, 'Lions barking up the right tree with Nunan ...', *Inside Football*, Vol. 26, No. 4, 13 March 1996.
42. Rohan Connolly, 'For Barter Or For Worse', *Sunday Age*, 3 December 1995; Anthony Mithen, 'Tigers Close On Holland', *Age*, 1 December 1995.
43. Joyce Brown, 'Lions barking up the right tree with Nunan ...', *Inside Football*, Vol. 26, No. 4, 13 March 1996.
44. Interview, Alan McConnell, 10 August 2018; Interview, Marty Warry, 18 January 2020.
45. Jake Niall, 'For richer or for poorer?', *Sunday Age*, 11 May 1997.
46. Russell Holmesby, *The Death of Fitzroy Football Club: The Story of Fitzroy's Demise in the Words of the Men & Women Who Lost Their Club*, Melbourne: Hardie Grant Books, 2020, p. 178.
47. Greg Denham, 'Baldwin sees end to dark days', *Age*, 13 December 1996.
48. Geoff Poulter, 'Battle Weary Lion To Return', *Herald Sun*, 26 February 1996; Daryl Timms, 'Injury May Finish Zanotti', *Herald Sun*, 12 April 1996; Interview, Nick Mitchell, 24 September 2019.
49. Greg Hobbs, 'The First Annual Football Record List: Our Top 100 AFL Players', *Football Record*, 29–31 March 1996, pp. 5–9.
50. Michael Horan, 'Boyd the Lionheart', *Herald Sun*, 2 August 1996; Stephen Rielly, 'Why this should be one of the best known faces in football', *Age*, 23 June 1995.
51. Stephen Rielly, 'Why this should be one of the best known faces in football', *Age*, 23 June 1995.
52. Michael Horan, 'Boyd the Lionheart', *Herald Sun*, 2 August 1996.
53. Stephen Rielly, 'Why this should be one of the best known faces in football', *Age*, 23 June 1995.
54. Ibid.
55. Stephen Linnell, 'Boyd's new dedication earns state selection', *Age*, 27 April 1994.
56. Len Johnson, 'Lions find heart to bounce back', *Age*, 4 April 1994.
57. Damien Barrett, 'A broken heart, but no regrets', *Herald Sun*, 30 June 2006.
58. Philip Johnson, 'Boyd get No 1 billing at Fitzroy', *Age*, 27 March 1995.
59. Donald, *Fitzroy*, p. 286.
60. Chloe Saltau, 'The Last Roy Boyd', *Age*, 2 September 2006.
61. Interview, Stephen Paxman, 10 July 2018.
62. Interview, Chris Johnson, 11 May 2020.
63. Interview, Matthew Primus, 26 September 2019.
64. Interview, John Rombotis, 13 July 2018.
65. Interview, John Barker, 14 August 2019.
66. Chloe Saltau, 'The Last Roy Boyd', *Age*, 2 September 2006; Interview, Chris Johnson, 11 May 2020.
67. Interview, Simon Hawking, 14 April 2020.
68. Interview, John McCarthy, 8 January 2019; Interview, Matthew Primus, 26 September 2019.

69 Coventry, *Time and Space*, pp. 269-73; Jim Main, 'Life After the Boot', *Inside Football*, Vol. 26, No. 3, 6 March 1996.
70 Michel Stevens, 'Captain Shocked', *Herald Sun*, 29 June 1996.
71 Hore-Lacy, *Fitzroy*, pp. 139–40.

Chapter Three

1 Stephen Howell, 'Lion Will', *Sunday Age*, 25 August 1996.
2 Cartledge, *Footy's Revolution*, p. 91.
3 AFL, *Annual Report 1996*, p. 30.
4 AFL, *99th Annual Report 1995*, p. 3.
5 Muyt, *Maroon & Blue*, p. 220.
6 Interview, Stephen Paxman, 10 July 2018.
7 Interview, Chris Johnson, 11 May 2020.
8 Interview, John McCarthy, 8 January 2019.
9 'Star Profile: Chris Johnson', *Football Australia*, April 1995.
10 Interview, Chris Johnson, 11 May 2020.
11 Interview, John Barker, 14 August 2019.
12 Interview, Matthew Primus, 26 September 2019.
13 Muyt, *Maroon & Blue*, p. 222.
14 Interview, Chris Johnson, 11 May 2020.
15 Muyt, *Maroon & Blue*, p. 215.
16 Ibid., p. 220.
17 Interview, Stephen Paxman, 10 July 2018; Scott Gullan, 'Man In the Middle Of Roys' Last Rites', *Herald Sun*, 31 August 1996.
18 Interview, Stephen Paxman, 10 July 2018.
19 Kym Morgan, 'AFL journey ends where it started', *Advertiser*, 19 September 2015.
20 Interview, Brett Chandler, 10 July 2018.
21 Ian Munro, 'Lion Heart', *Sunday Age*, 18 August 1996.
22 Ibid.
23 Hore-Lacy, *Fitzroy*, p. 15.
24 Ian Munro, 'Lion Heart', *Sunday Age*, 18 August 1996.
25 Ibid.
26 Alan Attwood, 'A job for the Lion-hearted is not for the faint-hearted', *Age*, 27 November 1993; Ian Munro, 'Lion Heart', *Sunday Age*, 18 August 1996.
27 Alan Attwood, 'A job for the Lion-hearted is not for the faint-hearted', *Age*, 27 November 1993.
28 Hore-Lacy, *Fitzroy*, p. 15.
29 Ian Munro, 'Lion Heart', *Sunday Age*, 18 August 1996.
30 Hore-Lacy, *Fitzroy*, pp. 17–8.
31 Ibid., p. 33.
32 Interview, Elaine Findlay, 12 November 2019.
33 Hore-Lacy, *Fitzroy*, p. 104.
34 Ibid., p. 105.
35 Hore-Lacy, *Fitzroy*, pp. 39–46.
36 Interview, Stephen Paxman, 10 July 2018; Muyt, *Maroon & Blue*, p. 216.
37 Muyt, *Maroon & Blue*, p. 218.
38 John Hamilton, 'Tradition Ends Without A Roar', *Herald Sun*, 2 July 1996.
39 Interview, Greg Swann, 14 January 2019.
40 Interview, Andrew Ireland, 23 January 2019.
41 Ashley Browne, 'The Last Days Of Fitzroy', *Age*, 23 August 1996.
42 Interview, Melanie Gibb, 18 February 2020; Interview, Fran Gazzola, 1 May 2020.
43 Interview, Fran Gazzola, 1 May 2020.
44 Stephen Linnell, 'Manager quits in new blow to Lions', *Age*, 14 May 1996.
45 Interview, Alan McConnell, 10 August 2018.
46 Interview, Fran Gazzola, 1 May 2020.

47 Interview, Melanie Gibb, 18 February 2020.
48 Interview, Glenn Warry, 15 November 2018.
49 Interview, Alan McConnell, 10 August 2018.
50 Ashley Browne, 'The Last Days Of Fitzroy', *Age*, 23 August 1996.
51 Interview, Alan McConnell, 10 August 2018.
52 Ashley Browne, 'The last of the Lions', *Age*, 2 May 1997.
53 Interview, Tim Renwick, 14 May 2019.
54 Jake Niall, 'How Fitzroy lost the Lions' share', *Sunday Age*, 5 May 1996.
55 Interview, Leon Harris, 17 June 2020.
56 Interview, Greg Freemantle, 12 August 2019.
57 Interview, Tim Renwick, 14 May 2019.
58 Daryl Timms, 'Lions mourn an old mate', *Herald Sun*, 30 April 2004.
59 Interview, Tony Mazoski, 18 January 2020.
60 Interview, Simon Hawking, 14 April 2020.
61 Stephen Howell, 'Lion Will', *Sunday Age*, 25 August 1996.
62 Interview, Lance Upton, 29 June 2020.
63 Interview, John McCarthy, 8 January 2019.
64 Stephen Howell, 'Lion Will', *Sunday Age*, 25 August 1996.
65 Ibid.
66 Interview, Tim Renwick, 14 May 2019.
67 John Hamilton, 'Tradition Ends Without A Roar', *Herald Sun*, 2 July 1996; G.K. Miller, 'Fitzroy Footballers in the Forces', *Weekly Times*, 17 June 1942; Alf Brown, 'Fitzroy's football president resigns', *Herald*, 8 January 1952.
68 Linda Pearce, 'Fitzroy's nomads face a life-and-debt situation', *Sunday Age*, 4 September 1994; Ben Collins, 'The Lion Trainer', *AFL Record*, 15–16 September 2017.
69 Interview, Tim Renwick, 14 May 2019.
70 Ben Collins, 'The Lion Trainer', *AFL Record*, 15–16 September 2017.
71 Ibid.
72 Hore-Lacy, *Fitzroy*, p. 112; Greg Denham, 'AFL withholds Lions' cash', *Age*, 27 August 1994.
73 Interview, Glenn Warry, 15 November 2018.
74 Interview, Alan McConnell, 10 August 2018.
75 Hore-Lacy, *Fitzroy*, p. 112.
76 Interview, Alan McConnell, 10 August 2018; Interview, John Rombotis, 13 July 2018.
77 Stephen Howell, 'A season to end all season', *Sunday Age*, 1 September 1996.
78 Interview, Matthew Primus, 26 September 2019; Interview, Simon Hawking, 14 April 2020.
79 Muyt, *Maroon & Blue*, p. 218.
80 Fitzroy Football Club Newsletter, c. March 1996, Skott Dean papers.
81 Glenn McFarlane, 'Power of One', *Herald Sun*, 20 July 2014.
82 Muyt, *Maroon & Blue*, pp. 162–63.
83 Ibid., pp. 162–66.
84 Interview, Bill Atherton, 10 September 2019.
85 Interview, Jan Wright, 3 December 2018.
86 Martin Flanagan, 'The club they hold so dear', *Age*, 20 May 1996.
87 Interview, Jan Wright, 3 December 2018.
88 Interview, Rick Lang, 2 March 2020.
89 Geoff Easdown, 'Old Lions Back For a Final Roar', *Herald Sun*, 26 August 1996.

90 Correspondence, Kathy Doyle, 29 July 2020.
91 Muyt, *Maroon & Blue*, p. 216; Interview, Brett Chandler, 10 July 2018; Interview, Marty Warry, 18 January 2020.
92 Stephen Howell, 'Lion Will', *Sunday Age*, 25 August 1996.

Chapter Four

1   'Pledging Their Best In 1996', *Herald Sun*, 1 January 1996.
2   'Ah, well, happy New Year anyway', *Age*, 1 January 1996.
3   Michelle Griffin, 'Good fortune makes the stars shine', *Sunday Age*, 31 December 1995.
4   Michael Dimock, 'Defining generations: Where Millennials end and Generation Z begins', *Pew Research Centre*, 17 January 2019, accessed 23 April 2019, https://www.pewresearch.org/fact-tank/2019/01/17/where-millennials-end-and-generation-z-begins/.
5   Interview, Rohan Connolly, 1 October 2018.
6   Australian Bureau of Statistics, *1996 Census of Population and Housing: Selected Social and Housing Characteristics for Statistical Local Areas Victoria* (Canberra: Australian Bureau of Statistics, 1997), p. 1.
7   Peter Abelson and Demi Chung, 'The Real Story of Housing Prices in Australia from 1970 to 2003', Macquarie University, 2006, p. 10; W. McLennan, *Australian Statistician, Average Weekly Earning States and Australia November 1996* (Canberra; Australian Government Publishing Service, 1997), p. 7.
8   Martin Flanagan, '1996, The Year That Was', *Age*, 28 December 1996.
9   Tony Parkinson, *Jeff: The Rise and Fall of a Political Phenomenon*, Melbourne: Viking, 2000, pp. 169–206.
10 'Pledging Their Best In 1996', *Herald Sun*, 1 January 1996.
11 Patrick Smith, 'New supremo will give footy the soft sell', *Age*, 3 October 1996.
12 Garry Linnell, *Football Ltd: The Inside Story of the AFL*, Sydney: Pan Macmillan, 1995, p. 147; Martin Blake and Len Johnson, 'The Oakley Years, 1986-96', *Age*, 18 June 1996.
13 Linnell, *Football Ltd*, p. 160.
14 Ross Oakley with Jonathan Green and Geoff Slattery. *The Phoenix Rises: The amazing story of the salvation of Australian Football*. Richmond: Slattery Media Group, 2014, p. 317
15 Linnell, *Football Ltd*, p. 80.
16 Ibid., p. 118.
17 Oakley et al, *The Phoenix Rises*, pp. 216–17; Linnell, *Football Ltd*, p. 125.
18 Linnell, *Football Ltd*, p. 87; Michael Gawenda, 'Mover and Shaker', *Age*, 7 September 1996; Oakley et al, *The Phoenix Rises*, p. 300.
19 Michael Gawenda, 'Mover and Shaker', *Age*, 7 September 1996; Linnell, *Football Ltd*, p. 87.
20 Michael Gawenda, 'Mover and Shaker', *Age*, 7 September 1996.
21 Ross Oakley, 'Victoria cannot support 11 clubs', *Football Record*, 3–5 May 1996.
22 AFL, *Annual Report 1996*, p. 4.
23 Ross Oakley, 'Emotion aside, mergers the only answer', *Sunday Age*, 2 June 1996.
24 Ross Oakley, 'Victoria cannot support 11 clubs: Inequalities will force rationalisation', *Football Record*, 3–5 May 1996.
25 AFL, *99th Annual Report 1995*, pp. 37–39.

26 Ibid., p. 2.
27 'Pledging Their Best In 1996', *Herald Sun*, 1 January 1996; AFL, *99th Annual Report 1995*, p. 2.
28 Oakley et al, *The Phoenix Rises*, p. 292.
29 Patrick Smith, 'Footy tradition a lot more than beanie and scarf', *Age*, 8 May 1996.
30 Oakley et al, *The Phoenix Rises*, p. 295.
31 T. Trimble, 'Lions being badly mauled', *Herald Sun*, 20 April 1996.
32 Oakley et al, *The Phoenix Rises*, p. 250.
33 Hore-Lacy, *Fitzroy*, p. 133.
34 Ibid., pp. 78–79; Patrick Smithers and Greg Denham, 'Threats, acrimony as Fitzroy, AFL do battle', *Age*, 10 July 1993; Hore-Lacy, *Fitzroy*, p. 81; Patrick Smith, 'Struggling Lions turn to drink to help stay alive', *Age*, 27 August 1993.
35 Patrick Smith, 'AFL gets wires crossed over footy cable channel', *Age*, 28 February 1996.
36 Peter Allen and Alistair Macrae, 'A footy merger worth its weight', *Age*, 4 May 1996.
37 Tom Hafey and Bert Newton, 'Has the AFL Too Many Melbourne-Based Clubs?', *Herald Sun*, 23 May 1996.
38 Muyt, *Maroon & Blue*, pp. 201–02.
39 Lorraine Wilson, *Carn the Lions*, second edition, Melbourne: Cardigan Street, 1996.
40 Patrick Smith, 'Once every 100 years is plenty after frosty night at the MCG', *Age*, 9 February 1996; Rohan Connolly, 'The Centenary Balls-Up', *Sunday Age*, 1 September 1996.
41 Patrick Smith, 'Once every 100 years is plenty after frosty night at the MCG', *Age*, 9 February 1996.

Chapter Five

1 Hore-Lacy, *Fitzroy*, p. 114.
2 Ibid., p. 141.
3 Fitzroy Football Club, *1995 Annual Report and Audited Financial Statements*, pp. 4, 11; AFL, *Annual Report 1995*, p. 37.
4 Stephen Linnell and Greg Denham, 'Winning Blues net profit of $600,000', *Age*, 7 December 1995; Stephen Linnell and Len Johnson, 'Healthy profit but hard to repeat, say Cats', *Age*, 13 December 1995.
5 Jason Dowling, 'Saving football: New documents reveal how close the VFL came to shutting down', *Age*, 6 May 2016.
6 Daryl Timms, 'Hawthorn Debt Rise', *Herald Sun*, 16 November 1996.
7 James Button, *Comeback: The Fall and Rise of Geelong*, Carlton: Melbourne University Press, 2016, p. 64.
8 Stephen Linnell and Greg Denham, 'AFL solves Fitzroy's cash-flow problems', *Age*, 5 July 1996.
9 Oakley et al, *The Phoenix Rises*, pp. 279–81.
10 Hore-Lacy, *Fitzroy*, p. 124.
11 Interview, Colin Hobbs, 12 August 2019.
12 Hore-Lacy, *Fitzroy*, pp. 112, 153.
13 Hore-Lacy, *Fitzroy*, p. 92; Stephen Linnell, 'Fitzroy's future again at risk', *Age*, 5 February 1994.
14 Linnell, *Football Ltd*, pp. 364–65.
15 Oakley et al, *The Phoenix Rises*, p. 282; AFL, *Annual Report 1996*, p. 4; 'Mergers: what 5-year plan says', *Football Record*, 5–7 May 1995.
16 Stephen Rielly, 'Now it's time for clubs to pay and play', *Age*, 23 August 1994.
17 Ashley Browne and Greg Denham, 'Geelong delays decision on Ablett', *Age*, 3 September 1994.

18. Michael Smith, 'National blueprint says "RIP Fitzroy"', *Canberra Times*, 27 August 1994; Stephen Rielly, 'Now it's time for clubs to pay and play', *Age*, 23 August 1994.
19. Stephen Rielly, 'Now it's time for clubs to pay and play', *Age*, 23 August 1994.
20. Dyson Hore-Lacy, 'Footy and friends – good for Nauru', *Age*, 15 November 1994.
21. Interview, Elaine Findlay, 12 November 2019.
22. Hore-Lacy, *Fitzroy*, p. 123.
23. Ashley Browne, 'Nauru millions save the Lions', *Age*, 26 October 1994.
24. Hore-Lacy, *Fitzroy*, p. 123.
25. Ibid., pp. 126–27.
26. Ibid., pp. 142–43.
27. Ibid., p. 143.
28. Ibid., p. 151.
29. Ibid., pp. 142–48, 152.
30. Ibid., p. 114.
31. Peter Nixon, *An Active Journey: The Peter Nixon Story*, Ballan: Connor Court Publishing, 2012, p. 263.
32. Linnell, *Football Ltd*, p. 289.
33. Oakley et al, *The Phoenix Rises*, p. 220.
34. Ibid., pp. 224–26.
35. Ibid., pp. 227–32.
36. Ibid., p. 250.
37. Jake Niall, 'How Fitzroy lost the Lions' share', *Sunday Age*, 5 May 1996.
38. Oakley et al, *The Phoenix Rises*, p. 251; Hore-Lacy, *Fitzroy*, pp. 114–17.
39. Oakley et al, *The Phoenix Rises*, p. 251.
40. Martin Blake and Len Johnson, 'The Oakley Years, 1986-96', *Age*, 18 June 1996.
41. Stephen Linnell, 'AFL's $4m merger plan – Crunch time for Fitzroy', *Age*, 14 June 1995.
42. 'What Graeme Samuel actually said: Supporter base is key issue', *Football Record*, 5–7 May 1995.
43. Stephen Linnell, 'AFL's merger stakes jump by $2 million', *Age*, 20 June 1995.
44. Patrick Smith, 'Clubs snub commission on night of the battler', *Age*, 20 June 1995.
45. Stephen Linnell, 'AFL's $4m merger plan – Crunch time for Fitzroy', *Age*, 14 June 1995.
46. Ibid.
47. Geoff Poulter, 'Clubs Vote No To Lord', *Herald Sun*, 20 February 1996.
48. Hore-Lacy, *Fitzroy*, p. 154.
49. Letter, Dyson Hore-Lacy to Fitzroy Members and Shareholders, c. May 1996, Skott Dean Papers.
50. Hore-Lacy, *Fitzroy*, p. 154.
51. Letter, Dyson Hore-Lacy to Fitzroy Members and Shareholders, c. May 1996, Skott Dean Papers.
52. Hore-Lacy, *Fitzroy*, p. 148.
53. Ibid., pp. 154–55.
54. Ibid., p. 155.
55. Ibid., pp. 154–55; Bears, Lions In Merger Row', *Herald Sun*, 13 June 1996; Interview, Bill Atherton, 10 September 2019.
56. Hore-Lacy, *Fitzroy*, p. 156.
57. Ibid., p. 156.
58. Oakley et al, *The Phoenix Rises*, p. 251; Stephen Linnell, 'AFL gives Fitzroy ultimatum', *Age*, 1 March 1996.
59. Minutes, AFL Commission Meeting, 23 January 1996; Hore-Lacy, *Fitzroy*, p. 155.
60. Hore-Lacy, *Fitzroy*, p. 161.
61. Minutes, AFL Commission Meeting, 9 February 1996.
62. Minutes, AFL Commission Meeting, 19 February 1996.
63. Stephen Linnell, 'Players' group fears on Lions', *Age*, 2 March 1996.

64 Stephen Linnell, 'AFL gives Fitzroy ultimatum', *Age*, 1 March 1996.
65 Stephen Linnell, 'Players' group fears on Lions', *Age*, 2 March 1996.
66 Ibid.
67 Ibid.
68 Minutes, AFL Commission Meeting, 7 March 1996; Stephen Linnell and Ashley Browne, 'Fitzroy solvency on agenda today', *Age*, 7 March 1996; Stephen Linnell, 'AFL turns up heat on Lions', *Age*, 8 March 1996.
69 Oakley et al, *The Phoenix Rises*, p. 252.
70 Stephen Linnell, 'AFL likely to veto Magpies' soccer bid', *Age*, 13 March 1996.
71 Patrick Smith, 'Cash and now time run out for Lions', *Age*, 13 March 1996.
72 Hore-Lacy, *Fitzroy*, p. 168.
73 Ibid., pp. 156–57.

Chapter Six

1 Gerard Healy, 'The Burning Question', *Herald Sun*, 22 March 1996.
2 Cash and Damousi, *Footy Passions*, p. 48.
3 Michael Roberts and Michael Winkler, 'Why I love football', *Football Record*, Centenary Souvenir Edition 1996.
4 Fitzroy Football Club newsletter, c. March 1996, Skott Dean papers.
5 Stephen Linnell, 'Clubs angry at lightning deficit', *Age*, 17 April 1996; Rohan Connolly, 'The Centenary Balls-Up', *Sunday Age*, 1 September 1996.
6 Daryl Timms, 'Nunan Lashes Lazy Lions', *Herald Sun*, 19 February 1996.
7 Stephen Linnell, 'Bulldogs fend off the Lions', *Age*, 27 February 1996; Richard Hinds, 'The Lion tamer', *Sunday Age*, 3 March 1996.
8 Stephen Linnell, 'Bulldogs fend off the Lions', *Age*, 27 February 1996; Anthony Mithen, 'Lion outed two for headbutting', *Age*, 5 March 1996.
9 Anthony Mithen and Greg Denham, 'Cats counting cost after Gabba loss', *Age*, 6 March 1996.
10 Stephen Howell, 'Ablett show back to the road again', *Sunday Age*, 10 March 1996.
11 'Weekend Details', *Age*, 18 March 1996.
12 Interview, Stephen Paxman, 10 July 2018; Interview, John McCarthy, 8 January 2019; Interview, Chris Johnson, 11 May 2020.
13 Ashley Browne, 'For Fitzroy and Hawthorn, new coaches are old hands', *Age*, 30 March 1996.
14 Charles Happell, 'Fitzroy v Hawthorn', *Age*, 29 March 1996.
15 'Primus primed for the job', *Football Record*, 6–8 April 1996.
16 Andrew Maher, 'Prime Time', *Inside Football*, Vol. 26, No. 4, 13 March 1996.
17 Peter Hackett, 'The Men Behind the Might; Matthew Primus', *Advertiser*, 27 March 1999.
18 Interview, Matthew Primus, 26 September 2019.
19 'Lightning premiership: you team', *Age*, 5 February 1996.
20 Charles Happell, 'Fitzroy v Hawthorn', *Age*, 29 March 1996; Geoff Poulter, 'Rare Chance For Hopeful Roys', *Herald Sun*, 29 March 1996.
21 Michelangelo Rucci, 'Crowds to flock in', *Advertiser*, 30 March 1996.
22 'Weekend Weather', *Age*, 30 March 1996.
23 Interview, Greg Freemantle, 12 August 2019.

24. Interview, Tony Mazoski, 18 January 2020.
25. Rohan Connolly, 'New coach Michael Nunan rolls up his sleeves and – The rebuilding begins', *Sunday Age*, 29 October 1995; Stephen Howell, 'A season to end all seasons', *Sunday Age*, 1 September 1996; Jon Anderson, 'A Day in the Sun', *Herald Sun*, 16 May 2009.
26. 'David Hookes: A life', *Age*, 20 January 2004.
27. Correspondence, Kathy Doyle, 29 July 2020.
28. *Football Record*, 29–31 March 1996.
29. Geoff Poulter, 'A Little More Roy Joy', *Herald Sun*, 22 March 1996.
30. Rohan Connolly, 'Fitzroy and Canberra: lost opportunity', *Sunday Age*, 17 March 1996.
31. Mike Sheahan, 'Not So Dingy In Lions' Den', *Herald Sun*, 22 March 1996.
32. Gerard Healy, 'The Burning Question', *Herald Sun*, 22 March 1996.
33. Interview, Fran Gazzola, 1 May 2020.
34. Scott Gullan, 'Fitzroy Firm Sparks Lions', *Herald Sun*, 28 March 1996.
35. Correspondence, C. Hobbs, 29 August 2019.
36. Interview, Leon Harris, 17 June 2020.
37. Anthony Mithen, 'Hawks' Experience Telling', *Age*, 1 April 1996.
38. Michael Stevens, 'Hawks Warm To Task', *Herald Sun*, 1 April 1996.
39. Michael Lovett, 'Lions lamenting', *Sunday Age*, 31 March 1996.
40. Interview, Chris Johnson, 11 May 2020 'Footy Snapshot', *Herald Sun*, 1 April 1996.
41. Michael Lovett, 'Lions lamenting', *Sunday Age*, 31 March 1996.
42. Michael Stevens, 'Hawks Warm To Task', *Herald Sun*, 1 April 1996; Michael Lovett, 'Lions lamenting', *Sunday Age*, 31 March 1996.
43. Michael Stevens, 'Hawks Warm To Task', *Herald Sun*, 1 April 1996.
44. Michael Lovett, 'Lions lamenting', *Sunday Age*, 31 March 1996.
45. Ibid.
46. 'Primus primed for the job', *Football Record*, 4–6 April 1996.
47. Michael Stevens, 'Hawks Warm To Task', *Herald Sun*, 1 April 1996; Michael Lovett, 'Lions lamenting', *Sunday Age*, 31 March 1996; Jon Anderson, 'Did You Know?', *Herald Sun*, 3 April 1996.
48. Anthony Mithen, 'Hawks' experience telling', *Age*, 1 April 1996.
49. Michael Lovett, 'Lions lamenting', *Sunday Age*, 31 March 1996.
50. Interview, Chris Johnson, 11 May 2020.
51. Michael Stevens, 'Hawks Warm To Task', *Herald Sun*, 1 April 1996.
52. Fitzroy Football Club Newsletter, c. March 1996, Skott Dean papers.
53. Mike Sheahan, 'From Spirits To Spirit', *Herald Sun*, 13 April 1996.
54. Melissa Fyfe, 'Fitzroy hits rock-bottom', *Age*, 22 April 1996.
55. Linda Pearce, 'Saints feast on hangover cure', *Sunday Age*, 21 April 1996.
56. Mal Brown, 'In the Jaws of a Lions', *Inside Football*, Vol. 26, No. 13, 15 May 1996.
57. Interview, John McCarthy, 8 January 2019.
58. Ted Hopkins, 'Lions Not Roar Material', *Herald Sun*, 3 May 1996; Geoff Poulter, 'Richo the Key To Big Tigers Win', *Herald Sun*, 3 May 1996.
59. Gareth Andrews, 'Fitzroy in the throes of death', *Sunday Age*, 21 April 1996.

60 Interview, Alan McConnell, 10 August 2018; Interview, Greg Freemantle, 12 August 2019.
61 Joyce Brown, 'Lions barking up the right tree with Nunan …', *Inside Football*, Vol. 26, No. 4, 13 March 1996.
62 Interview, Alan McConnell, 10 August 2018.
63 Richard Hinds, 'The Lion Tamer', *Sunday Age*, 3 March 1996.
64 Hore-Lacy, *Fitzroy*, pp. 139–40.
65 Ibid., p. 140.
66 Darren Pearce, 'Lionising a great Bear', *Sunday Age*, 28 April 1996.
67 Darren Pearce, 'Bears stroll to the top', *Age*, 29 April 1996.
68 Mike Sheahan, 'Lions Stand Firm – Brisbane Leads Queue of Merger Suitors', *Herald Sun*, 29 April 1996.
69 Darren Pearce, 'Bears stroll to the top', *Age*, 29 April 1996.
70 Ibid., Steve Perkin, 'Good News, Bears', *Herald Sun*, 29 April 1996.

Chapter Seven

1 Ross Fitzgerald, *The Footy Club: Inside the Brisbane Bears*, St. Lucia: University of Queensland Press, 1996, p. 86.
2 Hore-Lacy, *Fitzroy*, p. 160.
3 Ibid., pp. 156–57.
4 Rohan Connolly, 'Lions chief says it's time for the truth', *Sunday Age*, 7 July 1996.
5 Interview, Elaine Findlay, 12 November 2019.
6 Hore-Lacy, *Fitzroy*, p. 141.
7 Ibid., p. 160.
8 Interview, Andrew Ireland, 23 January 2019.
9 Fitzgerald, *The Footy Club*, p. 5.
10 Linnell, *Football Ltd*, p. 234.
11 Ibid., pp. 216–43, 321–30.
12 Interview, Andrew Ireland, 23 January 2019.
13 Fitzgerald, *The Footy Club*, p. 10.
14 'Help! The Record Answer the Tough Ones', *Football Record*, 12–14 July 1996.
15 Fitzgerald, *The Footy Club*, p. 56.
16 Ibid., p. 86.
17 Hore-Lacy, *Fitzroy*, p. 158.
18 Ibid., p. 158.
19 Ibid., pp. 159–60.
20 Bob Hart, 'Fitzroy Rumour', *Herald Sun*, 18 April 1996.
21 'Merger Denials', *Herald Sun*, 12 April 1996.
22 Anthony Mithen, 'Roos deny reports of merger with Lions', *Age*, 12 April 1996; 'Merger Denials', *Herald Sun*, 12 April 1996.
23 Michael Stevens, 'Lions face Cash Query', *Herald Sun*, 26 April 1996.
24 Correspondence, Kathy Doyle, 29 July 2020.
25 Interview, Alan McConnell, 10 August 2018.
26 Greg Denham, 'Q&A Simon Hawking, Fitzroy', *Age*, 20 May 1996.
27 Interview, Stephen Paxman, 10 July 2018; Muyt, *Maroon & Blue*, p. 220.
28 'Lions Set Date', *Herald Sun*, 23 April 1996.
29 Fitzroy Football Club, *1994 Annual Report and Audited Financial Statements*.
30 Hore-Lacy, *Fitzroy*, pp. 160–61.
31 Ibid., p. 162; Minutes, AFL Commission Meeting, 19 April 1996.
32 Hore-Lacy, *Fitzroy*, pp. 163–64.
33 Ibid., p. 163.
34 Ibid., p. 163.
35 Stephen Linnell, 'Roys to ask for merger talks', *Age*, 29 April 1996.
36 Hore-Lacy, *Fitzroy*, p. 163.
37 Interview, Andrew Ireland, 23 January 2019.
38 Ibid.
39 Stephen Linnell, 'Bears wait to step in', *Age*, 20 May 1996.

40 Stephen Linnell, 'League may step in after Fitzroy meeting', *Age*, 24 April 1996.
41 Mike Sheahan, 'Lions Stand Firm – Brisbane Leads Queue of Merger Suitors', *Herald Sun*, 29 April 1996.
42 Stephen Linnell, 'Roys to ask for merger talks', *Age*, 29 April 1996.
43 'What the club faithful think', *Age*, 30 April 1996.
44 Stephen Linnell and Martin Blake, 'Lions admit merge option', *Age*, 30 April 1996; Ron Reed, 'Eloquent Call To Arms', *Herald Sun*, 30 April 1996.
45 Michael Stevens, 'Lions face Cash Query', *Herald Sun*, 26 April 1996.
46 Hore-Lacy, *Fitzroy*, p. 165.
47 Ron Reed, 'Eloquent Call To Arms', *Herald Sun*, 30 April 1996.
48 Stephen Linnell and Martin Blake, 'Lions admit merge option', *Age*, 30 April 1996.
49 Patrick Smith, 'Chairman smooths ruffled fur', *Age*, 30 April 1996.
50 Hore-Lacy, *Fitzroy*, p. 166.
51 Ibid., p. 165; Stephen Linnell and Martin Blake, 'Lions admit merge option', *Age*, 30 April 1996.
52 Muyt, *Maroon & Blue*, p. 190.
53 Hore-Lacy, *Fitzroy*, p. 165; Daryl Timms, 'Lions Reveal '95 Loss', *Herald Sun*, 25 April 1996.
54 Stephen Linnell and Martin Blake, 'Lions admit merge option', *Age*, 30 April 1996.
55 Hore-Lacy, *Fitzroy*, pp. 188–89.
56 Stephen Linnell and Martin Blake, 'Lions admit merge option', *Age*, 30 April 1996.
57 Oakley et al, *The Phoenix Rises*, p. 252.
58 'What the club faithful think', *Age*, 30 April 1996.
59 Philip Cullen, 'Fitzroy Defiant We Won't Merge Or Die', *Herald Sun*, 30 April 1996.
60 Patrick Smith, 'Chairman smooths ruffled fur', *Age*, 30 April 1996.
61 Mike Sheahan, 'Lions' Brave Stand May Lead To Downfall', *Herald Sun*, 4 May 1996.
62 Ron Reed, 'Eloquent Call To Arms', *Herald Sun*, 30 April 1996.

Chapter Eight

1 Hore-Lacy, *Fitzroy*, p. 174.
2 Jarrod Molloy, 'The heartbreak of losing Fitzroy', *Age*, 31 August 2006.
3 Rohan Connolly, 'Respect, just a little bit', *Sunday Age*, 21 July 1996.
4 Rohan Connolly, 'Respect, just a little bit', *Sunday Age*, 21 July 1996.
5 Luke West, 'Time at the Top – Carter's AFL stints with Fitzroy, Brisbane and Melbourne in the '90s', *Bendigo Advertiser*, 1 May 2020.
6 Stephen Rielly, 'Fitzroy v Richmond', *Age*, 3 May 1996.
7 Stephen Howell, 'Lions get within a roar, then …', *Sunday Age*, 5 May 1996.
8 Tony de Bolfo, 'Tigers With Ease', *Herald Sun*, 6 May 1996.
9 Stephen Howell, 'Lions get within a roar, then …', *Sunday Age*, 5 May 1996.
10 Ibid.
11 Tony de Bolfo, 'Tigers With Ease', *Herald Sun*, 6 May 1996.
12 Stephen Howell, 'Lions get within a roar, then …', *Sunday Age*, 5 May 1996.
13 Anthony Mithen, 'Richmond cuts loose', *Age*, 6 May 1996.
14 Ibid.
15 Tony de Bolfo, 'Tigers With Ease', *Herald Sun*, 6 May 1996; Michael Lovett, 'Ex-Roys remain hopeful for club', *Sunday Age*, 5 May 1996.
16 Stephen Howell, 'Lions get within a roar, then …', *Sunday Age*, 5 May 1996.

17 Tony de Bolfo, 'Tigers With Ease', *Herald Sun*, 6 May 1996.
18 Ibid.
19 Greg Leech, 'Double Disillusioned', *Inside Football*, Vol. 26, No. 35, December 1996.
20 Mike Sheahan, 'Hogg comes home', *Herald Sun*, 1 March 2002.
21 Michael Manley, 'Jeff Gone? Hogwash!', *Inside Football*, Pre-season Special 1996.
22 Greg Leech, 'Double Disillusioned', *Inside Football*, Vol. 26, No. 35, December 1996.
23 Patrick Smith, 'Chairman smooths ruffled fur', *Age*, 30 April 1996.
24 Stephen Linnell, 'Roys to ask for merger talks', *Age*, 29 April 1996.
25 Ross Oakley, 'Victoria cannot support 11 clubs: Inequalities will force rationalisation', *Football Record*, 3–5 May 1996.
26 Daryl Timms, 'Debt Rule Secure', *Herald Sun*, 6 May 1996.
27 Gerard Healy, 'Merger Would Revive Old Roars', *Herald Sun*, 1 May 1996; Jon Anderson, 'The Ins and Outs of a Merger', *Herald Sun*, 2 May 1996.
28 Oakley et al, *The Phoenix Rises*, p. 252; Minutes, AFL Commission Meeting, 3 May 1996.
29 Hore-Lacy, *Fitzroy*, pp. 168–70.
30 Stephen Linnell, 'AFL's $4m merger plan – Crunch time for Fitzroy', *Age*, 14 June 1995.
31 Stephen Linnell, 'Lions, Bears in merger fight', *Age*, 13 June 1996.
32 Minutes, AFL Commission Meeting, 9 May 1996.
33 'What the club faithful think', *Age*, 30 April 1996.
34 Ibid.
35 Interview, Bill Atherton, 10 September 2019.
36 Hore-Lacy, *Fitzroy*, p. 167.
37 Interview, Bill Atherton, 10 September 2019.
38 Hore-Lacy, *Fitzroy*, pp. 167–68.
39 Interview, Mark Dawson, 8 October 2019.
40 Interview, Greg Miller, 30 January 2019.
41 Linnell, *Football Ltd*, pp. 318, 324; Interview, Mark Dawson, 8 October 2019.
42 Interview, Greg Miller, 30 January 2019.
43 Interview, Bill Atherton, 10 September 2019.
44 Rohan Connolly, 'Roos, Lions: how it would operate', *Sunday Age*, 12 May 1996.
45 Hore-Lacy, *Fitzroy*, p. 142.
46 Interview, Bill Atherton, 10 September 2019.
47 Hore-Lacy, *Fitzroy*, p. 142.
48 Stephen Linnell, 'Magpies "open to name change" in Fitzroy union', *Age*, 30 May 1996.
49 Hore-Lacy, *Fitzroy*, pp. 168–70.
50 Stephen Linnell, 'AFL's $4m merger plan – Crunch time for Fitzroy', *Age*, 14 June 1995.
51 Minutes, AFL Commission Meeting, 26 May 1996.
52 Interview, Mark Dawson, 8 October 2019.
53 Hore-Lacy, *Fitzroy*, pp. 168–69.
54 Interview, Andrew Ireland, 23 January 2019.
55 Hore-Lacy, *Fitzroy*, p. 169.
56 Ibid., p. 170.
57 Ross Oakley, 'Time to look back', *Football Record*, 8–12 May 1996.
58 Muyt, *Maroon & Blue*, p. 191.
59 Anthony Mithen, 'Carlton v Fitzroy', *Age*, 10 May 1996.
60 Geoff Poulter, 'Sad Days For Lions', *Herald Sun*, 10 May 1996.
61 Melissa Fyfe, 'Blues win big, lose big', *Age*, 13 May 1996; 'Blues Never In Doubt', *Herald Sun*, 13 May 1996.
62 Melissa Fyfe, 'Blues win big, lose big', *Age*, 13 May 1996.

63 Jake Niall, 'Re-enactment best forgotten', *Sunday Age*, 12 May 1996.
64 Hore-Lacy, *Fitzroy*, pp. 170–72.
65 Ibid., pp. 172–73.
66 Ibid., p. 174.

Chapter Nine

1   Ron Reed, 'Lion Hearts Find Wealth Of Pride', *Herald Sun*, 20 May 1996.
2   Hore-Lacy, *Fitzroy*, p. 175.
3   Ibid., p. 173.
4   Patrick Smith, 'How Hore-Lacy lost his beloved Lions', *Age*, 5 July 1996.
5   Rohan Connolly and Geoff Stong, 'Secret AFL merger talks', *Sunday Age*, 12 May 1996.
6   Interview, Rohan Connolly, 1 October 2018.
7   Rohan Connolly, 'Roos, Lions: how it would operate', *Sunday Age*, 12 May 1996; Rohan Connolly and Geoff Stong, 'Secret AFL merger talks', *Sunday Age*, 12 May 1996.
8   'Let us not lose our Lions' heart', *Sunday Age*, 12 May 1996.
9   Stephen Linnell and Greg Denham, 'Roos deny merger with Lions imminent', *Age*, 13 May 1996.
10 Jon Ralph, 'Richmond Football Club in 1990: How the Tiger Army saved its own skin', *Herald Sun*, 26 September 2017; Oakley et. al., *The Phoenix Rises*, pp. 213–14.
11 Stephen Linnell and Greg Denham, 'Roos deny merger with Lions imminent', *Age*, 13 May 1996.
12 Stephen Linnell and Greg Denham, 'Roos deny merger with Lions imminent', *Age*, 13 May 1996.
13 Rohan Connolly and Geoff Stong, 'Secret AFL merger talks', *Sunday Age*, 12 May 1996.
14 Hore-Lacy, *Fitzroy*, pp. 175–76.
15 Ibid., p. 176.
16 Mike Sheahan and Daryl Timms, 'It's a Deal', *Herald Sun*, 15 May 1996.
17 Mike Sheahan, 'Historic Step Forward', *Herald Sun*, 15 May 1996.
18 Stephen Linnell, 'It's a done deal: Bears', *Age*, 15 May 1996.
19 Hore-Lacy, *Fitzroy*, p. 175.
20 Mike Sheahan and Daryl Timms, 'It's a Deal', *Herald Sun*, 15 May 1996.
21 Hore-Lacy, *Fitzroy*, pp. 175, 177.
22 Stephen Linnell, 'Carey worry on merger', *Age*, 16 May 1996; Hore-Lacy, *Fitzroy*, p. 177.
23 Scott Gullan and Daryl Timms, 'Talks Are On, But Deal Denied', *Herald Sun*, 16 May 1996.
24 Stephen Linnell, 'Carey worry on merger', *Age*, 16 May 1996.
25 Patrick Smith, 'Merger mind games can shred a flag', *Age*, 16 May 1996.
26 Scott Gullan and Daryl Timms, 'Talks Are On, But Deal Denied', *Herald Sun*, 16 May 1996.
27 Interview, Greg Miller, 30 January 2019.
28 Greg Miller, 'To the Members of the North Melbourne Football Club', *Age*, 18 May 1996.
29 Daryl Timms and Michael Stevens, 'Sponsor Flop Sparked Talks', *Herald Sun*, 17 May 1996.
30 Ibid.
31 Daryl Timms and Michael Stevens, 'Sponsor Flop Sparked Talks', *Herald Sun*, 17 May 1996; Stephen Linnell and Len Johnson, 'Roos won't risk losing stars over merger', *Age*, 17 May 1996.
32 Hore-Lacy, *Fitzroy*, p. 178.
33 Stephen Howell, 'A season to end all seasons', *Sunday Age*, 1 September 1996; Hore-Lacy, *Fitzroy*, p. 179.
34 Stephen Howell, 'A season to end all seasons', *Sunday Age*, 1 September 1996.

35 Interview, Stephen Paxman, 10 July 2018; Interview, John McCarthy, 8 January 2019; Andrew Bain, 'The Axe Comes Down On Fitzroy', *Inside Football*, Vol. 26, No. 21, 10 July 1996.
36 Stephen Linnell and Len Johnson, 'Roos won't risk losing stars over merger', *Age*, 17 May 1996.
37 Interview, Stephen Paxman, 10 July 2018.
38 Interview, Brett Chandler, 10 July 2018; Interview, John Rombotis, 13 July 2018.
39 Patrick Smith, 'Brisbane suddenly back in merger running', *Age*, 17 May 1996.
40 Mike Sheahan, 'Door Ajar For Bears', *Herald Sun*, 17 May 1996.
41 Patrick Smith, 'Brisbane suddenly back in merger running', *Age*, 17 May 1996.
42 Mike Sheahan, 'Door Ajar For Bears', *Herald Sun*, 17 May 1996.
43 Hore-Lacy, *Fitzroy*, p. 182.
44 Daryl Timms, 'Lions reveal '95 Loss', *Herald Sun*, 25 April 1996.
45 Patrick Smith, 'Top Roys on secret prowl for a partner', *Age*, 15 May 1996; Patrick Smith, 'Reported and missing, inaction', *Sunday Age*, 19 May 1996.
46 Patrick Smith, 'Top Roys on secret prowl for a partner', *Age*, 15 May 1996.
47 Anthony Mithen, 'Fitzroy v Fremantle', *Age*, 17 May 1996.
48 Ron Reed, 'Lion Hearts Find Wealth Of Pride', *Herald Sun*, 20 May 1996.
49 Richard Hinds, 'A rare moment of joy for lion-hearted Roys', *Sunday Age*, 19 May 1996.
50 Ron Reed, 'Lion Hearts Find Wealth Of Pride', *Herald Sun*, 20 May 1996; Rohan Connolly and Jake Niall, 'Lions warn clubs', *Sunday Age*, 19 May 1996.
51 Ron Reed, 'Lion Hearts Find Wealth Of Pride', *Herald Sun*, 20 May 1996.
52 Charles Happell, 'Carter looks a Lion with a future', *Age*, 24 May 1996.
53 Jake Niall, 'Lions end losing streak', *Sunday Age*, 19 May 1996.
54 Greg Denham, 'Young Lions savor glory', *Age*, 20 May 1996.
55 Interview, Matthew Primus, 26 September 2019.
56 Muyt, *Maroon & Blue*, p. 191.
57 Ron Reed, 'Lion Hearts Find Wealth Of Pride', *Herald Sun*, 20 May 1996.
58 Ibid.
59 Ibid.
60 Richard Hinds, 'Roys roar at last', *Sunday Age*, 19 May 1996.
61 Richard Hinds, 'A rare moment of joy for lion-hearted Roys', *Sunday Age*, 19 May 1996.
62 Jake Niall, 'Lions end losing streak', *Sunday Age*, 19 May 1996.
63 Muyt, *Maroon & Blue*, p. 198.
64 Tony de Bolfo, 'Roys Shrug Aside Abnormal Week', *Herald Sun*, 20 May 1996.
65 Greg Denham, 'Q&A Simon Hawking, Fitzroy', *Age*, 20 May 1996.
66 Greg Denham, 'Young Lions savor glory', *Age*, 20 May 1996.
67 Jon Anderson, 'A Day in the Sun', *Herald Sun*, 16 May 2009.
68 Jake Niall, 'Lions end losing streak', *Sunday Age*, 19 May 1996; Ted Hopkins, 'Pike Just Plain Productive On Roys' Big Day', *Herald Sun*, 21 May 1996.
69 Greg Denham, 'Young Lions savor glory', *Age*, 20 May 1996.
70 'Lion Nick Star In Rise', *Herald Sun*, 24 May 1996.
71 Charles Happell, 'Carter looks a Lion with a future', *Age*, 24 May 1996.

72 Tony de Bolfo, 'Roys Shrug Aside Abnormal Week', *Herald Sun*, 20 May 1996.
73 Jon Anderson, 'A Day in the Sun', *Herald Sun*, 16 May 2009.
74 Tony de Bolfo, 'Footy Snapshot', *Herald Sun*, 20 May 1996.
75 Interview, Tim Renwick, 14 May 2019.
76 Greg Denham, 'Young Lions savor glory', *Age*, 20 May 1996.
77 Ibid.
78 Muyt, *Maroon & Blue*, p. 198; Interview, John Barker, 14 August 2019.
79 Interview, Fran Gazzola, 1 May 2020.
80 Martin Flanagan, 'The club they hold so dear', *Age*, 20 May 1996; Muyt, *Maroon & Blue*, p. 198.

Chapter Ten

1 Phil Cullen, 'Debt No Hurdle – Miller', *Herald Sun*, 28 June 1996.
2 Mark Buttler and Rebecca Lang, 'A Nation Mourns', *Herald Sun*, 1 May 1996.
3 Robert Fidgeon and Simon Pristel, 'Riveting Drama Off Screen and On', *Herald Sun*, 16 May 1996; Alen Rados, 'Hotel Boost For City', *Herald Sun*, 22 May 1996.
4 Robert Ridgeon, 'Seven Well-Heeled In Drama Footy', *Herald Sun*, 15 May 1996.
5 Hore-Lacy, *Fitzroy*, p. 193; Alan Attwood, 'A job for the Lion-hearted is not for the faint-hearted', *Age*, 27 November 1993.
6 'AFL's green light to Port', *Daily Telegraph*, 22 May 1996.
7 Hore-Lacy, *Fitzroy*, pp. 183–85.
8 Craig Hutchison, 'Club Woes Bite Deep', *Herald Sun*, 2 July 1996.
9 Letter, Dyson Hore-Lacy to Fitzroy Members and Shareholders, c. May 1996, Skott Dean Papers.
10 Daryl Timms and Tony de Bolfo, 'Humane Act Says Wiegard', *Herald Sun*, 15 May 1996.
11 Greg Denham, 'Anger and frustration at an old club under siege', *Age*, 15 May 1996.
12 Correspondence, Kathy Doyle, 29 July 2020.
13 'Anthony Mithen, 'Ex-Lion hits out at his old club', *Age*, 16 May 1996.
14 Jonathan Brown, *Life and Football*, p. 57.
15 Greg Denham, 'Anger and frustration at an old club under siege', *Age*, 15 May 1996.
16 Philip Culen, 'We're Gone', *Herald Sun*, 15 May 1996.
17 Terry Brown, 'Hard To Imagine No Roys', *Herald Sun*, 16 May 1996.
18 Daryl Timms and Tony de Bolfo, 'Humane Act Says Wiegard', *Herald Sun*, 15 May 1996.
19 'Family Lives To Cheer For Their Club', *Herald Sun*, 2 July 1996.
20 Tony de Bolfo, 'A Question Of Loyalty', *Herald Sun*, 28 June 1996.
21 Stephen Linnell, 'Merged board a 50/50 split', *Age*, 27 June 1996; Bill Brennan, 'Merger 10 years too late', *Herald Sun*, 6 July 1996.
22 Stuart Potter, 'History lost in North deal', *Herald Sun*, 25 May 1996.
23 Philip Culen, 'We're Gone', *Herald Sun*, 15 May 1996.
24 Linda Pearce, 'I'm a Roo, merger or no merger, says Carey', *Sunday Age*, 19 May 1996.
25 Jake Niall, 'No "get-out" clause in Roostars' contracts', *Sunday Age*, 19 May 1996.
26 Mike Sheahan, 'Fitzroy-North Melbourne Roos', *Herald Sun*, 25 May 1996.
27 Patrick Smith, 'Bears' offer hard to pass up', *Age*, 24 May 1996.
28 Stephen Linnell, 'Roos, Roys may tell all soon', *Age*, 25 May 1996.

29 Scott Gullan, 'Kangas Crush Hapless Lions', *Herald Sun*, 25 May 1996; Anthony Mithen, 'Carey at his peak as Roos demolish Lions', *Age*, 25 May 1996; Dwayne Russell, 'A training run for the Roos', *Sunday Age*, 26 May 1996.
30 Dwayne Russell, 'A training run for the Roos', *Sunday Age*, 26 May 1996.
31 Ibid.; Scott Gullan, 'Kangas Crush Hapless Lions', *Herald Sun*, 25 May 1996.
32 Andrew Baln. 'Fitzroy v Melbourne: Time On', *Sunday Age*, 9 June 1996.
33 Greg Baum, 'Fitzroy v Melbourne', *Age*, 14 June 1996.
34 Muyt, *Maroon & Blue*, p. 216.
35 Len Johnson, 'Roys KO'd by teenager', *Age*, 17 June 1996.
36 Bruce Matthews, 'Club Future Unsettles Lions', *Herald Sun*, 17 June 1996.
37 Scott Gullan, 'Nunan: Fines Only Option', *Herald Sun*, 21 June 1996.
38 Ibid.
39 Mike Sheahan, 'Collins Wary of Fitzroy Fines', *Herald Sun*, 21 June 1996; Phil Cullen, 'Lions Stand By Fines', *Herald Sun*, 20 June 1996.
40 Phil Cullen, 'Lions Stand By Fines', *Herald Sun*, 20 June 1996.
41 Anthony Mithen and Stephen Linnell, 'Nunan defends fines', *Age*, 21 June 1996.
42 Scott Gullan, 'Fines the Only Option: Lions', *Herald Sun*, 21 June 1996; Philip Cullen, 'Lions' Spur', *Herald Sun*, 21 June 1996.
43 Michael Horan, 'Holland Blunder – Former Charge Comes Back To Haunt Roys' Coach', *Herald Sun*, 24 June 1996
44 Stephen Cauchi, 'Hawks middle of road', *Age*, 24 June 1996
45 Nick Place, 'Time On', *Sunday Age*, 23 June 1996; Stephen Cauchi, 'Hawks middle of road', *Age*, 24 June 1996.
46 Gerard Whateley, 'Chief Wins Merge Votes', *Herald Sun*, 29 May 1996.
47 Hore-Lacy, *Fitzroy*, pp. 183–85.
48 Daryl Timms, 'Key Lion Hits Out', *Herald Sun*, 31 May 1996.
49 Mike Stevens and Mark Duffield, 'AFL Considers Night Farewell', *Herald Sun*, 7 June 1996.
50 Patrick Smith, 'Clubs have no right to mislead, misinform', *Age*, 30 May 1996.
51 *David Syme & Co. Ltd v Hore-Lacy* [2000] VSCA 24 (2000) 1 VR 667.
52 'Apology to Dyson Hore-Lacy', *Age*, 20 December 2000.
53 Darren Pearce and Stephen Howell, 'Bears still open to merger approaches', *Sunday Age*, 16 June 1996.
54 Mike Sheahan, 'Roys Tell: Why Roo Bid's Better', *Herald Sun*, 29 May 1996; Daryl Timms, 'Roys Fans "Silenced"', *Herald Sun*, 30 May 1996.
55 'Bears, Lions In Merger Row', *Herald Sun*, 13 June 1996; Stephen Linnell, 'Lions, Bears in merger fight', *Age*, 13 June 1996.
56 'North: Lions' Debt No Fear', *Herald Sun*, 13 June 1996.
57 Hore-Lacy, *Fitzroy*, p. 194.
58 Minutes, AFL Commission Meeting, 26 May 1996.
59 'Roo chief in hospital', *Mercury*, 16 May 1996; Hore-Lacy, *Fitzroy*, p. 196.
60 Hore-Lacy, *Fitzroy*, pp. 195–96.
61 Stephen Linnell, 'Fitzroy anger on Ross changes', *Age*, 26 June 1996; Hore-Lacy, *Fitzroy*, p. 197.
62 Hore-Lacy, *Fitzroy*, p. 196.
63 Ibid., p. 196.
64 Ibid., p. 196.
65 Ibid., pp. 196–97.
66 Ibid., p. 197.
67 Stephen Linnell, 'Roos, Lions merger stumbles on a name', *Age*, 25 June 1996.

68. Mike Sheahan, 'Roys Find Ally In Name Game', *Herald Sun*, 25 June 1996.
69. Interview, Andrew Ireland, 23 January 2019.
70. Stephen Linnell, 'Fitzroy anger on Ross changes', *Age*, 26 June 1996.
71. Hore-Lacy, *Fitzroy*, p. 198.
72. Ibid., p. 198.
73. Phil Cullen, 'Debt No Hurdle – Miller', *Herald Sun*, 28 June 1996.

Chapter Eleven

1. Greg Denham, '"Insolvent" Lions to fold?', *Age*, 29 June 1996.
2. Dyson Hore-Lacy, 'Footy and friends – good for Nauru', *Age*, 15 November 1994.
3. Ashley Browne, 'Nauru millions save the Lions', *Age*, 26 October 1994.
4. J. Wright, 'Cash-Strapped Nauru Seeks our Expert Help', *Courier-Mail*, 3 February 1996.
5. 'Pacific blues rock tiny island nation', *Mercury*, 21 June 1996.
6. Hore-Lacy, *Fitzroy*, pp. 185–86.
7. Ibid., pp. 186, 189.
8. Stephen Linnell, 'Ten-day deadline for Lions', *Age*, 21 May 1996.
9. Hore-Lacy, *Fitzroy*, pp. 182–87.
10. Stephen Linnell, 'Concern mounts over Lions' payments', *Age*, 22 May 1996; Stephen Linnell, 'Ten-day deadline for Lions', *Age*, 21 May 1996; Philip Cullen, 'We Can Pay', *Herald Sun*, 21 May 1996.
11. Hore-Lacy, *Fitzroy*, p. 199.
12. Ibid., p. 195.
13. Ibid., p. 195.
14. John Hurley, 'Nauru's city projects in doubt', *Age*, 13 August 1996.
15. Hore-Lacy, *Fitzroy*, p. 199.
16. Ibid., p. 199.
17. Ibid., p. 200.
18. Interview, Glenn Warry, 15 November 2018.
19. Interview, Alan McConnell, 10 August 2018; Interview, Greg Freemantle, 12 August 2019.
20. Lucinda Schmidt, 'Fitzroy's day of truth: football is business', *Financial Review*, 15 July 1996; Michael Stevens and Scott Gullan, 'Lions On the Brink', *Herald Sun*, 29 June 1996.
21. Interview, Melanie Gibb, 18 February 2020.
22. Greg Denham, '"Insolvent" Lions to fold?', *Age*, 29 June 1996; Lucinda Schmidt, 'Fitzroy's day of truth: football is business', *Financial Review*, 15 July 1996.
23. Michael Stevens and Scott Gullan, 'Lions On the Brink', *Herald Sun*, 29 June 1996.
24. Interview, Greg Swann, 14 January 2019.
25. Hore-Lacy, *Fitzroy*, pp. 200–01.
26. Greg Denham, '"Insolvent" Lions to fold?', *Age*, 29 June 1996; Anthony Mithen, 'Nowhere to run in the darkness', *Age*, 29 June 1996; Lucinda Schmidt, 'Fitzroy's day of truth: football is business', *Financial Review*, 15 July 1996.
27. Greg Denham, '"Insolvent" Lions to fold?', *Age*, 29 June 1996.
28. Ibid.
29. Michelangelo Rucci, 'Nunan awaits next opening', *Advertiser*, 13 July 1996.
30. Interview, Jan Wight, 3 December 2018.
31. Interview, Greg Freemantle, 12 August 2019.
32. Muyt, *Maroon & Blue*, p. 192.
33. Michel Stevens, 'Captain Shocked', *Herald Sun*, 29 June 1996.
34. Anthony Mithen, 'Nowhere to run in the darkness', *Age*, 29 June 1996.
35. Andrew Bain, 'The Axe Comes Down On Fitzroy', *Inside Football*, Vol. 26, No. 21, 10 July 1996.

36 Stephen Howell, 'A season to end all seasons', *Sunday Age*, 1 September 1996.
37 Ibid.
38 Michael Stevens and Scott Gullan, 'Lions On the Brink', *Herald Sun*, 29 June 1996.
39 Greg Denham, '"Insolvent" Lions to fold?', *Age*, 29 June 1996.
40 Hore-Lacy, *Fitzroy*, p. 201.
41 Greg Denham, '"Insolvent" Lions to fold?', *Age*, 29 June 1996.
42 Michael Stevens and Scott Gullan, 'Lions On the Brink', *Herald Sun*, 29 June 1996.
43 Ibid.
44 'A sad, but inevitable, farewell to Fitzroy', *Age*, 29 June 1996.
45 Anthony Mithen, 'Nowhere to run in the darkness', *Age*, 29 June 1996.
46 'A sad, but inevitable, farewell to Fitzroy', *Age*, 29 June 1996.
47 Hore-Lacy, *Fitzroy*, p. 201.
48 Ibid., p. 202.
49 Anthony Mithen, 'Fitzroy v Geelong', *Age*, 28 June 1996.
50 Ibid.
51 Stephen Howell, 'A season to end all season', *Sunday Age*, 1 September 1996; Michel Stevens, 'Captain Shocked', *Herald Sun*, 29 June 1996.
52 Tony de Bolfo, 'Off-Field Woes Affect On-Field Performances', *Herald Sun*, 1 July 1996.
53 Michael Lovett, 'Player pay fears as the end looms', *Sunday Age*, 30 June 1996.
54 Stephen Howell, 'Lamentable Lions', *Sunday Age*, 30 June 1996.
55 Ibid.
56 Anthony Mithen, 'Captain down as club sinks', *Age*, 1 July 1996; 'Boyd points the finger at adversity', *Age*, 1 July 1996.
57 Stephen Howell, 'Lamentable Lions', *Sunday Age*, 30 June 1996; Michael Lovett, 'Player pay fears as the end looms', *Sunday Age*, 30 June 1996.
58 Melissa Fyfe, 'Lions fans in mourning', *Age*, 1 July 1996.
59 Anthony Mithen, 'Fitzroy v Essendon', *Age*, 5 July 1996.
60 Stephen Howell, 'A season to end all seasons', *Sunday Age*, 1 September 1996.
61 Ibid.
62 Anthony Mithen, 'Captain down as club sinks', *Age*, 1 July 1996.

Chapter Twelve

1 'The merger: your club's view', *Age*, 3 July 1996.
2 Andrew Cummins, 'Fans Mourn Loss To History', *Herald Sun*, 1 July 1996.
3 Hore-Lacy, *Fitzroy*, p. 203.
4 Ibid., pp. 201–02.
5 Ibid., p. 202.
6 Interview, Colin Hobbs, 12 August 2019.
7 Stephen Linnell, 'AFL fixture in chaos', *Age*, 1 July 1996.
8 Oakley et al, *The Phoenix Rises*, p. 254; Patrick Smith, 'How they took the Lions from Hore-Lacy', *Age*, 5 July 1996.
9 Rohan Connolly and Jake Niall, 'AFL set to take back $6m offer', *Sunday Age*, 30 June 1996.
10 Stephen Linnell, 'Bulldogs in queue for North merger', *Age*, 1 July 1996.
11 Roban Connolly and Jake Niall, 'AFL set to take back $6m offer', *Sunday Age*, 30 June 1996.

12. Karen Collier, 'Fans Rush For Final Souvenir', *Herald Sun*, 2 July 1996; John Hamilton, 'Tradition Ends Without A Roar', *Herald Sun*, 2 July 1996.
13. Ed Gannon, 'Lions Stripped', *Herald Sun*, 11 July 1996.
14. John Hamilton, 'Tradition Ends Without A Roar', *Herald Sun*, 2 July 1996.
15. Ibid.
16. Sian Watkins, 'League's fault, say loyal Roys', *Age*, 2 July 1996.
17. Rohan Connolly and Jake Niall, 'AFL set to take back $6m offer', *Sunday Age*, 30 June 1996.
18. Hore-Lacy, *Fitzroy*, pp. 202–03.
19. Greg Denham, 'Hotel "mystery" stumps administrator', *Age*, 2 July 1996; Stephen Linnell, 'Bulldogs in queue for North merger', *Age*, 1 July 1996.
20. Stephen Linnell, 'Bulldogs in queue for North merger', *Age*, 1 July 1996; Greg Denham, 'Hotel "mystery" stumps administrator', *Age*, 2 July 1996.
21. Charles Happell and Stephen Rielly, 'Players "forgotten" in battle for survival', *Age*, 2 July 1996.
22. Ron Reed, 'A Proud Old Club Runs Out of Choices', *Herald Sun*, 2 July 1996.
23. Stephen Linnell and Charles Happell, 'Protection for Oakley after threats', *Age*, 2 July 1996.
24. Interview, Matthew Primus, 26 September 2019.
25. Stephen Howell, 'Swans open floodgates', *Sunday Age*, 9 June 1996.
26. Charles Happell, 'Forgotten players search for goals', *Age*, 2 July 1996.
27. Greg Denham, 'Nunan may stand down today', *Age*, 2 July 1996.
28. Charles Happell, 'Forgotten players search for goals', *Age*, 2 July 1996.
29. Greg Denham, 'Nunan may stand down today', *Age*, 2 July 1996.
30. Minutes, AFL Commission Minutes, 1 July 1996.
31. Brett Quine, 'Hopes High On Merger', *Herald Sun*, 2 July 1996; Stephen Linnell and Charles Happell, 'Protection for Oakley after threats', *Age*, 2 July 1996.
32. Minutes, AFL Commission Minutes, 1 July 1996.
33. Ibid.
34. Hore-Lacy, *Fitzroy*, p. 203.
35. Minutes, AFL Commission Meeting, 1 July 1996.
36. Hore-Lacy, *Fitzroy*, p. 205.
37. Ibid., pp. 205–06; Minutes, AFL Commission Meeting, 1 July 1996.
38. Minutes, AFL Commission Meeting, 1 July 1996.
39. Brett Quine, 'Hopes High On Merger', *Herald Sun*, 2 July 1996.
40. Minutes, AFL Commission Meeting, 1 July 1996.
41. Tony de Bolfo, 'Off-Field Woes Affect On-Field Performances', *Herald Sun*, 1 July 1996.
42. Anthony Mithen and Charles Happell, 'North star cleared of biting', *Age*, 4 July 1996.
43. Hore-Lacy, *Fitzroy*, p. 206.
44. Minutes, AFL Commission Meeting, 1 July 1996.
45. Ron Reed, 'A Proud Old Club Runs Out Of Choices', *Herald Sun*, 2 July 1996; Stephen Linnell, 'Friday Lions' new D-Day', *Age*, 2 July 1996; Hore-Lacy, *Fitzroy*, p. 206.
46. Muyt, *Maroon & Blue*, p. 192.
47. Stephen Linnell, 'Friday Lions' new D-Day', *Age*, 2 July 1996; Michael Horan and Daryl Timms, 'Deadline – Merge By Friday Noon Or Die – AFL', *Herald Sun*, 2 July 1996.
48. Brett Quine, 'Hopes High On Merger', *Herald Sun*, 2 July 1996.
49. 'Angry But Resigned', *Herald Sun*, 3 July 1996.

50 Hore-Lacy, *Fitzroy*, p. 207.
51 Peter Ker, 'The merger that never got across the line', *Age*, 13 July 2003.
52 Hore-Lacy, *Fitzroy*, p. 208.
53 Ibid., p. 208.
54 Ibid., p. 208.
55 Scott Gullan, 'Coach Threat To Quit Over Merge', *Herald Sun*, 2 July 1996.
56 Mike Sheahan, 'Lions Salvage Pride', *Herald Sun*, 2 July 1996.
57 Greg Denham, 'Collins heads off boycott by Lions', *Age*, 3 July 1996.
58 Michael Horan, 'Boyd the Lionheart', *Herald Sun*, 2 August 1996.
59 Scott Gullan, 'Collins Averts Lions Walkout', *Herald Sun*, 3 July 1996.
60 Oakley et al, *The Phoenix Rises*, p. 254.
61 Andrew Bain, 'The Axe Comes Down On Fitzroy', *Inside Football*, Vol. 26, No. 21, 10 July 1996.
62 Jarrod Molloy, 'The heartbreak of losing Fitzroy', *Age*, 31 August 2006.
63 Scott Gullan, 'Collins Averts Lions Walkout', *Herald Sun*, 3 July 1996.
64 Greg Denham, 'Collins heads off boycott by Lions', *Age*, 3 July 1996; Michael Horan, 'Boyd the Lionheart', *Herald Sun*, 2 August 1996.
65 Interview, Stephen Paxman, 10 July 2018.
66 Greg Denham, 'Collins heads off boycott by Lions', *Age*, 3 July 1996.
67 Ibid.
68 Minutes, AFL Commission Meeting, 1 July 1996.
69 Rohan Connolly and Richard Hinds, 'Roo-Lions draw flak', *Sunday Age*, 26 May 1996.
70 'The merger: your club's view', *Age*, 3 July 1996.
71 Daryl Timms, 'Merge Doubt', *Herald Sun*, 3 July 1996.
72 Mike Sheahan, 'Super Team Fears Grow', *Herald Sun*, 3 July 1996.
73 Daryl Timms, 'Merge Doubt', *Herald Sun*, 3 July 1996.
74 Hore-Lacy, *Fitzroy*, p. 209; Oakley et al, *The Phoenix Rises*, p. 254.
75 Hore-Lacy, *Fitzroy*, p. 209.
76 Oakley et al, *The Phoenix Rises*, p. 255.
77 Hore-Lacy, *Fitzroy*, p. 210.
78 Ibid., p. 210; Mike Sheahan, 'Super Team Fears Grow', *Herald Sun*, 3 July 1996; Patrick Smith, 'Clubs have every right to be suspicious', *Age*, 3 July 1996.
79 Hore-Lacy, *Fitzroy*, p. 211.
80 Daryl Timms, 'Last-Ditch Bid – Bears Put Offer On the Table', *Herald Sun*, 4 July 1996.
81 Interview, Andrew Ireland, 23 January 2019.
82 Hore-Lacy, *Fitzroy*, p. 232; Interview, Andrew Ireland, 23 January 2019.
83 Interview, Andrew Ireland, 23 January 2019.
84 Lucinda Schmidt, 'Fitzroy's day of truth: football is business', *Financial Review*, 15 July 1996.
85 Philip Cullen, 'Footscray Court Bid', *Herald Sun*, 3 July 1996.
86 Stephen Linnell, 'Bulldogs threat to merger', *Age*, 3 July 1996.
87 Stephen Linnell, 'Roys to ask for merger talks', *Age*, 29 April 1996.
88 Mike Sheahan, 'Super Team Fears Grow', *Herald Sun*, 3 July 1996; Stephen Linnell, 'Merger in doubt as clubs hesitate', *Age*, 3 July 1996.
89 Hore-Lacy, *Fitzroy*, p. 211.
90 Ibid., p. 213.
91 Interview, Greg Miller, 30 January 2019.
92 Stephen Linnell, 'No compromise, say Roos', *Age*, 4 July 1996.
93 Philip Cullen, 'A Vital Vote Oakley', *Herald Sun*, 3 July 1996.
94 Oakley et al, *The Phoenix Rises*, p. 255.

Chapter Thirteen

1. Hore-Lacy, *Fitzroy*, pp. 213–14.
2. Ibid., p. 216.
3. Daryl Timms, 'Last-Ditch Bid – Bears Put Offer on the Table', *Herald Sun*, 4 July 1996.
4. 'AFL's moment of truth', *Age*, 4 July 1996.
5. Philip Cullen, '"Mayhem" Warning', *Herald Sun*, 4 July 1996.
6. Hore-Lacy, *Fitzroy*, p. 216.
7. Ibid., p. 216.
8. Mike Sheahan, 'Bears Can Save Roys', *Herald Sun*, 4 July 1996.
9. 'How the day of drama unfolded', *Age*, 5 July 1996; Daryl Timms, 'Last-Ditch Bid – Bears Put Offer on the Table', *Herald Sun*, 4 July 1996.
10. News item, *Ten News*, Channel Ten, 4 July 1996.
11. Philip Cullen, 'Merger On Track', *Herald Sun*, 4 July 1996.
12. 'The Deed of Arrangement between Fitzroy and the Brisbane Bears – August 4th 1996'.
13. 'How the day of drama unfolded', *Age*, 5 July 1996.
14. Ibid.; Stephen Linnell and Peter Gregory, 'Merger crisis as Dogs issue legal challenge', *Age*, 4 July 1996; Peter Gregory, 'Bulldogs to pursue $1.3m damages', *Age*, 5 July 1996.
15. Russell Coulson, 'Dogs Fail To Halt Merger', *Herald Sun*, 5 July 1996.
16. Hore-Lacy, *Fitzroy*, pp. 216–17, 232.
17. Interview, Colin Hobbs, 12 August 2019.
18. 'How the day of drama unfolded', *Age*, 5 July 1996; Interview, Colin Hobbs, 12 August 2019.
19. Hore-Lacy, *Fitzroy*, pp. 217–18.
20. Ibid., p. 218; 'How the day of drama unfolded', *Age*, 5 July 1996.
21. Interview, Greg Miller, 30 January 2019.
22. 'How the day of drama unfolded', *Age*, 5 July 1996.
23. Hore-Lacy, *Fitzroy*, p. 219.
24. Interview, Andrew Ireland, 23 January 2019; 'How the day of drama unfolded', *Age*, 5 July 1996.
25. 'How the day of drama unfolded', *Age*, 5 July 1996.
26. Minutes, AFL Commission Meeting, 4 July 1996.
27. Hore-Lacy, *Fitzroy*, p. 219.
28. 'How the day of drama unfolded', *Age*, 5 July 1996.
29. Interview, Greg Miller, 30 January 2019.
30. Minutes, AFL Commission Meeting, 4 July 1996.
31. Hore-Lacy, *Fitzroy*, p. 246.
32. Interview, Andrew Ireland, 23 January 2019.
33. Minutes, AFL Commission Meeting, 4 July 1996.
34. Oakley et al, *The Phoenix Rises*, p. 257.
35. News item, *Ten News*, Channel Ten, 4 July 1996.
36. Peter Ker, 'The merger that never got across the line', *Age*, 12 July 2003.
37. Hore-Lacy, *Fitzroy*, p. 219–20.
38. Minutes, AFL Commission Meeting, 4 July 1996.
39. Ibid.; Oakley et al, *The Phoenix Rises*, p. 257; 'How the day of drama unfolded', *Age*, 5 July 1996; Peter Ker, 'The merger that never got across the line', *Age*, 12 July 2003.
40. Hore-Lacy, *Fitzroy*, p. 220.
41. Ibid., p. 220.
42. Minutes, General Meeting of the Clubs, 4 July 1996; 'How the day of drama unfolded', *Age*, 5 July 1996.
43. Minutes, General Meeting of the Clubs, 4 July 1996.
44. Ibid.
45. Patrick Smith, 'How Hore-Lacy lost his beloved Lions', *Age*, 5 July 1996.

46   Hore-Lacy, *Fitzroy*, p. 220.
47   Interview, Colin Hobbs, 12 August 2019.
48   Hore-Lacy, *Fitzroy*, p. 220.
49   Interview, Colin Hobbs, 12 August 2019.

Chapter Fourteen

1   Charles Happell, 'Diehards take it hard in heart of Roys' territory', *Age*, 5 July 1996.
2   Peter Ker, 'The merger that never got across the line', *Age*, 12 July 2003.
3   Phil Skeggs, 'Hungry For A Future', *Herald Sun*, 5 July 1996.
4   Michael Horan, 'Boyd the Lionheart', *Herald Sun*, 2 August 1996.
5   Phil Skeggs, 'Hungry For A Future', *Herald Sun*, 5 July 1996.
6   'How the day of drama unfolded', *Age*, 5 July 1996.
7   Northey's Amazing Account of Brisbane-Fitzroy Merger', *SEN Website*, 20 June 2017, https://www.sen.com.au/news/2017/06/20/northeys-amazing-account-of-brisbane-fitzroy-merger/, accessed on 21 July 2019.
8   Lynch, *Taking Nothing For Granted*, p. 126.
9   Hore-Lacy, *Fitzroy*, p. 221; Trevor Grant, 'Dog Eats Dog In Feeding Frenzy', *Herald Sun*, 5 July 1996.
10   Stephen Linnell, 'It's the Brisbane Lions', *Age*, 5 July 1996.
11   Oakley et al, *The Phoenix Rises*, p. 258.
12   Minutes, AFL Commission Meeting, 4 July 1996.
13   Ibid.
14   Stephen Linnell, 'It's the Brisbane Lions', *Age*, 5 July 1996; Stephen Linnell and Greg Denham, 'AFL solves Fitzroy's cash-flow problems', *Age*, 5 July 1996; Craig Hutchison, 'Nauru To Get Lion's Share', *Herald Sun*, 5 July 1996.
15   Stephen Linnell and Greg Denham, 'AFL solves Fitzroy's cash-flow problems', *Age*, 5 July 1996; Craig Hutchison, 'Nauru To Get Lion's Share', *Herald Sun*, 5 July 1996.
16   Peter Ker, 'The merger that never got across the line', *Age*, 12 July 2003.
17   Stephen Linnell, 'It's the Brisbane Lions', *Age*, 5 July 1996.
18   Peter Ker, 'The merger that never got across the line', *Age*, 12 July 2003.
19   Holmesby, *The Death of Fitzroy Football Club*, p. 195.
20   Trevor Grant, 'Dog Eats Dog In Feeding Frenzy', *Herald Sun*, 5 July 1996.
21   Stephen Linnell, 'It's the Brisbane Lions', *Age*, 5 July 1996.
22   Peter Ker, 'The merger that never got across the line', *Age*, 12 July 2003; Daryl Timms, 'Bitter Roos', *Herald Sun*, 5 July 1996.
23   Charles Happell, 'Diehards take it hard in heart of Roys' territory', *Age*, 5 July 1996.
24   Tim Stoney, 'Fans Farewell the Glory Days', *Herald Sun*, 5 July 1996.
25   Charles Happell, 'Diehards take it hard in heart of Roys' territory', *Age*, 5 July 1996.
26   Stephen Linnell, 'It's the Brisbane Lions', *Age*, 5 July 1996.
27   Oakley et al, *The Phoenix Rises*, p. 258.
28   Hore-Lacy, *Fitzroy*, p. 221.
29   Interview, Tim Renwick, 14 May 2019.
30   Paul Riding, 'Fifty Fifty Sport', *Herald Sun*, 13 July 1996.
31   Andrew Roberts, 'Humiliation Shows Fitzroy Has No Future', *Herald Sun*, 10 July 1996.
32   Felicity Lewis and Terry Brown, 'Outraged Fans To Quit Footy', *Herald Sun*, 6 July 1996.
33   Mike Sheahan, 'Jokes Leave Sour Taste', *Herald Sun*, 6 July 1996.

34 Felicity Lewis and Terry Brown, 'Outraged Fans To Quit Footy', *Herald Sun*, 6 July 1996.
35 Tim Stoney, 'Fans Farewell the Glory Days', *Herald Sun*, 5 July 1996.
36 James Button, 'The lionhearts of Fitzroy', *Age*, 6 July 1996.
37 Felicity Lewis and Terry Brown, 'Outraged Fans To Quit Footy', *Herald Sun*, 6 July 1996.
38 Hore-Lacy, *Fitzroy*, p. 221.
39 Hore-Lacy, *Fitzroy*, p. 223.
40 Philip Cullen, 'Last-Gasp Bid', *Herald Sun*, 5 July 1996.
41 Hore-Lacy, *Fitzroy*, pp. 225–26.
42 Stephen Linnell, 'It's the Brisbane Lions', *Age*, 5 July 1996.
43 Mike Sheahan, 'Bears Steal Prize', *Herald Sun*, 5 July 1996.
44 Ibid.
45 Patrick Smith, 'High drama, pain, but it's good for football', *Age*, 5 July 1996.
46 Minutes, AFL Commission Meeting, 5 July 1996.
47 Daryl Timms, 'Not To Be Swayed', *Herald Sun*, 6 July 1996.
48 Geoff Poulter, 'Lions In Another Mauling', *Herald Sun*, 5 July 1996.
49 Michael Horan, 'Dons At End Of the Lion', *Herald Sun*, 8 July 1996.
50 Ibid.
51 Martin Flanagan, 'Support – it has to be won, not bought', *Age*, 8 July 1996.
52 Michael Lovett, 'Lions roar in vain', *Sunday Age*, 7 July 1996.
53 Stephen Howell, 'A season to end all seasons', *Sunday Age*, 1 September 1996.
54 Leon Wiegard, 'Roys' Roar Deal', *Herald Sun*, 8 July 1996.
55 Michael Lovett, 'Lions roar in vain', *Sunday Age*, 7 July 1996; Michael Horan, 'Dons At End Of the Lion', *Herald Sun*, 8 July 1996; Stephen Howell, 'A season to end all seasons', *Sunday Age*, 1 September 1996.
56 Michael Lovett, 'Lions roar in vain', *Sunday Age*, 7 July 1996.
57 Ibid.
58 Daryl Timms, 'Not To Be Swayed', *Herald Sun*, 6 July 1996.
59 Justin Brasier, 'Nunan bows out with shot at his old Lions bosses', *Australian*, 8 July 1996.
60 Charles Happell, 'Start of the end for Lions', *Age*, 8 July 1996; Stephen Howell, 'A season to end all seasons', *Sunday Age*, 1 September 1996.
61 Stephen Howell, 'Lion Will', *Sunday Age*, 25 August 1996.
62 Michelangelo Rucci, 'Where are they now: Michael Nunan Coach who close book with 'Roys', *Advertiser*, 21 May 2016.
63 Mike Sheahan and Daryl Timms, 'It's a Deal', *Herald Sun*, 15 May 1996; Jake Niall and Michael Lovett, 'Nunan quits the Roys', *Sunday Age*, 7 July 1996.
64 Charles Happell, 'Start of the end for Lions', *Age*, 8 July 1996.
65 Jon Anderson, 'A Day in the Sun', *Herald Sun*, 16 May 2009.
66 Interview, Chris Johnson, 11 May 2020.
67 Stephen Howell, 'A season to end all seasons', *Sunday Age*, 1 September 1996.
68 Dwayne Russell, 'Pssst', *Sunday Age*, 14 August 2005; Muyt, *Maroon & Blue*, p. 220.
69 Charles Happell, 'Q&A: Matthew Primus, Fitzroy', *Age*, 8 July 1996.
70 Stephen Howell, 'A season to end all seasons', *Sunday Age*, 1 September 1996; Charles Happell, 'Start of the end for Lions', *Age*, 8 July 1996.
71 Gareth Andrews, 'Fitzroy in the throes of death', *Sunday Age*, 21 April 1996.
72 Trevor Grant and Mike Sheahan, 'The Coaches' Mid-Term Report', *Herald Sun*, 21 June 1996.

73 Ibid.
74 'Rev Footy Rankings', *Herald Sun*, 29 May 1996.
75 Geoff Poulter, 'Bears To Enjoy Picnic', *Herald Sun*, 26 April 1996; Geoff Poulter, 'Roos Too Good', *Herald Sun*, 24 May 1996.
76 Patrick Smith, 'When fact merges with fiction', *Age*, 20 May 1996.
77 Charles Happell, 'Q&A: Matthew Primus, Fitzroy', *Age*, 8 July 1996.

Chapter Fifteen

1 'Murray: Support Brisbane', *Herald Sun*, 25 July 1996.
2 Stephen Linnell, 'Birth of Brisbane Lions', *Age*, 5 July 1996.
3 Martin Flanagan, 'Support – it has to be won, not bought', *Age*, 8 July 1996.
4 Tony de Bolfo, 'Last Rites In a Faraway Place', *Herald Sun*, 2 September 1996.
5 Barry Dickins, 'Last rites for the Royboys', *Age*, 6 July 1996.
6 Oakley et al, *The Phoenix Rises*, p. 259.
7 Martin Flanagan, 'Support – it has to be won, not bought', *Age*, 8 July 1996.
8 Jake Niall, 'Fans forgotten in Roys ritual', *Sunday Age*, 7 July 1996.
9 Martin Flanagan, 'Support – it has to be won, not bought', *Age*, 8 July 1996.
10 Stephen Linnell, 'Lions 'shafted' in merger, says Hore-Lacy', *Age*, 6 July 1996.
11 Bruce Ferrall, 'It's a great result', *Herald Sun*, 6 July 1996.
12 Alan Harrison, 'Now for a flag in '97', *Herald Sun*, 8 July 1996.
13 Jake Niall, 'Fans forgotten in Roys ritual', *Sunday Age*, 7 July 1996.
14 'Brisbane Offer Avoids A Takeover', *Herald Sun*, 6 July 1996.
15 Letter, Birt and Ireland to Fitzroy members, 16 July 1996, Skott Dean papers.
16 Interview, Sam Lord, 21 February 2020.
17 John Wood, 'Brisbane Deal A Disgrace', *Herald Sun*, 8 July 1996; Will Hessler, 'Their wool and our eyes', *Age*, 11 July 1996; Michael Plowright, 'Where the big dollars fly', *Age*, 11 July 1996.
18 'Dogs Roos Merge Plan', *Herald Sun*, 6 July 1996.
19 Henry Landini, 'Sting of the Century', *Herald Sun*, 6 July 1996.
20 Daniel Zavattiero, 'Dignity stripped', *Herald Sun*, 8 July 1996.
21 Stephen Rielly, 'Bears target 10,000 Lions', *Age*, 24 July 1996.
22 Harry (Tom) Balaam, 'Lions Sent To the Gallows', *Herald Sun*, 6 July 1996.
23 A Disgruntled Football Supporter, 'Footy Murder Most Foul', *Herald Sun*, 9 July 1996.
24 Keith Lofthouse, 'Thanks for the misery, Mr Oakley', *Age*, 16 September 1996.
25 Merv Wilson, 'Disgrace to stop Roos', *Herald Sun*, 6 July 1996.
26 John Wood, 'Brisbane Deal A Disgrace', *Herald Sun*, 8 July 1996.
27 Arthur Paul, 'Fifty Fifty Sport', *Herald Sun*, 13 July 1996.
28 Daryl Timms, 'Not To Be Swayed', *Herald Sun*, 6 July 1996.
29 Peter Allen, 'Fitzroy supporters aren't transferable', *Age*, 10 July 1996.
30 'Dogs Roos Merge Plan', *Herald Sun*, 6 July 1996.
31 Julian Agius, 'A farewell to the Roys', *Age*, 12 July 1996.
32 Daryl Timms and Michael Stevens, 'Pay Demand: Alan McConnell – Here We Go Again', *Herald Sun*, 9 July 1996.

33. Jake Niall and Michael Lovett, 'Nunan quits the Roys', *Sunday Age*, 7 July 1996; Stephen Howell, 'A season to end all seasons', *Sunday Age*, 1 September 1996.
34. Stephen Howell, 'A season to end all seasons', *Sunday Age*, 1 September 1996.
35. Michael Horan, 'No Rush For Lions' Job', *Herald Sun*, 8 July 1996.
36. Ibid.
37. Interview, Alan McConnell, 10 August 2018.
38. Interview, Leon Harris, 17 June 2020.
39. Interview, Brett Chandler, 10 July 2018; Interview, Stephen Paxman, 10 July 2018; Interview, Chris Johnson, 11 May 2020.
40. 'Body and Mind: The Caretaker Lion', *Football Record*, 16–18 August 1996.
41. Ibid.
42. Daryl Timms and Michael Stevens, 'Pay Demand: Alan McConnell – Here We Go Again', *Herald Sun*, 9 July 1996.
43. Interview, Alan McConnell, 10 August 2018; Stephen Howell, 'A season to end all seasons', *Sunday Age*, 1 September 1996.
44. 'Lions Appreciate Quiet Week', *Herald Sun*, 12 July 1996.
45. Charles Happell, 'West Coast v Fitzroy', *Age*, 12 July 1996.
46. James Foster, 'Eagles Show No Mercy', *Herald Sun*, 13 July 1996; Tim Atkinson, 'Eagles' class buries Lions'. *Age*, 13 July 1996.
47. Interview, Glenn Warry, 15 November 2018.
48. David Aldridge, 'Merger Is 10 Years Too Late', *Herald Sun*, 13 July 1996.
49. Daryl Timms and Michael Stevens, 'Pay Demand: Alan McConnell – Here We Go Again', *Herald Sun*, 9 July 1996.
50. Tony de Bolfo, 'Armbands For the Love of Fitzroy', *Herald Sun*, 19 July 1996; 'The Footy Panel: Roy-Mania', *Age*, 12 July 1996.
51. Daryl Timms, 'Roos Bid For Lion Logo', *Herald Sun*, 16 July 1996; Hore-Lacy, *Fitzroy*, p. 230.
52. Daryl Timms, 'Bears Unveil Lions' Colours and Anthem', *Herald Sun*, 19 July 1996.
53. Darren Pearce, 'Bear fans angry as Roys live on in club jumper and song', *Age*, 19 July 1996. Another example of animosity to the incorporation of so much Fitzroy into Brisbane: W.G. Brooks, 'Lions in Brisbane', *Australian*, 24 August 1996.
54. Tony de Bolfo, 'New Guernsey Irritates Bears Members', *Herald Sun*, 20 July 1996.
55. Daryl Timms, 'Bears Unveil Lions' Colours and Anthem', *Herald Sun*, 19 July 1996.
56. Ibid.
57. Stephen Rielly, 'Collingwood v Fitzroy', *Age*, 19 July 1996.
58. Tony de Bolfo, 'Boyd Injury A Roy Blow', *Herald Sun*, 20 July 1996.
59. Anthony Mithen, 'Fitzroy waiting on banner backlash', *Age*, 22 July 1996.
60. Oakley et al, *The Phoenix Rises*, p. 259.
61. Bruce Matthew, 'Lions' Demise Even Touches Pies', *Herald Sun*, 22 July 1996.
62. 'Banner Ignored', *Herald Sun*, 23 July 1996.
63. Tony de Bolfo, 'Armbands For the Love of Fitzroy', *Herald Sun*, 19 July 1996.
64. Bruce Matthew, '"Lions" Demise Even Touches Pies', *Herald Sun*, 22 July 1996.
65. Anthony Mithen, 'Lions let chance slip', *Age*, 22 July 1996; Michael Horan, 'Lions Give Pies Fright of a Lifetime', *Herald Sun*, 22 July 1996.

66 Michael Horan, 'Lions Give Pies Fright of a Lifetime', *Herald Sun*, 22 July 1996; Anthony Mithen, 'Lions let chance slip', *Age*, 22 July 1996.
67 Bruce Matthew, 'Lions' Demise Even Touches Pies', *Herald Sun*, 22 July 1996.
68 Anthony Mithen, 'Lions let chance slip', *Age*, 22 July 1996.
69 Grantley Bernard, 'Spirited Lions let Magpies off the hook', *Australian*, 22 July 1996.
70 Bruce Matthew, '"Lions" Demise Even Touches Pies', *Herald Sun*, 22 July 1996.
71 Stephen Rielly, 'Bears target 10,000 Lions', *Age*, 24 July 1996.
72 Darren Pearce, 'Big Bear to court Roy fans', *Sunday Age*, 21 July 1996.
73 Stephen Rielly, 'Bears target 10,000 Lions', *Age*, 24 July 1996.
74 Letter, Birt and Ireland to Fitzroy members, 16 July 1996, Skott Dean papers.
75 Darren Pearce, 'Big Bear to court Roy fans', *Sunday Age*, 21 July 1996; Daryl Timms, 'Bears Unveil Lions' Colours and Anthem', *Herald Sun*, 19 July 1996.
76 Daryl Timms, 'Bears Unveil Lions' Colours and Anthem', *Herald Sun*, 19 July 1996.
77 Stephen Rielly, 'Bears target 10,000 Lions', *Age*, 24 July 1996.
78 Interview, Kinnear Beatson, 11 November 2019.
79 Interview, Andrew Ireland, 23 January 2019.
80 Stephen Rielly, 'Fitzroy's legends differ on merger', *Age*, 25 July 1996.
81 Darren Pearce, 'Big Bear to court Roy fans', *Sunday Age*, 21 July 1996.
82 Stephen Rielly, 'Fitzroy's legends differ on merger', *Age*, 25 July 1996.
83 Hore-Lacy, *Fitzroy*, p. 225.
84 Stephen Rielly, 'Fitzroy's legends differ on merger', *Age*, 25 July 1996; 'Murray: Support Brisbane', *Herald Sun*, 25 July 1996; Grantley Bernard, 'Record saves Couch from longer ban', *Australian*, 25 July 1996.
85 AAP, 'Murray: Support Brisbane', *Herald Sun*, 25 July 1996.
86 Malcolm Conn, 'Hawks, Demons eye marriage as Lions merger ratified', *Australian*, 26 July 1996.
87 Muyt, *Maroon & Blue*, p. 168.
88 Jeff Sayers, 'What the Fitzroy Supporters Say', *Age*, 3 May 1997.
89 Minutes, AFL Commission Meeting, 21 July 1996.
90 Lucinda Schmidt, 'Revived Fitzroy finds game has moved on', *Financial Review*, 9 February 1998.
91 Hore-Lacy, *Fitzroy*, pp. 233–34.
92 Hore-Lacy, *Fitzroy*, pp. 233–47; Malcolm Conn, 'Hawks, Demons eye marriage as Lions merger ratified', *Australian*, 26 July 1996.
93 'Club Cash Flow Worry', *Herald Sun*, 26 July 1996; Stephen Rielly and David Saunders, 'Fitzroy creditors accept deal', *Age*, 26 July 1996.
94 Stephen Rielly and David Saunders, 'Fitzroy creditors accept deal', *Age*, 26 July 1996.

Chapter Sixteen

1 Daryl Timms, 'Birt's Dignity Plea', *Herald Sun*, 5 August 1996.
2 Charles Happell and Stephen Rielly, 'Players "forgotten" in battle for survival', *Age*, 2 July 1996.
3 Stephen Linnell, 'October deadline for eight Lions', *Age*, 11 July 1996; Daryl Timms, 'No To Bears – Lion Threatens Legal Action', *Herald Sun*, 12 July 1996.
4 Interview, Andrew Ireland, 23 January 2019.

5. Interview, Kinnear Beatson, 11 November 2019; Interview, Andrew Ireland, 23 January 2019.
6. Interview, Alan McConnell, 10 August 2018; Interview, Glenn Warry, 15 November 2018.
7. Jake Niall, 'For richer or for poorer?', *Sunday Age*, 11 May 1997.
8. Caroline Overington, 'Team glad of pay, but who gets a guernsey?', *Age*, 5 July 1996.
9. Michael Horan, 'Boyd the Lionheart', *Herald Sun*, 2 August 1996.
10. Anthony Mithen, 'Captain down as club sinks', *Age*, 1 July 1996.
11. Linda Pearce, 'Emotions run high for finale at "home"', *Sunday Age*, 18 August 1996.
12. Rohan Connolly, 'Respect, just a little bit', *Sunday Age*, 21 July 1996.
13. Donald, *Fitzroy*, p. 288.
14. Bruce Matthews, 'Big V Call-Ups For Barnes Johnson', *Herald Sun*, 21 May 1996.
15. Bryce Lewis, 'A Lion With a Burning Desire', *Inside Football*, Vol. 26, No. 8, 10 April 1996.
16. Interview, Chris Johnson, 11 May 2020.
17. Ibid.; 'Star Profile: Chris Johnson', *Football Australia*, April 1995, p. 62.
18. Donald, *Fitzroy*, p. 288; Paul Heinrichs, 'Heroes rise above the heartbreak', *Age*, 26 August 1994.
19. Interview, Chris Johnson, 11 May 2020.
20. Daryl Timms and Michael Stevens, 'Top Lion Pay Demand', *Herald Sun*, 9 July 1996.
21. Interview, Chris Johnson, 11 May 2020.
22. Charles Happell, 'Q&A: Matthew Primus, Fitzroy', *Age*, 8 July 1996.
23. Interview, Matthew Primus, 26 September 2019.
24. Daryl Timms, 'No To Bears – Lion Threatens Legal Action', *Herald Sun*, 12 July 1996.
25. Bruce Matthews, 'Player Union Rebuff For Roy', *Herald Sun*, 13 July 1996.
26. Interview, John Barker, 14 August 2019.
27. Muyt, *Maroon & Blue*, p. 216.
28. Interview, Alan McConnell, 10 August 2018; Muyt, *Maroon & Blue*, p. 216.
29. Michael Stevens, 'Nunan Yet To Make A Choice', *Herald Sun*, 5 July 1996.
30. Linda Pearce, 'Emotions run high for finale at "home"', *Sunday Age*, 18 August 1996.
31. Muyt, *Maroon & Blue*, p. 216.
32. Greg Denham, 'Baldwin sees end to dark days', *Age*, 13 December 1996.
33. Jake Niall, 'Second bite at success', *Age*, 29 May 1998.
34. Interview, Alan McConnell, 10 August 2018; Muyt, *Maroon & Blue*, p. 216.
35. Luke West, 'Time At The Top – Rowan Warfe's 110 AFL games with Fitzroy and Sydney', *Bendigo Advertiser*, 10 May 2020.
36. Interview, John Rombotis, 13 July 2018.
37. Emma Quayle, 'Too much, too young?', *Sunday Age*, 11 June 2006.
38. Luke West, 'Time At The Top – Carter's AFL stints with Fitzroy, Brisbane and Melbourne in the '90s', *Bendigo Advertiser*, 1 May 2020.
39. Stephen Rielly, 'Lion and family face yet another upheaval', *Age*, 31 August 1996.
40. Interview, Stephen Paxman, 10 July 2018; Martin Flanagan, 'Sounds of silence', *Age*, 19 August 1996.
41. Martin Blake, 'Roos revive pain for old Lions', *Sunday Age*, 29 April 2007.
42. Ibid.
43. Stephen Rielly, 'Lion and family face yet another upheaval', *Age*, 31 August 1996.

44 Ibid.
45 Interview, Glenn Warry, 15 November 2018.
46 Glenn McFarlane, 'Fallen Lion beating demons', *Herald Sun*, 27 August 2006.
47 Michelangelo Rucci, 'Crows Dine Out On Lion Carcass', *Herald Sun*, 29 July 1996.
48 Michelangelo Rucci, 'Crows Dine Out On Lion Carcass', *Herald Sun*, 29 July 1996; Ashley Porter, 'Crows pick on Lion bones', *Age*, 29 July 1996.
49 Michelangelo Rucci, 'Crows Dine Out On Lion Carcass', *Herald Sun*, 29 July 1996.
50 Ibid.; John Kerin, 'Adelaide rout sparks scramble for record books', *Australian*, 29 July 1996.
51 Alastair Lynch, 'Bears Will Hit the Jackpot in Fitzroy Lottery', *Courier-Mail*, 6 August 1996.
52 Stephen Rielly, 'Robert Shaw and the Taming of a Young Lion', *Age*, 27 May 1994; Mark Ray, 'Hawking A Chance For Swans', *Age*, 4 June 1998.
53 Alastair Lynch, 'Bears Will Hit the Jackpot in Fitzroy Lottery', *Courier-Mail*, 6 August 1996.
54 Interview, Simon Hawking, 14 April 2020.
55 Bruce Matthews, 'Lions Labor After Early Morning Call', *Herald Sun*, 5 August 1996.
56 Stephen Cauchi, 'Dogs stand on record against the Lions', *Age*, 5 August 1996; Glenn McFarlane, 'Fallen Lion beating demons', *Herald Sun*, 27 August 2006.
57 Stephen Cauchi, 'Dogs stand on record against the Lions', *Age*, 5 August 1996.
58 Ibid.; Bruce Matthews, 'Lions Labor After Early Morning Call', *Herald Sun*, 5 August 1996.
59 Bruce Matthews, 'Lions Labor After Early Morning Call', *Herald Sun*, 5 August 1996.
60 Geoff Poulter, 'Roys' Joy', *Herald Sun*, 7 August 1996.
61 Ted Hopkins, 'Pike Just Plain Productive On Roys' Big Day', *Herald Sun*, 21 May 1996.
62 Donald, *Fitzroy*, p. 298.
63 Mike Sheahan, 'From Spirits To Spirit', *Herald Sun*, 13 April 1996.
64 Ibid.
65 Steve Butcher, 'Footballer spared jail for drink driving', *Sunday Age*, 7 July 1996.
66 Ibid.
67 Chloe Saltau, 'Pike finds life and football rosier', *Age*, 27 September 2003.
68 Jake Niall, 'Saints stay alive', *Sunday Age*, 11 August 1996.
69 Ibid.
70 Stewart Oldfield, 'Saints beat Lions, mud', *Age*, 12 August 1996.
71 Jake Niall, 'Saints stay alive', *Sunday Age*, 11 August 1996.
72 Stewart Oldfield, 'Saints beat Lions, mud', *Age*, 12 August 1996.
73 Interview, Martin Pike on 'The Lead', *ABC Grandstand*, 10 May 2020.
74 Linda Pearce, 'Is Pike worth the risk?', *Sunday Age*, 1 September 1996.
75 Michelangelo Rucci, 'Power, Crows in race for Pike', *Advertiser*, 12 September 1996.
76 Muyt, *Maroon & Blue*, p. 217.
77 Interview, Brett Chandler, 10 July 2018; Interview, John Rombotis, 13 July 2018.
78 Interview, Simon Hawking, 14 April 2020.
79 Interview, Stephen Paxman, 10 July 2018.
80 Interview, Marty Warry, 18 January 2020.

81 Muyt, *Maroon & Blue*, p. 216.
82 Damian Barrett, 'Hungry For Success', *Inside Football*, Vol. 26, No. 34, November 1996.
83 Michael Horan, 'Boyd the Lionheart', *Herald Sun*, 2 August 1996.
84 Muyt, *Maroon & Blue*, p. 224.
85 Interview, Alan McConnell, 10 August 2018.

Chapter Seventeen

1 Stephen Howell, 'Lion Will', *Sunday Age*, 25 August 1996.
2 Doug Stewart, 'Angry Vics on the outer', *Daily Telegraph*, 15 August 1996.
3 Mike Sheahan, 'Face It, Interstate Finals Are Here To Stay', *Herald Sun*, 13 August 1996.
4 Stephen Linnell, 'Future of Whitten Oval "questionable"', *Age*, 15 August 1996.
5 Bresnehan James, 'AFL push on', *Mercury*, 14 August 1996.
6 AAP, 'We Paid Players Too Well: Hawks', *Herald Sun*, 15 August 1996.
7 AAP, 'Merger Inevitable For Hawks', *Courier-Mail*, 16 August 1996; Tony De Bolfo, 'New Face of Footy', *Herald Sun*, 16 August 1996.
8 'Greats support merger', *Age*, 14 August 1996.
9 Stephen Linnell and Ashley Browne, 'Oakley lashes at Scott group', *Age*, 15 August 1996; Stephen Linnell, 'Hawthorn claims most members favour merger', *Age*, 16 August 1996.
10 Daryl Timms, 'Birt's Dignity Plea', *Herald Sun*, 5 August 1996.
11 Interview, Alan McConnell, 10 August 2018; Interview, Greg Swann, 14 January 2019.
12 Interview, Fran Gazzola, 1 May 2020.
13 Interview, Rick Lang, 2 March 2020; Geoff Poulter, 'A Walk Through Football History', *Herald Sun*, 3 April 1996.
14 Interview, Rick Lang, 2 March 2020.
15 Interview, Fran Gazzola, 1 May 2020.
16 Interview, Greg Freemantle, 12 August 2019.
17 Ashley Browne, 'The Last Days Of Fitzroy', *Age*, 23 August 1996.
18 Interview, Leon Harris, 17 June 2020.
19 Scott Gullan, 'Big Finish To Tumultuous Season', *Herald Sun*, 22 August 1996.
20 Anthony Mithen, 'Fitzroy v Brisbane', *Age*, 16 August 1996.
21 Martin Flanagan, 'Sounds of silence', *Age*, 19 August 1996.
22 Martin Flanagan, 'Sounds of silence', *Age*, 19 August 1996; Linda Pearce, 'Emotions run high for finale at "home"', *Sunday Age*, 18 August 1996; Michael Lovett, 'Bears romp home to end Lion hopes', *Sunday Age*, 18 August 1996; Tony de Bolfo, 'Brisbane Coup', *Herald Sun*, 17 August 1996.
23 Ashley Browne, 'Bears' bit-players star', *Age*, 19 August 1996.
24 Ibid.; Ashley Browne, 'The Last Days Of Fitzroy', *Age*, 23 August 1996; Justin Brasier, 'Lions "not in hunt" as fans turn on Bears', *Australian*, 19 August 1996.
25 Michael Lovett, 'Bears romp home to end Lion hopes', *Age*, 18 August 1996.
26 Malcolm Conn, 'Boyd in fear from angry Lions fans', *Australian*, 22 August 1996.
27 Bruce Matthews, 'No Fairytale Ending For Lions' Faithful', *Herald Sun*, 26 August 1996; Malcolm Conn, 'Boyd in fear from angry Lions fans', *Australian*, 22 August 1996.
28 Ashley Browne, '100 Moments from the AFL Centenary Season', *Age*, 28 September 1996.

29 Linda Pearce, 'Emotions run high for finale at "home"', *Sunday Age*, 18 August 1996.
30 Patrick Smith, 'Fitzroy Fans', *Sunday Age*, 25 August 1996.
31 Justin Brasier, 'Lions "not in hunt" as fans turn on Bears', *Australian*, 19 August 1996.
32 Linda Pearce, 'Emotions run high for finale at "home"', *Sunday Age*, 18 August 1996.
33 Stephen Howell, 'A season to end all seasons', *Sunday Age*, 1 September 1996.
34 Jake Niall, 'Tough farewell for a poor relation', *Sunday Age*, 25 August 1996.
35 Stephen Howell, 'A season to end all seasons', *Sunday Age*, 1 September 1996.
36 Interview, Stephen Paxman, 10 July 2018.
37 Muyt, *Maroon & Blue*, p. 207.
38 Correspondence, Simon McLaughlin, 26 September 2020.
39 Patrick Smith, 'Finally, fans arrived in force for Fitzroy', *Age*, 26 August 1996.
40 Mark Dees, 'Royboys' Last Rites A Farce', *Herald Sun*, 31 August 1996; Mark Dees, 'Why I skipped the Fitzroy tearfest', *Age*, 29 August 1996.
41 Muyt, *Maroon & Blue*, p. 208.
42 Ibid., p. 207.
43 Jim Pollard, 'A Day For Grieving', *Herald Sun*, 26 August 1996; Stephen Howell, 'Lions pair on outer', *Sunday Age*, 25 August 1996.
44 Jim Pollard, 'A Day For Grieving', *Herald Sun*, 26 August 1996; Patrick Smith, 'Finally, fans arrive for Fitzroy', *Age*, 26 August 1996.
45 Grantley Bernard, 'Pride of Lions remains as Tigers douse failing flame', *Australian*, 26 August 1996
46 Interview, Greg Freemantle, 12 August 2019.
47 Jarrod Molloy, 'The heartbreak of losing Fitzroy', *Age*, 31 August 2006; Ashley Browne, 'Richmond v Fitzroy', *Age*, 23 August 1996.
48 Muyt, *Maroon & Blue*, p. 219; Interview, Brett Chandler, 10 July 2018.
49 Scott Gullan, 'Man In the Middle Of Roys' Last Rites', *Herald Sun*, 31 August 1996.
50 Stephen Howell, 'A season to end all seasons', *Sunday Age*, 1 September 1996.
51 Anthony Mithen, 'Lions to the slaughter', *Age*, 26 August 1996.
52 Patrick Smith, 'Finally, fans arrive for Fitzroy', *Age*, 26 August 1996.
53 Stephen Howell, 'Lions pair on outer', *Sunday Age*, 25 August 1996.
54 Patrick Smith, 'Finally, fans arrive for Fitzroy', *Age*, 26 August 1996.
55 Ibid.
56 Stephen Howell, 'A season to end all seasons', *Sunday Age*, 1 September 1996.
57 Anthony Mithen, 'Lions to the slaughter', *Age*, 26 August 1996.
58 Grantley Bernard, 'Pride of Lions remains as Tigers douse failing flame', *Australian*, 26 August 1996.
59 Muyt, *Maroon & Blue*, p. 221.
60 Interview, Alan McConnell, 10 August 2018.
61 Muyt, *Maroon & Blue*, p. 196.
62 Scott Gullan, 'Fitzroy Down and Well and Truly Out', *Herald Sun*, 26 August 1996.
63 Interview, Stephen Paxman, 10 July 2018.
64 Interview, Alan McConnell, 10 August 2018.
65 Stephen Howell, 'A season to end all seasons', *Sunday Age*, 1 September 1996; Patrick Smith, 'Finally, fans arrive for Fitzroy', *Age*, 26 August 1996.

66. Interview, Alan McConnell, 10 August 2018.
67. Ibid.
68. Stephen Linnell, 'Media shut out as last rites loom for Lions', *Age*, 26 August 1996.
69. Patrick Smith, 'Finally, fans arrive for Fitzroy', *Age*, 26 August 1996.
70. Stephen Linnell, 'Media shut out as last rites loom for Lions', *Age*, 26 August 1996.
71. Andrew Cummins, 'Fan: My Fear In Clash at the MCG', *Herald Sun*, 29 August 1996.
72. Geoff Easdown, Ed Gannon and Daryl Timms, 'Anger and Tears As Roys Fade', *Herald Sun*, 26 August 1996.
73. Benjamin Haslem, 'Tears as Lions end century of memories', *Australian*, 26 August 1996.
74. Scott Gullan, 'Man In the Middle Or Roys' Last Rites', *Herald Sun*, 31 August 1996; Stephen Howell, 'A season to end all seasons', *Sunday Age*, 1 September 1996.
75. Bruce Matthews, 'No Fairytale Ending For Lions' Faithful', *Herald Sun*, 26 August 1996.
76. Ibid.
77. Correspondence, Simon McLaughlin, 26 September 2020.
78. Tom Reynolds, 'Long Live Lions', *Herald Sun*, 26 August 1996.
79. Muyt, *Maroon & Blue*, p. 206.
80. Geoff Easdown, Ed Gannon and Daryl Timms, 'Anger and Tears As Roys Fade', *Herald Sun*, 26 August 1996.
81. Ibid.
82. Patrick Smith, 'Finally, fans arrive in force for Fitzroy', *Age*, 26 August 1996.
83. Ibid.
84. Hore-Lacy, *Fitzroy*, p. 231.
85. Donna Harris, 'Don't Go the Way of Fitzroy', *Herald Sun*, 27 August 1996.
86. 'Collectors can't get enough of the Lions', *Football Record*, 9–11 August 1996.
87. Jim Pollard, 'A Day For Grieving', *Herald Sun*, 26 August 1996; Scott Gullan, 'Man In the Middle Of Roys' Last Rites', *Herald Sun*, 31 August 1996.

Chapter Eighteen

1. Interview, Leon Harris, 17 June 2020.
2. Ross Brundrett, 'Glorious Roys Head North To Oblivion', *Herald Sun*, 31 August 1996.
3. Fiona Whitlock, 'Near the end of the Lion', *Age*, 27 August 1996.
4. Martin Flanagan, 'The End', *Age*, 2 September 1996.
5. Barry Dickins, 'Farewell Fitzroy', *Age*, 31 August 1996.
6. Ross Oakley, 'Future for Lions', *Football Record*, 30 August – 1 September 1996.
7. Geoff Slattery, 'Farewell Fitzroy, we love you well', *Football Record*, 23–25 August 1996.
8. Patrick Smith, 'Lions should have a dignified death', *Age*, 5 June 1996.
9. Greg Denham, 'Lions game switch ruled out', *Age*, 4 June 1996.
10. Mike Sheahan, 'Lions Farewell At Home Just Not Worth Fuss', *Herald Sun*, 8 June 1996.
11. Interview, Fran Gazzola, 1 May 2020.
12. Mike Stevens and Mark Duffield, 'AFL Considers Night Farewell', *Herald Sun*, 7 June 1996.
13. Oakley et al, *The Phoenix Rises*, p. 259.
14. Mike Sheahan, 'Lions Farewell At Home Just Not Worth Fuss', *Herald Sun*, 8 June 1996.

15 Muyt, *Maroon & Blue*, p. 210; Interview, Fran Gazzola, 1 May 2020.
16 Interview, Glenn Warry, 15 November 2018; Interview, Simon Hawking, 14 April 2020.
17 Interview, Stephen Paxman, 10 July 2018.
18 Stephen Howell, 'A season to end all seasons', *Sunday Age*, 1 September 1996.
19 Scott Gullan, 'Man In the Middle Of Roys' Last Rites', *Herald Sun*, 31 August 1996.
20 Tony de Bolfe and Philip Cullen 'Fans' Tearful Last Kick-To-Kick', *Herald Sun*, 30 August 1996.
21 Ibid.
22 Interview, Greg Freemantle, 12 August 2019.
23 Scott Gullan, 'Man In the Middle Of Roys' Last Rites', *Herald Sun*, 31 August 1996.
24 Interview, John McCarthy, 8 January 2019.
25 Scott Gullan, 'Man In the Middle Of Roys' Last Rites', *Herald Sun*, 31 August 1996; Stephen Howell, 'A season to end all seasons', *Sunday Age*, 1 September 1996.
26 Tony de Bolfe and Philip Cullen 'Fans' Tearful Last Kick-To-Kick', *Herald Sun*, 30 August 1996.
27 Scott Gullan, 'Man In the Middle Of Roys' Last Rites', *Herald Sun*, 31 August 1996.
28 Interview, Alan McConnell, 10 August 2018.
29 Holmesby, *The Death of Fitzroy Football Club*, p. 210.
30 'Weekend AFL Teams', *Herald Sun*, 31 August 1996.
31 Stephen Howell, 'A season to end all seasons', *Sunday Age*, 1 September 1996.
32 Tony de Bolfo, 'Last Rites In a Faraway Place', *Herald Sun*, 2 September 1996.
33 Brunswick Street BBQ invitation, nd, Skott Dean papers.
34 Muyt, *Maroon & Blue*, p. 196.
35 Tim Atkinson, 'Freo sends Roys packing', *Age*, 2 September 1996.
36 Tony de Bolfo, 'Last Rites In a Faraway Place', *Herald Sun*, 2 September 1996.
37 Interview, Tim Renwick, 14 May 2019.
38 Martin Flanagan, '1996, The Year That Was', *Age*, 28 December 1996.
39 Ashley Browne, '100 Moments from the AFL Centenary Season', *Age*, 28 September 1996.
40 Interview, Fran Gazzola, 1 May 2020.
41 Tony de Bolfo, 'Last Rites In a Faraway Place', *Herald Sun*, 2 September 1996.
42 Interview, Rick Lang, 2 March 2020.
43 Jarrod Molloy, 'The heartbreak of losing Fitzroy', *Age*, 31 August 2006.
44 Karen Collier and Andrew Cummins, 'Lion Hearts Broken By Final Thrashing', *Herald Sun*, 2 September 1996.
45 Post-game interview, Channel Seven broadcast.
46 Tim Atkinson, 'Freo sends Roys packing', *Age*, 2 September 1996.
47 Correspondence, Simon McLaughlin, 26 September 2020.
48 Martin Flanagan, 'The End', *Age*, 2 September 1996.
49 Muyt, *Maroon & Blue*, p. 210.
50 Martin Flanagan, 'The End', *Age*, 2 September 1996.
51 Karen Collier and Andrew Cummins, 'Lion Hearts Broken By Final Thrashing', *Herald Sun*, 2 September 1996; Andrew Cummins and Craig Binnie, 'Lions Fans Weep At Team's Finale', *Herald Sun*, 2 September 1996.
52 Glen Quartermain, 'Defiant Spirit To the End', *Herald Sun*, 2 September 1996.

53 Holmesby, *The Death of Fitzroy Football Club*, p. 212.
54 '48 hours: The End (3)', *Age*, 2 September 1996.
55 Interview, Leon Harris, 17 June 2020.
56 Tony de Bolfo, 'Last Rites In a Faraway Place', *Herald Sun*, 2 September 1996.
57 Martin Flanagan, 'The End', *Age*, 2 September 1996.
58 Interview, Marty Warry, 18 January 2020.
59 Interview, Brett Chandler, 10 July 2018.
60 Interview, Alan McConnell, 10 August 2018.
61 Tony de Bolfo, 'Last Rites In a Faraway Place', *Herald Sun*, 2 September 1996.
62 Interview, Tim Renwick, 14 May 2019.
63 Jarrod Molloy, 'The heartbreak of losing Fitzroy', *Age*, 31 August 2006.
64 Interview, John Barker, 14 August 2019.
65 Muyt, *Maroon & Blue*, p. 210.
66 Ibid., p. 211.
67 Interview, Fran Gazzola, 1 May 2020.
68 Muyt, *Maroon & Blue*, p. 212.
69 Karen Collier and Andrew Cummins, 'Lion Hearts Broken By Final Thrashing', *Herald Sun*, 2 September 1996.
70 Muyt, *Maroon & Blue*, p. 223.
71 Interview, Alan McConnell, 10 August 2018.
72 Glen Quartermain, 'Defiant Spirit To the End', *Herald Sun*, 2 September 1996.
73 Karen Collier and Andrew Cummins, 'Lion Hearts Broken By Final Thrashing', *Herald Sun*, 2 September 1996.
74 Chloe Saltau, 'The Last Roy Boyd', *Age*, 2 September 2006.
75 Interview, Alan McConnell, 10 August 2018.
76 Interview, Marty Warry, 18 January 2020; Interview, Chris Johnson, 11 May 2020.
77 Interview, Glenn Warry, 15 November 2018.
78 Geoff Slattery, 'So Long, It's Been Good To Know You', *Football Record*, 30 August – 1 September 1996.
79 Gareth Andrews, 'Fitzroy in the throes of death', *Sunday Age*, 21 April 1996.
80 Rod Nicholson, 'Where are they now?', *Herald Sun*, 26 April 2009.

Chapter Nineteen

1 Ben Collins, 'The Lion Trainer', *AFL Record*, 15–16 September 2017.
2 Mike Sheahan, 'Merge – It's Time To Look Ahead, Not Back', *Herald Sun*, 16 September 1996.
3 Alan Stockdale, *Victorian Parliamentary Debates*, Legislative Assembly, Vol. 431, 11 September 1996, p. 155–57.
4 Mark Buttler, 'No Merger – Vote Goes Against Plan', *Herald Sun*, 17 September 1996.
5 Daryl Timms, 'AFL Maintains Tough Stance', *Herald Sun*, 18 September 1996.
6 Hore-Lacy, *Fitzroy*, p. 231.
7 Stephen Lennell, 'Sydney debts worse than Fitzroy: papers', *Age*, 26 September 1996.
8 Patrick Smith, 'AFL baby bites the hand that feeds it', *Age*, 26 September 1996.
9 Interview, Glenn Warry, 15 November 2018.
10 Interview, Kinnear Beatson, 11 November 2019; Interview, Greg Freemantle, 12 August 2019.
11 Interview, Greg Freemantle, 12 August 2019.

12 Interview, Alan McConnell, 10 August 2018.
13 Kendall Hill, 'Metropolitan: Travel Alert', *Age*, 5 September 1996; Terry Brown and Phil Skeggs, 'Footy Shame. Lions Accused of Bali Resort Rampage', *Herald Sun*, 19 September 1996; Muyt, *Maroon & Blue*, p. 223.
14 Jason Koutsoukis, 'Fitzroy players ruined our holiday', *Age*, 19 September 1996.
15 Jason Koutsoukis, 'Fitzroy players ruined our holiday', *Age*, 19 September 1996; Ed Gannon, 'Club Defends Bali Behaviour', *Herald Sun*, 26 September 1996.
16 'Fitzroy In Clear On Bali', *The Herald Sun*, 26 November 1996, p. 64; Interview, Brett Chandler, 10 July 2018; Interview, John Rombotis, 13 July 2018.
17 Muyt, *Maroon & Blue*, p. 197.
18 'Pickled Pike', *The Herald Sun*, 21 September 1996.
19 Michael Horan, 'Pike Is Top Lion', *Herald Sun*, 17 September 1996.
20 Muyt, *Maroon & Blue*, p. 197.
21 Linda Pearce, 'Johnson heads for Brisbane', *Sunday Age*, 1 September 1996; 'Five New Lions', *Herald Sun*, 9 September 1996; Anthony Mithen, 'Brisbane Lions sign five Roys: Football', *Age*, 9 September 1996.
22 Greg Denham and Stephen Rielly, 'Primus, Holland heading for Port', *Age*, 9 October 1996.
23 Linda Pearce, 'Is Pike worth the risk?', *Sunday Age*, 1 September 1996.
24 Daryl Timms, 'Pride Of Lions Surprised By Disinterest', *Herald Sun*, 19 October 1996.
25 Daryl Timms, 'AFL Cooked Up Deal On Primus, Say Clubs', *Herald Sun*, 9 October 1996.
26 Interview, Andrew Ireland, 23 January 2019.
27 Tony de Bolfo, 'Power Makes Primus Priority', *Herald Sun*, 7 October 1996; Mike Sheahan, 'Brisbane Takes the Lions' Share', *Herald Sun*, 26 October 1996.
28 Daryl Timms, 'AFL Cooked Up Deal On Primus, Say Clubs', *Herald Sun*, 9 October 1996.
29 ''96 Nominees', *Advertiser*, 24 October 1996; Ashley Browne, 'Roy boys in demand as 11 find new homes', *Age*, 26 October 1996.
30 Ashley Browne, 'Roy boys in demand as 11 find new homes', *Age*, 26 October 1996.
31 Ibid.
32 Daryl Timms, 'Probe On Paxman', *Herald Sun*, 25 October 1996.
33 Simon Atkins, Peter Bird, Frank Bizzotto, Peter Doyle, Darren Holmes, Wayne Lamb, Adam McCarthy, John McCarthy, Anthony McGregor, Nick Mitchell and Danny Morton.''96 Nominees', *Advertiser*, 24 October 1996.
34 Jon Anderson, 'A Day in the Sun', *Herald Sun*, 16 May 2009; Interview, Nick Mitchell, 24 September 2019.
35 Interview, John McCarthy, 8 January 2019.
36 Greg Denham, 'Baldwin sees end to dark days', *Age*, 13 December 1996.
37 Stephen Rielly, 'Careers come to an end for Hawthorn premiership pair', *Age*, 25 October 1997.
38 'Lion Pub Decision', *Herald Sun*, 7 August 1996.
39 Hore-Lacy, *Fitzroy*, p. 249.
40 'Lions Reborn', *Herald Sun*, 2 November 1996.
41 Stephen Linnell, 'Fitzroy given the final rites', *Age*, 1 November 1996.
42 Christopher Webb, 'Lions' share paid out', *Age*, 3 December 1996.
43 Stephen Linnell, 'Fitzroy saga ends with little left for creditors', *Age*, 14 November 1997.

44 Stephen Linnell, 'Brisbane Lions: it's official', *Age*, 26 February 1997.
45 Interview, Andrew Ireland, 23 January 2019.
46 Interview, Alan McConnell, 10 August 2018.
47 Chloe Saltau, 'The last Roy Boyd', *Age*, 2 September 2006.
48 Interview, Lance Upton, 29 June 2020.
49 Ben Collins, 'The Lion Trainer', *AFL Record*, 15–16 September 2017.
50 Ian Munro, 'Lion Heart', *Sunday Age*, 18 August 1996.
51 Ron Reed, 'Lion Hearts Find Wealth Of Pride', *Herald Sun*, 20 May 1996.
52 Mike Sheahan, 'Lions' Roar Fades To a Death Rattle', *Herald Sun*, 29 June 1996.
53 Jake Niall, 'Fans forgotten in Roys ritual', *The Sunday Age*, 7 July 1996, p. 5
54 'Apology to Dyson Hore-Lacy', *Age*, 20 December 2000.
55 Hore-Lacy, *Fitzroy*, p. 259.
56 Scott Spits, 'Ezard heading for job with Coburg', *Age*, 18 October 1996; Greg Denham, 'MCG may host night grand final', *Age*, 15 November 1996
57 Interview, Glenn Warry, 15 November 2018.
58 Interview, Leon Harris, 17 June 2020.
59 Interview, Greg Freemantle, 12 August 2019.
60 Interview, Tim Renwick, 14 May 2019.
61 Interview, Tony Mazoski, 18 January 2020; Interview, Tim Renwick, 14 May 2019.
62 Stephen Howell, 'Lion Will', *Sunday Age*, 25 August 1996; Interview, Lance Upton, 29 June 2020.
63 Ben Collins, 'The Lion Trainer', *AFL Record*, 15–16 September 2017.
64 Ashley Browne, 'The Last Days Of Fitzroy', *Age*, 23 August 1996.
65 Emma Quayle, 'Too much, too young?', *Sunday Age*, 11 June 2006.
66 Glenn McFarlane, 'End of road for many: Nunan', *Sunday Mail*, 1 September 1996; Interview, Alan McConnell, 10 August 2018.
67 Interview, Glenn Warry, 15 November 2018.
68 Interview, John Rombotis, 13 July 2018.
69 Emma Quayle, 'Too much, too young?', *Sunday Age*, 11 June 2006.
70 Darren Pearce with Jake Niall, 'Missing the action', *Sunday Age*, 1 June 1997.
71 Interview, Stephen Paxman, 10 July 2018.
72 Interview, Matthew Primus, 26 September 2019.
73 Interview, Simon Hawking, 14 April 2020.
74 Interview, Marty Warry, 18 January 2020.
75 Tony de Bolfo, 'Collins Misses Oakley', *Herald Sun*, 18 December 1996.
76 Oakley et al, *The Phoenix Rises*, p. 261.
77 Ibid., p. 261.
78 Jesse Hogan, 'Man who took football to a nation', *Age*, 10 June 2013.
79 Barry Dickins, 'From the Footy Almanac vault: Barry Dickins remembers mud', *Guardian*, 20 September 2016.
80 Glenn McFarlane, 'A Lion's lament for Martin Pike', *Herald Sun*, 26 June 2011; Holmesby, *The Death of Fitzroy Football Club*, p. 218.
81 Oakley et al, *The Phoenix Rises*, p. 261.

Chapter Twenty

1. Luke West, 'Time at the Top – Carter's AFL stints with Fitzroy, Brisbane and Melbourne in the '90s', *Bendigo Advertiser*, 1 May 2020.
2. Interview, John Barker, 14 August 2019.
3. Rohan Connolly, 'Worth the weight', *Age*, 18 November 2000.
4. 'Up Where He Belongs', *Herald Sun*, 25 August 2001.
5. Interview, Chris Johnson, 11 May 2020.
6. Greg Denham, 'Hawks' Hudson set to become a Bulldog', *Age*, 20 December 1996.
7. Damian Barrett, 'A broken heart, but no regrets', *Herald Sun*, 30 June 2006.
8. Jon Anderson, 'Fitzroy Meeting', *Herald Sun*, 16 July 1998.
9. Daryl Timms, 'Fitzroy Meeting Worries Lions', *Herald Sun*, 21 July 1998.
10. Rohan Connolly, 'Lions look at VFL merge bid', *Sunday Age*, 1 September 1996; '"Yes" To Union', *Herald Sun*, 2 September 1996; Adrian Dunn, 'Lion Camps Still Keen On Alliance', *Herald Sun*, 13 September 1996; Scott Spits, 'Fitzroy faces more battles as it contemplates a VFL marriage', *Age*, 6 September 1996.
11. Martin Blake, 'Royboys' heart still beating', *Age*, 1 September 2006.
12. Jon Anderson, 'Fitzroy Meeting', *Herald Sun*, 16 July 1998.
13. Interview, Bill Atherton, 10 September 2019.
14. Mike Sheahan, 'Lions seal deal to win over fans', *Sunday Mail*, 29 July 2001.
15. Michael Stevens, 'New Lions "raped" Fitzroy', *Herald Sun*, 2 May 2001.
16. Mike Sheahan, 'Lion bond grows', *Herald Sun*, 28 September 2001.
17. Tony de Bolfo, 'Last Rites In a Faraway Place', *Herald Sun*, 2 September 1996.
18. Russell Jackson, 'What becomes of the broken hearted: the footy stalwarts who kept Fitzroy alive', *Guardian*, 25 August 2016.
19. 'Long Trip For Lions', *Herald Sun*, 15 August 1996; The Footy Panel: Recruiting Drive (1)', *Age*, 26 July 1996.
20. Tim Stoney and Daryl Timms, 'Bear's Blast: Gordon Launches Attack On Roos', *Herald Sun*, 21 August 1996; Daryl Timms and Tim Stoney, 'Gordon Faces $2000 Fine', *Herald Sun*, 21 August 1996.
21. Patrick Smith, 'Roasted Roos: Gordon blue', *Sunday Age*, 25 August 1996.
22. Wade Britnell, 'What the Fitzroy Supporters Say', *Age*, 3 March 1997.
23. North Melbourne Football Club, *1997 Annual Report and Balance Sheet*, pp. 3, 7; North Melbourne Football Club, *1998 Season Annual Report and Balance Sheet*, pp. 6–7.
24. Letter, John Birt to Fitzroy members and shareholders, 12 September 1996, privately held.
25. Jake Niall, 'Fans forgotten in Roys ritual', *Sunday Age*, 7 July 1996.
26. Interview, Lance Upton, 29 June 2020.
27. Interview, Skott Dean, 11 January 2020.
28. Scott Gullan, 'Man In the Middle Or Roys' Last Rites', *Herald Sun*, 31 August 1996.
29. Michael Plowright, 'Where the big dollars fly', *Age*, 11 July 1996.
30. Barry Dickins, 'Neither bear nor lion, a bewildering animal called Nothing', *Age*, 27 September 2003.
31. Interview, Rick Lang, 2 March 2020.

32 Gary Coomber, 'What the Fitzroy Supporters Say', *Age*, 3 March 1997.
33 Stephen Howell, 'Push to win the hearts of diehard Fitzroy fans', *Sunday Age*, 11 May 1997.
34 Alan Munro, 'What the Fitzroy Supporters Say', *Age*, 3 March 1997.
35 Ken Bailey, 'What the Fitzroy Supporters Say', *Age*, 3 March 1997.
36 Greg Baum, 'For some Fitzroy fans, the pride lives on', *Age*, 26 September 2001.
37 Shaun Phillips, 'Truly beats the heart of a Lion', *Herald Sun*, 26 September 2001.
38 Michael Davis, 'Fitzroy's fans roar approval – AFL Grand Final', *Weekend Australian*, 29 September 2001.
39 Glenn Mitchell, 'Lions legend flies the flag', *Herald Sun*, 28 September 2001.
40 Martin Flanagan, 'Lion Pride On Parade', *Age*, 29 September 2001.
41 Interview, Rob Clancy, 12 November 2019.
42 Interview, Sam Lord, 21 February 2020.
43 Ben Collins, 'The Lion Trainer', *AFL Record*, 15–16 September 2017.
44 Chris Donald, *Kevin Murray: Heart of the Lion*, Essendon: Pennon Publishing, 2005, p. 249.
45 Muyt, *Maroon & Blue*, p. 266.
46 Shaun Phillips and Philip Cullen, 'Spirit of '44 lives on in Roy heartland', *Herald Sun*, 1 October 2001.

Conclusion

1 Ashley Browne, 'The last of the Lions', *Age*, 2 May 1997.
2 Cash and Damousi, *Footy Passions*, p. 22.
3 AFL, *Annual Report 1996*, p. 28.
4 Oakley et al, *The Phoenix Rises*, p. 251
5 'Fitzroy Football Club', *Age*, 9 April 1897.
6 'Fitzroy Football Club', *Fitzroy City Press*, 31 March 1898.
7 'Exit University. Football League Retirement', *Argus*, 17 October 1914.
8 Cartledge, *Footy's Glory Days*, p. 18.
9 Michael Stevens, 'Fans Back Optus Move', *Herald Sun*, 28 October 1996.
10 Peter Temple, *Black Tide*. Melbourne: The Text Publishing Company, 2012, p. 22.
11 Stephen Rielly, 'Fitzroy's legends differ on merger', *Age*, 25 July 1996.
12 AFL, *Annual Report 1996*, p. 25.
13 Ibid., pp. 6, 25.
14 Tony De Bolfo, 'Mergers Off – Jackson's First Big Action', *Herald Sun*, 3 October 1996.
15 AFL, *Annual Report 1996*, p. 25.
16 Interview, Rick Lang, 2 March 2020.
17 John Harms, *Play On: A Sporting Omnibus*, Fitzroy North: Malarkey Publications, 2015, p. 496.
18 Charles Happell, 'Start of the end for Lions', *Age*, 8 July 1996.
19 Cartledge, *Footy's Revolution*, p. 221.
20 Patrick Smith, 'Prepare for the scars of footy's evolution', *Age*, 31 August 1996.
21 'Samuel's biggest regret? Perpetuating a "myth"', *Age*, 23 June 2003.
22 Peter Temple, *Bad Debts*, Sydney: HarperCollins, 1996, p. 7.
23 Correspondence, Kathy Doyle, 29 July 2020.
24 Interview, Skott Dean, 11 January 2020.
25 Interview, Stuart Winstanley, 12 November 2019.
26 Interview, Jan Wright, 3 December 2018.

27 Correspondence, William Oliver, 11 November 2019.
28 'Up there forever: it's time to let go', *Sunday Age*, 7 July 1996.
29 Ken Merrigan, 'Long live Fitzroy', *Sunday Age*, 7 July 1996.

Epilogue

1 Interview, Bill Atherton, 10 September 2019.
2 Peter Hanlon, 'Roars heard again in Fitzroy', *Brisbane Times*, 9 December 2008.
3 Interview, Bill Atherton, 10 September 2019.
4 Interview, David Leydon, 19 September 2019.
5 Jack Banister and Kasey Symons, interview with David Leydon, *The People's Game: An AFL Podcast*, podcast audio, 31 August 2019.
6 Interview, Elaine Findlay, 12 November 2019.
7 Interview, Joan Eddy on 'Afternoons with Jacinta Parsons', *ABC Radio Melbourne*, 5 May 2020.
8 'To win is a beautiful thing', Fitzroy Football Club website, 16 September 2018, www.fitzroyfc.com.au/latest-news/to-win-is-a-beautiful-thing, accessed 14 January 2019.

ACKNOWLEDGEMENTS

Writing a book about the Fitzroy Football Club was an ambition of mine for several years before I opened a Word document in March 2018 and decided to tell the story of the club's final year in the AFL. That I made it to the end of this long and, at times, difficult journey is a testament to the support and encouragement I received along the way, and I am deeply grateful to everyone who helped me bring this book to life.

First and foremost I must thank David Tenenbaum and his team at Melbourne Books. David had every reason not to publish this book, yet he decided to take a chance on me. I argued that this was an important story and one that needed to be told well — David and his team have been instrumental in realising that vision. Not only that, they have been a joy to work with throughout the process. In particular, I would like to thank Ben Knightand and Charlotte Gurtler for their studious and careful work in editing the manuscript.

In researching this book I had the great privilege of interviewing many people associated with the club and the events of 1996. All gave generously of their time and some kindly invited me into their homes.

These discussions provided rare insights into the club and the circumstances around its departure from the AFL and made the story really come alive for me. I owe everyone I spoke to a tremendous debt of gratitude.

For official records, I received valuable assistance from Patrick Keane and the Office of the AFL CEO, who helped me obtain AFL Commission minutes. The League was also kind enough, due to access problems caused by COVID-19, to grant me permission to use images as published in annual reports.

Throughout the crafting of this book Fitzroy supporters helped me in a variety of ways, from confirming small factual details to providing or confirming assessments of certain players to suggesting possible book titles. I hope the end result feels authentic to the experience of every supporter who lived through 1996. Specifically, I would like to thank fellow traveller Adam Muyt for his encouragement, David Leydon for reading parts of my book and for giving me a photo of his family and Skott Dean for sharing both his personal records and his story. Colin Hobbs, Bill Atherton, Elliot Cartledge and Philip Mendes read all or part of the book. Their advice and corrections on important details was much appreciated. Tim Renwick and Fran Gazzola were also invaluable in providing and confirming a variety of little details.

Jan Wright offered me photos from her extensive and remarkable collection, and although I was ultimately only able to use a handful, the gesture was greatly appreciated. Wilma Aylward, Kayleen Russell, Rick Lang and Simon McLaughlin also kindly donated photos. Anastasia Symeonides was instrumental in helping me obtain several images published in Fairfax newspapers, a task made all the more difficult by the restrictions imposed due to Covid-19.

I owe great thanks to Gerard Whateley for accepting my invitation to write this book's foreword. In the midst of a busy and uncertain period in the middle of 2020 he took the time to craft his reflections on the Fitzroy merger and he truly exceeded my expectations with his masterful contextualisation.

Two friends offered invaluable assistance in the development of this book. First, Mitchell Toy provided the front and back cover images for the book. He is an extraordinarily talented artist and a man of immense ability. Second, my erstwhile colleague Tom Richardson was a vital sounding board and draft reader, and I often deferred to his sharp and analytical historical mind.

This book is nothing if not about family, the one that we are born into and the ones that we make for ourselves. Accordingly I must thank my mother, who did more than her fair share of babysitting while I was engaged in seemingly endless interviewing, writing or editing. I must also thank my father for not only helping me find my love of football, but for working so hard for so many years to allow me to have a good upbringing, a good education and a chance to realise my dream of becoming a historian. He died the year before I began working on this project, and I hope that it is a fitting tribute to his memory.

Finally, my greatest thanks go to my beautiful wife, Alithea, whose forbearance was frequently tested on many occasions during the writing of this book but whose love and support was never taken for granted, and to my little lion men, Joel and Toby. I hope that one day they might read this book and learn what happened to the club that their grandfather held so dear.

THE AUTHOR

William Westerman is a Canberra-based historian, born and raised in Melbourne, currently working at the Australian War Memorial as the author of the *Official History of Australian Operations in Iraq, 2003–2011* and an author of the *Official History of Australian Peacekeeping Operations in East Timor, 2000–2012*. He completed a PhD at UNSW Canberra in 2014, researching Australian battalion commanders in the First World War. He has written two books, as well as numerous book chapters and journal articles, on aspects of the Australian Army and the First World War. He has also written a short biography of Lindsay Thompson, the 40th Premier of Victoria.

He has taught at Monash University and worked as an ANU Teaching Fellow with the Military and Defence Studies Program, Australian Command and Staff College, Canberra. He is also a Fellow of the Royal Historical Society and an Adjunct Lecturer at UNSW Canberra. He is a third-generation Roys supporter, and his sons, Joel and Toby, are — like their father — also members of the Fitzroy Football Club.